University of
Chester

**CHESTER CAMPUS**
**LIBRARY**
**01244 392738**

This book is to be returned on or before the last date stamped
below. Overdue charges will be incurred by the late return of
books.

D1349078

# Advances in the Sign Language
# Development of Deaf Children

Perspectives on Deafness

*Series Editors*
Marc Marschark
Patricia Elizabeth Spencer

*The World of Deaf Infants: A Longitudinal Study*
Kathryn P. Meadow-Orlans, Patricia Elizabeth Spencer,
and Lynn Sanford Koester

*Sign Language Interpreting and Interpreter Education:*
*Directions for Research and Practice*
Marc Marschark, Rico Peterson, and Elizabeth A. Winston

*Advances in the Spoken Language Development of Deaf and Hard-of-Hearing Children*
Edited by Patricia Elizabeth Spencer and Marc Marschark

*Advances in the Sign Language Development of Deaf Children*
Edited by Brenda Schick, Marc Marschark, and Patricia Elizabeth Spencer

ADVANCES IN THE

# Sign Language Development

OF DEAF CHILDREN

EDITED BY

Brenda Schick, Marc Marschark, and
Patricia Elizabeth Spencer

OXFORD
UNIVERSITY PRESS

2006

# OXFORD
UNIVERSITY PRESS

Oxford University Press, Inc., publishes works that further
Oxford University's objective of excellence
in research, scholarship, and education.

Oxford   New York
Auckland   Cape Town   Dar es Salaam   Hong Kong   Karachi
Kuala Lumpur   Madrid   Melbourne   Mexico City   Nairobi
New Delhi   Shanghai   Taipei   Toronto

With offices in
Argentina   Austria   Brazil   Chile   Czech Republic   France   Greece
Guatemala   Hungary   Italy   Japan   Poland   Portugal   Singapore
South Korea   Switzerland   Thailand   Turkey   Ukraine   Vietnam

Copyright © 2006 by Brenda Schick, Marc Marschark, and
Patricia Elizabeth Spencer

Published by Oxford University Press, Inc.
198 Madison Avenue, New York, New York 10016
www.oup.com

Oxford is a registered trademark of Oxford University Press

Library of Congress Cataloging-in-Publication Data
Advances in the sign language development of deaf children /
edited by Brenda Schick, Marc Marschark, and Patricia Elizabeth Spencer.
p.   cm.
Includes bibliographical references.
ISBN-13 978-0-19-518094-7
ISBN 0-19-518094-1
1. Sign language acquisition.   2. Deaf children—Language.
I. Schick, Brenda S. (Brenda Sue), 1952–   II. Marschark, Marc.
III. Spencer, Patricia Elizabeth.
HV2474.A38 2005
419—dc22      2004023070

9  8  7  6  5  4  3  2  1

Printed in the United States of America
on acid-free paper

# Preface

A colleague of ours once remarked (paraphrasing to protect the innocent): "Isn't it amazing how we can all know so much about this and still know so little?" Even if the comment was not quite as profound as it might appear, in this context, it is dead on. This volume came about because we felt that this is one of the most exciting times in the history of language development research and the *most* exciting with regard to sign language development of deaf children. Yet, for all of the research we have seen on the topic, the pieces of the puzzle still seem to be spread all over the table, in small interlocking clumps, but without revealing the bigger picture.

It is also a time of great changes in the larger field of research concerning deaf children, for a variety of reasons. Over the past couple of years, in our editorial roles for the *Journal of Deaf Studies and Deaf Education*, we have seen some subtle and not so subtle changes in the field. The 800-pound gorilla in this case is the cochlear implant.[1] With regard to spoken language development, the increasing popularity of cochlear implants, particularly in Australia (where approximately 80% of all deaf children now receive implants) and in the United States, is changing the lives of some investigators almost as much as it is changing the lives of deaf children and their parents (Spencer & Marschark, 2003). Research concerning the impact of implants on language

---

[1] Just in case there is some country that does not have this joke-turned-metaphor: Q: *Where does an 800-pound gorilla sit?* A: *Anywhere it wants!*

development in those children certainly has changed dramatically (see chapters in the companion to this volume, *Advances in the Spoken Language Development of Deaf and Hard-of-Hearing Children*). At the same time, research concerning the influence of cochlear implants on the larger mosaic of deaf children's development seems to be proceeding at a remarkably slow pace, and while we are learning about their effects on social and emotional development, we still know little if anything about their effects on academic achievement, peer interaction, and cognitive development. Most significantly for the present purposes (with the gorilla looming in the wing), research concerning sign language development and its use in deaf children with cochlear implants is just now making some tentative progress after a period of fervent—if unsupported—claims that sign language and implants do not mix. With memories of similar fervent, unsupported claims about sign language and spoken language not mixing still fresh, we leave that issue to others.

There are other changes happening in the field that are not so apparent, some of which are directly related to research on sign language development in deaf and hard-of-hearing children, some indirectly so, and some . . . well, it is still unclear. At the most general level, this is a time of expanded international research interest concerning sign language, Deaf studies, and the development and education of deaf children, with emphasis on sign language and how it influences all other aspects of deaf children's worlds. This change is evident in the increasing numbers of conferences, books, and professional journals devoted to sign language and to deaf children. But while research on the development of sign language in most countries is expanding at an impressive pace, it appears that it is slowing in those countries that are most quickly embracing cochlear implants. Big mistake. We never have been good at educating hard-of-hearing children—and most deaf children with implants are functionally hard of hearing even when their implants are functioning perfectly—and issues of how language is intertwined with literacy, academic achievement, and social-emotional functioning are still largely unresolved. Moreover, many children (and adults) with implants continue to acquire and use sign language, and yet there is little understanding of—and apparently little interest in (but see Hoiting, chapter 7 this volume)—the potential interplay of sign language, implants, development, and Deaf culture. Research is needed on this interplay more than ever.

At another level, as the chapters of this volume indicate, research concerning language development in deaf children is now reaching maturity (or at least puberty) and is leaping ahead with an enthusiasm and synergy that has not been seen previously (see Marschark, Schick, & Spencer, chapter 1 this volume). The field is now leaving behind much of the wishful-thinking simplicity of its youth and gaining a deeper understanding of the process and content of sign language development in deaf children and, importantly, its symbiotic relationship with all other aspects of deaf children's growth (e.g., Marschark, 2003; Schick, 2004; Shaffer, chapter 12 this volume; Spencer, 2000). As an indicator of that maturity, we are now recognizing ways in which sign language development varies with the context in which it is learned (e.g., Spencer & Harris, chapter 4 this volume; Volterra, Iverson, & Castrataro, chapter 3 this volume), its use in contexts beyond the developmental environment (e.g., G. Morgan, chapter 13 this volume; Singleton & D. Morgan, chapter 14 this volume), and theoretical implications of sign language as a visual-spatial language (e.g., Lillo-Martin & Chen Pichler, chapter 10 this volume; Slobin, chapter 2 this volume).

As our understanding of sign language development improves, so does our appreciation of subtleties we had either not noticed previously or had noticed but were not sure how to handle. For example, we have long recognized that sign languages have the potential for grammatical structures that are impossible or difficult to imagine in a spoken language. Thus, American Sign Language allows multiple layers of meaning to be communicated simultaneously, sometimes with different elements of meaning on different hands. This *simultaneity of expression* also reveals the gestural origins of sign language structure, one of several characteristics that make for interesting contrasts with spoken languages. Given the layering and spatial organization of meanings possible within even literal signing (ignoring, for the moment, the complexities of figurative language, cultural nuances, etc.), one would expect differences in development in signed and spoken modalities that could well affect both social and cognitive development. Development moves from the simple to the complex in both cases, but with a different set of complexities across the two modalities. What about the interactions between the two modes of communication—especially when most deaf children are exposed to both?

Similarly, although several of the contributors to this volume aptly demonstrate the importance of language learning contexts to the nature of development, we are just now coming to appreciate the possibility that relatively small differences in input may have significant effects on language structure and use. As we note in chapter 1, essentially all deaf children are exposed to a diversity of language models (not all of them good), a situation not encountered by hearing children. Approximately 95% of deaf children have hearing parents (Mitchell & Karchmer, 2004), most of whom will not become ideal models of sign language fluency, but even those deaf children who have deaf parents will be exposed to nonfluently signing peers and various adults who, themselves, had hearing parents and learned to sign later and in less-than-ideal circumstances. The long-term effects of learning language under such conditions—and its specific influence on sign language development in both ontogenetic and linguistic senses—remain to be determined. Recent research on the comprehension of sign language by older deaf children and adults, as well as the apparent ease of deaf people's communication at international gatherings, suggests either remarkable flexibility in sign language fluency or yet another divergence from spoken language. How does exposure to variable sign order influence syntactic development? Does variability in observed morphosyntactic regularity, classifier use (Schick, chapter 5), fingerspelling (Padden, chapter 8), and discourse structure (Morgan, chapter 13) affect children's ultimate sign language fluency—and, if so, for better or worse? Given the special options for incorporation of verb modulations and the apparent centrality of verb syntax in natural signed languages, does acquiring a sign language rather than a spoken language result in a different "view of the world"?

For the most part, our mention of these considerations pertains to their implications for sign language, but we also raise them at other levels of analysis. As we describe in chapter 1, the unique sociopolitical culture surrounding sign language and deafness not only influences research on sign language and its development but also affects the models and attitudes to which deaf children are exposed. Similarly, although the focus of this volume is on theoretical issues relating to language development in deaf children, we again have to remind ourselves of the potential for application as well as theory, for applied research as well as basic research. It is interesting that while research on spoken language in deaf children tends to focus on practical aspects of language comprehension and production (to the apparent exclusion of understanding the broader implications of having diminished speech intelligibility and comprehension skills), research on sign language in deaf children has been less concerned with the practical. In this volume, Spencer and Harris (chapter 4) discuss the considerable research literature on mother–child communication, and Singleton and D. Morgan (chapter 14) present a new perspective on learning sign language in the classroom. Still lacking, however, are considerations of how the use of sign language might affect classroom learning, how it (rather than school placement) might affect social-emotional development, and how the cognitive differences associated with sign language use (Marschark, 2003) might offer opportunities for improvement of educational methods.

There have been several points in the theoretical and chronological history of sign language research where these kinds of questions have emerged (and re-emerged), even if we have struggled with their answers. For example, early discussions concerning the importance of iconicity for learning a signed language appeared to conclude that, while they might be important for adult second language learners, to the extent to which signs mirror their referents, there was little effect on vocabulary learning by young children (see Emmorey, 2002). Yet, as several chapters in this volume make clear, the question may not be the existence or nonexistence of such effects as much as the extent and complexity of their impact on other aspects of development.

This situation is reminiscent of a similar debate, one that also seems not to be as simple as we once thought: the question of whether deaf children have the benefit of a *sign advantage*, wherein the first signs can be produced earlier than the first words. The relation of the first signs (and the possible advantage) to early gesture is certainly part of this, but together with the iconicity of both signs and gestures, several chapters in this volume make it clear that the question also bears on social and cognitive development as well as the origins of language (see also Stokoe, 2001). Importantly, the consideration of this issue in several chapters of this volume indicates both advances in our understanding of the nuances of sign language development in different contexts and a mature willingness of the field to revisit questions that we thought had been left behind. At the same time, if discussion of a sign language advantage 20 years ago appeared to dissipate with greater care to methodological issues, the re-emergence of the issue now points up the need to keep methodologically apace with theoretical progress lest we err on the side of either unnecessary conservatism or unrestrained generality.

Methodology, ah, that's the thing! As we note in chapter 1, investigators (and/or readers) in language development frequently forget just how thin our database on sign language development really is. Unlike research on language development in hearing children, the corpora used in even the benchmark studies in our field are not easily accessible (if at all) to other researchers and students of language. In large measure, this reflects the difficulty of trying to code a visual-spatial language with words and symbols on a printed page or computer disk. Underlying that issue, however, is the fact that there is not yet agreement on the mechanics of sign language coding (perhaps a sign of some lingering immaturity) or much cross-laboratory sharing of video-based language samples as there is among investigators of hearing children's language development.

If the existing generalities about sign language development in deaf children are based on relatively limited data, the onus on a maturing field of study is to check out the generalizability of earlier reports, develop alternative and convergent methodologies (see Meier, chapter 9 this volume), and be willing to reconsider conclusions that have been based on restricted samples and (now) questionable assumptions. The goal here is not to second-guess those who made earlier advances in the field, but to recognize that as we move forward, we want to avoid garden paths that fail to lead in the right direction. Our understanding of signed languages is now so much greater than it was 30 years ago, it seems inconceivable that we have not made some grievous errors along the way, that all of our earlier observations will be reliable, that experimental data are fully without confounds. It seems likely that this situation is a continuous one, and it would serve us well to remember it. For example, we have to wonder whether the fact that many (most?) investigators of sign language development in deaf children use some version of the MacArthur Communication Development Inventory to assess vocabulary and early sign combinations (see, just in this volume, Anderson, chap. 6; Hoiting, chap. 7; Spencer & Harris, chap. 4; Volterra et al., chap. 3) will turn out to be a strength or a weakness when reconsidered 10 or 20 years from now.

One value of volumes like this one is that it makes us think of such things and critically re-examine both our own work and that of others in the field. With a collection of chapters like that presented here and the time to read and reread them—in sharp contrast to a conference, which has both the value and the challenge of simultaneity—one has the time to allow some pieces of the puzzle fall together on their own. Other pieces are more difficult to fit into the picture, and the time and thought required to do so sometimes provide all new insights, either of new configurations that make more sense or the recognition that what made sense before no longer does.

In the case of this book, the chapters are compelling in their urging of investigators to pause for a metaphorical moment, to look for and acknowledge differences, and not just similarities, between signed and spoken languages. Such a re-examination is not just about possible differences in the ways that the same meanings are combined and expressed, but also about the dynamics of language interactions between deaf children and others that influence subsequent aspects of language development. We assume that such consideration will be revealing with regard to other domains of development as well—such is the potential synergy of good research.

At a theoretical level, these chapters—and the picture they reveal—have great value with regard to understanding language at large and the ways in which they appear different depending on how they are studied (a kind of linguistic Heisenberg Principle). Investigators inside and outside of this field need to recognize natural sign languages as a resource for learning about visual languages and about learning language "through noise." We have seen enough now to believe that there are significant differences between signed languages and spoken languages, as well as between users of signed languages and spoken languages. Each of these has an independent reality that is of theoretical interest and utility with regard to work in other areas, but it is still unclear how their unique qualities influence each other in cross-domain interactions.

At both theoretical and methodological levels, we have to remember that much of the research on sign language development in deaf children concerns the earliest stages of development, and the chapters of this book clearly reflect that situation. There have long been laments about the lack of research, in general, on semantic and syntactic development after the preschool years, but the issue is of particular importance with regard to deaf children, because of the diverse and variable language models to which they are exposed. Research involving older deaf children is now emerging, but it is necessarily more speculative at this time, and we are not even close to understanding how variability in early language development will play itself out in the later years. We all act as though the effects of atypical early language environments magically disappear by the time deaf children become adults; we know nothing of the course of that presumed convergence, and there are those among us who doubt its veracity.

To some degree, several of these issues are simply natural consequences of the relative youth of the field. One thing that would improve the situation considerably is the availability of better access to primary data repositories. As we noted above, this is not a trivial issue, as the impact that representation and tools have on research on sign language development can remain unclear for a long time, later requiring backing up and redirection along a different path. Although this may be a valuable experience in itself and yield insights that might have been missed otherwise, having to invent a form of representation or coding for each project one does provides little by way of intellectual advancement. Moreover, it prejudices future work by others who might benefit from having such data available—if only they could figure out the coding scheme.

If such issues appear problematic, the good news is that they are resolvable with current wills and ways. Volumes of this sort have the potential to spur such changes, and we have hope that the excitement generated by the pieces of this puzzle coming together will motivate action to tear down the methodological barriers to greater progress and to fill in the gaps that, for one reason or another, have been of lesser interest or urgency until now. There are, however, some gaps that are more difficult to fill. One of these results from the loss of the renown researcher of child language, Elizabeth Bates, a small part of whose work led to development of the MacArthur Communicative Development Inventory, which is being used (in various forms) in so much research about deaf children. Another gap, even closer to home, is that left by the loss of our colleague, friend, and contributor, David Stewart. David's untimely death at age 50, on June 7, 2004, came as he was putting his finishing touches on a chapter for this volume on language development in the context of sign language use. David's contributions to research on the development and education of deaf children stand on their own—he was both a capable and insightful investigator and a dedicated and respected teacher. More than that, he was a friend to many in our field and someone who had so much more to give. The gap he left in this book will not be filled, and the many more contributions he would have made to the field are now in want of someone to address. Happily, David's research and teaching inspired many others to follow in his footsteps, and this is perhaps the greatest testament of all.

## REFERENCES

Emmorey, K. (2002). *Language, cognition, and the brain: Insights from sign language research*. Mahwah, NJ: Lawrence Erlbaum Associates.

Marschark, M. (2004). Cognitive functioning in deaf adults and children. In M. Marschark & P. E. Spencer (Eds.), *Oxford handbook of deaf studies, language, and education* (pp. 464–477). New York: Oxford University Press.

Mitchell, R. E., & Karchmer, M. A. (2004). Chasing the mythical ten percent: Parental hearing status of deaf and hard of hearing students in the United States. *Sign Language Studies, 4*, 138–163.

Schick, B. (2004). How might learning through an educational interpreter influence cognitive development? In E. A. Winston (Ed.), *Educational interpreting: How might it succeed?* (pp. 73–87). Washington, DC: Gallaudet University Press.

Spencer, P. E. (2000). Looking without listening: Is audition a prerequisite for normal development of visual attention during infancy? *Journal of Deaf Studies and Deaf Education, 5*, 291–302.

Spencer, P. E., & Marschark, M. (2003). Cochlear implants: Issues and implications. In M. Marschark & P. E. Spencer (Eds.), *Oxford handbook of deaf studies, language, and education* (pp. 434–448). New York: Oxford University Press.

Stokoe, W. C. (2001). *Language in hand*. Washington, DC: Gallaudet University Press.

# Contents

# Contributors

Diane Anderson
Institute of Human Development
University of California, Berkeley
1235 Tolman Hall
Berkeley, CA 94720 USA

Marianna Castrataro
Istituto di Psicologia del CNR
Via Nomentana, 56
00161 Roma, Italy

Deborah Chen Pichler
Department of Linguistics
Gallaudet University
800 Florida Avenue NE
Washington, DC 20002
   USA

Margaret Harris
Department of Psychology
Royal Holloway, University of
   London
Egham Hill
Surrey TW20 0EX, UK

Nini Hoiting
Royal Effatha Guyot Group
Department of Diagnostics and
   Innovation
Rijksstraatweg 63
9752 AC Haren, The Netherlands

Jana M. Iverson
Department of Psychology
University of Pittsburgh
3415 Sennott Square
210 S. Bouquet Street
Pittsburgh, PA 15260 USA

Diane Lillo-Martin
Department of Linguistics
University of Connecticut
337 Mansfield Road, Unit 1145
Storrs, CT 06269-1145 USA

Marc Marschark
Department of Research
National Technical Institute for
   the Deaf

Rochester Institute of Technology
96 Lomb Memorial Drive
Rochester, NY 14623 USA
  and Department of Psychology
University of Aberdeen
Aberdeen AB24 2UB Scotland,
  UK

Richard P. Meier
Department of Linguistics
The University of Texas at Austin
1 University Station B5100
Austin, TX 78712 USA

Dianne D. Morgan
Department of Counseling,
  Educational Psychology,
  and Research
100 Ball Hall
College of Education
University of Memphis
Memphis, TN 38152 USA

Gary Morgan
Department of Language and
  Communication Science
City University
Northampton Square
London, EC1V 0HB UK

Carol A. Padden
Department of Communication
University of California, San
  Diego
9500 Gilman Drive
La Jolla, CA 92093-0503 USA

Judy Reilly
Department of Psychology
San Diego State University
  and Université of Poitiers

6330 Alvarado Court, 208
San Diego, CA 92120 USA

Brenda Schick
Department of Speech,
  Language, and Hearing
  Sciences
Campus Box 409
University of Colorado
Boulder, CO 80309-0409 USA

Barbara Shaffer
Department of Linguistics
Humanities 526
University of New Mexico
Albuquerque, NM 87131 USA

Jenny L. Singleton
Department of Educational
  Psychology
University of Illinois at
  Urbana-Champaign
1310 S. Sixth Street, 226 ED
Champaign, IL 61820 USA

Dan I. Slobin
Department of Psychology
University of California
3210 Tolman #1650
Berkeley, CA 94720-1650 USA

Patricia Elizabeth Spencer
Texas A&M University at
  Corpus Christi
6300 Ocean Drive
Corpus Christi, TX 78412 USA

Virginia Volterra
Istituto di Psicologia del CNR
Via Nomentana, 56
00161 Roma, Italy

# Advances in the Sign Language
# Development of Deaf Children

# 1

# Understanding Sign Language Development of Deaf Children

*Marc Marschark, Brenda Schick, &*
*Patricia Elizabeth Spencer*

*As long as we have deaf people on Earth, we will have Sign Language.*
*It is God's noblest gift to the Deaf.*

 —George W. Veditz, *Preservation of the Sign Language*

Sign language is not new. In fact, some investigators have argued that the first human languages were signed rather than spoken (see Armstrong, 1999; Stokoe, 2001). Discussions about the role of sign language in learning and in deaf education also have been around for a long time (e.g., Bartlett, 1850; Bell, 1898; James, 1893), as have descriptions of its place in the lives of deaf people and their communities (see Baynton, 1996; Woll & Ladd, 2003). Attempts to understand the structure of signed languages as linguistic systems, on the other hand, are relatively recent. At just more than 40 years old (Stokoe, 1960/2005; Stokoe, Casterline, & Croneberg, 1965), sign language linguistics is still quite young given the typical pace of scientific progress. On this time line, research on the sign language of deaf and hearing children acquiring it as a first language is still in its metaphorical childhood (e.g., Boyes Braem 1973/1990; Kantor, 1980; McIntire, 1977; Schlesinger & Meadow, 1972), and our understanding of deaf children's acquisition of specific sign language structures and their use in discourse is a mere babe in arms (see Morgan, chapter 13 this volume).

The earliest discussions of the development of sign language in deaf children, beginning in the mid-nineteenth century, relied primarily on theoretical/philosophical arguments. Over the next 50 years or so, observations of school-age deaf children were added to the argument, based on the dubious assumption that their language repertoires and performance reflected the impact of sign language as a first language (see below) and thus demonstrated its value—or lack thereof, depending on the particular observations cited and the perspective of the commentator. Today, investigators are examining deaf children's sign language development in both naturalistic contexts and controlled testing situations. Such studies are providing a better understanding of deaf children's language *competence* (their implicit knowledge of language), the course of development, and pragmatic aspects of their conversational interactions with language models.

With increasing breadth and depth in the study of children's sign language acquisition, we are now seeing advances in several domains at once, with evidence of research synergism that reveals generalizations about the nature of how deaf children learn language, the role of sign language in other aspects of development, and language itself. However, the history of signed languages within society and debate about its appropriateness in educating deaf children has influenced research and researchers in this field in ways that are not often obvious but always lurking in the background. The field also has been shaped by the fact that, as a young one, its investigators have come from diverse backgrounds: linguistics and language development to be sure, but also cognitive and developmental psychology, anthropology, communication science, sociology, neuropsychology, deaf education, sign language interpreting, and others. Moreover, in contrast with researchers studying development in most other languages, those involved in research on sign languages (given that they are usually hearing people) are often not native and sometimes are not even fluent users of those languages. Although these researchers are usually guided by deaf assistants and consultants, it is useful to keep in mind that had existing research been driven from within the community of deaf signers, rather than from outside, it might have taken a very different route—and it still may.

## HISTORICAL REPORTS OF SIGN LANGUAGE

The use of sign languages is well documented. Historical records from both Western and Middle Eastern cultures indicate that deaf people and Deaf[1] communities that used sign language have existed for at least 7,000 years. In Plato's *Cratylus* (360 B.C.), we see one of the earliest considerations of sign language, as Socrates poses the question, "Suppose that we had no voice or tongue and wanted to indicate objects to one another. Should we not, like the deaf and dumb, make signs with the hands, head, and the rest of the body?" In the fifteenth century, the courts of the Ottoman sultans included hundreds of deaf people whose responsibilities included teaching sign language to the rest of the court

---

[1] In this and the following chapters, "deaf" refers to audiological status, whereas "Deaf" refers to linguistic-cultural affiliation.

(Woll & Ladd, 2003). In this case the issue was a social-political one, as it was deemed inappropriate to speak in front of the sultan.

One of the best-known historical examples of a signing deaf community is from the North America in the 1600s, in Scituate, Massachusetts, the second oldest town in Plymouth Colony. Members of the large deaf population of Kent, England, had immigrated to Scituate, and their sign language took root in the New World. By the 1690s, many of those families and deaf families from other Massachusetts towns had moved to Martha's Vineyard. There, intermarriage led to an extremely high rate of deafness, and signing was a natural and accepted form of communication long before the first school for the deaf was established (Groce, 1985).

Such reports of communities of persons who signed provide us with some understanding of the lives of deaf people in earlier times. However, other than the occasional observation that a particular child or group used a signed language, there is little to be gleaned from such accounts that suggests any particular interest in sign language as an object of linguistic study or in the sign language development of deaf children. There are few documented accounts of how adults actually produced sign language, and no historic records of children's productions, as opposed to their interpretations, have come down to us.

## SIGN LANGUAGE IN THE EDUCATION OF DEAF CHILDREN

Looking to history for early uses of sign language in the education of deaf children, there is relatively little information beyond isolated descriptions of particular individuals and the occasional writings of several educational pioneers. For the most part, it appears that early efforts at deaf education involved a focus on language learning through reading and writing, what later came to be called the *natural* method, rather than either sign or speech. In the late 1400s, for example, the Dutch Humanist Rudolphus Agricola described a deaf person who had been taught to read and write, thus offering one of the first suggestions that deaf individuals could be educated effectively. His work was later elaborated by the Italian mathematician and physician Girolamo Cardano, who, in a 1575 book, advocated for the education of deaf children, citing their ability to "speak by writing" and "hear by reading." The Spanish Benedictine monk Pedro Ponce de Leon also is frequently noted as at least a candidate for the title of "father of deaf education." In Spain during the Renaissance, as in ancient Rome, sons could only inherit the wealth and power of aristocratic families if they were literate; thus, it was important that young deaf men acquire literacy skills. Ponce de Leon was highly regarded in this respect, and in his writings he described teaching the congenitally deaf sons of the nobility to read and write in Spanish, Latin, and Greek.

In the middle of the eighteenth century, sign language was used in the world's first government-sponsored school for deaf children, a national institution for deaf-mutes (now, the *Institut National des Jeunes Sourds de Paris*), established in Paris under the guidance of Charles Michel Abbé de l'Epée. Although he was not the first observer to recognize the use of sign language by deaf individuals (see Stokoe, 1960/2005), he developed a system of "methodical signs" (*signes methodiques*) by taking the natural sign language in use in the Paris deaf community and extensively modifying it to resemble spoken French. Most notably, de l'Epée added signs to represent various aspects of French grammar, such as tense, mood, articles, and prepositions, some of which are still parts of American Sign Language (ASL; e.g., indications of future and past). Later, Alexander Graham Bell (1898) referred to signing at the school as the "de l'Epée sign language." de l'Epée saw sign language as a natural way for deaf people to communicate and with his successor, Abbé Roch Ambroise Sicard, advocated for its use in education.

Thomas Hopkins Gallaudet, visiting from the United States, was impressed with the sign-language–based curriculum and spent several months at the institute with Sicard. It was there that he recruited Laurent Clerc, a deaf assistant teacher, to bring the curriculum, as well as the concept of methodical signs, to American and establish the Connecticut Asylum for the Deaf and Dumb (now the American School for the Deaf) in 1817. de l'Epée's "methodological" approach was not entirely a success in America, however, and Baynton (1996) reports that the "methodical signs were too unwieldy, slow, confusing, and difficult to remember for teachers and students alike" (p. 119). Other critics of the methodical signs argued that they were not natural and could not become a part of the language, and they were "opposed to the genius of the language" (Baynton, 1996, p. 121). Harvey Peet, a prominent educator of deaf children at the time, thought that while the methodical signs were useful for educational lessons designed to teach English, they would not be adopted into the natural sign language. He believed that in natural sign language, "syntax was not accidental," and that changing it would destroy the language (Peet, 1857, cited in Baynton, 1996, p. 119). By the mid-1800s, the "de l'Epée sign language" had only a small following in deaf education.

For Gallaudet, sign language helped solve one of the major problems related to deafness, that of access to the gospel and salvation (Baynton, 1996). Gallaudet believed that education should develop the conscience of a moral and religious human being. He argued that by using sign language "the deaf-mute can intelligibly conduct his private devotions, and join in social religious exercises with his fellow pupils" (Gallaudet, 1948, cited in Baynton, 1996, p.18).

Ironically, although sign language was considered a means by which one could address the consciousness and soul—and was thought to be superior to speech in the expression of emotions—even some of its supporters felt that sign language was inferior to speech in conveying abstract thought. Deaf leaders of the time, in contrast, expressed the value that sign language had in the deaf community. As expressed in the epigraph to this chapter by George W. Veditz, a leader in the Deaf community and a proponent of sign language in deaf education, who signed for one of the first recorded films of sign languages, sign language is "God's most noble gift to the Deaf."

Despite scientific observations indicating that spoken language was not necessary for deaf individuals in order to be able to think and reason (e.g., James, 1893), many hearing educators and philosophers still thought otherwise and claimed that deaf children must acquire vocal articulation and spoken language to be able to function cognitively at an abstract level. Adopting Samuel Heinicke's "oral approach" to schooling for deaf children, established in Leipzig in 1778, Preyer (1882) advocated education through spoken language only in the United States, arguing that without speech deaf children might understand "lower order" concepts and abstractions but not the "higher abstractions" required for education.

Among educators and philosophers, the debate about the utility of sign language in educating deaf children continued and is well documented in the *American Annals of the Deaf and Dumb* throughout the second half of the nineteenth century and beyond. Commentators in the *Annals* during this period struggled with how a deaf child could "naturally" learn spoken language and, conversely, how sign language could be "natural" in a hearing family. For many, sign language was seen as a way to "unlock" the deaf child's mind and provide an avenue for education. Bell (1898), for example—recognized as a vocal opponent of sign language for children with any hearing at all—nonetheless recognized that sign language might be useful for deaf children who could not learn language through any other modality. The majority of the educational establishment, meanwhile, saw sign language as dooming deaf children to limited intellectual growth.

Of course, there was ample practical evidence that sign language functioned as a real language within the Deaf community, and throughout the first half of the twentieth century, the Deaf community lamented that sign language had been excluded from the schools. Deaf adults rarely were given any substantial role in the governance of the school, however. Few deaf people served as school principals or superintendents, and probably no deaf person sat on a school governing board (Baynton, 1996). The Deaf community therefore fought back in the only manner available to them: They actively lobbied state legislatures and school boards to adopt sign language, and at each annual convention of the National Association of the Deaf, resolutions were passed that condemned the banishment of sign language from the schools. Stokoe (1960/2005, p. 9) provided this example of one such resolution:

> Resolved, that the oral method, which withholds from the congenitally and quasi-congenitally deaf the use of the language of signs outside the schoolroom, robs the children of their birthright; that those champions of the oral method, who have been carrying on a warfare, both overt and covert, against the use of the language of signs by the adult, are not friends of the deaf; and that in our opinion, it is the duty of every teacher of the deaf, no matter what method he or she uses, to have a working command of the sign language.

Nevertheless, while sign language continued to flourish in the Deaf community, it remained without a formal role in education as well as not seen as worthy of scientific investigation. As we now know, it eventually would take the civil rights movement in the United States and a new line of linguistic research before schools for the deaf would allow sign language a role in the classroom.

## ATTEMPTS AT COMPROMISE

Although each side in the "war of methods" clearly has had isolationist supporters, there also have been individuals who sought some middle ground, in order to match each child's abilities and needs. Several times over the past 150 years, there have been attempts to join the "oral" and "manual" approaches to education into what was originally referred to as "the combined system." These systems typically have come from educators more interested in practical results rather than philosophical orientation (e.g., Westervelt & Peet, 1880), in an effort to promote integration and assimilation into the larger hearing community, as well as to development literacy skills. The combined methods of the nineteenth century lost out to oral education, however, and it was to be almost 100 years before they re-emerged in the 1960s and 1970s. This time, the "combined" movement was fueled by a new recognition of the linguistic status of natural sign languages, the marked lack of success in teaching many deaf children spoken language, and, consequently, the need to rethink assumptions of some investigators about deaf children "lacking language" (e.g., Furth, 1966). There also were continuing concerns about low levels of literacy and other academic skills attained by most deaf students at a time when schools for the deaf in the United States were overcrowded, as a result of rubella epidemics.

In an attempt to teach deaf children the language that would be used in schools, several manual forms of spoken language were developed, collectively known in North America as manually coded English. These artificial systems (e.g., signed English, SEE1, SEE2) generally used individual signs from the community's indigenous, naturally developed sign language but followed rules of the spoken vernacular for syntax, word meaning, and morphology in order to allow (at least in theory) simultaneous signed and spoken language production (see Anthony, 1971; Bornstein, 1990; Gustason, Pfetzing, & Zawolkow, 1980). The reincarnation of the "methodological" approach largely disappointed again, however, and numerous reports exist of the difficulties faced in these attempts to adapt visual-manual language to grammatical structures of auditory-verbal languages (Gee & Goodhart, 1985; Mounty, 1986). Even today, there is little evidence that these systems increase the overall level of academic performance by deaf students, and they have not proven any more effective for promoting reading and writing than have natural signed languages, despite that being their *raîson d'etre* (Marschark, in press).

The lack of success evidenced by "combined" systems now has led us back to a re-emphasis on sign languages that developed naturally, over time, in various Deaf communities. By the late twentieth century, linguistic evidence of the sophistication and formal properties of these "natural" sign languages was available. In many countries, increased sensitivity to and valuing of the rights of minority populations led to greater recognition of Deaf people as members of a special group with its own language and, to some extent, cultural values and expectations and "ways of being." It has now been demonstrated that when appropriate language models are available, deaf children acquire these languages efficiently and at least as early as hearing children acquire their community's spoken language.

Some educational programs are beginning to support the development of deaf students as both bilingual—fluent in the sign language of the Deaf community and the language of the larger hearing community, perhaps in written form—and bicultural, with the ability to participate in both Deaf and hearing communities (see LaSasso & Lollis, 2003). There are also an increasing number of other countries who have adopted their Deaf community's natural sign language as the language of instruction (see Ahlgren & Hyltenstam 1994; Hoiting, chapter 7 this volume; Mahshie, 1995). Unfortunately, there are still few evaluations of the extent to which bilingual education has been successful in providing fluency either in language of instruction or in enhancing academic achievement in various content areas. The "method wars" thus continue, stronger in some countries than others, and deaf children and their parents continue to face sometimes acrimonious debate and conflicting advice about the type of language system they should use and the most effective means of communication in the classroom.

## LINGUISTIC STUDIES OF SIGN LANGUAGE DEVELOPMENT COME OF AGE

Around the time that American Sign Language (ASL)[2] was first recognized as a true language, following the work of Stokoe and his colleagues in the 1960s (e.g., Stokoe et al., 1965), there was rapid growth of
research on both the structure and function of language development
in hearing children.[2] While supporters of spoken language training for
deaf children continued their focus on improving speech articulation in
therapeutic settings, those interested in sign language began to examine the use of sign language in mother–child interactions and home
settings. The first such studies, appearing in the 1960s and 1970s, usually involved simple vocabulary comparisons between hearing children
and deaf children (almost always of hearing parents). Several studies,
however, sought to describe the linguistic and communicative aspects
of mother–deaf-child interactions. Consistent with the investigations by
Snow (1972), Newport (1977), and others focusing on the way that hearing mothers talk to their hearing children, most of that work examined
the language of the mothers (i.e., motherese)—and tangentially about
the reciprocal language produced by the children (see Volterra & Erting, 1990). These research studies were some of the first to consider
Deaf parents as a resource, to help us understand the dynamics of parent–
child interaction in a visual language, in comparison with a spoken
language.

Several early studies of mother–child communication involving deaf
children with hearing mothers suggested that poor maternal communication skills had negative effects on their children's language learning
(for discussion, see Beckwith, 1977; Goss, 1970; Schlesinger & Meadow, 1972). Comparisons with dyads in which the mother was deaf,
however, demonstrated that early interactions coupled with effective
communication had positive effects on language development as well
as social-emotional development (e.g., Kantor, 1982; Meadow, Greenberg, Erting, & Carmichael, 1981). In particular, the quality of the
mother–child relationship was found to be strongly related to children's communication competence, and mother–child communication
was strongly related to positive developmental outcomes in a variety of

---

[2] Throughout this chapter, "American Sign Language" (ASL) and "English" are used
generically to refer to all signed and spoken English languages. It is noteworthy that most
of the research conducted to date on sign language development in deaf children has
involved children in North America acquiring ASL. Although it is assumed that the
principles underlying the development of ASL in that context are representative of any
sign language in any naturalistic context, subtle and not-so-subtle variations due to culture, context, and educational methods suggest the potential for interesting study and
erroneous conclusions.

other domains. Findings indicating that gestural systems developed even when mothers and deaf children primarily used spoken language (e.g., Greenberg, Calderon, & Kusché, 1984; see Volterra, Iverson, & Castrataro, chapter 3 this volume) opened new doors of sign language development research, and the nature of this reciprocal communicative-social-linguistic dance has been of interest ever since (see, e.g., Meadow-Orlans, Spencer, & Koester, 2004).

In perhaps the first study of its kind, Schlesinger and Meadow (1972) examined the effects that deaf children's language had on their social interactions with their mothers, rather than the other way around. Their longitudinal study described the language development of four young deaf children (two of whom had deaf parents) acquiring sign language as a first language. Although the children varied greatly, Schlesinger and Meadow reported three consistent findings that were remarkable for the time and are still important today. First, they found that children's use of sign did not interfere with their spoken language development. Rather, spoken language skill increased as the children learned more sign, a finding also reported by Crittenden, Ritterman, and Wilcox (1986; see also Yoshinaga-Itano, in press). Second, Schlesinger and Meadow observed that the language milestones of the four children they studied paralleled those of hearing children (see Newport & Meier, 1985), suggesting innate (Lillo-Martin, 1997) or cognitive-social-environmental (Bates, Benigni, Bretherton, Camaioni, & Volterra, 1977) invariants underlying language acquisition, regardless of its mode. Third, Schlesinger and Meadow found that the availability of sign language in families with deaf children greatly decreased the amount of "communication frustration" between children and parents relative to deaf children, a finding that was to lead to many studies of mother–deaf-child dyads in the years following.

All three of these findings led to lines of programmatic research in several laboratories, and the apparent similarity of language development by deaf children with deaf parents and hearing children of hearing parents provided a context in which the study of sign language development in deaf children blossomed in its own right. Not only did such investigations offer pioneering (yet modern) investigations of a new "kind" of language development, but the comparisons of spoken and sign language acquisition yielded, and continues to yield, new insights into the nature of language, its origins, and the relation of language to other aspects of development.

Unfortunately, unlike contemporaneous research on the language development of hearing children (e.g., Brown, 1973), the transcripts used in most of the early and more recent sign language studies have not been made available to researchers outside the original teams that conducted the research. This may be, in part, because sign productions are more difficult to represent in writing than spoken productions, but a great deal is also lost in the written documentation of early spoken language, and investigators found ways to overcome that obstacle via the CHILDES project (see MacWhinney, 2001). Alternatively, this omission may simply reflect the youth of the field and the ongoing search for common methodologies—thus offering a new and exciting challenge (see Slobin, chapter 2 this volume).

## THE CONTEMPORARY CONTEXT FOR STUDIES OF SIGN LANGUAGE DEVELOPMENT

Today, ASL and other natural sign languages are again being used in schools, but still without widespread acceptance in the education community, which continues to favor manual versions of spoken language. This time, the use of sign languages found in Deaf communities is accompanied by somewhat greater if still limited efforts to document their appropriateness and utility for educational purposes and subsequent literacy development. In this context, sign language development is not just interesting to those who are motivated by theoretical reasons, but schools, teachers, and families are coming to recognize their need to understand how a visual language develops and how it interacts with other aspects of development.

The available research in this area is not yet sufficient to provide these audiences with a clear roadmap of sign language development. North American researchers do not even agree on what types of signing constitute ASL (see Kuntze, 1990; see also Anderson, chapter 6 this volume), a language that is changing as it is used by a larger community than previously, one with a large number of second-language learners, both hearing and deaf. This is an interesting, natural situation worthy of investigation in its own right, as the great number of linguistic variations within the Deaf community and the diversity in sign systems to which deaf children are exposed reflect the unusual milieu that surrounds deaf children as language learners. In this milieu, classroom teachers often are not fluent in sign language, even when it is the (or a) language of instruction. In the United States, neither national certification of deaf educators nor most teacher training programs in deaf education require any minimum competency in sign language in order to teach. In fact, each of us has heard hearing teachers of deaf children claim that they learned how to sign from the children they taught. Deaf children thus are often faced with language learning environments that few hearing children would ever encounter: For many deaf children, most of their early language models are not fluent users of the language the children are learning. Their parents, like most hearing people, learn sign language as a second language, often through informal coursework and self-instruction without the benefit of using it daily across various contexts or having fluent models (a challenge then shared by their children).

It is important to keep in mind here that the children we are describing represent approximately 95% of the population of deaf children (Mitchell & Karchmer, 2004). As a result of this situation, most deaf children do not encounter "good" examples of a full, rich language until they encounter deaf adults or deaf children from deaf families. Even in those cases, however, because most deaf adults were in a similar situation as children (i.e., with hearing parents), the signing they see from deaf adults as well as deaf peers will be quite variable. Together with the relatively degraded and restricted input they receive from their parents, this added variability in language models typically results in language delays that, in turn, make it all the more difficult to take advantage of fluent language when they are finally exposed to it (Erting, Prezioso, & O'Grady Hynes, 1990; Spencer, 1993a, 1993b).

The complexity of this language learning situation often appears to be missed or ignored. Research on sign language development has focused primarily on generalities, and most studies have involved a small number of children that are not necessarily representative of deaf children at large, and fairly brief language samples (see Tomasello & Stahl, 2004; see also Meier, chapter 9 this volume). All too often, in efforts to interpret data unambiguously and to demonstrate commonalities between deaf and hearing children, researchers have assumed simplistic accounts of development in which deaf children with deaf parents are presumed to be typically developing children. Little interest has been shown in determining the validity of this assumption or how to know whether any particular deaf child has a language disorder (vs. a typical delay). In reality, there is not research on what a language disorder looks like in ASL. In addition, only rarely has the possibility been considered that growing up with sign language might lead to cognitive and social differences worthy of investigation (Marschark, 1993; Stokoe, 2001).

Unfortunately, much of the available research on signed languages, particularly in developmental investigations, has minimized the linguistic diversity within the signing community. Kuntze (1990) thus argued that "an unfortunate side to the otherwise marvelous wealth of new information about ASL was that the focus of the linguistic analysis was unbalanced" (p. 76) in that linguistic study has focused on those aspects of ASL that seemed more ASL-like and put aside aspects of signing that seem to be influenced by English. As a Deaf adult and a researcher, Kuntze believes that linguistic inquiry has created artificial definitions of what is inside ASL, versus outside (reminiscent of earlier claims that signed languages were not worthy of study). At least with regard to ASL, the sociopolitical history of sign language alluded to above thus clearly has influenced what researchers have investigated, a situation not far below the surface in studies of other sign languages as well. Importantly, the pressure in this regard is not all from the "outside"; influences from within the Deaf community and its supporters are altering the course of language research as well.

Beyond these issues of research theory and methodology, there are a number of more subtle complexities in deaf children's language development that appear worthy of study. For example, those deaf mothers who grew up in hearing families may have very different social histories and parenting resources, as well as communication styles, from deaf mothers from multigenerational deaf families. These potential differences have usually been ignored when the language behaviors of "deaf mothers" are described. In addition, variations in the language-learning environments provided to deaf children by hearing parents are often also overlooked. Only more recently have researchers begun to address how deaf children from hearing families can learn natural sign languages as well, enriching our understanding of how children learn visual languages (see Lindert, 2001; see also Hoiting, chapter 7 this volume).

In considering sign language growth in young deaf children, it is also important to keep in mind that language development and language learning are not the same thing. *Language development* typically is used in the sense of a natural or automatic unfolding of language along a regular path, as indicated by universal milestones relevant to language *qua* language. *Language learning*, by comparison, refers to language acquisition that requires some amount of effort on the part of both a learner and teacher(s), that is, intentional rather than naturally occurring activity. Although this distinction is rarely important in studies of hearing children (viz., only when those children have special learning needs), it is not one that can be viewed lightly in studies of the language used by deaf children. Language appears to *develop* relatively naturally among deaf and hearing children of deaf parents (given the above caveats) and among hearing children of hearing parents. Deaf children of hearing parents, meanwhile, typically have been *taught* language from the time they enter early intervention programming through their college careers.

It appears likely that these language differences between deaf and hearing children have a variety of influences on other aspects of development. To the extent that we ignore them, we ignore much of the need for a greater understanding of sign language development in deaf children—the practical need for language in social and educational settings—and risk overly simplistic accounts of children's sign language that are applicable in only a minority of cases. Recognition and understanding of the complexity of this situation require concerted and collaborative efforts on both theoretical and practical fronts. But they also carry potential for considerable gains with regard to broad issues of language development and the education of deaf children (Marschark, 2002) as well as a greater understanding of the majority of individuals who make up the Deaf community and eventually watch sign language develop in their own children.

In a similar vein, much of the research on sign language development to date has implicitly attempted to show how the development of ASL or other sign languages is no different than the development of any spoken language. One would have thought that the years of study seeking to document the elusive *early sign advantage* would have shown the importance of recognizing variability both in sign language and in deaf children (e.g., Meier & Newport, 1990), but several related issues remain unsettled. Lillo-Martin and Pichler (chapter 10 this volume), for example, appear to accept the full comparability of signed and spoken languages as proven fact, while Spencer and Harris (chapter 4 this volume) and Marschark (in press) question whether the two modalities might have slightly different developmental consequences, as evidenced in a variety of cognitive, neuropsychological, and psycholinguistic studies involving adults. In the broader context, while sociocultural studies have emphasized the uniqueness of Deaf culture, language studies have sought commonality of signed and spoken languages, their underpinnings, and their consequences.[3]

Several of the other chapters in this volume either explicitly (e.g., Slobin, chapter 2) or implicitly (e.g., Reilly, chapter 11; Schick, chapter 5) acknowledge that sign languages, as a group, may have typological differences from spoken languages. Recognition that signed and spoken languages may not be strictly comparable allows us to see what is unique in the development of a visual language and potentially different about the development of deaf children. The benefits to the study of language and language development may be the first to appear, but the implications for other domains of development and for the education of deaf children would not be far behind. To achieve this end, however, the study of signed languages and language development will need to more focus more on individual variation and entail more cross-linguistic comparisons (Kuntze, 1990). As Slobin (chapter 2 this volume) notes, "In order to make cross-linguistic comparisons— between spoken and signed languages, or between the acquisition of

---

[3] It is tempting to suggest that this orientation is a symptom of the hearing status of the investigators. However, such "blinders" may be less the consequence of a hearing–speaking chauvinism than reflection of many investigators' reaction to such a possibility. All too often, an apparent desire to support Deaf individuals and the Deaf community results in an uncritical embrace of all things Deaf and an advocacy of "equality" that denies potentially interesting differences and important variability.

different languages—it is necessary to work in a linguistic framework that is not biased toward languages of a particular type." Slobin also notes that we need to be very careful that our tools and terms do not bias us toward making sign language look like spoken languages, lest those tools interfere with that which they are designed to investigate.

Despite the fact that researchers have focused on investigating those parts of the language that have fairly obvious counterparts in spoken language (e.g., phonology, syntax, pronouns, morphology), we have learned much about the different forms in which many of those aspects are expressed in visual versus auditory languages. This includes the use of space, nonmanual markers, or classifiers (see Lindert 2001; Loew, 1982; T. Supalla, 1982) to indicate meanings typically expressed by sequentially ordered bound and free morphemes in spoken languages. Some of these are described elsewhere in this volume (see, e.g., Hoiting, chapter 7; Meier, chapter 9; Reilly, chapter 11; Shaffer, chapter 12; Schick, chapter 5), but many more are to be explored. A better understanding of how visual languages develop will have direct impact on early intervention and educational programming for deaf children, improving opportunities and efficiency. Appreciating the language diversity among deaf children as well as between them and hearing children will allow new insights into both their language learning and the nature of signed languages. Perhaps most important, all of these advances will provide a context in which deaf children can thrive and be understood as individuals as well as members of diverse groups. And if some of them go on to join other investigators conducting research "from the inside," areas of study will emerge that are as new and exciting to them as their language is to us today. What more could one ask for?

## REFERENCES

Ahlgren, I., & Hyltenstam, K. (Eds.). (1994). Bilingualism in deaf education: Proceedings of the international conference on bilingualism in deaf education. Stockholm, Sweden [Special issue]. *International Studies on Sign Language and Communication of the Deaf, 27.*

Anthony, D. (1971). *Seeing essential English manual.* Anaheim, CA: Educational Services Division.

Armstrong, D. F. (1999). *Original signs.* Washington, DC: Gallaudet University Press.

Bartlett, D. E. (1850). The acquisition of language. *American Annals of the Deaf and Dumb, 3*(1), 83–92.

Bates, E., Benigni, L., Bretherton, I., Camaioni, L., & Volterra, V. (1977). From gesture to the first word: On cognitive and social prerequisites. In M. Lewis & L. A. Rosenblum (Eds.), *Interaction, conversation, and the development of language* (pp. 247–308). New York: Academic Press.

Baynton, D. C. (1996). *Forbidden signs: American culture and the campaign against sign language.* Chicago: University of Chicago Press.

Beckwith, L. (1977). Relationships between infants' vocalizations and their mothers' behaviors. *Merrill-Palmer Quarterly, 17,* 211–226.

Bell, A. G. (1898). *The question of sign-language and the utility of signs in the instruction of the deaf.* Washington, DC: Sanders Printing Office.

Bornstein, H. (Ed.). (1990). *Manual communication: Implications for education.* Washington, DC: Gallaudet University Press.

Boyes Braem, P. (1973). *The acquisition of the dez (handshape) in American Sign Language: A preliminary analysis.* Unpublished manuscript, Salk Working Papers, Salk Institute, San Diego, CA. (Published in *From gesture to language in hearing and deaf children,* by V. Volterra & C. J. Erting, Eds., (pp. 107–127). 1990, Berlin: Springer-Verlag.

Brown, R. (1973). *A first language.* Cambridge, MA: Harvard University Press.

Crittenden, J. B., Ritterman, S. I., & Wilcox, E. W. (1986). Communication mode as a factor in the performance of hearing-impaired children on a standardized receptive vocabulary test. *American Annals of the Deaf, 131,* 356–360.

Erting, C. J., Prezioso, C., & O'Grady Hynes, M. (1990). The interactional context of deaf mother-infant communication. In V. Volterra & C. J. Erting (Eds.), *From gesture to language in hearing and deaf children* (pp. 97–106). Berlin: Springer-Verlag.

Furth, H. G. (1966). *Thinking without language.* New York: Free Press.

Gee, J., & Goodhart, W. (1985). Nativization, linguistic theory, and deaf language acquisition. *Sign Language Studies, 49,* 291–342.

Goss, R. N. (1970). Language used by mothers of deaf children and mothers of hearing children. *American Annals of the Deaf, 115,* 93–96.

Greenberg, M., Calderon, R., & Kusché, C. (1984). Early intervention using simultaneous communication with deaf infants: The effect on communication development. *Child Development, 55,* 607–616.

Groce, N. E. (1985). *Everyone here spoke sign language: Hereditary deafness at Martha's Vineyard.* Cambridge, MA: Harvard University Press.

Gustason, G., Pfetzing, D., & Zawolkow, E. (1980). *Signing exact English.* Silver Spring, MD: National Association of the Deaf.

James, W. (1893). Thought before language: A deaf-mute's recollections. *American Annals of the Deaf and Dumb, 18,* 135–145.

Kantor, R. (1980). The acquisition of classifiers in American Sign Language. *Sign Language Studies, 28,* 193–208.

Kantor, R. (1982). Communicative interaction: Mother modification and child acquisition of American Sign Language. *Sign Language Studies, 36,* 233–278.

Kuntze, M. (1990). ASL: Unity and power: Communication issues among deaf people. *Deaf American Monograph, 40,* 75–77.

LaSasso, C., & Lollis, J. (2003). Survey of residential and day schools for deaf students in the united states that identify themselves as bilingual-bicultural programs. *Journal of Deaf Studies and Deaf Education, 8,* 79–91.

Lillo-Martin, D. (1997). The modular effects of sign language acquisition. In M. Marschark, P. Siple, D. Lillo-Martin, R. Campbell, & V. S. Everhart (Eds.), *Relations of language and thought: The view from sign language and deaf children* (pp. 62–109). New York: Oxford University Press.

Lindert, R. (2001). *Hearing families with deaf children: Linguistic and communicative aspects of American Sign Language development.* Unpublished doctoral dissertation, University of California, Berkeley.

MacWhinney, B. (2001). From CHILDES to TALKBANK. In M. Almgren, A. Barreña, M. Ezeizaberrena, I. Idiazabal, & B. MacWhinney (Eds.), *Research on child language acquisition* (pp. 17–34). Somerville, MA: Cascadilla.

Mahshie, S. (1995). *Educating deaf children bilingually: With insights and applications from Sweden and Denmark.* Washington, DC: Pre-College Programs, Gallaudet University.

Marschark, M. (1993). Origins and interactions in language, cognitive, and social development of deaf children. In M. Marschark & D. Clark (Eds.), *Psychological perspectives on deafness* (pp. 7–26). Hillsdale, NJ: Lawrence Erlbaum.

Marschark, M. (2002). Foundations of communication and the emergence of language in deaf children. G. Morgan & B. Woll (Eds.), *Current developments in child signed language research* (pp. 1–28). Amsterdam: John Benjamins.

Marschark, M. (in press). Developing deaf children or deaf children developing? In D. Power & G. Leigh (Eds.), *Educating deaf students: Global perspectives.* Washington, DC: Gallaudet University Press.

McIntire, M. L. (1977). The acquisition of American Sign Language hand configurations. *Sign Language Studies, 16,* 247–266.

Meadow, K. P., Greenberg, M. T., Erting, C., & Carmichael, H. (1981). Interactions of deaf mothers and deaf preschool children: Comparisons with three other groups of deaf and hearing dyads. *American Annals of the Deaf, 126,* 454–468.

Meadow-Orlans, K. P., Spencer, P. E., & Koester, L. S. (2004). *The world of deaf infants.* New York: Oxford University Press.

Meier, R. P., & Newport, E. L. (1990). Out of the hands of babes: On a possible sign advantage in language acquisition. *Language, 66,* 1–23.

Mitchell, R. E., & Karchmer, M. A. (2004). Chasing the mythical ten percent: parental hearing status of deaf and hard of hearing students in the United States. *Sign Language Studies, 4,* 138–163.

Mounty, J. (1986). *Nativization and input in the language development of two deaf children of hearing parents.* Unpublished doctoral dissertation, Boston University.

Newport, E. L. (1977). Motherese: The speech of mothers to young children. In J. J. Castellan, D. B. Pisoni, & G. R. Potts (Eds.), *Cognitive theory* (pp. 177–210). Hillsdale, NJ: Lawrence Erlbaum.

Newport, E. L., & Meier, R. (1985). Acquisition of American Sign Language. In D. I. Slobin (Ed.), *The crosslinguistic study of language acquisition* (pp. 881–938). Hillsdale, NJ: Lawrence Erlbaum.

Preyer, W. (1882). *Die Seele des Kindes.* Leipzig.

Schlesinger, H. S., & Meadow, K. P. (1972). *Sound and sign: Childhood deafness and mental health.* Berkeley, CA: University of California Press.

Snow, C. (1972). Mothers' speech to children learning language. *Child Development, 43,* 549–565.

Spencer, P. E. (1993a). Communication behaviours of infants with hearing loss and their hearing mothers. *Journal of Speech and Hearing Research, 36,* 311–321.

Spencer, P. E. (1993b). The expressive communication of hearing mothers and deaf infants. *American Annals of the Deaf, 138,* 275–283.

Stokoe, W. C. (1960). *Sign language structure: An outline of the visual communication system of the American deaf.* Studies in Linguistics, Occasional Papers 8. Buffalo, NY: Department of Anthropology and Linguistics, University of Buffalo. (Reprinted in *Journal of Deaf Studies and Deaf Education, 10,* 000–000, 2005).

Stokoe, W. C. (2001). *Language in hand.* Washington, DC: Gallaudet University Press.

Stokoe, W. C., Casterline, D. C., & Croneberg, C. G. (1965). *A dictionary of American Sign Language on linguistic principles.* Washington, DC: Gallaudet College Press.

Supalla, T. (1982). *Structure and acquisition of verbs of motion and location in American Sign Language.* Unpublished doctoral dissertation, University of California, San Diego.

Tomasello, M., & Stahl, D. (2004). Sampling children's spontaneous speech: How much is enough? *Journal of Child Language, 31,* 101–121.

Westervelt, Z., & Peet, H. P. (1880). The natural method. *American Annals of the Deaf, 25,* 212–217.

Volterra, V., & Erting, C. J. (Eds.). (1990). *From gesture to language in hearing and deaf children.* Berlin: Springer-Verlag.

Woll, B., & Ladd, P. (2003). Deaf communities. In M. Marschark & P. E. Spencer (Eds.), *Oxford handbook of deaf studies, language, and education* (pp. 151–163). New York: Oxford University Press.

Yoshinaga-Itano, C. (in press). Early identification, communication modality, and the development of speech and spoken language skills: Patterns and considerations. In P. E. Spencer & M. Marschark (Eds.), *Advances in the spoken language development of deaf and hard-of-hearing children.* New York: Oxford University Press.

# 2

# Issues of Linguistic Typology in the Study of Sign Language Development of Deaf Children

*Dan I. Slobin*

This chapter stands outside of the theme of "advances in the sign language development of deaf children." Those advances are admirably documented in the rest of this volume, and the development of sign languages has been illuminated by other recent collections as well (see Baker, van den Bogaerde, & Crasborn, 2003; Chamberlain, Morford, & Mayberry, 2000; Morgan & Woll, 2002). Indeed, this decade has begun with a flowering of crosslinguistic and interdisciplinary attention to signing children and their caregivers. My task in this chapter is twofold: first, to consider some lessons that have been learned from the crosslinguistic study of hearing children and their acquisition of a range of spoken languages (Berman & Slobin, 1994; Slobin, 1985a, 1985b, 1985c, 1992, 1997b, 1997c; Strömqvist & Verhoeven, 2004), and second, to attempt to situate the study of sign languages in a typological framework. My focus is thus on issues of linguistic analysis, with special attention to *typology* (Slobin, 1997e). The languages of the world—spoken and signed—present a kaleidoscopic array of diversity. Although linguists have striven, for centuries, to find an underlying uniformity, it now seems that the most interesting universals are revealed in systematic patterns of constrained variation, rather than in surface deviations from a single preordained formal structure. These universals are a collection of dimensions or parameters, making it possible to classify languages according to their positions on such dimensions, that is, to deal with *types* of languages.[1]

---

[1] In this chapter I use the term "dimension," rather than "parameter," as principles of constrained variation are central to both principles-and-parameters and functionalist-typological approaches.

**Table 2-1: Declensions of English Nominals**

| Case | Singular | Plural |
|------|----------|--------|
| Nominative | a king | kings |
| Genitive | king's, of a king | of kings |
| Dative | to a king | to kings |
| Accusative | a king | kings |
| Vocative | ó king! | ó kings! |
| Ablative | with, from, or by a king | by kings |

From da Silva (1809, p. 40).

Crosslinguistic studies of child language seek to compare the acquisition of comparable and contrasting languages in order to discover the mechanisms and processes that drive the course of development in general. A basic problem facing such investigation is to define the appropriate dimensions and comparison sets of languages. Many cautionary tales can be drawn from the history of linguistics and of developmental psycholinguistics. The relatively new field of sign language linguistics can learn from such tales when drawing comparisons between signed and spoken languages.

Perhaps the most elementary problem is to be aware of the presuppositions that the investigator brings from knowledge of a particular language or class of languages. We have learned to ridicule the early attempts of European explorers and missionaries to apply the terms of classical Greek and Latin grammar to the exotic languages they encountered in their new colonies. Even English was submitted to such analyses, as can be seen, for example, in table 2.1, which lists "declinations" provided in a Portuguese grammar of English from 1809 (da Silva, 1809).

How far have we come from the use of such traditional molds in the analysis of spoken languages, let alone sign languages? We still use many familiar classical categories in the description of English and other languages, albeit with increasing questioning of the universal applicability even of such time-worn notions as "noun," "verb," and "subject."[2] Grammars of sign languages also run the risk of uncritical

---

[2] Wolfgang Klein, a German linguist, points out somewhere that linguists must be wary of expecting to find familiar grammatical categories in unfamiliar languages. He takes issue with the general assumption of Western linguists that there must be verbs in Chinese, because we are used to languages with verbs. In a telling analogy, he suggests that Germans know that every cuisine includes potatoes, and so it is no surprise to find that the Chinese cuisine also relies on potatoes. It's just that their potatoes come in small grains and grow differently.

recourse to familiar linguistic terms and analyses. But just as English doesn't have a vocative case—even though classical languages did—American Sign Language (ASL), for example, may not have "pronouns" or "agreement" simply because these are found in descriptions of the language of the surrounding hearing community and the languages studied by English speakers. This is not the place for a detailed critique of linguistic analyses of sign languages; see, for example, Liddell (2003) and Taub (2001) for thoroughgoing and insightful attempts to take a fresh approach to the grammar of ASL, as well as chapters in Emmorey (2003) for concerns about the applicability of the category of "classifier" to signed languages.

Here I present some small case studies to demonstrate how child language research over the past decades has been forced to move away from the impulse to take a familiar language—generally English—as representing the child's initial assumptions about the nature of language. These case studies have implications for the description and analysis of children's acquisition of signed languages. The problem, in each instance, is to select an appropriate linguistic exemplar as the starting point for crosslinguistic comparison and generalization. Over time, American investigators have learned that English is not the best starting point for predicting patterns of child language development overall. Rather, English has come to be seen as an exemplar of a particular type of language—or, better, as an exemplar of the interplay of particular points on universal dimensions of variation. With regard to the investigation of sign languages—as suggested later in this chapter—the entire collection of comparison languages has been skewed because the sign languages that have been described differ in fundamental typology from the structures of the surrounding speaking communities in Eurasia and the Americas.

## SELECTING APPROPRIATE STARTING POINTS FOR THE PREDICTION OF PATTERNS OF LANGUAGE DEVELOPMENT

### Starting Point: The Primacy of Word Order

It is hard to escape the illusion that patterns of native-language thinking for speaking directly reflect the structure of human cognition. In the early years of American psycholinguistics, it was assumed that English subject–verb–object (SVO) word order follows the underlying logic of thought. For example, Osgood and Tanz (1977) proposed: "Our intuition about the nature of simple cognitions is . . . that they have an SVO structure. . . . Regardless of the dominant order type, in the process of language development in children there is initially a relatively fixed SVO ordering in 'sentence' productions" (pp. 539–540). And Bruner

(1975) suggested "that a concept of agent–action–object–recipient at the pre-linguistic level aids the child in grasping the linguistic meaning of appropriately ordered utterances involving such case categories as agentive, action, object, indirect object and so forth" (p. 17).

These intuitions led to crosslinguistic studies of early word order in children's production and comprehension, with the expectation that early stages of development would be characterized by fixed word order, and that the dominant early order would be SVO. The strategy of such comparative research is to pick languages that contrast on the relevant dimension. For example, in one study (Slobin, 1982; Slobin & Bever, 1982) we selected three SVO languages (English, Italian, Serbo-Croatian) and one SOV language (Turkish). The choice of languages reflected another principle of typologically oriented research—the interaction of several dimensions. The four languages lie on a scale of increasing flexibility in word order, due to the availability of inflectional cues to verb–argument structure, as shown in table 2.2. The English-based expectation was that children in all four languages would begin with reliance on a fixed word order, probably reflecting the dominant order in the input, and that inflectional marking of grammatical relations would be a later development.

Briefly stated, these expectations were not confirmed. Turkish, with its transparent and regular agglutinative inflectional morphology, allows for all six orders of S, V, and O; children as young as 24 months (2;0) had already mastered the case markers, used pragmatically appropriate word-order variation in their production, and comprehended all six orders. Serbo-Croatian has a complex, synthetic, and only partially reliable case-marking system; still, children of 2;0 had extracted the principle of case marking in their speech and correctly comprehended SVO sentences—but only if appropriate case marking

**Table 2-2: Grammatical Features of Four Languages**

|  | English | Italian | Serbo-Croatian | Turkish |
|---|---|---|---|---|
| Basic word order | SVO | SVO | SVO | SOV |
| Degree of word-order flexibility | Low | Medium | High | Very high |
| Rich verbal inflection (person/number) | No | Yes | Yes | Yes |
| Case-inflectional morphology | No | No | Yes (synthetic) | Yes (agglutinative) |
| Nominal case inflection | No | No | Sometimes | Always |

was present.[3] To our surprise, English- and Italian-speaking children did not reliably use word order as a comprehension cue until age 2;6. The message of these findings is that children are sensitive to both word order and affixes on individual words, that perceptually salient affixes attract attention, and that such "local cues" (Ammon & Slobin, 1979) can guide sentence interpretation early in development. In brief, young learners are sensitive to many types of devices for encoding meaning.

### Starting Point: The Inaccessibility of Passive Constructions

Beginning again with English, it has long been noted that passives are a relatively late acquisition, appearing in speech around age 3;6, and presenting comprehension problems as late as age 5 (Pinker, Lebeaux, & Frost, 1987; Maratsos, Kuczaj, Fox, & Chalkley, 1979). For example, long after children can correctly manipulate toys in response to instructions such as "the horse kicks the cow," they are confused by passive equivalents such as "the cow is kicked by the horse." To account for this phenomenon, nativist theorists proposed that the relevant syntactic principle did not mature until some time after age 3;6 (Borer & Wexler, 1987). However, the picture is quite different in children's acquisition of Sesotho, a Bantu language studied by Demuth (1992). At around age 2;8, Sesotho-speaking children show good control of passives in both production and comprehension. Because it is unlikely that their biological maturation has been speeded up in comparison with American children, it is necessary to seek alternative explanations. Passives are highly frequent in Sesotho because they serve salient discourse functions. Sesotho is a topic-oriented language in which the subject position in a sentence is restricted to topical information, that is, information that is given or old. Therefore, the only way to ask questions is to use a passive or a cleft construction, since it is the function of questions to focus on what is *not* given. Thus, for example, it is ungrammatical to say the equivalent of "Who wants the food?" The only option is to ask, "The food is wanted by who?" or "It's who that wants food?" Accordingly, children are exposed to many passive constructions and must learn them early on in order to carry out basic speech functions. The message of these findings is that one can't generalize across languages on the basis of morphology and syntax alone; rather, one must attend equally

---

[3] In an agglutinative morphological system, elements of meaning line up with separate elements of form, and are "glued together" in a series. For example, the Turkish nominal suffix *-ler* indicates plural: *turist-ler*, "tourists"; *-i* indicates accusative: *turist-i*, "tourist"-accusative; in combination: *turist-ler-i*, "tourists"-accusative. In Serbo-Croatian, each case suffix is a synthetic form that combines case, gender, animacy, and number in a single form: *turist-a*, "tourist"-accusative:masculine:animate:singular; *turist-e*, "tourist"-accusative:masculine:animate:plural.

to frequency of occurrence of constructions and to the discourse functions that they serve. These factors influence the accessibility of linguistic forms and construction types.

## Starting Point: The Accessibility of General-Purpose Verbs

In many languages, first verbs in children's vocabularies include general-purpose verbs such as "go," "do," "make," and "put," with early uses extended across a range of specific purposes (e.g., Clark, 1978, for English, Finnish, French, Japanese, Korean; Hollebrandse & van Hout, 1984, for Dutch; Ninio, 1999, for Hebrew). For example, when an English-speaking 2-year-old says "make" followed by a noun, "make" could mean "write," "draw," "move," "cut out," "build," and so on, depending on the noun and the context. We might expect, then, that early lexical acquisition is facilitated by the use of a few verbs with general meanings, leaving the specific meanings to be inferred from the possible or ongoing actions with objects in the situation. Again, however, crosslinguistic comparison is necessary, because there are languages that "specialize" in a more "granular" analysis of high-frequency semantic domains, that is, languages that have many specific verbs where familiar languages can get along with nonspecific, general-purpose verbs. Such a language, for example, is the Mayan language Tzeltal (Brown, 2001). Tzeltal verbs in many domains remind one of "classifier verbs" in sign languages. For example, instead of a general verb meaning "carry" or "hold," Tzeltal cares about how something is supported by use of the body, as shown in example 2.1; instead of a general eating verb, Tzeltal cares about what kinds of substances are being eaten and in what way, as shown in example 2.2, and so forth (Brown, 2001, p. 529).

(2.1) Tzeltal verbs of carrying/holding
   *pet*, "in both arms"
   *kuch*, "weight on head/back"
   *k'ech*, "weight across shoulders"
   *lik*, "in hand, supported from top"
   *tuch'*, "vertically extending from hand"
   *tzak*, "grasp in hand"

(2.2) Tzeltal verbs of eating
   *lo'*, "bananas, soft thing"
   *k'ux*, "beans, crunchy things"
   *we'*, "tortillas, bread"
   *tz'u'*, "sugarcane"
   *uch'*, "corn gruel, liquids"

If children begin with nonspecific or general concepts of basic activities, a language like Tzeltal (or ASL) might present problems; perhaps the strategy would be to pick one high-frequency verb from a set and use it in a general fashion. This is not what Brown found for Tzeltal. Many specific verbs are found in children's first vocabularies, in the age range of 1;3–2;2. For example, early lexical items for one Mayan child included appropriate uses of *we'*, "eat tortillas," versus *lo'*, "eat soft things"; *pet*, "carry in arms," versus *tzak*, "grasp in hand," and so forth. Early verbs in the acquisition of sign languages often show similar specificity, as we have been finding in studies of early acquisition of ASL (Lindert, 2001) and SLN (Sign Language of the Netherlands) (Slobin et al., 2003). Explanations have been proposed on the basis of factors of iconicity and gestures that simulate motor activities. However, although those mimetic factors may well play a role, verb specificity is apparently accessible to beginning learners of spoken languages as well.

Brown suggests that children develop expectations about the level of semantic granularity that is encoded in lexical items in their language, that is, a particular sort of verb-learning bias arises as the result of learning more and more verbs in a language. As a result, patterns of early language come to reflect typological characteristics of the exposure language. In this instance, the relevant dimensions are semantic, rather than morphological or syntactic, but the underlying message is the same: It is necessary to attend to relevant typological dimensions in picking a set of spoken languages to be used as standards of comparison for the development of particular sign languages.

## FROM CROSSLINGUISTIC FINDINGS TO ACQUISITION MECHANISMS

Crosslinguistic findings such as these lead to the postulation of learning strategies that may account for contrasting developmental patterns: "operating principles" (Peters, 1985, 1997; Slobin, 1973, 1985a), "procedures" (Pinker, 1984), and a large collection of "constraints" proposed by various theorists. For example, on the basis of earlier mastery of suffixes than prefixes, holding semantic content roughly constant, I proposed that child learners "pay attention to the ends of words" (Slobin, 1973). Pye (1992) went on to refine this proposal, demonstrating that the critical factor in acquisition is a morpheme's perceptual saliency, finding that syllabicity and stress are more important than utterance-final position. Peters (1997) refined the perceptual dimension further, proposing a systematic set of prosodic and phonological dimensions that influence morphological acquisition. Again, generalizations require data from a range of contrasting languages, in this instance, contrasting on acoustic, rather than syntactic or semantic dimensions.

## FROM ACQUISITION MECHANISMS TO TYPOLOGY

Perceptual saliency and frequency, along with dominant construction types and semantic patterns, all work together to reinforce the overall typological characteristics of the language being acquired by the child. As more and more morphemes, constructions, and lexical items come to require the same kinds of processing, the typology of the language begins to emerge as a sort "habit" in acquisition; that is, the learner is predisposed to apply familiar patterns to new instances. For example, research on a number of Indo-European suffixing languages led to the generalization that children will select a stem and overgeneralize a dominant affix, such as English-speaking children's past-tense and plural regularizations (e.g., *falled, breaked, sheeps, mans*) or Russian-speaking children's use of a single case suffix for all nouns (e.g., a uniform accusative or instrumental or dative marker across genders), although the input provides distinct suffixes on the basis of gender. Bantu languages such as Sesotho provide an important counterexample. In these languages, there are a number of noun classes (15 in Sesotho) as compared with the two or three genders of Indo-European languages (masculine, feminine, and sometimes neuter). The classes are marked by prefixation, and there are no free-standing nouns; that is, there is no parallel model to English "chair"/"chair-s" or Dutch *stoel/stoel-en*. For example, the noun stem *-tho*, "person," does not stand on its own but requires either the singular prefix *mo-*, forming *mo-tho*, "person," or the plural prefix *ba-*, forming *ba-tho*, "persons." Similarly, for other noun classes, there are pairs such as *mo-sé*, "dress"/*me-sé*, "dresses"; *se-fate*, "tree"/*di-fate*, "trees," and so on, across an array of noun classes. The prefix that marks a particular noun class is repeated on lexical elements throughout a clause to mark agreement with that noun: Prefixes occur on nouns, demonstratives, adjectives, possessives, and so forth. For example, the *se-* prefix indicates a singular for a noun that belongs to class 7 (one of the "gender" classes in Sesotho), such as *se-fate*, "tree." That prefix is repeated across morphemes in a construction that makes reference to a noun belonging to that class: *se-*, subject; *-se-*, object; *se-se-*, adjective; *sena*, demonstrative pronoun; *se*, relative pronoun; and more. The utterances that a Sesotho-learning child hears always include repeated instances of the same type of prefixed morpheme throughout a clause. Demuth (1992) found that children quickly identified the role of prefixes in the language. At first they isolated noun stems, then began adding prefixes, and by about 2;6 used distinct prefixes for both singular and plural. That is, they did not follow the Indo-European model of using a bare noun stem for singulars and adding an affix to indicate plural; rather, they worked on the entire system, adding both singular and plural prefixes.

Clearly, repetitive use of a principle across lexical items and constructions makes the principle itself salient—in the case of Sesotho, the principles of prefixing and agreement. Children are not learning isolated pieces of a linguistic system; rather, they seem to make use of a sort of "typological bootstrapping" (Slobin, 1997d) to identify new constructions as similar to already learned constructions. Construction types become available patterns or templates for the learner. Thus, the Sesotho-learning child begins to expect repeated use of noun class prefixes to mark agreement through a construction, the Turkish-learning child comes to expect that suffixes will carry grammatical information, and the Yucatec Mayan child will look for highly specific verb meanings. Repeated solutions of linguistic problems by using a particular strategy thus reinforce the typological consistency of the language. That is, with increasing mastery of morphosyntactic and semantic patterns, a sense of the overall typology of the exposure language begins to play a role in guiding acquisition.

This line of research emphasizes that one cannot pull out one system from a particular language—prefixes or suffixes, case marking, agreement, word order, general verbs, and so forth—and compare that system across languages. Each individual language presents its own "ecological balance" of grammatical forms and lexical patterns, and crosslinguistic comparisons must pay close attention to the interaction of sets of dimensions in acquisition. Note, too, that languages differ with regard to their placement on individual typological dimensions. For example, as shown in table 2.2, Serbo-Croatian and Turkish are both case-marking inflectional languages, but the former is SVO and the latter is SOV; the former relies on synthetic morphology and the latter on agglutinative morphology. English, Italian, and Serbo-Croatian are all SVO languages, but they differ considerably in pragmatic word-order flexibility. One cannot draw generalizations, for example, about the acquisition of SVO languages, or case-marking inflectional languages, without paying attention to a network of cross-cutting construction types.

The caution for researchers investigating the acquisition of signed languages is to be very careful in drawing generalizations from the literature on spoken languages and to carefully pick appropriate comparisons on typological dimensions of morphosyntax, lexical organization, and pragmatics. In the rest of this chapter, therefore, I propose some typological dimensions that seem to be particularly relevant to the analysis of signed languages—as well as some that seem to have been uncritically transferred from some spoken languages. To begin with, though, it will be necessary to critically examine the sort of information that is presented by conventions of transcription and glossing, since the format and content of linguistic examples and transcribed discourse influence the conclusions that can be drawn from the data. As Elinor

Ochs (1979) succinctly phrased the problem many years ago: "Transcription is theory." That is, there is no "objective" or theory-neutral way in which to represent linguistic data.

## GLOSSING AND TRANSLATING: EXPLICIT AND IMPLICIT ANALYSIS

### How Linguists Deal With Foreign Language Examples

The field of linguistics has established generally accepted standards for presenting linguistic examples in publications, with only minor variation between journals, theorists, and countries (see, e.g., the style sheet of any linguistics journal). A simple example will demonstrate how many choices are made at the levels of transcription, glossing, and translation. Consider the German sentence in example 2.3:

> (2.3) *die frau liebt den mann*
> DEF.ART.FEM.SG.NOM woman love:3SG.PRES
> DEF.ART.MASC.SG.ACC man
> 'The woman loves the man.'

The first line is an orthographic transcription. This is already a theoretical decision, because it could have been a phonetic transcription, and it could have included prosodic information (if it were a sentence from a spoken discourse, rather than a written example). The second line is a morpheme-by-morpheme gloss, using standard linguistic abbreviations for grammatical forms and English translations of lexical items. This line is rich with theory-relevant decisions. For example, the first article, *die*, is glossed as definite article feminine singular nominative, but, in fact, *die* could also be an accusative form. Here, the fact that the second article, of the clause, *den*, is accusative means that the first article, *die*, can be glossed as nominative. Glossing thus requires knowledge of the grammar and attention to other items in a construction. The third line gives a free translation into English. In both the second and third lines, *frau* is translated as "woman," rather than "wife," and *mann* is translated as "man" rather than "husband." But this sentence could also mean "the wife loves the husband." In brief, how much information is given in the choices of grammatical glosses and English equivalents, and how much is presupposed at the level of glossing?

Example 2.3 was invented to simply set forth the standard three lines of a linguistic example: foreign language form, morpheme-by-morpheme gloss, and free translation (sometimes also called gloss). As soon as we move beyond "simple" examples, the terrain gets very rocky indeed. Example 2.4a is from a paper written in Spanish about a Mayan language called Lowland Chontal (O'Connor, in press). I've picked this example intentionally to make a point that will become important in considering the glossing of sign language examples. Lowland Chontal is spoken in Mexico, where the surrounding language is Spanish, and it seems unexceptional to find it glossed and translated in Spanish. In similar fashion, sign language examples tend to be glossed and translated in the spoken language of the surrounding community (English for ASL, Dutch for SLN, etc.). Many types of problems arise. Compare example 2.4a with my English version in example 2.4b:

(2.4a) *iyasa -k'o -may -pa*
       1SG.AGT -V.POS:boca.abajo -V.DIR:quedar -PFV.SG
       'Yo me embroqué en el suelo.'

(2.4b) *iyasa -k'o -may -pa*
       1SG.AGT -V.POS:face.down -V.DIR:remain -PFV.SG
       'I lay face down on the ground.'

Fortunately, there is a fairly "universal" system of grammatical glossing, still in progress, but quite well established over the past century or so. So we do not have to translate the grammatical glosses, which stand for: first singular agent, verb posture, verb directional, and perfective singular. Linguists are pretty good at reading across and between the three lines of an example, trying to build up an impression of what the foreign language example might mean and how it is constructed. But note that there are some differences between the English and Spanish glosses, and we have no further access to the original meanings without further information from the linguist (often provided elsewhere in the paper or in related publications). Here O'Connor glossed the postural verb as *boca abajo*, "mouth down," in Spanish, and I assumed that this verb describes a posture that we would call *face down* in English. The Chontal example is a polymorphemic verb (like a sign language verb), and this is lost in both the English and Spanish third lines—because both languages are of a different type (discussed further below). The Spanish verb *embrocarse* means something like "put oneself in an inverted position"; I picked "lie face down" as an English equivalent. And both the Spanish and English versions add information about the location: *en el suelo*, "on the ground." But this is not the structure of the Chontal verb, which has a directional verb form that O'Connor glosses as *quedar*, "remain." The best I can make out is that this particle means to move in a direction in which one then remains—and in a face-down posture. But the directional element disappears in both the Spanish and English versions, because neither of these languages has a simple way of saying something like "lie down onto the ground." Note, too, that the final Chontal particle indicates the tense/aspect of the verb, perfective singular. Both of these features are maintained in the Spanish *embroqué*, which happens to mark both perfective aspect and number on the verb (but also adds person), but they are lost in English, which provides only a simple past.

The purpose of this long example is to raise several critical issues for the comparative study of sign languages in general and, particularly here, of the acquisition of sign languages.

## Problems of Transcribing and Glossing Sign Language

Without making use of line drawings or video clips, consider a simple example from ASL (and its equivalents in many other sign languages). The hand is placed palm down with an inverted V pointing downward; the hand moves forward while wiggling the fingers. Clearly, the sign means something like "two-legged being walks forward." But how can we preserve this example for subsequent linguistic analysis? We could decide to gloss it as WALK, following the familiar shortcut of capital letters, with a subscript indicating direction, such as WALK$_{FORWARD}$. This gives us the illusion that ASL has a verb that is parallel to the English verb "walk," and that it can take a directional adverb, parallel to "walk forward" in English. But, of course, there's no reason that ASL can only be glossed in English. ASL can just as well be described by Spanish, Dutch, or Japanese linguists, in their spoken/written languages—in the same way that an investigator of Lowland Chontal can choose to gloss that language into Spanish, or English, or whatever the language of the investigator may be—or, more precisely, the language of the publication. (O'Connor is an English speaker who publishes about Chontal in both Spanish and English.) This simple ASL example could best be glossed into Spanish as *avanzar caminando*, "advance walking." This is because the typology of Spanish prefers that the main verb indicate direction and that manner be specified by a nonfinite adjunct, in this case a gerund.[4]

It should be obvious, though, that the signed example corresponds neither to WALK$_{FORWARD}$ nor to *avanzar caminando*. It is, rather, more like a Mayan verb, with a collection of meaning elements that, taken together, mean something like "two-legged figure move forward in a walking manner." How can this be rendered in a format that allows for cross-linguistic and developmental analysis—both between sign languages and in comparison to spoken languages? Glosses in any given spoken language are misleading. The only solution is to follow the lead of

---

[4] In Talmy's (1985, 1991, 2000) terms, Spanish is a *verb-framed* language and English is *satellite framed*. This distinction has widespread consequences for cognition and discourse (Slobin, 1996, 1997a, 2000, 2002). Independent analysis is required to determine if Chontal or ASL falls into one of these typological categories or represent a different sort of typology (Slobin, 2004; Slobin & Hoiting, 1994).

linguistics and agree upon ways to break signs down into meaning components and to gloss them in a theory-neutral and language-neutral way. One such attempt is the Berkeley Transcription System (BTS) that a group of us has developed over the past decade, in working with transcription of sign language videotapes in several different sign languages.[5] This is not the place to lay out how BTS works, but I do give one example that is parallel to the Lowland Chontal example. This provides a bridge to examine the typology of sign languages with regard to complex verb constructions.

BTS treats verbs as polycomponential, with a separate symbol for each type of component and its realization in a particular verb. For this example, we will need the following BTS components (including only manual components). The sign has a "classifier" handshape—referred to as "property marker" in BTS. (For a justification of this reanalysis of classifiers, see Slobin et al. [2003].) This handshape is in a particular posture, follows a particular path, and demonstrates a particular movement pattern. Each of these types of meaning component ("morpheme") is indicated by a lower-case abbreviation in BTS: pm = prop-property marker, pst = posture, pth = path, mvt = movement. These are the kinds of elements out of which sign language verbs are constructed. The "lexical" instantiations of these components are indicated by associated capital letters: TL = two legs, ERC = erect, F = forward, WIG = wiggle. Putting all of this together, the example takes the form presented in example 2.5.

(2.5) pm'TL-pst'ERC-pth'F-mvt'WIG
    'walk forward'

Note that this format does not require any capital letter glosses into English words (and the formal components of BTS have been translated into Dutch to provide exactly equivalent transcriptions of ASL and SLN). The transcription in example 2.5 can be read, in English, as, for example, "inverted V handshape moves forward wiggling." In similar fashion, the Lowland Chontal in example 2.4 can be read, in English, as

[5] Current versions and continuing discussion of BTS are available on a website organized by Brenda Schick (http://www.Colorado.EDU/slhs/btsweb/). The rationale for BTS can be found in Slobin et al. (2001), along with the transcription manual; an introduction is provided in Hoiting and Slobin (2002). The system is still under construction, but the following examples will give some idea of the level of granularity that is used in BTS transcriptions. Property markers distinguish a large collection of meaningful handshapes, such as shape (pm'CIR = circular object, pm'STK = stick like object), handling configuration (pm'BO = baby O, pm'FF = flattened F), and tracing handshape (CS = curved surface, TUBE = tube). A range of movement patterns are distinguished, such as mvt'BOUNCE and mvt'JAB. Many path types are transcribed, such as pth'A = arc and pth'Z = zigzag.

"first person agent moved into a face-down posture, remaining there." I suggest that transcriptions and analyses on this level—although certainly prone to various kinds of errors and misinterpretations—provide a clearer idea of the nature of such languages as ASL and Chontal.

BTS representations make it clear that sign language verbs are not at all like the verbs of English or Dutch or German or French; that is, they are not at all like the verbs of the surrounding spoken languages. Capital-letter glosses, even with subscripts and superscripts, mask the deep typological differences between the sign languages that have been studied and the spoken languages of the community—be they Indo-European, Chinese, Japanese, or Turkish. All of those spoken languages belong to one typological class, but this is not due to modality. We have already seen that one Mayan verb looks quite different from the structure of these familiar spoken languages. The next step, therefore, is to explore the relevant typological dimension and its consequences for analyses of sign languages and their acquisition.

## DEPENDENT-MARKED AND HEAD-MARKED LANGUAGES

"Dependent marked" and "head marked" are relatively unfamiliar terms in sign language linguistics (Hoiting & Slobin, 2003). This typological dimension was introduced by Nichols (1986) and plays an important role in her typological and historical explorations of spoken languages (Nichols, 1992). Nichols (1986) defines the "head" as "the word which governs, or is subcategorized for—or otherwise determines the possibility of occurrence of—the other word. It determines the category of its phrase" (p. 57). For example, a predicate is the head of its phrase, and the arguments and adjuncts are dependents; a noun is the head of its phrase, and modifying adjectives are dependents. Syntactic relations such as subject or object can be morphologically marked on the *dependent* (noun) or on the *head* (verb) of a construction. Of most relevance to us here is marking on the verb—because I argue that sign languages are head marked, in distinction to the dependent-marked languages of the surrounding speaking worlds. I focus on clause relations, that is, the relations of the arguments of a verb (the dependents) to the verb (the head). As an example, consider a simple transitive clause of the standard SVO variety in English. I first use examples with pronouns, because these are the only forms in English with case marking, and then replace a pronoun with a noun in following examples. Begin with the sentence in example 2.6:[6]

---

[6] Abbreviations used are as follows: ACC = accusative case, HAB = habitual aspect, INCOMPL = incompletive aspect, MASC = masculine, NOM = nominative case, OBJ = object, PRO = pronoun, SG = singular, SUBJ = subject, TOP = topic.

(2.6) *He see -s me.*
   3SG.MASC.PRO.SUBJ see -3SG.PRES 1SG.PRO.OBJ

The dependents are the two pronouns, and those elements bear the case marking (i.e., "he" rather than "him," "me" rather than "I"). The verb does not indicate the argument roles but only indicates inherent characteristics of the arguments (in this case, the singularity and person of the subject). With regard to clause relations, example 2.6 is consistently dependent marked.

The same is true of Turkish—a language that is otherwise typologically quite different from English, in that it is an SOV language with agglutinative morphology and no gender. But with regard to dependent marking, example 2.7 is identical to example 2.6:[7]

(2.7) *O ben -i gör -üyor*
   3SG.PRO.NOM 1SG.PRO -ACC see -PRES
   'He/she sees me.'

The word order is different, and the realization of case marking is different. In Turkish it is the agglutinative suffix *-i* on the first-person pronoun *ben* that indicates the role of that argument in the clause. Nonetheless, Turkish is a dependent-marked language, as are all of the Germanic and Romance languages, Japanese, Chinese, and many others. (Head-marked languages are common in the Americas and elsewhere in the world, but they are not common in standard linguistic approaches to morphosyntax that sign language linguists rely upon.)

Yucatec—another Mayan language—is presented in example 2.8. Like Lowland Chontal and ASL, all of the grammatical indicators of argument roles (the equivalents case marking on noun arguments in dependent-marked languages) occur as elements of the verb.

(2.8) *k -uy -il -ik -en*
   HAB -3SG.ACTOR -see -INCOMPL -1SG.UNDERGOER
   'He/she sees me.'

The corresponding ASL construction is formally parallel to example 2.8. It consists of a horizontal V-handshape, indicating the gaze,

---

[7] Turkish is a "pro-drop" language, that is, a language with usual subject ellipsis unless the subject is in focus. (Accordingly, the designation "null-subject" language would be more appropriate for pro-drop languages that do not use head marking to mark argument relations on the verb.) Thus, example 2.7 is not strictly parallel to example 2.6; either the subject pronoun, *o*, should be elided, or the English subject pronoun "he" in example 2.6 should receive contrastive stress. (The lack of consistent prosodic notation for written languages has caused serious misunderstandings with regard to their syntax, which is primarily based on written examples.)

moving from a locus established for a third person (in discourse or the physical setting) and moving toward the face of the signer. Beyond this description, there is no standard way of notating such a construction in publications of sign language. What we find are variants of $_{HE}$LOOK-AT$_{ME}$ and/or pictures. A BTS transcription reveals the head-marked character of the ASL verb. The following symbols are used in example 2.9: pm = property marker ("classifier") GAZE = horizontal V-handshape indicating act of looking, ori = orientation of property marker handshape, D = palm down, B = fingertips back, src = source, 3 = locus established for third person (participant other than signer and recipient), gol = goal, 1 = signer. (Note that example 2.9 provides only the second and third lines of the standard format of linguistic examples. The first line would be a phonological description, using one of a variety of available notations, preferably accompanied by a video clip.)

> (2.9) pm'GAZE-ori'DB-src'3-gol'1
> 'He/she looks.at me.'

ASL and Yucatec are both head-marked languages, with polycomponential verbs that indicate the roles of arguments without the use of pronouns that carry grammatical marking of those roles. Because argument roles are indicated on the verb, these are technically "pro-drop" languages. The term, however, is misleading. It is not that there are pronouns that need to be "dropped." Rather, if a pronoun or overt noun participant is used, it must be *added*. This is because the default clause in such head-marked languages carries all of the essential syntactic information within the verb. Explicit arguments are needed only when they are in focus, that is, when they are introduced as topics or when they contrast with other possible participants. It therefore would be more appropriate to call these "pro-*add*" languages.[8]

What happens to our examples if we replace "he/she" by an explicit noun, for example, a name? In English and Turkish nothing essential changes. The pronoun is simply replaced: "John sees me," *John beni görüyor* (the Turkish proper noun has a "zero suffix," indicating that it is nominative case). In Mayan, though, *John* does not serve as the subject of the verb; rather, the external noun must be introduced as a topic, with a suffixed marker in first position, as in example 2.10 (or

---

[8] Sebastián and Slobin (1994) introduced this term in analyzing Spanish child language. Spanish is also "pro-drop," though for other reasons, as discussed below with regard to agreement morphology (see also footnote 7). But with regard to acquisition, children learning all types of "pro-drop" or "argument-ellipsis" or "null-subject" languages face the task of knowing when to explicitly mention an argument. This is the opposite problem to English-learning children, who must be sure to always explicitly encode the arguments that are required by the verb, regardless of their pragmatic status.

with the noun after the verb, in a pragmatically marked position that does not require a topic marker; thanks to William Hanks for elucidating this construction).

> (2.10) *John -e' k -uy -il -ik -en*
> John -TOP HAB -3SG.ACTOR -see -INCOMPL -1SG.UN-
> DERGOER
> 'As for John, he-sees-me.'

Note that the verb in example 2.10 is the same as the verb in example 2.8. If John is interpreted as a topic, the *-uy-* marker indicating third person singular actor on the verb is not an "agreement" marker. It remains an element on the head that indicates the role of the third person participant.

The pattern in ASL is identical. "John" is introduced by pointing to him, if he is present, or to a locus that has been established for him, or by giving his name in fingerspelling or as a name sign in a particular locus. This can be accompanied by a nonmanual topic marker. Having done this, the verb in example 2.9 displays an unchanged head-marked pattern, with no "agreement." ASL, and other sign languages I know of, are *topic-prominent* rather than *subject-prominent* languages. The introduction of a topic establishes a universe of discourse, sets up a mental space (Liddell, 2003; Taub, 2001). Meaning components on verbs index established referents, but there is no evident syntactic reason to treat them formally as markers of agreement between an argument of the verb and a topic.

If we allow ourselves to treat languages like ASL as head marked and topic prominent, we free ourselves of the syntactic machinery based on dependent-marked and subject-prominent languages such as English. As a consequence, rather different questions arise with regard to children's acquisition of sign languages. As a start, for example, analyses of the signing of ASL and SLN toddlers, using BTS, indicates an early grasp of principles of polycomponential verbs (Slobin et al., 2003), and I expect to find similar reports in this volume.

### Head Marking, Agreement, and Pro-drop

There is, in fact, more to marking on the verb than indicating argument roles (i.e., expressing clause relations). Markers on the verb can also index inherent categories of arguments, such as number and gender. This is the familiar domain of agreement in classical syntax. In the head-marked languages discussed above, marking on the verb serves, in Nichols's (1986) terms, to mark "the presence or type of dependency" (p. 59). As she points out, this sort of relation is what Sapir (1921) called "pure relational concepts" (p. 101). In his words, the marking elements "serve to relate the concrete elements of the proposition to each other, thus giving it definite syntactic form." The movement of the ASL "classifier" indicated by pm'GAZE does just this: It relates the source and goal elements of the proposition, without providing further information about inherent qualities of those elements. What has traditionally been termed "agreement" is the use of markers to "index categories of one member on the other" (Nichols, 1986, p. 59). Sapir used the term "concrete relational concepts" to refer to this kind of marking. These are the categories that underlie subject–verb agreement—such as person, gender, number—and they do not seem to play a central role in sign language syntax.

Nevertheless, both kinds of verb marking of relational concepts allow for argument ellipsis ("pro-drop"). That is, in languages like Spanish and Turkish, where person/number marking on the verb indicates inherent qualities of the grammatical subject, it is possible to elide the subject when it is no longer topical in discourse. Languages with this kind of argument ellipsis, however, cannot elide *all* of the arguments of a predicate, whereas fully head-marked languages do so normally and easily. We must be careful, therefore, not to draw upon "pro-drop" languages like Spanish and Turkish when making comparisons to a quite different motivation for "pro-drop" in languages like ASL and SLN. What is important in a sign language is that, except for "plain verbs" (i.e., verbs that cannot move in space), the normal procedure is to establish topics at loci and then embed those loci in movement trajectories of verbs (whether indicating physical or metaphorical movement). Note that even for "plain verbs," many sign languages make use of auxiliary verbs that *do* move in space, retaining the dominant head-marked typology of those languages (e.g., for SLN: Bos, 1994; Hoiting & Slobin, 2001; for Taiwan Sign Language: Smith, 1990).

### Consequences for Acquisition

The use of motion as a feature of head-marked languages does not pose a problem to young learners of sign languages—at least on the basis of the limited evidence currently available. The most detailed study that I'm aware of is Casey's recent dissertation (2003a; also see Casey, 2003b), where extensive evidence is presented for the elementary use of motion of the hand from one locus to another to indicate relations between participants. Casey uses the cover term *directionality* to deal with "person agreement verbs," "spatial verbs," and "verbal clitics," providing a useful definition of directionality: "the use of movement, spatial displacement, and/or palm orientation in the production of a manual action gesture or sign to indicate an additional referent involved in the action" (Casey, 2003a, p. 28). Note that the definition applies to sign as well as gesture. Marking argument relations on the verb is thus a basic element of sign languages—and indeed, of the gestural modality generally, including homesign, children's adaptations of sign systems, and co-speech gestures of hearing people.

Children acquiring spoken head-marked languages are also adept at manipulating verbal affixes to indicate source and goal, agent and patient, giver and recipient, and so forth. Example 2.11 is an utterance of an Eskimo child of 3;2 speaking Inuktitut, a head-marked language (Allen, in press; also see Allen, 1996). The child is referring to a puppy in the porch, which she saw her friend bring in and can hear but not see. Her utterance is a single verb indicating that a first-person singular subject (the child) wants a third-person singular object (the dog) to come in. Because the dog's presence is known, it is a presupposed topic and does not have to be lexicalized. There is therefore no agreement here, but simply an indication of Nichols's "type of dependency" or Sapir's "pure relational concept," that is, the child's desired action on the dog. This is indicated by the verb particle -jara, which encodes a relation between a first singular participant and a third singular transitive participant (roughly, agent and patient).

> (2.11) *itiq -guma -jara*
>         enter -want -1SG.3SG.TRANSITIVE
>         'I want to take him/her/it in.'

## SIGN LANGUAGES IN A NETWORK OF TYPOLOGICAL DIMENSIONS

Table 2.3 represents an attempt to demonstrate the complexity of finding typological comparison languages for the investigation of acquisition, and psycholinguistics generally. The table compares ASL with six spoken languages—the five studied by Berman and Slobin (1994), plus Yucatec Mayan, an example of the sort of head-marked language discussed above. The rows provide ten typological dimensions along which the languages can be compared and contrasted, with my best estimate of the position of each of the seven languages on those dimensions. The cell entries represent the dominant option used in a language (there are almost always minority constructions that differ). To summarize the dimensions:

- *Marking type*: the head-/dependent-marking typology discussed above.
- *Nominal case inflectional*: the presence or absence of case marking on the dependent arguments in a clause.
- *Grammatical morphology*: grammatical morphemes that are arranged in sequence (prefixes, suffixes, infixes) versus those that occur simultaneously with root forms. Much has been made of the simultaneous morphology of sign languages (manual plus

Table 2-3: Some Grammatical Features of ASL Compared With Six Spoken Languages: Typological Summary

| | ASL | English | German | Spanish | Hebrew | Turkish | Yucatec |
|---|---|---|---|---|---|---|---|
| Marking type | Head | Dependent | Dependent | Dependent | Dependent | Dependent | Head |
| Nominal case inflection | − | − | + | − | − | + | − |
| Grammatical morphology | Simultaneous | Prefix, suffix | Prefix, suffix | Prefix, suffix | Prefix, suffix, simultaneous | Suffix | Prefix, suffix |
| Word-order variability | Medium | None | Medium | Medium | Low | High | ? |
| Pro-drop | + | − | − | + | +/− | + | + |
| Topic/subject prominent | Topic prominent | Subject prominent | Subject prominent | Subject prominent | Subject prominent | Subject prominent | Topic prominent |
| Classifiers | + | − | − | − | − | − | + |
| Motion lexicalization | Verb framed? | Satellite framed | Satellite framed | Verb framed | Verb framed | Verb framed | Verb framed? |
| Grammaticized tense | − | + | + | + | + | + | − |
| Grammaticized aspect | + | + | − | + | − | + | + |

nonmanual features, co-placement of handshapes, etc.).[9] Among spoken languages, Semitic languages such as Hebrew and Arabic have another kind of simultaneity. Briefly, a lexical item is represented by an unpronounceable consonant frame that becomes pronounceable with the intercalation of vowel patterns that express grammatical morphemes. For example, the Hebrew root *s-g-r*, "close," can be realized in many forms with various intercalated vowels (+ prefix and/or suffix); the present tense masculine singular is *soger*, and the past tense masculine third person is *sagar*, where the vowel frames (*-o-e-* and *-a-a-*) are the tense markers.

- *Word-order variability*: the degree to which the order of words in a clause can be varied for pragmatic purposes, without additional grammatical morphology.
- *Pro-drop*: the option of eliding one or more arguments in a clause. (ASL and Yucatec allow eliding of several arguments; Spanish and Turkish, only of subjects; Hebrew, only of first- and second-person subjects in past and future.)
- *Topic-/subject prominent*: relative importance of topic or subject in overall grammatical organization:
  - *Topic prominent*: topic is overtly marked and is critical in syntactic organization.
  - *Subject prominent*: subject controls verb agreement, co-reference, and a number of other constructions, forming the grammatical pivot for structuring the clause.
- *Classifiers*: obligatory marking of semantic categories of nouns ("property markers" in sign languages).
- *Motion lexicalization*: the expression of path of motion in a directional verb (*verb framed*) or directional satellite (affix, adjunct) (*satellite framed*).
- *Grammaticized tense*: formal marking of tense on the verb.
- *Grammaticized aspect*: formal marking of aspect on the verb (e.g., durative, completive, habitual, etc.).

Note that no two languages line up identically on all ten dimensions. In addition, the dimensions interact in various ways. For example,

---

[9] Perhaps the simultaneity of sign language morphology has been overstated. Although handshapes are placed together simultaneously in two-handed signs, and property marker handshapes move as simultaneous parts of directional verbs, the movement from source to goal (however defined) is of necessity sequential. That is, there is no way to simultaneously encode source and goal. Also note that the simultaneity of nonmanual and manual expressions is comparable in many ways to the simultaneity of suprasegmental features of spoken languages (intonation, stress, rhythm, etc.), which are all too often ignored in transcription and linguistic analysis.

word-order variability is more likely in case-inflectional languages (because case marking makes it possible to keep track of argument roles regardless of word order). Pro-drop is likely to be the norm in head-marked languages but may be an option—as null subject—in dependent-marked languages. The message is that there is no simple way to pick comparison spoken languages in making predictions about the acquisition or use of particular construction types in a sign language. Prediction is only feasible if one attends to interaction among dimensions, along with data on frequency of use and discourse functions of the forms under consideration. And this can only be done in a psycholinguistic framework that includes attention to processing mechanisms along with strategies of learning, memory, and communication.

## SUMMARY AND CONCLUSIONS

In order to make crosslinguistic comparisons—between spoken and signed languages or between the acquisition of different languages—it is necessary to work in a linguistic framework that is not biased toward languages of a particular type. Beginning with several case studies of the acquisition of spoken languages, I have tried to demonstrate the progress that has been made by moving away from predictions based on patterns of the structure and acquisition of particular languages, generally English or, more broadly, Indo-European languages. The examination of several case studies from the child language literature demonstrates the importance of typological analysis, as well as attention to factors of frequency and discourse function of grammatical forms and constructions.

Crosslinguistic analysis on the linguistic level also requires standards of morphosyntactic and lexical analysis that are not biased toward one language or type of language. I have argued that sign languages differ systematically from the spoken languages of the surrounding communities, across Eurasia and America. In particular, sign languages are head marked, whereas the surrounding languages are dependent marked. Close attention to these typological dimensions calls for a reorientation in which traditional notions such as "subject," "agreement," and "pro-drop" are replaced by analyses more appropriate to the typology of signed languages.

In sum, then, this brief overview of several critical typological and psycholinguistic issues is a call for continued careful research across a variety of disciplines and language types. This volume is best seen as an attempt to fill in the blanks and seek the connections between language type, modality, acquisition, and communication.

## REFERENCES

Allen, S. E. M. (1996). *Aspects of argument structure acquisition in Inuktitut.* Amsterdam: John Benjamins.

Allen, S. E. M. (in press). Interacting pragmatic influences on children's argument realization. In M. Bowerman & P. Brown (Eds.), *Crosslinguistic perspectives on argument structure: Implications for learnability.* Mahwah, NJ: Lawrence Erlbaum.

Ammon, M. S., & Slobin, D. I. (1979). A cross-linguistic study of the processing of causative sentences. *Cognition, 7*, 3–17.

Baker, A., van den Bogaerde, B., & Crasborn, O. (Eds.). (2003). *Cross-linguistic perspectives in sign language research: Selected papers from TISLR 2000.* Hamburg: Signum.

Berman, R. A., & Slobin, D. I. (1994). *Relating events in narrative: A crosslinguistic developmental study.* Hillsdale, NJ: Lawrence Erlbaum.

Borer, H., & Wexler, K. (1987). The maturation of syntax. In T. Roeper & E. Williams (Eds.), *Parameter-setting and language acquisition* (pp. 123–172). Dordrecht: D. Reidel.

Bos, H. F. (1994). An auxiliary verb in Sign Language of the Netherlands. In I. Ahlgren, B. Bergman, & M. Brennan (Eds.), *Perspectives on sign language structure* (pp. 37–53). Durham, UK: International Sign Linguistics Association.

Brown, P. (2001). Learning to talk about motion UP and DOWN in Tzeltal: Is there a language-specific bias for verb learning? In M. Bowerman & S. C. Levinson (Eds.), *Language acquisition and conceptual development* (pp. 512–543). Cambridge: Cambridge University Press.

Bruner, J. S. (1975). The ontogenesis of speech acts. *Journal of Child Language, 2*, 1–19.

Casey, S. K. (2003a). *"Agreement" in gestures and signed languages: The use of directionality to indicate referents involved in actions.* Unpublished doctoral dissertation, University of California, San Diego.

Casey, S. (2003b). Relationships between gestures and signed languages: Indicating participants in actions. In A. Baker, B. van den Bogaerde, & O. Crasborn (Eds.), *Cross-linguistic perspectives in sign language research: Selected papers from TISLR 2000* (pp. 95–118). Hamburg: Signum.

Chamberlain, C., Morford, J. P., & Mayberry, R. I. (Eds.). (2000). *Language acquisition by eye.* Mahwah, NJ: Lawrence Erlbaum.

Clark, E. V. (1978). Discovering what words can do. In D. Farkas, W. M. Jacobsen, & K. W. Todrys (Eds.), *Papers from the parasession on the lexicon* (pp. 34–57). Chicago: Chicago Linguistics Society.

da Silva, A. N. (1809). *Nova grammatica da lingua ingleza.* Lisbon: Typografia Lacerdina.

Demuth, K. (1992). The acquisition of Sesotho. In D. I. Slobin (Ed.), *The crosslinguistic study of language acquisition* (Vol. 3, pp. 557–638). Hillsdale, NJ: Lawrence Erlbaum.

Emmorey, K. (Ed.). (2003) *Perspectives on classifier constructions in sign languages.* Mahwah, NJ: Lawrence Erlbaum.

Hoiting, N., & Slobin, D. I. (2001). Typological and modality constraints on borrowing: Examples from the sign language of the Netherlands. In

D. Brentari (Ed.), *Foreign vocabulary in sign languages* (pp. 121–137). Mahwah, NJ: Lawrence Erlbaum.

Hoiting, N., & Slobin, D. I. (2002). Transcription as a tool for understanding: The Berkeley Transcription System for sign language research (BTS). In G. Morgan & B. Woll (Eds.), *Directions in sign language acquisition* (pp. 55–75). Amsterdam: John Benjamins.

Hoiting, N., & Slobin, D. I. (2003, November). *Motion and space in sign languages.* Colloquium held at the Max Planck Institute for Psycholinguistics, Nijmegen.

Hollebrandse, B., & van Hout, A. (1994). Light verb learning in Dutch. In *Amsterdam series in child language development: No. 3. Papers from the Dutch-German Colloquium on Language Acquisition.* Groningen: University of Groningen.

Liddell, S. K. (2003). *Grammar, gesture, and meaning in American Sign Language.* Cambridge: Cambridge University Press.

Lindert, R. B. (2001). *Hearing families with deaf children: Linguistic and communicative aspects of American Sign Language development.* Doctoral dissertation, University of California, Berkeley.

Maratsos, M., Kuczaj, S., Fox, D., & Chalkley, M. A. (1979). Some empirical studies in the acquisition of transformational relations: Passives, negatives, and the past tense. In W. A. Collins (Ed.), *Children's language and communication* (pp. 1–45). Hillsdale, NJ: Lawrence Erlbaum.

Morgan, G., & Woll, B. (Eds.). (2002). *Directions in sign language acquisition.* Amsterdam: John Benjamins.

Nichols, J. (1986). Head-marking and dependent-marking grammar. *Language, 62,* 56–119.

Nichols, J. (1992). *Linguistic diversity in space and time.* Chicago: University of Chicago Press.

Ninio, A. (1999). Pathbreaking verbs in syntactic development and the question of prototypical transitivity. *Journal of Child Language, 26,* 619–653.

Ochs, E. (1979). Transcription as theory. In E. Ochs & B. B. Schieffelin (Eds.), *Developmental pragmatics* (pp. 43–72). New York: Academic Press.

O'Connor, L. (in press). Acerca de los predicados complejos en el chontal de la baja. In A. Oseguera & M. Hope (Eds.), *Historia y etnografía entre los Chontales de Oaxaca.* Mexico City: Instituto Nacional de Antropología e Historia.

Osgood, C. E., & Tanz, C. (1977). Will the real direct object in bitransitive sentences please stand up? In A. Juilland (Ed.), *Linguistic studies offered to Joseph Greenberg on the occasion of his sixtieth birthday.* Saratoga, CA: Anna Libri.

Peters, A. M. (1985). Language segmentation: Operating principles for the analysis and perception of language. In D. I. Slobin (Ed.), *The crosslinguistic study of language acquisition: Vol. 1. The data* (pp. 1029–1067). Hillsdale, NJ: Lawrence Erlbaum.

Peters, A. M. (1997). Language typology, prosody, and the acquisition of grammatical morphemes. In D. I. Slobin (Ed.), *The crosslinguistic study of language acquisition: Vol. 5. Expanding the contexts* (pp. 135–198). Mahwah, NJ: Lawrence Erlbaum.

Pinker, S. (1984). *Language learnability and language development.* Cambridge, MA: Harvard University Press.

Pinker, S., Lebeaux, D., & Frost, L. A. (1987). Productivity and constraints in the acquisition of the passive. *Cognition, 26*, 196–267.

Pye, C. (1992). The acquisition of K'iche' Maya. In D. I. Slobin (Ed.), *The crosslinguistic study of language acquisition* (Vol. 3, pp. 221–308). Hillsdale, NJ: Lawrence Erlbaum.

Sapir, E. (1921). *Language: An introduction to the study of speech*. New York: Harcourt Brace.

Sebastián, E., & Slobin, D. I. (1994). Development of linguistic forms: Spanish. In R. A. Berman & D. I. Slobin (Eds.), *Relating events in narrative: A crosslinguistic developmental study* (pp. 239–284). Hillsdale, NJ: Lawrence Erlbaum.

Slobin, D. I. (1973). Cognitive prerequisites for the development of grammar. In C. A. Ferguson & D. I. Slobin (Eds.), *Studies of child language development* (pp. 175–208). New York: Holt, Rinehart & Winston.

Slobin, D. I. (1982). Universal and particular in the acquisition of language. In E. Wanner & L. R. Gleitman (Eds.), *Language acquisition: The state of the art* (pp. 128–172). Cambridge: Cambridge University Press.

Slobin, D. I. (1985a). Crosslinguistic evidence for the Language-Making Capacity. In D. I. Slobin (Ed.), *The crosslinguistic study of language acquisition: Vol. 2. Theoretical issues* (pp. 1157–1256). Hillsdale, NJ: Lawrence Erlbaum.

Slobin, D. I. (Ed.). (1985b). *The crosslinguistic study of language acquisition: Vol. 1. The data*. Hillsdale, NJ: Lawrence Erlbaum.

Slobin, D. I. (Ed.). (1985c). *The crosslinguistic study of language acquisition: Vol. 2. Theoretical issues*. Hillsdale, NJ: Lawrence Erlbaum.

Slobin, D. I. (Ed.). (1992). *The crosslinguistic study of language acquisition*. Vol. 3. Hillsdale, NJ: Lawrence Erlbaum.

Slobin, D. I. (1996). Two ways to travel: Verbs of motion in English and Spanish. In M. Shibatani & S. A. Thompson (Eds.), *Grammatical constructions: Their form and meaning* (pp. 195–220). Oxford: Clarendon Press.

Slobin, D. I. (1997a). Mind, code, and text. In J. Bybee, J. Haiman, & S. A. Thompson (Eds.), *Essays on language function and language type: Dedicated to T. Givón* (pp. 437–467). Amsterdam: John Benjamins.

Slobin, D. I. (Ed.). (1997b). *The crosslinguistic study of language acquisition*. Vol. 4. Mahwah, NJ: Lawrence Erlbaum.

Slobin, D. I. (Ed.). (1997c). *The crosslinguistic study of language acquisition: Vol. 5. Expanding the contexts*. Mahwah, NJ: Lawrence Erlbaum.

Slobin, D. I. (1997d). The origins of grammaticizable notions: Beyond the individual mind. In D. I. Slobin (Ed.), *The crosslinguistic study of language acquisition: Vol. 5. Expanding the contexts* (pp. 265–323). Mahwah, NJ: Lawrence Erlbaum.

Slobin, D. I. (1997e). The universal, the typological, and the particular in acquisition. In D. I. Slobin (Ed.), *The crosslinguistic study of language acquisition: Vol. 5. Expanding the contexts* (pp. 1–39). Mahwah, NJ: Lawrence Erlbaum.

Slobin, D. I. (2000). Verbalized events: A dynamic approach to linguistic relativity and determinism. In S. Niemeier & R. Dirven (Eds.), *Evidence for linguistic relativity* (pp. 107–138). Amsterdam: John Benjamins.

Slobin, D. I. (2002). Language and thought online: Cognitive consequences of linguistic relativity. In D. Gentner & S. Goldin-Meadow (Eds.), *Advances in the investigation of language and thought*. Cambridge, MA: MIT Press.

Slobin, D. I. (2004). The many ways to search for a frog: Linguistic typology and the expression of motion events. In S. Strömqvist & L. Verhoeven (Eds.), *Relating events in narrative: Vol. 2. Typological and contextual perspectives* (pp. 219–257). Mahwah, NJ: Lawrence Erlbaum.

Slobin, D. I., & Bever, T. G. (1982). Children use canonical sentence schemas: A crosslinguistic study of word order and inflections. *Cognition, 12*, 229–265.

Slobin, D. I., & Hoiting, N. (1994). Reference to movement in spoken and signed languages: Typological considerations. *Proceedings of the Berkeley Linguistics Society, 20*, 487–505.

Slobin, D. I., Hoiting, N., Anthony, M., Biederman, Y., Kuntze, M., Lindert, R., Pyers, J., Thumann, H., & Weinberg, A. (2001). Sign language transcription at the level of meaning components: The Berkeley Transcription System (BTS). *Sign Language & Linguistics, 4*, 63–96.

Slobin, D. I., Hoiting, N., Kuntze, K., Lindert, R., Weinberg, A., Pyers, J., Anthony, M., Biederman, Y., & Thumann, H. (2003). A cognitive/functional perspective on the acquisition of "classifiers." In K. Emmorey (Ed.), *Perspectives on classifier constructions in sign languages* (pp. 271–296). Mahwah, NJ: Lawrence Erlbaum.

Smith, W. H. (1990). Evidence for auxiliaries in Taiwan Sign Language. In S. D. Fischer & P. Siple (Eds.), *Theoretical issues in sign language research: Vol. 1. Linguistics* (pp. 211–228). Chicago: University of Chicago Press.

Strömqvist, S., & Verhoeven, L. (Eds.). (2004). *Relating events in narrative: Vol. 2. Typological and contextual perspectives*. Mahwah, NJ: Lawrence Erlbaum.

Talmy, L. (1985). Lexicalization patterns: Semantic structure in lexical forms. In T. Shopen (Ed.), *Language typology and lexical description: Vol. 3. Grammatical categories and the lexicon* (pp. 36–149). Cambridge: Cambridge University Press.

Talmy, L. (1991). Path to realization: A typology of event conflation. *Proceedings of the Berkeley Linguistics Society, 17*, 480–519.

Talmy, L. (2000). *Toward a cognitive semantics: Vol. 2. Typology and process in concept structuring*. Cambridge, MA: MIT Press.

Taub, S. F. (2001). *Language from the body: Iconicity and metaphor in American Sign Language*. Cambridge: Cambridge University Press.

# 3

# The Development of Gesture in Hearing and Deaf Children

*Virginia Volterra, Jana M. Iverson, & Marianna Castrataro*

In this chapter, we present a survey of the current body of knowledge on the role of gesture in the development of language by hearing and deaf children. Our goal is to demonstrate how variation in the type of linguistic input to which children are exposed influences the extent to which the manual modality is employed for communicative purposes and assumes linguistic properties. To this end, we present evidence from research on children who vary widely in the nature and organization of the input to which they are exposed.

The chapter is organized into five sections. The first three focus on hearing children exposed to gestural input of varying degrees of complexity. Thus, we begin by describing the development of gesture in children exposed only to speech and follow this with a discussion of gesture in children exposed to speech with enhanced gestural input. We then consider instances in which children are simultaneously exposed to spoken and signed linguistic input. In the final two sections, we focus on deaf children who vary in terms of their access to sign language input. We first discuss research regarding the use of gesture by deaf children with no sign language input, and we then review what is

---

[1] Although the term "homesign" is usually adopted to refer to the gestural communication of deaf individuals who are not exposed to spoken or sign language (see Schick, chap. 5, this volume), we avoid this term here because our focus is on the early stages of communicative and linguistic development and similarities and differences with respect to children (hearing and deaf) discussed in the other sections.

currently known about gesture development in deaf children exposed to sign language. We conclude with a summary of the main points of this chapter.

## THE ROLE OF GESTURE IN THE ACQUISITION AND DEVELOPMENT OF SPOKEN LANGUAGE BY HEARING CHILDREN

Historically, the field of language acquisition has focused on the development of speech and, more recently, on the development of sign language. However, a large body of work carried out over the past 25 years includes many studies indicating that, in the early stages of development, hearing children's communicative repertoires are not limited to the vocal symbols of spoken languages (for a recent review, see Volterra, Caselli, Capirci, & Pizzuto, 2005). They also include gestures, and these gestures have been found to play an important role in the initial stages of communicative development. Indeed, recent research suggests that the speech and gesture system may draw on underlying brain mechanisms common to both language and motor functions (Corballis, 2002; Iverson & Fagan, 2004; Iverson & Thelen, 1999; Kimura, 1993). Following a brief description of the types of gestures produced by young hearing children exposed to spoken language only, we describe research examining the role of gesture in early lexical development and in the transition to two-word speech.

### Types of Gestures

Two types of gestures have been observed in the communicative repertoires of young children exposed only to speech. The first category, *deictic gestures* (also known as performatives; Bates, 1976; Bates, Camaioni, & Volterra, 1975), typically appears between the ages of 9 and 13 months (0;9–1;1) and marks the onset of intentional communication. The deictic gesture category includes four distinct gestures: ritualized requests, GIVE, SHOW, and POINT. For example, a child might extend the hand toward an object, repeatedly opening and closing the palm and looking toward the adult, or extend the index finger to ask for or to indicate a desired toy. Deictic gestures are nonsymbolic; they express communicative intent on the part of the child, but their content can only be interpreted by referring to the extralinguistic context in which communication occurs. Of the four deictic gestures, pointing is the most frequently observed and the most closely linked with later language development (Bruner, 1983; Locke, 1980). For instance, Bates, Benigni, Bretherton, Camaioni, and Volterra (1979) reported strong positive correlations between emergence of pointing and first word onset, but no such relationship was found for other deictic gestures and the onset of first words.

The second type of gesture, which we will call *representational gestures* (also referred to as symbolic, characterizing, iconic, or referential), appears in children's production during roughly the same age period. Some representational gestures are conventional and culturally defined (e.g., clapping hands, "all gone"); some are specific to particular cultures (e.g., among Italians, bringing the index finger to the cheek and rotating it signifies "good"). Still others are action-related (e.g., bringing the hand to the mouth for "eat") or object-related (e.g., bringing the hand to the ear for "telephone"). Despite this variability, all representational gestures share a common characteristic, namely, that they have a reasonably consistent form that is used intentionally to express a reasonably consistent meaning. In other words, unlike deictic gestures, representational gestures express a meaning that can be interpreted without reference to contextual information.

## The Role of Gesture in Early Lexical Development

In the initial stages of communicative development, many of the meanings expressed by children's representational gestures (e.g., EAT) are equivalent to those conveyed by first words (e.g., "yum yum"). First words and gestures appear to undergo a similar process of progressive decontextualization. They are initially found as parts of routines from which they are progressively detached until they are used in a referential manner to name new objects or events in multiple and varying contexts (Acredolo & Goodwyn, 1988; Caselli, 1983a, 1990; Goldin-Meadow & Morford, 1985; Iverson, Capirci, & Caselli, 1994; Volterra, 1984). Research to date suggests that at around 1 year of age, there is a basic equipotentiality between the gestural and vocal channels (Erting & Volterra, 1994). Children make relatively equal use of both the vocal and gestural modalities when communicating, and the sizes of the gestural and vocal repertoires are similar. At this point in development, the only difference between the two domains is in the modality of expression. In short, there is little evidence to suggest that a 13-month-old is biased in any way toward the development of vocal as opposed to gestural language.

Data from a longitudinal study of 12 Italian children suggest that during the first half of the second year, gestures may even account for a larger proportion of children's communicative repertoires and overall production than do words (Capirci et al, 2002; Iverson et al., 1994). Children were videotaped at home when they were 16 and 20 months of age. Results indicated that while gestures accounted for a substantial portion of the children's repertoires at both ages, gestures were most prevalent in children's communication at 16 months. At this age, 6 of the 12 children had more or as many gestures as words in their communicative repertoires. Interestingly, however, some of the children who had more words than gestures in their repertoires nevertheless made greater communicative use of the gestural modality, producing gestures more frequently than words despite their relatively larger word vocabularies. By 20 months, a clear shift toward a preference for communication in the vocal modality was observed: 10 of 12 children had more words than gestures at this age.

With regard to gesture types, there were differences and developmental changes in these children in the distributions of deictic and representational elements in the gestural as compared to the vocal modality. While all children had deictic gestures in their repertoires at both 16 and 20 months (with POINT being most frequently used compared to REQUEST and SHOW), the same was not true of deictic words (demonstrative and locative expressions, e.g., "this" and "there"): Gestural deixis preceded vocal deixis in the repertoire of half the children in the group. Representational gestures were present in the repertoires of all children at both ages, and in many children representational gesture types moderately increased from 16 to 20 months. This suggests that, for representational as well as for deictic elements, the clear shift toward the vocal modality observed at 20 months cannot be attributed simply to a contraction of the children's gestural repertoire, but was due to a parallel and relatively greater expansion of the vocal repertoire.

These observations from a relatively small number of children have been confirmed by more recent data collected using parental questionnaires. These studies have explored gestural and spoken vocabulary size in a sample of about 300 children from 8 to 17 months of age using the *Primo Vocabolario del Bambino* (PVB; the Italian version of the MacArthur-Bates Communicative Development Inventory (CDI); Casadio & Caselli, 1989; Caselli & Casadio, 1995). Consistent with observational accounts, children at the beginning of the second year are reported to produce more action gestures than words; at 12 months, the mean number of action gestures is 29, while the mean number of words produced is only 8. In the next months, the two modalities appear to develop in parallel. By 16–17 months, children are reported to use a mean of about 40 action gestures and 32 words.

## Gesture and the Transition to Two-Word Speech

Just as gestures provide a way for young children to communicate meaning during early lexical acquisition, so too do they play a transitional role in the development of the ability to convey two pieces of information within a single, communicative utterance. Recent research has examined this issue with regard to developmental changes in the *structure* and *informational content* of children's utterances.

With regard to the structure of early gestural and vocal utterances, Capirci, Iverson, Pizzuto, and Volterra (1996) reported clear developmental changes in gesture production in single- as compared to two-element utterances produced by the previously described Italian 16- and

20-month-olds. In line with findings reported by other researchers (e.g., Butcher & Goldin-Meadow, 2000; Goldin-Meadow & Morford, 1994), they noted that all of the children in their sample produced cross-modal combinations consisting of a single gesture and a single word while they were still one-word speakers. Indeed, at both ages, the most frequent two-element utterances were gesture—word combinations, and production of these combinations increased significantly from 16 to 20 months.

In addition, despite the fact that children readily combined gestures, combinations of two gestures were infrequent, and combinations of two representational gestures were never observed. When children combined two representational elements, they did so in the vocal modality. This suggests that, for hearing children, there is a constraint on the extent to which gestures become productive elements in communicative utterances. This may be due to the fact that representational gestures are relatively infrequent in the input provided to hearing children exposed only to speech, an issue to which we return below.

With regard to the informational content of two-element utterances, Capirci et al. (1996) classified two-element utterances into three major categories: *equivalent, complementary,* and *supplementary. Equivalent* combinations included only cross-modal productions of two representational units that typically referred to the same referent and conveyed the same meaning (e.g., BYE BYE + *ciao,* "bye-bye"). *Complementary* combinations typically referred to a single referent, but they always included a deictic element (gestural or vocal) that provided nonredundant information, singling out or disambiguating the referent indicated by the accompanying representational element or by another, co-occurring deictic element (e.g., POINT [to flowers] + *fiori,* "flowers"; *questa + pappa,* "this + food"; POINT [to toy] + *etto,* "this"). *Supplementary* combinations differed from the other two combination types in that each of the combined elements added information to the other (e.g., *piccolo + miao miao,* "little + kitty"; POINT [to pigeon] + *nanna,* "sleep"; ALL GONE + *acqua,* "water").

At both ages, complementary gesture—word combinations were by far the most frequent. Supplementary combinations were observed in some children at 16 months and were evident in the production of 10 children by 20 months. Interestingly, no child was observed to produce two-word combinations without having first produced supplementary gesture—word combinations (either in the same or at the previous session). This suggests that the ability to combine two distinct pieces of information within a single, tightly timed communicative utterance is first established in the context of gesture—word combinations and that the development of this ability may be related to the onset of two-word speech. This notion is supported by more recent data suggesting that onset of supplementary gesture—word combinations is a reliable predictor of the emergence of two-word utterances (Butcher & Goldin-Meadow, 2000).

## Gesture in Parental Input to Young Children

As noted above, although young hearing children exposed only to spoken language make extensive use of gesture in the early stages of communicative development, gesture never acquires languagelike properties. Specifically, children exposed exclusively to spoken input never combine two gestural symbols, although they frequently combine single words with single gestures and eventually words with other words. One possibility is that children's patterns of gesture use may mirror patterns of gesture production accompanying spoken input provided by mothers.

To address this issue, Iverson, Capirci, Longobardi, and Caselli (1999) analyzed the gestures and gesture—speech co-productions of the mothers of the 12 children who participated in the studies described above. Mothers' gestures were identified and classified into three major categories: deictic, representational, and emphatic. This third category included gestures that were comparable to the "beats" described by McNeill (1992): They do not have a well-identifiable meaning and are often executed during speech in a rhythmic fashion to stress or highlight aspects of discourse structure and/or the content of accompanying speech.

The majority of gestures produced by mothers at both observations were deictic, with pointing being the most common. Emphatic gestures were relatively rare, accounting for a relatively small proportion of gestures at both child ages. In addition, comparison of maternal gesture patterns at 16 months with those at 20 months revealed no significant differences in the production of any of the gesture types over time. In other words, mothers tended to produce informationally simple pointing gestures that referred to the immediate context; abstract gestures (e.g., beats) that are frequently observed in interactions between adults were virtually absent from these mother—child interactions (see also Bekken, 1989).

With regard to the relationship between gesture and co-occurring speech, a majority of maternal gestures at both observations served to reinforce the message conveyed in speech (e.g., NO + no in bocca, "not in your mouth"). Mothers' gestures, in other words, rarely provided information that was not already present in the spoken message. This stands in contrast to adult—adult interactions, in which gesture generally provides additional information beyond that conveyed in speech (see McNeill, 1992, 2000).

In summary, analyses of maternal gesture production revealed that mothers appear to be using a kind of "gestural motherese" characterized by fewer and more concrete gestures redundant with and reinforcing the message conveyed in speech. Not only are mothers' gestures tightly linked to the immediate linguistic and extralinguistic context, but also they appeared to be used with the goal of underscoring, highlighting, and attracting attention to particular words and/or objects. Gestures that cannot be used for this purpose (e.g., beats) are virtually eliminated from the communicative repertoire when mothers speak to their young children. Thus, the pattern of gesture production observed in young children exposed only to speech is parallel to that seen in maternal input. Although children make more frequent use of gesture than their caregivers, the predominance of pointing gestures, the absence of combinations of representational gestures, and the production of gestures with speech are characteristic of both child and caregiver productions.

## HEARING CHILDREN EXPOSED TO AN
## ENHANCED GESTURAL INPUT

In the preceding section, we presented findings from studies of children growing up in naturally occurring input situations in which parents make some use of gesture but primarily communicate via a structured spoken language. We now turn to a review of current research examining the effects of enhanced gestural input (provided in conjunction with spoken input) on early communicative and linguistic development. While much of this work (e.g., Acredolo & Goodwyn, 1988; Goodwyn & Acredolo, 1998) has focused on typically developing children, some (see Abrahamsen, 2000, for a review) has been carried out with children with developmental disorders.

In initial observational work, Acredolo and Goodwyn (1988) noted the ease and frequency with which young children spontaneously acquire and utilize symbolic gestures (akin to the representational gestures described above) to communicate (e.g., Acredolo & Goodwyn, 1988) despite the fact that parents tend naturally to emphasize vocal and devalue gestural communication. These findings led naturally to the question of whether encouraging infants to use symbolic gestures might have an effect on the course of early communicative and language development. Thus, they conducted a 2-year longitudinal study in which parents were instructed to encourage their infants to acquire and make use of symbolic gestures.

More than 130 families participated in the study. Infants entered the study at 11 months and were assigned to one of three groups. In the Gestural Training group, parents were provided with a set of eight toys, with a target gesture associated with each toy. Parents were asked to incorporate the toys into everyday routines and to model the gestures at the same time, along with the related verbal label for the object. Thus, for example, when parents introduced the toy fish, they might label the fish while simultaneously producing the related target gesture (lip smacking): "See the fishie? [FISHIE gesture] Fishie! It's a fishie!" [FISHIE gesture]. Parents were also instructed to encourage the use of gestures for communicative purposes by inventing their own gestures or borrowing signs from American Sign Language (ASL) and using them simultaneously with selected words in the speech stream (Goodwyn, Acredolo, & Brown, 2000).

In the Verbal Training group, parents were asked to encourage vocal development, but they were provided with a somewhat different set of target symbols than the Gesture Training group. However, parents in the Verbal Training group were simply instructed to model the target words for their child; no specific instructions about gesture use were provided. The final group was a Nonintervention control group, in which parents were not aware that the focus of the research was specifically on language development.

Results indicated that children in the Gesture Training group easily acquired symbolic gestures, and these gestures were used in productive combinations with other gestures and words to express two-symbol propositions. Despite clear individual differences in the propensity to learn symbolic gestures, infants in the Gestural Training group acquired significantly more of the target items than did infants in the Verbal Training group. In addition, although they found no reliable advantage for the emergence of the first symbol, they did demonstrate a small but statistically significant advantage in the attainment of a number of early language milestones (e.g., the 10-word milestone).

Infants' cognitive and language abilities (both receptive and expressive) were assessed using standardized measures at 15, 19, 24, 30, and 36 months. Comparisons between the Gestural Training and Nonintervention groups on these measures revealed that the experience with enhanced symbolic gesturing seemed to benefit Gesture Training infants' receptive and expressive language development. These findings stand in sharp contrast to the common expectation that additional emphasis on gestures might interfere with the development of spoken words. Rather, enhanced gestural input may have a facilitating effect on language development.

Along these lines, Goodwyn et al. (2000) have suggested that exposure to symbolic gesturing may provide added "practice" for the emerging symbolic function, thereby accelerating the development of object-related words. Not only do symbolic gestures provide a way around obstacles posed by the intricacies of spoken words, but they may also enable children to gather information about the symbolic function in general and about objects, events, and conditions that make up their world. The child with a symbolic gesture for "flower," for example, learns that one entity (the gesture) can stand for a very different entity (the flower) for the purpose of communication. The child also learns that buttercups and dandelions are flowers but that a potato is not. In their view, repeated experiences of this sort allow for advances at a conceptual level that may in turn contribute to language learning.

Abrahamsen, Cavallo, and McCluer (1985) analyzed data from the Toddler Sign Program, a 9-month program of bimodal input and assessment that involved 25 handicapped and nonhandicapped toddlers between the ages of 11 and 33 months at the program onset. The program environment was generally speech oriented, but some words were accompanied by manual signs from ASL. Nevertheless, the two youngest children and two speech-delayed children with Down syndrome exhibited a sign advantage in their early vocabularies, although the advantage had disappeared by the onset of syntax, suggesting that it is primarily a prelinguistic phenomenon.

In a subsequent discussion of the extent to which exposure to ordinary versus enhanced gestural input conditions may influence early symbolic development, Abrahamsen (2000) compared data from the Toddler Sign Program to data from Goodwyn and Acredolo's (1993) Gesture Training group and from infants exposed to ASL and spoken English from birth (Folven & Bonvillian, 1991; see below). This comparison revealed that exposure to enhanced gestural input conferred little or no developmental advantage in the emergence of the first symbolic form: Children exposed to enhanced gesturing reached this milestone at approximately the same ages as did children exposed to sign and speech from birth. However, consistent with Goodwyn et al.'s (2000) claims, Abrahamsen argued that although exposure to enhanced gestural input may not influence the emergence of first symbols, the effects of such exposure may become apparent somewhat later in development, when children are faced with the problem of rapidly mastering new forms for vocabulary acquisition. In Abrahamsen's view, an integral component of vocabulary growth is the ability to master new forms rapidly. Exposure to enhanced gesturing provides children with opportunities to master new forms in both the vocal and manual modalities. To the extent that procedures for mastering new forms can draw on abilities shared by the two modalities, rapid acquisition of new vocabulary items may be facilitated.

In summary, the available evidence suggests that although exposure to enhanced gestural input (in the form of "baby sign," or ASL signs used in conjunction with the speech stream) may not affect the onset of symbolic communication, its effects may become apparent somewhat later in development, as children build concepts and acquire new lexical items at a rapid pace. While it is clear that enhanced experience with gestural communication does not interfere with (and may even facilitate) the development of spoken language, the mechanisms by which enhanced gestural input influences language development are as yet unknown.

## HEARING CHILDREN EXPOSED TO A SPOKEN
## AND SIGNED LANGUAGE INPUT

Children exposed to a signed and a spoken language from birth provide researchers with an opportunity to examine directly the question
of whether the relatively late emergence of words can be attributed to
constraints imposed by production in the vocal modality. The issue has
to do with the fact that although many children demonstrate the desire
and skills required for intentional communication between the ages of
9 and 12 months, most do not produce first words until several months
later (e.g., Bates, 1976; Bates et al., 1979). This gap between the onset of
intentional communication via gesture and the onset of first words has
been interpreted by some as reflecting specific demands involved in
vocal production. Production of words requires coordination of numerous muscles in the vocal tract, and thus even when children are
cognitively and communicatively ready to produce first words, their
progress toward this milestone may be slowed due to the additional
difficulty of coordinating production in the vocal modality.

Some researchers have proposed that acquisition of a manual language may not be similarly constrained, and that this may confer an
advantage on the attainment of early sign relative to speech milestones
(Meier & Newport, 1990). Their argument is based on the developmental fact that manual dexterity is well developed by the time children are
ready to begin communicating intentionally, and because parents can
take their infant's hands and shape them into sign forms, providing
children with visual feedback about the relationship between their own
forms and target forms, children might be expected to reach early
communicative milestones in sign earlier than comparable milestones in
speech. Data in support of this claim come from longitudinal studies of
children exposed to sign from birth by their deaf parents. In comparison
to children with no sign exposure, the children exposed to sign in these
studies were reported to reach early language acquisition milestones
(e.g., first word/sign, 10-item vocabulary, first combination) at significantly younger ages (e.g., Bonvillian, Orlansky & Novack, 1983; Meier
& Newport, 1990; Orlansky & Bonvillian, 1985).

One limitation of these studies, however, is that they fail to distinguish between early gesture and early sign productions. Manual productions were defined as signs when they resembled an adult sign
form, but some of the gestures produced spontaneously by hearing
children with no sign exposure look remarkably like the signs of a sign
language (e.g., the repeated opening and closing of the child's hand is
both a gesture to request produced by young children with no sign
experience and a sign in ASL for "milk"). Thus, it is difficult to determine whether such a form should be counted as a sign when produced by a young signing child, or whether it should more properly be

considered a gesture. Because the available data do not provide a means for distinguishing between clear-cut instances of signs and instances of forms that could be gestures, we do not know whether the reported modality advantage for early language development is a reliable phenomenon, or whether it can instead be attributed to the early advantage for communication in the gestural modality that is also demonstrated by children who have not been exposed to signed input (Volterra & Iverson, 1995).

To address this issue, we examined the spontaneous communication of a bilingual hearing child of deaf parents exposed to sign and spoken language from birth, focusing on both manual (gestures and signs) and vocal production (Capirci, Iverson, Montanari, & Volterra, 2002; Capirci, Montanari, & Volterra, 1998). The child (Marco) was observed at monthly intervals between the ages of 10 and 30 months. Both of his parents were deaf, but they employed Italian Sign Language (LIS), spoken Italian, and simultaneous communication when interacting with their child. While Marco's father preferred to use only LIS, his mother made use of all three modes of communication. Marco also spent an average of approximately 30 hours a week in day care, where he was exposed to spoken Italian. Marco was thus exposed from the beginning of his life to LIS and simultaneous communication at home and to spoken Italian at day care.

Because the focus of the study required making clear distinctions between signs and gestures, conservative criteria were developed to distinguish signs from gestures and to avoid overestimating Marco's sign production. Communicative gestural signals were defined as signs only when (a) they resembled adult LIS forms and (b) their form differed from those produced by Italian monolingual children with no sign exposure. All of Marco's manual signals that failed to meet these criteria were classified as gestures. Thus, for example, although the LIS sign for "good" is executed by rotating the index finger on the cheek, instances of this form were classified as gestures for Marco because the gesture GOOD is produced in the same way by monolingual Italian children. To explore potential effects of simultaneous exposure to signed and spoken languages on early communicative development, Marco's gestural and verbal production was compared to that of a group of 12 monolingual children observed at 16 and 20 months.

Marco's earliest communications consisted primarily of gestures, a finding consistent with numerous other reports in the literature indicating that children's earliest communicative signals are produced in the gestural modality (Capirci et al., 1998). Sign language acquisition did not precede spoken language acquisition. Furthermore, the rapid growth in acquisition of new words and signs often termed the "vocabulary burst" occurred first in the vocal (between the ages of 19 and 22 months) and then in the manual (beginning at 25 months) modality.

In addition, Marco's overall vocabulary size and verbal/manual productivity fell within the range obtained for monolingual children. Marco's communication patterns generally followed those observed among children exposed only to speech. There was, in other words, no evidence of a sign advantage for early production in Marco's data. These results are consistent with other studies of bilingual sign—speech acquisition (Van den Bogaerde, 2000) that indicate that the course of spoken and sign language development is quite similar, with the emergence of two-word and two-sign combinations occurring after Marco had acquired a vocabulary of around 50 words and 50 signs, respectively.

However, an interesting difference was observed when the proportions of deictic and representational gestures produced by Marco were compared to those from the monolingual children. While Marco used proportionately more representational than deictic gestures at both comparison points, monolingual children produced deictic gestures much more frequently than representational gestures (see also Van den Bogaerde, 2000). It seems likely that Marco's relatively extensive use of representational gestures was a result of increased facility in the manual modality. Specifically, exposure to sign language may enhance children's appreciation of the representational potential of the manual modality; this may, in turn, generalize to gesture use.

With regard to the production of two-element combinations, since bilingual signers/speakers have linguistic symbols in two modalities, they have combination structures available to them (i.e., gesture + sign, sign + sign, word + sign) that are not available to monolingual children. Two of these combination structures (gesture + word and sign + word) are cross-modal and can potentially convey two different pieces of information in a single, integrated utterance, thereby eliminating the problem of coordinating articulatory movements necessary for the production of two words (Capirci et al., 1996).

Marco and the monolingual children all produced gesture—word combinations before word—word combinations, and gesture—word combinations also appeared before sign—word combinations in Marco's production. By 20 months, however, Marco was producing many more cross-modal combinations than were the monolingual children. This may be in part a reflection of his exposure to simultaneous communication, which was used extensively by his mother. In addition, at both ages, Marco combined two representational gestures, structures that were never used by his monolingual peers. The ability to combine two representational gestural elements does not appear to develop spontaneously in children who are not exposed to a sign language input, and not even in children who are immersed in a rich gestural environment, as Italian children are. The absence of representational gesture combinations seems to reflect a deeper constraint on production in the gestural modality in children exposed only to speech and suggests that the capacity to combine two representational elements in the gestural modality may be an effect of exposure to a signed input.

A final question is whether the large number of cross-modal combinations produced by Marco enhanced his communicative potential relative to his monolingual peers. In other words, did Marco make use of sign + word (in addition to gesture + word) combinations to convey two different pieces of information, something that his nonsigning peers could only do using gesture + word combinations? To address this issue, all of Marcos' combinations were categorized as equivalent, complementary, or supplementary according to the informational content they conveyed. While at 16 months of age, the overall pattern of production of equivalent, complementary, and supplementary combinations for Marco was roughly similar to that of the monolingual children, at 20 months, however, a striking difference emerged. While Marco's production of complementary and supplementary combinations remained similar to that of the monolingual children, he produced many more equivalent combinations than did the monolingual children taken as a group. This may again be a reflection of exposure to simultaneous communication, in which signs and words are co-produced. There was no evidence of an advantage in the production of supplementary combinations.

In summary, although these data are from a single case study, they are consistent with findings reported by other researchers who have developed criteria to distinguish between early gesture and sign production in children exposed to sign language (e.g., Meier & Willerman, 1995; Petitto, 2000; Petitto et al. 2001). When such criteria are employed, there is no indication that children exposed to sign reach early language milestones earlier than do their peers exposed only to spoken language. However, exposure to sign may have an effect on the extent to which children use the gestural modality for representational purposes. Representational gesture production was enhanced relative to monolingual children, and combinations of two representational gestures were produced by Marco, but not by the monolingual comparison children.

## THE USE OF GESTURE BY DEAF CHILDREN
## WITHOUT SIGN LANGUAGE INPUT

For ethical reasons, it is difficult to do research on language acquisition under restricted input conditions. However, this opportunity is naturally provided by some deaf children. A majority of deaf children are born to hearing parents who have little or no experience with sign language. Because of their acoustic deficits, these children do not have access to the spoken language used in the surrounding environment, and they are not able to acquire sign language spontaneously because it is not used by their families.

To date, several studies have been conducted on the gestures produced by deaf children not exposed to a sign language input (Goldin-Meadow, 2003; Goldin-Meadow & Mylander, 1984, 1990a, 1990b; Goldin-Meadow & Morford, 1985; Mohay, 1994; Morford, 1996; Pereira & De Lemos, 1994; Volterra, Beronesi, & Massoni, 1994). All of the deaf children in these studies had hearing parents and were not systematically exposed to a natural sign language input, but their cultural, linguistic, and educational backgrounds differed.

In general, all of these studies have demonstrated that despite impoverished learning conditions, these children develop gestural communication (both deictic and representational gestures), and that their gestures serve many of the communicative functions as the gestures of young children learning language in typical linguistic environments. Like young hearing children, their early communication consists primarily of single points or single representational gestures (e.g., pointing out the window to comment on a dog, patting the head to request a hat). There is also a clear transition from single-gesture utterances to two-element combinations. However, the overall pace of communicative development appears to be somewhat slower relative to hearing children. For instance, the acquisition of new communicative elements tends to proceed more slowly than for hearing children, with the gestural equivalent of the "vocabulary spurt" occurring at later ages (between 18 months and 2 years) relative to hearing children (Fenson et al., 1994).

While these data are a powerful testimony to the strength and resilience of the human drive to communicate, researchers differ in their interpretations of the data and of the gestural behaviors of the deaf children. Goldin-Meadow and her colleagues have conducted detailed longitudinal analyses of the production of 10 American deaf children of hearing parents followed from approximately 2–5 years of age. In these analyses, they credit the children with considerable creativity in their use of characterizing signs (i.e., representational gestures). Examination of the gestural communication of the children's mothers has revealed clear differences between mothers' gestures and those produced by their children, suggesting that the children's gestures were probably not shaped by communicative input from the environment.

Goldin-Meadow and colleagues have also argued that the deaf children's gestural systems are organized hierarchically. In their coding scheme, pointing is generally considered a deictic sign and classified as a nominal, while other characterizing signs are classified as predicates (either verbs or adjectives). Gestural strings consisting of two pointing gestures or pointing with a characterizing sign are labeled "sentences." Longer strings of pointing in combination with two action gestures are treated as complex sentences containing two propositions. For example, one child pointed at a tower and produced the HIT sign and then the FALL sign (flat palm flops over in the air) to comment on the fact that he had hit the tower and that the tower had fallen (for a critical review, see Bates & Volterra, 1984). Using this classification system, Goldin-Meadow and colleagues have reported that all of the children in their sample produced simple grammatical structures displaying recursion and developed systems with a number of lexical and syntactic and semantic properties comparable to those found in early child language.

In contrast, other authors have give more weight to the role of input in the development of deaf children's communication system, pointing out that these children are nonetheless immersed in a communicative environment even if it is not fully accessible to them. For instance, Pereira and De Lemos (1994) followed three Brazilian deaf children from the ages of 2–7 to about 5 years, focusing their analyses on the children's interactions with their hearing mothers. Their results highlight the importance of interactional processes in the negotiation of meaning between the conversational partners. Other studies have examined both gestural communication and spoken production, since many deaf children of hearing parents are enrolled in intensive oral education programs. For example, Mohay's (1990) longitudinal study of two deaf children (from 18 months to about 3 years) focused on both gestural and spoken production and the interaction between the two. In their single case study of an Italian deaf child from 6 to 7 years of age, Volterra et al. (1994) analyzed the relationship between his gestural and spoken production, noting that the child made use of aspects of the gestural input of which his hearing speech therapist (with whom he was interacting) was unaware.

Although the deaf children in all of the studies just described developed communication systems, these systems were idiosyncractic to individual children and presumably shared by their caregivers. The developmental importance of a shared communicative system is underscored by a study of two American deaf children raised by oral deaf parents (DeVilliers, Bibeau, Ramos, & Gatty, 1993). The input of these children was quite different from that of the deaf children discussed above. The deaf parents gestured while they spoke, and they produced combinations of up to four or five gestures. (Such combinations are rarely observed in the production of other hearing parents.) In addition, the parents were familiar with deafness and with visual interaction strategies used to communicate with deaf persons. Analyses of the children's production indicated that they were able to communicate about the same topics as children acquiring spoken language, and they went on to acquire spoken English with greater ease than did oral deaf children who did not share a communicative system with their parents.

To summarize, deaf children not exposed to a sign language input are nevertheless able to express the same range of semantic functions and pragmatic intents as those expressed gesturally and vocally by young hearing children. The gestures and, in particular, the gestural strings used by these deaf children are more *complex* relative to those used by nonsigning hearing children, but they are more *simple* in comparison to the signed utterances of deaf signing children and the spoken (or cross-modal) utterances of hearing children exposed to spoken language. Deaf children not exposed to a sign language input produce combinations of two or more representational gestures (in contrast to hearing children in natural input conditions), but this ability appears at a much older chronological age than the age at which children exposed to a systematic linguistic input usually produce their first two-word or two-sign combinations. The evidence reviewed here leaves little doubt that human children are active and creative participants in the language acquisition process, and that they are able to go well beyond the input offered in their efforts to communicate. At the same time, however, the issue of whether the "languagelike" structures in these gestural systems might simply be more general features of communicative systems in the visual modality remains unresolved and merits future investigation.

## THE USE OF GESTURE BY DEAF CHILDREN
## EXPOSED TO A SIGN LANGUAGE INPUT

As discussed above, the distinction between the linguistic signal and gesture is relatively straightforward in the case of spoken language acquisition because language and gesture occur in separate modalities. However, the distinction is much more difficult to make in the case of sign languages, in which gestures and signs are produced in the same modality. Two major questions have thus been of interest with regard to deaf children exposed to sign language input. The first has to do with the role of gesture in the development of language; the second, with whether gesture is a consistent feature of sign language production.

With regard to the question of the role of gesture in sign language acquisition, Bonvillian and colleagues (Folven & Bonvillian, 1991), studying a group of children (eight hearing, one deaf) whose primary linguistic input was ASL, have reported a sequence in the appearance of deictic gestures (ritualized request, showing, giving, and pointing) consistent with studies of speech-exposed children (e.g., Bates et al., 1979) in which pointing preceded the first symbolic word. Comparisons between deaf children exposed to a signed input and hearing children suggest that all children, regardless of whether their primary linguistic input is spoken or signed, acquire a small inventory of gestures prior to the onset of symbolic communication. Thus, for example, in a comparison of the early production of a hearing child acquiring vocal language (Italian) to that of a deaf girl acquiring sign language (ASL), Caselli (1983b) found that both children followed a similar developmental sequence, progressing from initial context-bound use of communicative signals to production of more flexible, decontextualized signs or words. Caselli and Volterra (1990) analyzed the communication of three hearing children learning Italian and one deaf child learning LIS and reported that development in the manual modality was similar until the point at which the child learning LIS produced combinations of two representational items in the manual modality. In contrast, the hearing children learning Italian produced combinations of representational items only in the vocal modality.

These findings underscore the integral role of gesture in the early stages of communicative development. Even deaf children exposed to a signed input make use of gestures to communicate, and like hearing children exposed to speech, they do so at a time when they are working out the problem of symbolic communication.

With regard to the question of whether gesture is a consistent feature of sign language production, surprisingly little attention has been focused on the relationship between gesture and sign language development in older deaf children or on the role of gesture in communication in adult native signers. In a recent chapter, Emmorey (1999) explored whether a parallel to the co-speech gestures produced by hearing people is evident in signers' production. Her analysis suggests that signers do gesture, but not in the way that speakers do. In contrast to speakers, signers do not produce idiosyncratic, spontaneous movements of the hands and arms while they are signing. However, they do produce component gestures (also defined as "constructed action") as a separate component of a signed utterance, and signing comes to a halt while the gesture is produced. The meanings of such manual gestures are clear even outside of the sign context. For example, in a description of a scene from the *Frog Story*, a signer reproduced the boy's "be quiet" gesture that was directed to the dog. Gestures may be more apparent in the production of nonnative signers, who tend to intermix gestures with signing when communicating with one another (Messing, 1999).

In addition to manual gestures, body gestures that are not components of the signed utterance can be produced concurrently with signing (e.g., the body rocks back and forth while describing a scene of a child on a swing). Such gestures are not linguistic: They express how referents move their bodies during the action described by the concurrent signing, particularly during narratives. Similarly, facial gestures convey information about emotion or attitude; such gestures are distinct from the facial markers used for grammatical purposes (e.g., marking adverbials, topics, wh-questions). Finally, while mouth movements can serve linguistic functions, they can also be produced to provide emotional stress or to comment on ongoing signed productions.

Examples such as these lead naturally to the question of how to determine whether a given expression is a gesture or a sign. Marschark (1994) has proposed that if a manual expression resembles a gesture produced by speakers, then that expression should be considered gesticulation rather than signing. However, the issue is complicated by the fact that the form of some gestures mirrors that of linguistic signs. Thus, a gesture tracing the shape of an object could be a gesture, or it could be a morphologically complex sign language classifier predicate. A similar problem is apparent with respect to pointing gestures. In many sign languages, pointing gestures/signs are lexicalized and used as pronouns that can be directed toward persons, objects, or locations in the real word or toward locations in signing space to refer to nouns associated with those locations. Analyses of longitudinal data on deaf children acquiring ASL have revealed a developmental progression from production of pointing as a deictic gesture to production of pointing gestures as deictic signs for pronominal reference (for further details, see Petitto, 1994; Pizzuto, 1994). In these examples, the critical issue has to do with the extent to which such expressions may be nonlinguistic or linguistic, and in analyses of children's acquisition and production of specific language forms, the question of whether to credit them with production of complex linguistic forms (e.g., classifiers, pronouns) or gestures is a crucial one.

To summarize, the question of the relationship of gesture to sign has been relatively unexplored, likely due to concern that it would devalue the linguistic status of sign. Research conducted to date suggests that gesture is as essential a part of sign language as it is of speech-based communication. As Stokoe and Marschark (1999) have pointed out, "In both signed and spoken languages gesture serves as a complement to, and in many ways an essential component of, linguistic communication. Insofar as spoken and signed languages represent coordinate, functionally equivalent modes of communication, gesture should serve the same psychological and linguistic role in both" (p. 164).

## SUMMARY AND CONCLUSIONS

Gesture is a robust feature of communicative development in young children. The evidence reviewed in this chapter suggests that all children, regardless of their hearing status or the modality of the linguistic input to which they are exposed, make use of gestures to communicate. At the beginning of the second year, children do not appear to be biased in any way toward the acquisition of a vocal versus a manual language. Although the gestural modality appears to be "advantaged" for early communication in all children, the extent to which the gestural modality becomes elaborated for communicative and linguistic purposes depends on the nature of the input to which the child is exposed. We have reviewed research on five different populations of children who vary in their hearing status (hearing, deaf) and the nature of the input to which they are exposed (typical, enhanced, restricted), and as we have discussed above, these variations in input have important implications for the way in which gesture is used. Gesture can be integrated with and an accompaniment to a fully elaborated linguistic system (speech or sign); its use and complexity can be enhanced by altering linguistic input; and it can serve as the primary mode of communication when access to linguistic input is restricted.

In the case of children exposed to typical linguistic input (spoken or signed), gestures emerge before first words or signs and co-exist with words and signs during the early stages of communicative development. For hearing children exposed only to speech, the vocal and manual modalities initially seem to enjoy a sort of equipotentiality: Children readily acquire and produce both gestures and words and frequently combine gestures with words to convey multiple ideas. However, by 20 months, the vocal modality becomes the primary one for linguistic communication. At this point, most hearing children have begun to demonstrate a preference for vocal communication, and constraints on the development of gestural communication have become evident. Thus, children exposed only to speech never combine two representational elements in the manual modality; when two-element combinations of representational elements emerge, they are produced exclusively in the vocal modality. The absence of representational gesture combinations is fully consistent with the nature of the linguistic input that hearing children receive. Although their caregivers gesture as they speak, their gestures tend to occur in a one-to-one relationship with verbal utterances, and production of two gestures within the bounds of a single verbal utterance is rare. However, combinations of representational words occur regularly in the spoken portion of the input, and it is ultimately this pattern that is followed by speech-exposed children.

For children exposed to a sign language from birth, the developmental progression from communication to language is strikingly parallel to that observed among young speaking children. Even signing children use gestures to communicate, and gestures typically emerge before the onset of first signs. Signing children also combine gestures with signs to form combinations like the gesture—word combinations observed in speech-exposed children. However, unlike speaking children, signing children do combine representational elements in the manual modality. Production of sign combinations is, of course, completely consistent with the fact that the input to which they are exposed regularly contains combinations of representational elements in the manual modality.

By the end of the second year, both speech- and sign-exposed children come to rely progressively less and less on gestures for communicative purposes as they begin to master their respective linguistic systems. Importantly, however, gestures do not simply disappear at this point in development. Among adult speakers, gestures are produced with speech in a temporally and semantically integrated fashion (McNeill, 1992, 2000). And although continued research is clearly needed to tease apart the relationship between gesture and sign in both mature and child signers, the available evidence indicates that signers do gesture, and that these gestures are distinct from linguistic manual and nonmanual expressions.

The cases of hearing children exposed to spoken language and deaf children exposed to sign language can be thought of as the endpoints on a continuum of complexity in the manual modality. Speaking children represent the least elaborated end of the continuum; despite the initial equipotentiality of the vocal and manual modalities, gestures become integrated with and secondary to the primary spoken linguistic system. Deaf children represent the most elaborated end of the continuum; in their case, the manual modality assumes the properties of a fully fledged language.

By contrast, the instances of altered input, in which hearing children are exposed to enhanced gesture or to a combination of sign and speech and in which deaf children of hearing parents are deprived of sign input, represent intermediate points on the continuum. Thus, for example, hearing children exposed to enhanced gesturing readily acquire novel target gestures and do so at a more rapid pace than do children exposed to enhanced verbal input. This enhanced input appears to result in a potentiation of gestural communication, but this advantage is most apparent between the ages of 12 and 15 months and relatively short-lived. This is not surprising given that gestural input, albeit enhanced, is nonetheless produced in conjunction with speech, the child's primary input modality, and is not organized into a structured linguistic system. Interestingly, there is surprisingly little variability in the age of onset of first manual symbols across groups of children with exposure to gestural input that ranges from asystematic (i.e., the spontaneous gestures accompanying parental speech to children with no sign training experience) to enhanced gestural input (i.e., sign training) to a fully fledged linguistic system (i.e., ASL). Exposure to enhanced gesturing, however, had positive effects on the children's development of *spoken* language. Although the mechanisms underlying this effect are not known, one possibility is that enhanced gesturing introduced additional variability into the input, variability that children can then use to advance their understanding of the nature of symbols and symbolic communication.

Linguistic input is sometimes also altered by introducing both spoken and signed languages (produced separately and in conjunction in the form of bimodal communication) to the child from birth. When this occurs, there are clear effects on the nature and organization of gestural communication. Thus, for example, the child Marco not only combined two representational elements in the manual modality (as would be expected on the basis of exposure to sign language), but also acquired a large representational *gesture* repertoire and produced such gestures with much greater frequency than did children with no sign language exposure. These findings suggest that exposure to sign language attunes children to ways in which the manual modality can be used for representational purposes.

Finally, when access to linguistic input is restricted, as in the case of deaf children with no sign language exposure, gesture becomes the primary mode of communication. Such children invent their own gestures and use these gestures to express a range of semantic functions and pragmatic intents similar to those expressed by children who have access to a more complete linguistic input. While these gestures are clearly more elaborate than those produced by hearing children, however, they do not appear to attain anything like the level of complexity that is apparent in sign languages. Thus, while the use of gesture for communication is a robust phenomenon, appearing even in the absence of exposure to systematic linguistic input, input shapes the gestural system and plays an especially important role in the transition from gestural communication to spoken or signed language.

## ACKNOWLEDGMENTS

Portions of the research presented in this chapter are supported in the framework of the European Science Foundation EUROCORES programme "The Origin of Man, Language and Languages" (OMLL) to V.V. and by NIH R01 HD41677 to J.M.I.

## REFERENCES

Abrahamsen, A. A., Cavallo, M. M., & McCluer, J. A. (1985). Is the sign advantage a robust phenomenon? From gesture to language in two modalities. *Merrill-Palmer Quarterly, 31,* 17–209.

Abrahamsen, A. (2000). Explorations of enhanced gestural input to children in the bimodal period. In K. Emmorey & H. Lane (Eds.), *The signs of language revisited: An anthology to honor Ursula Bellugi and Edward Klima* (pp. 357–399). Hillsdale, NJ: Erlbaum.

Acredolo, L. P., & Goodwyn, S. W. (1988). Symbolic Gesturing in Normal Infants. In *Child Development, 59,* 450–456.

Bates, E. (1976). *Language and context. The acquisition of pragmatics.* New York: Academic Press.

Bates, E., Benigni, L., Bretherton, I., Camaioni, L., & Volterra, V. (1979). *The emergence of symbols: Cognition and communication in infancy.* New York: Academic Press.

Bates, E., Camaioni, L., & Volterra, V. (1975). The acquisition of performatives prior to speech. *Merril Palmer Quarterly, 21*(3), 205–226.

Bates, E., & Volterra, V. (1984). On the invention of language: An alternative view. Commentary to S. Goldin-Meadow & C. Mylander, Gestural communication in deaf children: The effect and non-effects of parental input on early language development. *Monographs of the Society for Research in Child Development, 49*, 3–4, 130–142.

Bekken, K. (1989). *Is there motherese in gesture?* Unpublished doctoral dissertation, University of Chicago.

Bonvillian, J. D, Orlansky, M. D., & Novack, L. L. (1983). Developmental milestones: Sign language acquisition and motor development. *Child Development, 54*, 1435–1445.

Bruner, J. (1983). *Child's talk: learning to use language.* New York: Norton.

Butcher, C., & Goldin-Meadow, S. (2000). Gesture and the transition from one- to two-word speech: When hand and mouth come together. In D. McNeill (Ed.), *Language and gesture* (pp. 235–257). Cambridge: Cambridge University Press.

Capirci, O., Montanari, S., & Volterra, V. (1998). Gestures, signs, and words in early language development. In M. Iverson & S. Goldin-Meadow (Eds.), *The nature and function of gesture in children's communication* (pp. 45–60). New Directions for Child Development, 79. San Francisco: Jossey-Bass.

Capirci, O., Iverson, J., Montanari, S., & Volterra, V. (2002). Gestural, signed and spoken modalities in early language development: The role of linguistic input. *Bilingualism Language and Cognition, 5*(1), 25–37.

Capirci, O., Iverson, J. M., Pizzuto, E., & Volterra, V. (1996). Gestures and words during the transition to two-word speech. *Journal of Child language, 23*, 645–673.

Capirci, O., Caselli, M. C., Iverson, J. M., Pizzuto, E., & Volterra, V. (2002). Gesture and the nature of language in infancy: The role of gesture as transitional device enroute to two-word speech. In D. Armstrong, M. Karchmer, & J. Van Cleeve (Eds.), *The study of sign languages—essays in honor of William C. Stokoe* (pp. 213–246). Washington, DC: Gallaudet University Press.

Casadio, P., & Caselli, M. C. (1989). Il primo vocabolario del bambino. Gesti e parole a 14 mesi. *Età Evolutiva, 33*, 32–42.

Caselli, M. C. (1983a). Gesti comunicativi e prime parole. *Età Evolutiva, 16*, 36–51.

Caselli, M. C. (1983b). Communication to language: Deaf children's and hearing children's development compared. *Sign Language Studies, 39*, 113–144.

Caselli, M. C. (1994). Communicative gestures and first words. In V. Volterra & C. J. Erting (Eds.), *From gesture to language in hearing and deaf children* (pp. 56–67). Washington, DC: Gallaudet University Press.

Caselli, M. C., & Casadio, P. (1995). *Il primo vocabolario del bambino. Guida all'uso del questionario MacArthur per la valutazione della comunicazione e del linguaggio nei primi anni di vita.* Milano: Franco Angeli.

Caselli, M. C., & Volterra, V. (1994). From communication to language in hearing and deaf children. In V. Volterra & C. Erting (Eds.), *From gesture to language in hearing and deaf children* (pp. 263–277). Washington, DC: Gallaudet University Press.

Corballis, M. C. (2002), *From hand to mouth—the origins of language.* Princeton, NJ: Princeton University Press.

DeVilliers, J., Bibeau, L., Ramos, E., & Gatty, J. (1993). Gestural communication in oral deaf mother-child pairs: language with a helping hand? *Applied Psycholinguistics, 14,* 319–47.

Emmorey, K. (1999). Do signers gesture? In L. Messing & R. Campbell (Eds.), *Gesture, speech, and sign* (pp. 133–159). New York: Oxford University Press.

Erting, C., & Volterra, V. (1994). Conclusion. In V. Volterra, & C. Erting (Eds.), *From gesture to language in hearing and deaf children* (pp. 299–303). Washington, DC: Gallaudet University Press.

Fenson, L., Dale, P., Reznick, J., Bates, E., Thal, D., & Pethick, S. (1994). *Monographs of the Society for Research in Child Development: Vol. 59, No. 5. Variability in early communicative development.* (Serial No. 242).

Folven, R., & Bonvillian, J. D. (1991). The Transition from nonreferential to referential language in children acquiring American Sign Language. *Developmental Psychology, 27,* 806–816.

Goldin-Meadow, S. (2003). The resilience of language: What gesture creation in deaf children can tell us about how all children learn language. *Essays in Developmental Psychology.*

Goldin-Meadow, S., & Morford, M. (1985). Gesture in early child language: Studies of hearing and deaf children. *Merrill-Palmer Quarterly, 31,* 145–176.

Goldin-Meadow, S., & Morford, M. (1994). Gesture in early child language. In V. Volterra & C. J. Erting (Eds.), *From gesture to language in hearing and deaf children* (pp. 249–262). New York: Springer-Verlag.

Goldin-Meadow, S., & Mylander, C. (1984). Gestural communication in deaf children: The effect and non-effects of parental input on early language development. *Monographs of the Society for the Research in Child Development, 49,* 1–121.

Goldin-Meadow, S., & Mylander, C. (1990a). Beyond the input given: The child's role in the acquisition of language. *Language, 66,* 323–355.

Goldin-Meadow, S., & Mylander, C. (1990b). The role of parental input in the development of a morphological system. *Journal of Child Language, 17,* 527–563.

Goodwyn, S. W. & Acredolo, L. P. (1993). Symbolic gesture versus word: Is there a modality.

Goodwyn, S. W., & Acredolo, L. P. (1998). Encouraging symbolic gestures: A new perspective on the relationship between gesture and speech. In J. Iverson & S. Goldin-Meadow (Eds.), *The nature and functions of gesture in children's communication* (pp. 61–73). New directions for child development, 79. San Francisco: Jossey-Bass.

Goodwyn, S. W., Acredolo, L. P., & Brown C. A. (2000). Impact of symbolic gesturing on early language development. *Journal of Nonverbal Behavior 24(2),* 81–103.

Iverson, J. M., Capirci, O., & Caselli, M. C. (1994). From communication to language in two modalities. *Cognitive Development, 9,* 23–43.

Iverson, J. M., Capirci, O., Longobardi, E., & Caselli, M. C. (1999). Gesturing in mother-child interaction. *Cognitive Development, 14,* 57–75.

Iverson, J. M., & Fayan, M. K. (2004). Infant vocal-motor coordination: Precursor to the gesture-speech system? *Child Development, 75* 1053–1066.

Iverson, J. M., Thelen, E. (1999). Hand, mouth, and brain: The dynamic emergence of speech and gesture. *Journal of Consciousness Studies, 6,* 19–40.

Kimura, D. (1993). *Neuromotor mechanisms in human communication*. New York: Oxford University Press.

Locke, A. J. (1980). *The guided reinvention of language*. London: Academic Press.

Marschark, M. (1994). Gesture and sign. *Applied Psycholinguistics, 15*, 209–36.

Meier, R. P., & Newport, E. (1990). Out of the hands of babes: On a possible sign advantage in language acquisition. *Language, 6*, 1–23.

Meier, R. P., & Willerman, R. (1995). Prelinguistic gestures in deaf and hearing infants. In K. Emmorey & J. Reilly (Eds.), *Language, gesture and space* (pp. 391–409). Hillsdale, NJ: Erlbaum.

Messing, L. (1999). Two modes-two languages? In L. Messing & R. Campbell (Eds.), *Gesture, speech, and sign* (pp. 183–199). New York: Oxford University Press.

McNeill, D. (1992). *Hand and mind—what gestures reveal about thought*. Chicago: University of Chicago Press.

McNeill, D. (Ed.). (2000). *Language and gesture*. Cambridge: Cambridge University Press.

Mohay, H. (1994). The interaction of gesture and speech in the language development of two profoundly deaf children. In V. Volterra & C. Erting (Eds.), *From gesture to language in hearing and deaf children* (pp. 187–204). Washington, DC: Gallaudet University Press.

Morford, J. P. (1996). Insights to language from the study of gesture: A review of research on the gestural communication of non-signing deaf people. *Language and Communication, 16*(2), 165–178.

Orlansky, M. D., & Bonvillian, J. D. (1985). Sign Language Acquisition: Language Development in children of deaf parents and implications for other populations. *Merrill Palmer Quarterly, 31*, 127–143.

Pereira, C., & De Lemos, C. (1994). Gesture in hearing mother-deaf child interaction. In V. Volterra & C. Erting (Eds.), *From gesture to language in hearing and deaf children* (pp. 178–186). Washington, DC: Gallaudet University Press.

Petitto, L. A. (1994). The transition from gesture to symbol in American Sign Language. In V. Volterra & C. Erting (Eds.), *From gesture to language in hearing and deaf children* (pp. 153–161). Washington, DC: Gallaudet University Press.

Petitto, L. A. (2000). On the biological foundations of human language. In K. Emmorey & H. Lane (Eds.), *The signs of language revisited: An anthology to honor Ursula Bellugi and Edward Klima* (pp. 449–473). Hillsdale, NJ: Erlbaum.

Petitto, L. A., Katerelos, M., Levy, B. G., Gauna, K., Tétrault, K., & Ferraro, V. (2001). Bilingual signed and spoken language acquisition from birth: Implications for the mechanisms underlying early bilingual language acquisition. *Journal of Child Language, 28*, 453–496.

Pizzuto, E. (1994). The early development of deixis in American Sign Language: What is the point? In V. Volterra & C. Erting (Eds.), *From gesture to language in hearing and deaf children* (pp. 142–152). Washington, DC: Gallaudet University Press.

Pizzuto, E. (2004). Review of "The hands are the head of the mouth—the mouth as articulat or in sign languages." P. Boyes Braem & R. Sutton-Spence (Eds.), Hamburg: Signum, 2001 *Sign language and linguistics, 6:2*, 300–305.

Stokoe, W. C., & Marschark, M. (1999). Sign, gestures, and signs. In L. Messing & R. Campbell (Eds.), *Gesture, speech, and sign* (pp. 161–181). New York: Oxford University Press.

Van den Bogaerde, B. (2000). *Input and interaction in deaf families.* doctoral dissertation, University of Amsterdam, Utrecht.

Volterra, V. (1981). Gestures signs and words at two years: When does communication become language? *Sign Language Studies, 33,* 351–362.

Volterra, V., Beronesi, S., & Massoni, P. (1994). How does gestural communication become language? In V. Volterra & C. Erting (Eds.), *From gesture to language in hearing and deaf children* (pp. 205–218). Washington, DC: Gallaudet University Press.

Volterra, V., & Erting, C. (Eds.). (1994). *From gesture to language in hearing and deaf children.* Washington, DC: Gallaudet University Press.

Volterra, V., & Iverson, J. M. (1995). When do modality factors affect the course of language acquisition? In K. Emmorey & J. Reilly (Eds.), *Language, gesture, and space* (pp. 371–390). Hillsdale, NJ: Erlbaum.

Volterra, V., Caselli, M. C., Capirci, O., Pizzuto, E. (2005). Gesture and the emergence and development of language. In M. Tomasello & D. Slobin (Eds.), *Beyond nature-nurture! Essays in honor of Elizabeth Bates.* Mahwah, NJ.: Erlbaum.

# 4

# Patterns and Effects of Language Input to Deaf Infants and Toddlers From Deaf and Hearing Mothers

*Patricia Elizabeth Spencer & Margaret Harris*

This chapter addresses characteristics of input that are especially facil-
itative of the development of a signed visual-gestural language. We
begin by considering some key beneficial characteristics of language
addressed to young children learning a spoken language and then explore similarities and differences between these characteristics and
those that influence early sign development. We describe how deaf
mothers adapt their signing to benefit young deaf children who are just
beginning to learn sign, and we consider similarities and differences in
the sign adaptations of deaf mothers who are fluent signers and hearing
mothers who are new signers. The focus in the last part of the chapter is
on children's emerging sign communication and how that relates to sign
input and patterns of shared attention that operate within mother—
child dyads.

Recent studies of behavior genetics are shedding new light on
environmental influences on the development of language. In an extensive study of the incidence of typical and atypical language development in a large population of twins, Spinath, Price, Dale, and Plomin
(2004) concluded "the greatest effect on language disability and ability
in early childhood is shared environmental influence" (p. 445). Such an
emphasis on the significance of the environment may come as a surprise
to many researchers who have worked exclusively on the development
of spoken language. Within that research community there have
been—and will no doubt continue to be—many powerful advocates for
the innate basis of language (e.g., Pinker, 2002). Indeed, we agree that

humans are genetically predisposed to organize communicative input and to develop linguistic systems in specific ways. However, for those familiar with research into sign language, the evidence that language development is strongly influenced by the kind of input that children receive is striking. It is possible to observe what occurs across a wide range of situations in which the signed input varies from optimal to nonexistent.

Studies of deaf children also serve as a powerful reminder of the innate tendency of humans to find ways to communicate. Even when deaf children are not given language input that they can perceive and process, that is, when they are not given exposure to signed language, they develop systematic gestural means for communicating (Goldin-Meadow & Mylander, 1990). This phenomenon has long been noted in "home-signs," the gestural systems developed by deaf children when they must create their own ways of communicating within the family without reference to previously established, culturally transmitted forms of sign language. The children Goldin-Meadow and Mylander studied were developing their communication systems on their own by using gestures replicating actions and characteristics of objects. Although spontaneously generated gestural communication systems can serve a number of functions, especially with regard to sharing topics of interest and indicating needs, they are inherently limited in a number of ways (Emmorey, 2002). Such communications are generally easily understood only among family members or others very familiar with each other. The communicative productions are also limited in the degree to which they form systems of combined meanings and in their degree of abstractness. Thus, despite evidence that children have innate tendencies to construct functional communication systems from even somewhat degraded input (e.g., Goldin-Meadow & Mylander, 1990; Singleton, 1989; Singleton & Newport, 1987), there are clearly limits below which the input is insufficient to lead to development of a well-articulated, formal language system.

The language of deaf children who are exposed to sign language in their early home environments is not restricted in the ways discussed above for children without such exposure. Of course, as with spoken languages, early sign productions are limited by the children's still emerging cognitive, social, and linguistic skills. Sign language produced by toddlers and young children thus fails to represent the sophistication and complexity of the adult form of the language. However, unlike the primarily idiosyncratic communications that deaf children develop in the absence of a language model, sign language that is learned from more experienced users undergoes continued development as its young learners mature.

Given the difference in the end product of gestural communication created without access to a language model, as opposed to that of a language based on exposure to formal sign language, it is obvious that the language input provided to a deaf child plays a critical developmental role. Furthermore, because there are important similarities between the development of sign and spoken language, we could expect many of the features that affect the rate of acquisition to be identical (Harris, 1992). At the same time, because of the difference in the primary modalities used in spoken and signed language, we would expect some of features of the input to apply uniquely to one and not the other system.

## CHILD-DIRECTED SPEECH

Early studies of hearing mothers' talk to their young hearing children (e.g., Snow, 1977) revealed certain characteristic features, including simplicity, brevity, and accuracy. In other words, hearing mothers tend to speak in short, simple, and error-free utterances when talking to language-learning hearing children. Subsequent studies, however, have revealed that the *grammatical* characteristics of mothers' speech have little direct effect on their children's language development. Two observational studies, in which researchers analyzed samples of mothers' speech collected in the United Kingdom (Ellis & Wells, 1980) and in the United States (Gleitman, Newport, & Gleitman, 1984), showed that the length and complexity of maternal utterances failed to predict the speed of children's language development. However, Ellis and Wells collected extensive notes about nonverbal activities occurring in each recorded session, revealing other aspects of mothers' speech that were related to (and predicted) children's language development. A major finding related to the strong relationship between what mothers *said* to their children and the *activity* that was taking place at the time. Mothers of children with the most precocious language development asked them more questions and gave more instructions than did mothers of children with less precocious development. They were also more responsive to the children's utterances, producing more acknowledgments and imitations than mothers of less precocious children, and they frequently referred to ongoing activities in which both they and their child were involved.

Ellis and Wells thus demonstrated that, in the early stages of learning to talk, mothers who ask questions, give instructions, and generally comment on their toddlers' ongoing activity have children with more precocious language development (see also Harris, Jones, Brookes, & Grant, 1986; Tomasello & Todd, 1983). The importance of supplying young children with language that has an accessible nonverbal context becomes clear when the way in which children first begin to use and understand words is examined. Harris, Barrett, Jones, and Brookes (1988) compared the pattern of use of each of the first 10 words produced by children with their mothers' use of these same words when talking to the children during the preceding month. The researchers found considerable overlap between the context of a word's use by children and their mothers. Out of the 40 words studied, there were only three where there was no apparent relationship between a child's use and the mother's use of that word in the preceding month; in 33 of the cases, the child's use was identical to the mother's most frequent use. This relationship was particularly striking when the child's first use of a word appeared to be idiosyncratic, as in the example of James saying "mummy" only when he was holding out a toy for his mother to take. This pattern of use was explained by the fact his mother most commonly used "mummy" herself when holding out her hand to take a toy from James and asking "Is that for mummy?"

This close relationship between children's words and their mother's speech is of strictly limited duration because, when a child acquires a *new* use of the same word a few weeks later, it is much less likely to mirror a preceding maternal use. Barrett, Harris, and Chasin (1991) found that fewer than 50% of second uses were similar to prior maternal uses, and they were identical to the most frequent maternal use in only 24% of cases. This contrasts sharply with over 80% of initial uses of the same words by the same children. However, at the beginning of vocabulary development, the opportunity for a young child to experience frequent pairings of a word and a familiar nonverbal context can facilitate lexical development. Data from Hart (1991) suggest that children's first words are heard many times in the speech of their parents. On average, these words occurred 30 times in a monthly observation session, compared with a frequency of only two occurrences for words acquired 6 months later.

The content of children's early vocabulary input varies to some extent across cultures. For example, Todo, Fogel, and Kawai (1990) found that Japanese mothers were more concerned with their babies' feelings and emotions and less concerned with questioning and directing their babies in the manner that is so characteristic of Western mothers. Similar findings were reported by Fernald and Morikawa (1993). Other culturally specific topic patterns may be expected but have not yet been fully explored.

The content of children's early vocabulary also appears to be influenced by some of the formal properties of the particular language to which they are exposed. The emerging lexicon of children acquiring English contains more nouns (object names) than verbs (Fenson et al., 1994). However, Gopnik and Choi (1995) found that verbs appear earlier, and comprise a greater proportion of early vocabulary, for children acquiring Korean, and Tardif (1996) reports a similar finding for 21-month-old children learning Mandarin Chinese. This vocabulary difference between English and the other two languages reflects the fact that Korean- and Mandarin-speaking mothers use more verbs when talking to their children than do mothers who speak English.

A study of acquisition of Italian (Camaioni & Longobardi, 2001) highlighted the importance not only of the relative frequency of nouns and verbs but also of their relative morphological complexity and their position within an utterance. Camaioni and Longobardi argue that children's early vocabularies reflect not only the frequency with which they encounter particular words—and classes of words—but also the consistency of the form of a particular word from utterance to utterance. If there are few morphological inflections that can attach to a particular word stem, the form of a word will be similar whenever a child hears it. However, if there are many inflections, the form of the word will vary from utterance to utterance. Camaioni and Longobardi argue that stability of form will make an item easier to acquire. They also suggest that words which often occur in initial position (which is assumed to be particularly salient) are more likely to be acquired.

In summary, studies of hearing mothers' child-directed speech indicate that some features of language input are common across languages while others are language specific. Two input features that appear to be important for all young children who are learning a first language are (1) the relationship of adult language to the nonverbal context and (2) the stability of form of individual lexical items. Consistent relationships between what is being said and what is going on should be important for all children, irrespective of the language they are learning. As we discuss below, such relationships are commonly observed in the language that both deaf and hearing mothers address to deaf infants and young children; however, the two groups of mothers tend to differ in the degree to which they make their language perceptually accessible to the children. Stability of form of maternal utterances can present special issues for dyads with deaf children when mothers are hearing and are new signers. Like any adults acquiring a new language, new signers produce expressions that are often ungrammatical and produce individual signs with variable and not always accurate form.

Other language input features that relate to acquisition patterns (including the relative preponderance of words from different grammatical classes, their morphological variation from utterance to utterance, and their position within an utterance) vary from language to language. Because important aspects of grammar differ between adult versions of spoken English and both American Sign Language (ASL) and British Sign Language, this characteristic of child-directed signing will be explored below. Although existing cross-cultural research with hearing families indicates some culturally specific topics and content in parent–child conversations, we are not aware of studies of this phenomenon in families with deaf children.

## CHILD-DIRECTED SIGNING

One obvious difference between signed and spoken input is that the former is received primarily through vision. This has important implications for the way in which mothers demonstrate the relation between the topic of their conversation and the child's current activity. This is not to deny, of course, the importance of visual information to hearing children learning a spoken language. Visual information typically provides context for a spoken message. For example, mothers of hearing children often point to an activity or hold up an object to identify a conversation topic. One indication of the importance of visual support for the context of spoken language is evident in reports that blind children's initial language acquisition is often delayed (Dunlea, 1989; Moore & McConachie, 1994). In addition, much of the affective meaning of a spoken utterance is carried in the speaker's facial expression, posture, and other "body language." Such information may be especially important for a child who is not yet fluent in the language and for whom nonlinguistic or paralinguistic information serves as an important aid to understanding. However, the linguistic, referential content of a spoken language message is almost always represented in the sounds produced by the speaker and received and processed auditorily by the listener. In contrast, a message expressed in sign language typically requires that linguistic as well as paralinguistic and contextual information be received and processed using the visual sense.

An important difference between audition and vision as the means through which language input is received is that auditory information can be received even when the listener is not looking at the speaker. This is obviously not the case when vision is being used in the receipt of a signed message. For hearing children, there is an early and apparently innate link between hearing and looking behavior (see Fernald, 2001, for a review). In a classic study, Wertheimer (1961) showed that newborn hearing infants will turn their head to the right or the left to roughly localize a sound source. Wertheimer's observation has been confirmed by more recent studies (Castillo & Butterworth, 1981; Muir & Field, 1979). By 4 months of age, hearing infants can localize a sound source to within 22 degrees, and this ability increases steadily over time. By the end of the first year of life, sound becomes a very reliable cue to the source location (Morrongiello, Fenwick, Hillier, & Chance, 1979). In addition, even as early as 3 months of age, hearing infants show that they can identify their mothers' and fathers' voices and will look toward the presumed speaker even when that voice is played from a recording (Spelke & Owsley, 1979). Typically, of course, speech is directed to infants by adults who are present and are attempting to establish interaction with the infant. Looking toward the source of the sound will direct the infant's attention to the speaker.

To the degree that speech automatically captures hearing infants' attention to faces, there are important implications for the dynamics of communication with deaf infants. Mothers of deaf children often have to actively engage their visual attention in a way that mothers of hearing children do not. To do so, deaf mothers employ a set of attention-getting and directing strategies that are not often used by mothers of hearing infants. This results in differences in the timing and structure of effective language input to young children acquiring signed rather than spoken language. Moreover, because making child-directed language modifications is usually an "intuitive" or nonconscious process, it is probable that mothers communicating in their own well-practiced, commonly used language will make modifications more effectively than mothers using a new, relatively unpracticed language or language modality (Koester, 1992). In the case of children learning signed language, attention has therefore been focused on the language behaviors of mothers who are deaf and whose everyday communication is expressed through sign. How do these mothers comfortably establish an association between their signed language and the activity or attention focus in which their deaf children are engaged?

### Deaf Mothers with Young Deaf Children

Since the 1980s, studies from the United Kingdom (e.g., Harris, Clibbens, Chasin, & Tibbitts, 1989), Australia (e.g., Mohay, Milton, Hindmarsh, & Ganley, 1998), the United States (e.g., Erting, Prezioso, & O'Grady Hynes, 1990; Spencer, Bodner-Johnson, & Gutfreund, 1992), and Japan (e.g., Masataka, 1992) have resulted in an amazingly consistent set of descriptions of signing deaf mothers' child-directed language. Much of the focus of these reports has been on deaf mothers' accommodations to deaf children's need for a visual language model. Researchers have identified differences in the specific techniques or strategies used to establish associations between signed (compared to spoken) language and the context of activities and interests in which they are used. Differences tend to occur in the frequency or intensity with which these maternal behaviors are produced, rather than in the repertoire of interactive behaviors displayed. The kinds of accommodations shown in the child-directed signing of deaf mothers also differ over time: Different modifications occur in communications addressed to young infants (up to about 6 months in age) and those addressed to older infants, toddlers, and preschool children whose attention skills are more advanced and who give overt evidence of the emergence of formal language skills. Changes over time in mothers' communicative behaviors are, of course, gradual and seem to be responsive to their children's maturation and responses during interactions.

*Accommodations to Associate Language Input with*
*Child Attention and Nonlinguistic Context*

Like hearing mothers speaking to hearing infants, deaf mothers signing
to young deaf infants tend to use strong and varied facial expressions.
In fact, deaf mothers are reported to produce even stronger facial expressions than hearing mothers (Erting et al., 1990; Meadow-Orlans,
MacTurk, Prezioso, Erting, & [Spencer]Day, 1987), a difference that may
serve to increase the general stimulation level to infants who do not
receive auditory information as well as to increase infants' tendencies
to attend to their mothers' faces (Meadow-Orlans, Spencer, & Koester,
2004). Like hearing mothers, deaf mothers emphasize expressions
of positive affect and often playfully imitate their babies' expressions. Much early "dialogue" occurs through these imitated expressions, sometimes produced in a simultaneous or "mirroring" fashion and
sometimes occurring in a turn taking sequence. Affect seems to dominate
message content in early exchanges. For example, ASL-signing mothers
have been reported to substitute positive facial expressions for the
grammatically correct but less positive-looking expressions that are
obligatory with question forms signed to adults (Reilly & Bellugi, 1996).

   Also like hearing mothers interacting with young infants, deaf
mothers tend to produce multimodal communications. In addition to
enhanced and exaggerated facial expressions, deaf mothers combine
tactile, vocal, and kinesthetic stimulation for their infants. For example,
tactile signs, made directly on a child's body, have been noted in interactions between deaf mothers and younger deaf infants (Harris et al.,
1989; Koester, Traci, Brooks, Karkowski, & Smith-Gray, 2004; Maestas
y Moores, 1980) and are usually produced while the infant also has
access to visual information from the mother's facial expressions.

   A characteristic shared by speech of hearing mothers and the signing
of deaf mothers to their infants is rhythmicity. Signing to young infants
often has almost dancelike characteristics. Not surprisingly, researchers
have found that both signed and spoken utterances with these qualities tend to attract and hold the attention of infants better than do less
rhythmic, typical adult-directed utterances (Masataka, 1992, 2000). An
additional advantage to rhythmic signed utterances is that the signs
themselves tend to be prolonged (produced more slowly) and larger
than is typical in adult conversations (Erting et al., 1990; Ackerman,
Kyle, Woll, & Ezra, 1990; Masataka, 1992, 2000). The extended duration
of the signs may provide signals that are easier for infants to recognize and remember. The rhythm as well as slowed and enlarged sign
productions may also serve to emphasize segmentation between signs.

   Deaf mothers of younger infants often accommodate immature patterns of visual attention by producing signs in a location where the
infants can see them without having to redirect their gaze (Harris et al.,

1989; Waxman & Spencer, 1997). This can result in signs being produced in a location that would be considered inappropriate in a conversation with an older child or other adult signer. The strategy of sign relocation provides a referent–symbol association without requiring the infant to redirect his or her attention. Waxman and Spencer (1997), who documented deaf mothers' use of this and other attention-related strategies longitudinally from infant ages 9 through 18 months, found that use of this strategy significantly decreased as children approached and passed their first birthday. The drop in frequency may have been a natural reaction to either or both the children's increased mobility (limiting mothers' opportunities to sign in an existing field of visual attention) and the children's demonstrating more flexible patterns of visual attention.

Deaf mothers do not *always* accommodate their infants' pre-existing focus of visual attention; they often employ special means to redirect the infant's attention. For example, deaf mothers often move an object through an infant's visual field, with the termination of that movement being near the mother's face. The mother then usually signs the object name or provides other information about the object or its characteristics (Spencer, Swisher, & Waxman, 2004; Waxman & Spencer, 1997). Hearing mothers also move objects often to obtain or direct an infant's attention. However, probably because hearing infants can receive spoken messages without looking directly at their mothers, hearing mothers tend to move objects away from instead of toward themselves. This makes it difficult for a child to attend to the object and simultaneously see the mother's face or signing hand.

Although the incidence of signing directly on infants' bodies drops precipitously with maturation, some researchers (e.g., Erting et al., 1990) have reported generally elevated levels of tactile contact between deaf mothers and infants compared to hearing mothers and infants. The overall greater tactile contact is due at least in part to deaf mothers' use of tactile signals to obtain or redirect the attention of their young children (see, e.g., Koester et al., 2004). With younger infants, it may be difficult to distinguish tactile signals for attention redirection from other kinds of mothers' touching of the infants. For example, a deaf mother may gently rub the arm or leg of a 3-month-old infant and alternate this with rhythmically lifting and lowering the infant's feet. Often, the mother's facial expression and reaction when the infant looks up at her indicate that re-establishing face-to-face visual attention was her goal. With a 6-month-old infant, however, the mother may be more inclined to tap on the infants' shoulder repeatedly, and if necessary move an object through the infants' visual field and up to her face to obtain the infants' visual attention for a signed message. Over time, the infant will learn that the tapping signal means to look up for language. By the middle of the second year of life, tapping may be produced by the mother so quickly and gently, and the child's response obtained so quickly, that the two actions seem to happen almost simultaneously (Swisher, 2000). Tactile attention-getting signals continue to be modified and remain part of the communicative behavior associated with adult-to-adult signing. Although hearing adults sometimes use a similar tapping signal to request the attention of a child or even another adult, its use is quite rare even with infants and toddlers (Waxman & Spencer, 1997).

Despite the above generalizations, it should not be thought that deaf mothers form a completely homogeneous group that implements attention and communication strategies uniformly. Swisher (2000), who looked more closely at a subgroup of the deaf mothers and deaf infants observed by Meadow-Orlans and her colleagues (Meadow-Orlans et al., 2004; Waxman & Spencer, 1997), found that the mothers, all of whose infants were judged to have age appropriate visual attention and language skills at 18 months, had different patterns of use of the tactile attention redirecting signals. Several mothers tended to use the signals more often when their children were younger. Several others used the signal more frequently when the children were somewhat older. One mother rarely used tapping and was observed often to sign in what seemed to be her child's peripheral visual field. Harris and Mohay (1997) also noted variability in the attention behaviors of deaf mothers. They found that the proportion of occasions in which deaf mothers redirected attention during interactions with their infants ranged from just under 30% to just under 5%. Thus, influences in addition to infant maturation appear to relate to deaf mothers' production of tapping for attention and use of other attention-related communicative behaviors. These influences include differences in infants' inclinations to focus on potential communications and, perhaps, differences in mothers' assumptions about where and what their infants can see.

Characteristics of child-directed signing seem designed (even if intuitively or unconsciously) to promote deaf infants' and young children's ability to associate visual language input with the objects and events to which it refers. Making such associations, of course, depends upon the degree to which mothers' language is actually related to the context of the child's activity and attention focus. Spencer and her colleagues (Spencer, 2004; Spencer & Lederberg, 1997; Wilson & Spencer, 1997) found that, between infant ages 9 through 18 months, the content of approximately 80% of both deaf and hearing mothers' language related to the infants' focus of attention.

When children begin to give evidence of learning vocabulary, deaf mothers use child-directed language modifications that appear to be aimed at making the establishment of the association between sign and referent more transparent. For example, deaf mothers have been observed to point repeatedly to an activity or object, then sign its name or label, and then point again. Points and the signs may be repeated multiple times within a single "bout" or utterance (Waxman & Spencer, 1997).

Repetitions of a single sign, with or without accompanying points, can be extensive—often five to eight times or even more in a single utterance. This pattern of repetition provides multiple opportunities for language learning. A child who attends to the repetitions has many chances to make the association between the referent and its signed symbol; infants who do not yet give extended attention to their mothers' messages have a chance of seeing one or more of the sign repetitions and, therefore, of making the referent-symbol association. Although hearing mothers frequently repeat words and phrases directed to their young hearing children, deaf mothers tend to use this language modification to a much greater degree. Deaf mothers' signed utterances to infants and toddlers also tend to be short, including few linguistic units. Most are the rough equivalent of one- or two-word spoken utterances (albeit with multiple repetitions). This is, again, apparently an accommodation for immature visual attention.

The number of signed utterances deaf mothers produce during interactions with infants and toddlers is also low when compared to the typical frequency of hearing mothers' spoken utterances (Harris, 1992; Spencer & Lederberg, 1997). The lower rate of signed communications seems to be another natural consequence of deaf mothers' sensitivity to their children's immature patterns of visual attention in that deaf mothers almost never sign when they know their young child is not attending or ready to receive. Consequently, although hearing mothers' rate of production of spoken utterances decreases somewhat between 12 and 18 months, as their hearing children begin to participate more linguistically, deaf mothers' rate of production increases as their deaf children become more adept at shifting visual attention (see figure 4.1).

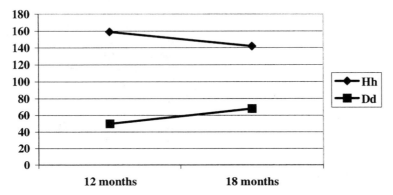

Figure 4-1. Mean frequency of signed utterances produced by deaf mothers with deaf infants (Dd) and spoken utterances produced by hearing mothers with hearing infants (Hh) at 12 and 18 months of age.

Examples of some of the challenges to providing language contingent upon a young deaf child's visual attention, and deaf mothers' responses to those challenges, are illustrated in table 4.1 (from Harris, 2000), which gives examples from transcripts of interactions with 18-month-olds. The examples show a variety of maternal strategies. Sometimes, as in example 2 in table 4.1, the mother has to work hard to attract the child's attention before she can sign but, in other cases, such as example 4, the child has been looking toward the mother for some time before she signs. The examples selected also show the characteristic short length of mothers' signed utterances and the linear structure of some longer productions.

*Accommodations Enhancing Stability of Form of Lexical Items*

We proposed earlier that stability of form of lexical items in mothers' language input would affect the speed and the order of acquisition of vocabulary. In fact, a phenomenon has been noted that appears to increase the stability of form of lexical items produced in child-directed

**Table 4-1: Contingency of Maternal Signing**

| Example | Sign Gloss | Context |
|---------|-----------|---------|
| 1 | CRY | C hits big teddy that M is holding. C steps back, turning to look at M. M *signs* and then points to teddy's eye. |
| 2 | I PHONE YOUR BROTHER | C is playing at some distance from M, who is holding receiver of toy telephone. M waves telephone receiver, her movements becoming more exaggerated. C looks up at M. M *signs*. |
| 3 | GIVE | C picks up beaker from floor. C turns toward M. M *signs*. |
| 4 | DOG | M turns pages of picture book on her knee as C watches. M turns to new page, points at picture of dog, *signs* (one-handed, close to book). |
| 5 | SHARP | C drops small object on floor. M picks it up. C watches her hands. M feels object with her fingers. C looks up at M's face. M *signs* with right hand, bringing hand down into contact with left hand, holding object. |
| 6 | BIRD | C sees something move outside window. M, who has back to window, turns to look and then *signs* so that her hands are between C and window. |

Adapted from Harris (2000).

signing. A characteristic of adult-directed ASL is the simultaneous or near-simultaneous "layering" of morphemes or morphemic-like elements. For example, the canonical form of the sign GIVE might be altered in its direction of movement to indicate both the giver and the recipient of the gift. It could even be produced with a specific brow-raise, head-tilt expression that would convert it to a yes-no question: (Did) HE GIVE-it-to HER? This and similar syntactic devices in ASL that allow simultaneous expression of meaning units could result in a considerable lack of stability of form as what children see as signs are produced simultaneously with one, then another morpheme.

However, there is some evidence that deaf mothers rarely present such complex syntactic structures when signing to infants and toddlers. Kantor (1982) observed that deaf mothers do not use all aspects of ASL morphology when signing to young deaf children. Instead, they offer a model of ASL in which signs are presented in a more linear and explicit manner. That is, Kantor reported that mothers' signed utterances consisted primarily of lexical signs in their "citation" or canonical form plus deictic points to persons, locations, or objects that were in the immediate environment. As an example, Kantor reported that one deaf mother signed, "She's watching you," to her child in a form clearly different from that which would be used with another adult. If signed to an adult, the movement of the sign WATCH, in its beginning and ending position, would incorporate both the agent of the verb and its object. However, this mother indicated the agent with a separate point, making separation of the meaning units more explicit and the production more linear. Spencer and Lederberg (1997) report a similar occurrence in which a deaf mother signed, "She's looking at you," to her deaf toddler. In this case, the signs were produced slowly and deliberately in the following order: POINT (to agent) + LOOK-AT (produced in canonical form without incorporation of direction) + POINT (to child). These productions simplify syntax, using a simple subject-verb-object (SVO) linear order and employing canonical forms of signs in lieu of the layered simultaneous grammatical conventions of adult-directed ASL. They also result in presenting more stable and predictable forms for the lexical items. Kantor indicated that this child-directed modification was time/age limited and that mothers produce more complex syntactic forms as their children approach the age of 2.5 or 3 years. Although this reported modification is intriguing, it has not yet been sufficiently studied to determine how widespread it is or how the structure of mothers' expressions change over time.

## Summary

There is evidence that characteristics of deaf mothers' child-directed signing changes as the children mature and begin to develop their language skills. With young infants, deaf mothers' sign language expressions are most often characterized as highly rhythmic and multimodal, accompanied by strongly positive facial expressions and frequent tactile contact. Signs are brought to infants' attention by mothers' moving their hands and bodies to be in the infants' existing field of vision and sometimes by mothers producing signs on infants' bodies. As infants mature, mothers tend to shorten their language productions and give infants multiple opportunities to associate language with current activities by waiting for attention before signing, by repeating single signs many times in an utterance, and by tapping on or pointing to the activity or object being labeled. Mothers also actively elicit their infants' visual attention by tapping on them, with or without the accompaniment of moving an object to obtain attention. Some observations also indicate that signs tend to be presented in a linear manner, frequently in SVO order, and in their canonical form.

After about 15 months of age, infants are more likely to spontaneously look at their mothers, and, perhaps in response to this, deaf mothers' use of the tapping signal changes. Taps are often quick, almost abbreviated. Frequency, length, and syntactic complexity of mothers' signed utterances increase as the children near their third year of life, and it appears that mothers incorporate more adultlike grammar in their signed utterances as children near 3 years of age.

Overall, differences between adult-directed and child-directed ASL employ modality-specific strategies to accomplish the two goals that we initially proposed to impact child language across cultures: (1) association of language with context and (2) stability of form of lexical items. Reports that deaf mothers use simplified, linear syntax and delay use of sign-specific indicators of topicalization, grammatically relevant facial expressions, and incorporation of manner and direction into verbs is deserving of further study. Specific content of deaf mothers' communications to deaf infants and toddlers also remains to be documented.

## Hearing Mothers with Deaf Children

So far we have been focusing on the way that deaf mothers who are native or near-native users of a sign language adapt their signing to meet the communicative needs of their children. The great majority of deaf children are not born into deaf families (Mitchell & Karchmer, 2004), but they nevertheless learn to sign. For this reason, a number of researchers have studied the interaction of deaf infants and toddlers with their hearing mothers and compared the mothers' communications with those of deaf mothers.

In the great majority of cases, hearing mothers are not familiar with the dynamics of visual communication before their child is born, and they are unlikely to be fluent signers. However, hearing parents react in a number of different ways to the identification of their child's hearing loss. Although some elect to rely exclusively on oral communication or cued speech, others actively embrace signing as part of their communicative repertoire. Some begin with one communicative approach and then change to another, and of those who consistently use signing, there is considerable variation in the level of sign competence that is achieved.

The variety of different communication systems used by hearing mothers, together with varying levels of competence of those using signs, mean that it is difficult to make overall comparisons between deaf and hearing mothers. Given the typically small numbers of participants in studies of interactions between mothers and deaf infants or toddlers, it is not surprising that there have been mixed findings regarding the degree to which hearing mothers use accommodations similar to those of deaf mothers in their interactions with young deaf children.

*Accommodations to Associate Language Input with Child Attention and Nonlinguistic Context*

Since hearing mothers will be familiar with the structure and dynamics of spoken language, we would expect them to be most similar to deaf mothers in those aspects of language input that are common to speech and sign. The most obvious candidate for similarity is the extent to which both deaf and hearing mothers talk about currently observable events and objects. As we noted above, deaf mothers tend to produce language that directly relates to their children's focus of attention, and they also emphasize the referential nature of their utterances (Harris et al., 1989; Spencer et al., 1992; Waxman & Spencer, 1997). The same close relationship between maternal speech and nonverbal context is also evident when hearing mothers talk to their hearing children. Thus, we would expect the signing of hearing mothers to deaf children to have similar characteristics.

Spencer et al. (1992) found that hearing mothers were as likely as deaf mothers to comment when their 12-month-old deaf infants looked at an object. In addition, at both 12 and 18 months, Spencer (2004) reported that the proportion of maternal linguistic utterances that followed or matched the child's activity or attention focus was similar for hearing and deaf mothers, regardless of child hearing status. Harris (2001) independently found that hearing as well as deaf mothers of 18-month-old deaf children used language mainly to comment on an object or event currently engaging their child's attention. Waxman and Spencer (1997) found that hearing and deaf mothers of 12-month-old deaf infants were similarly inclined to move their signs so that they were produced within the infants' existing visual fields. This tendency declined for both groups of mothers as their children reached 18 months of age.

In contrast with the above similarities in the child-directed language of deaf and hearing mothers of deaf children, Harris (2001) found that the total number of signed utterances produced and visually accessible to deaf 18-month-olds was smaller for hearing than for deaf mothers. There are a number of reasons why deaf mothers are usually better at presenting signs so that children can see them without having to disengage from their current activity. One important factor is timing. Spencer et al. (1992) found that hearing mothers often sign about an object or event while the child's attention is still engaged with it, whereas deaf mothers most often wait until their infants look back at them before signing. Similar differences in the timing of signs by hearing and deaf mothers have been reported by a number of other researchers including Ackerman et al. (1990) and Mohay, Luttrell, and Milton (1991). It is important to note, however, that there is considerable variability within the group of hearing mothers on their tendency to make their signs visible. Harris pointed out that three of the hearing mothers she observed produced more than 80% of their utterances within their children's line of sight, a proportion matching that of the deaf mothers. In contrast, another hearing mother failed to produce any signs that her child could see, and another accomplished signing in her child's visual attention field only 20% of the time.

As a group, hearing mothers with deaf children are more likely than those with hearing children to use the tactile strategies such as tapping on the child's body to redirect visual attention (Harris & Mohay, 1997; Waxman & Spencer, 1997). However, hearing mothers with deaf children use this kind of signal far less than deaf mothers do (Harris & Mohay, 1997; Waxman & Spencer, 1997). Not only do deaf mothers produce more successful attempts to redirect their deaf infants' attention, but they also produce more failed attempts (Harris & Mohay, 1997). This is the case during the first year of life, when infants apparently do not recognize the intent or function of the tactile signals (Waxman & Spencer, 1997), and also during the second and third years when toddlers are striving for independence and are no longer content to sit beside their mother.

Spencer (2000) found that, by 18 months of age, deaf children spent more time in coordinated joint attention with deaf than with hearing mothers. Coordinated joint attention occurs when children actively switch attention between a communication partner and an event or object in the environment and has been associated with language development in both deaf and hearing children (Smith, Adamson, & Bakeman; 1988; Meadow-Orlans & Spencer, 1996). It appears that the attention accommodating and directing behaviors used by deaf mothers support more joint attention by 18 months by deaf infants. Interestingly, the *frequency* of such attention bouts did not differ between the two groups of deaf children (or, for that matter, between them and the hearing children). Instead, the joint attention bouts lasted *longer* for the deaf children with deaf parents. In addition, children with deaf parents also showed longer times in another category of attention referred to as "onlooking" (in which the infant gazes directly at mother for an extended period, resulting in their being visually engaged with their mothers). They were therefore available to receive *visual* communications more of the time than either deaf or hearing children with hearing parents.

Hearing mothers talk to deaf children about as often as hearing mothers with a hearing child. Spencer (1993a) reports that, at 12 months, hearing mothers of deaf children produced an average of 154 utterances in 10 minutes while those with a hearing child produced 159 utterances; and at 18 months the mean was 142 utterances for both groups. However, on average, hearing mothers with deaf children produce fewer signed utterances than deaf mothers although this average disguises considerable variability. Spencer (1993b) reports that the number of signed utterances produced by hearing mothers with deaf infants who were in signing programs ranged from zero to 51 during 10 minutes of interaction at 12 months. The range was even broader at 18 months, and several of the hearing mothers matched the average rate of signed utterance production of deaf mothers (68 signed utterances in 10 minutes). Harris and Mohay (1997) reported similar findings. Comparing deaf and hearing mothers of 18-month-old deaf children, the highest rate of signed utterances production was 84 (in 10 minutes), from a deaf mother. However, the second highest production rate was from a hearing mother who signed 47 utterances in the same length of time.

Overall, the rate of signed utterances is lower than for spoken utterances produced by deaf as well as hearing mothers and this reflects, in part, the different turn taking and visual attention patterns required for presenting contextually and perceptually salient signed versus spoken language input. However, the extremely low rate of signed utterance production of some of the hearing mothers of deaf children also reflects their status as new, nonfluent users of sign language. It may also reflect the degree to which they actually accept and support the use of sign language. Spencer (1993b) found that the number of signed utterances produced by individuals in a small sample ($n = 7$) strongly correlated across the 12- and 18-month sessions. Mothers who began learning and using signs quickly continued to do so. Those who were initially reticent remained that way.

Both the requirements of visual communication and status as new sign language learners may also be reflected in the fact that the signed productions of hearing mothers of deaf children tend to be short, containing one or two signs. This is the case even with hearing mothers who are attempting simultaneous sign and vocal communication. Their spoken utterances frequently contain multiple words but only one or two of the major lexical items are signed. Although this has been taken as evidence of language input that is defective, it may be an automatic and unconscious pattern that is, in fact, a better match with the visual attention skills of toddlers than would be longer and more complex productions. Unfortunately, Waxman and Spencer (1997) found that hearing mothers are less likely to use the multiple points or taps on a referenced object than are deaf mothers; thus, hearing mothers' signed utterances may be less readily associated with their referent.

In summary, direct comparisons of the communicative behaviors of hearing and deaf mothers of deaf children show that both groups are (perhaps intuitively) inclined to produce language input that matches their young children's activities and interests. Perhaps in response to infants' still-developing visual attention skills, both groups of mothers produce fewer and shorter signed utterances compared with the spoken language production of hearing mothers with hearing or with deaf infants. Deaf mothers make more of their productions accessible to their deaf children, however, through greater use of a specified set of visual attention accommodations, such as moving the location of signs and waiting for attention before signing, and visual attention redirecting signals, primarily tactile in nature. Although both groups of mothers display sensitivity to their deaf children's needs for contextually related sign language input, mothers used to visually based communication promote more effective "uptake" (Harris, 1992) of the input they provide.

*Accommodations to Enhance Stability of Form*

A second principle that we proposed would affect language acquisition across cultures and modalities is the stability of lexical forms displayed to a young child. Input of more stable or consistent forms should be more easily acquired. Because hearing mothers of deaf children tend to speak simple English while signing, their sign productions will tend to follow simple SVO order as has also been suggested to be characteristic of input from deaf mothers (Kantor, 1982; Spencer & Lederberg, 1997). Thus, although the sign models provided by hearing mothers of deaf children typically lack indications of grammatical inflections, the word order is probably relatively stable. It is not clear, however, how consistently new signers articulate sign forms, and we know of no published research documenting this phenomenon. Given our own experience as hearing adults learning sign language, and the feedback of deaf students and colleagues, we think it can be assumed that the way in which many hearing adults articulate signed productions is neither accurate nor consistent. Furthermore, children may interact with teachers, therapists, and other interventionists whose sign production does not match that of their parents and in some cases may be no more consistently

articulated. A general lack of consistency of form in sign inpu
adults who are new signers, in addition to a generally low quan
visually accessible signed input, may be an important factor depre
the rate at which deaf children with hearing parents acquire sign
guage. Of course, there are individual differences among hea  .s
parents of deaf children. In addition, there are factors beyond sign
input that will influence a child's uptake of a sign language model that
we do not discuss here, such as child behaviors, presence or absence
of cognitive, or neurological or social disabilities, and general levels of
environmental support for learning.

## ASSOCIATION OF LANGUAGE INPUT WITH
## LANGUAGE ACQUISITION AND GROWTH

This chapter began with the assertion that observation of acquisition of
sign language produced by deaf children can tell us about relations
between language input provided by adults and early child language
development. Given that deaf children with signing deaf parents are exposed to language from birth, we might expect that their language
development and the emergence of formal language would progress on
a schedule like that documented for hearing children's spoken language. However, to the extent that differences in modality are relevant,
there would be differences.

By about 1 year of age, deaf children with signing deaf parents
typically produce actual signs—usually in the form of single-sign
utterances—during interactions with others. There is some disagree-
ment, however, about the timing of these first expressive signs. In an
early study, Orlansky and Bonvillian (1985) documented deaf mothers'
reports of their (hearing) infants who produced signs well before 1
year of age. The researchers concluded that earlier development of
manual than oral articulators allowed this advantage and showed that
cognitive readiness for language exists at earlier ages than is apparent
in observations of hearing infants. However, other investigators (e.g.,
Petitto, 1988; Volterra, Beronesi, & Massoni, 1994) have suggested
that the so-called "sign advantage" is a misinterpretation of motor
behaviors common to deaf and hearing infants. Petitto and Marentette
(1991) documented "manual babbling," consisting of repetitive movements of hands and fingers approximating sign handshapes in children of native signers, at about the same age vocal canonical babbling
appears for hearing infants. Babbling is, by definition, nonmeaningful
in a semantic sense. Petitto suggests that some reported early "signs"
are actually babbles (e.g., a repeated opening and closing of both
hands similar in form to the signs "want" or "milk") produced as
deaf infants acquire and practice the phonology of their parents' sign
language.

This leads to questions about potential effects of deaf mothers' generally low rate of signed utterances. Differences in quantity of language input for these children compared with hearing children might suggest that the latter would have an advantage in language acquisition. As described above, no such advantage has been found. However, *within* the group of deaf infants with deaf mothers studied by Meadow-Orlans et al. (2004), there was a strong association between the number of linguistic communications produced by mother and child (Wilson & Spencer, 1997). Frequency of deaf mothers' signed communications at both 12 and 18 months was associated with deaf infants' frequency of signed communications and with the number of different signs they produced at 18 months. Despite the overall lower frequency of linguistic communications produced by deaf compared with hearing mothers, the underlying association between maternal and infant productions was the same as has been reported for hearing children (Hart & Risley, 1995; Hoff-Ginsberg, 1994).

Spencer, Meadow-Orlans, Koester, and Ludwig (2004) found that the following 12-month variables in combination predicted 53% of the variance in 18-month production of language by the deaf children (considering both those with deaf and with hearing parents): children's visual behaviors (including social referencing to parent and engagement in episodes of coordinated joint attention), the overall quality of children's behavior during the interaction, mothers' frequency of signed productions, and mothers' rate of responding to children's attention focus. After these variables were accounted for, mothers' hearing status failed to add significantly to the prediction of child language behaviors. This analysis may seem to be avoiding the obvious: Clearly, deaf mothers produced more signs on average than did hearing mothers, and it appears that deaf mothers of deaf infants more effectively encouraged advanced visual attending behaviors than did hearing mothers (Spencer, Swisher, & Waxman, 2004; Waxman & Spencer, 1997). However, the analysis helps to clarify what it is about deaf mothers' communications that tends to give such benefits toward deaf children's language learning. In short, the advantages boil down to mothers intuitively responding in a way that (at least during the first 2 years of life) follows established attention focus or proto-conversation topic and presents language with form and timing sensitive to the children's visual attention.

As originally proposed, the sign language development of deaf children with deaf parents may additionally be supported by input in which signs are made clearly and with a stable form. This "stability" feature results in part from the enlarged, slowed production that is characteristic with young deaf infants. Producing signs in canonical form and with a rhythm that emphasizes segmentation between signs, as well as providing simplified models of sign language grammar, may also support children's identifying stable sign forms.

Data reported by Anderson and Reilly (2002) for the norming sample on the ASL-CDI show that earliest signs of deaf children with deaf parents and spoken words of hearing children with hearing parents tend to be the same—representing objects and events common in the environment of both groups of infants and their families. In addition, Anderson and Reilly found that initial lexicons of both groups were biased toward nouns instead of verbs. With increasing age (past 2 years) and vocabulary size (greater than about 200 signs), however, the deaf infants began to show a greater proportional representation of verbs than is the case for hearing children. This pattern of increasing number of verbs is typical of hearing children, too, with development, but the increase appears to be greater at this stage for the deaf children (see Hoiting, chapter 7 this volume). This may reflect greater emphasis on verb forms in the input of deaf mothers as their children mature, but there are as yet no large-scale data to confirm such a pattern. To date, this is the only indication of differences in the content of early sign of deaf children learning ASL and hearing children learning spoken English that might be indicative of differences in their input models.

## SUMMARY AND CONCLUSIONS

The studies we have reviewed in this chapter indicate that sign input best facilitates children's acquisition of sign language when it meets two conditions also shown to affect the development of hearing children's language: (1) a match between the child's attention focus or activity and the mother's language input and (2) stability and clarity of form of the language units that occur in the input. Providing language input that is both responsive to deaf children's focus of attention and perceptually accessible to their immature visual attention skills requires attention-accommodating and redirecting strategies that are modality specific. These strategies are most often observed in the child-directed communications of mothers who are deaf and are fluent signers. However, it would be an oversimplification to identify differences in quality of sign input solely with maternal hearing status.

There is wide variation in the sign input provided by both deaf and hearing mothers. This is not surprising given the wide variations reported in studies of hearing mothers' child-directed speech to hearing children (e.g., Hoff-Ginsberg, 1994). However, it appears that child-directed signing from deaf mothers, most of whom provide intuitively modified sign input that supports their children's entry into the use of sign language, is less variable than that of hearing mothers. Some hearing mothers can provide sign input that is highly attuned to their

children's attention and language skills, but many who are not experienced using signs or interacting with deaf people provide less than
sufficient input. In many ways, deaf children's acquisition of sign language appears to be related to the input they receive, but deaf children
also show variability that is undoubtedly due to individual differences
in facility for and attention to communication.

A major goal for early intervention programs should be to identify
and evaluate various methods for providing hearing families with the
skills necessary to facilitate their natural inclinations to provide accessible language input to their deaf children. Steps have been made in
this direction by Mohay and her colleagues in Australia (Mohay, 2000;
Mohay et al., 1998), Delk and her colleagues at Gallaudet University
(Delk & Weidekamp, 2001; Mertens, Delk, & Weidekamp, 2003), and
the early intervention programming provided in the state of Colorado
(e.g., Yoshinaga-Itano, 2003), among others. However, many questions
about the most supportive ways to provide sign input to young deaf
children continue to need research. Although we stated earlier that the
grammatical aspects of hearing mothers' language to their hearing
children do not seem to have strong effects on their children's developing language, that aspect has not been systematically investigated
for children learning sign language. Reports of deaf mothers' early use
of simplified, linear syntax deserve further investigation, with an eye
toward identifying child behaviors that may prompt and reflect such
modifications. Similarly, potential influences of the structures signed
by hearing mothers who are new signers and their ability to modify
the grammar of their productions to match their children's comprehension abilities should be studied in more detail. The possibility, even
probability, of very early identification of hearing loss in children from
hearing families causes such investigations to be of more than academic interest. If parents can be guided in ways to provide their deaf
children with signed language input from their early months, the
specter of significant language delays may in most cases be banished.

## REFERENCES

Ackerman, J., Kyle, J., Woll, B., & Ezra, M. (1990). Lexical acquisition in sign
    and speech: Evidence from a longitudinal study of infants in deaf families. In
    C. Lucas (Ed.), *Sign language research: Theoretical issues* (pp. 337–345). Wash-
    ington, DC: Gallaudet University Press.
Anderson, J., & Reilly, J. (2002). The MacArthur Communicative Development
    Inventory: The normative data from American Sign Language. *Journal of
    Deaf Studies and Deaf Education, 7*, 83–106.
Barrett, M., Harris, M., & Chasin, J, (1991). Early lexical development and ma-
    ternal speech: A comparison of children's initial and subsequent uses. *Journal
    of Child Language, 18*, 21–40.

Bonvillian, J., Orlansky, M., & Folven, R. (1990/1994). Early sign language acquisition: Implications for theories of language acquisition. In V. Volterra & C. J. Erting (Eds.), *From gesture to language in hearing and deaf children* (pp. 219–232). Berlin/Washington, DC: Springer-Verlag/Gallaudet University Press.

Camaioni, L., & Longobardi, E. (2001). Noun versus verb emphasis in Italian mother-to-child speech. *Journal of Child Language, 28*, 773–785.

Castillo, M., & Butterworth, G. (1981). Neonatal localisation of sound in visual space. *Perception, 10*, 331–338.

Delk, L., & Weidekamp, L. (2001). *Shared Reading Project: Evaluating implementation processes and family outcomes. Sharing results series.* Washington, DC: Gallaudet University, Laurent Clerc National Deaf Education Center.

Dunlea, A. (1989). *Vision and the emergence of meaning.* Cambridge: Cambridge University Press.

Ellis, R., & Wells, G. (1980). Enabling factors in adult-child discourse. *First Language, 1*, 46–62.

Emmorey, K. (2002). *Language, cognition, and the brain: Insights from sign language research.* Mahwah NJ: Lawrence Erlbaum.

Erting, C. J., Prezioso, C, & O'Grady Hynes, M. (1990). The interactional context of mother-infant communication. In V. Volterra & C. J, Erting (Eds.), *From gesture to language in hearing and deaf children* (pp. 97–106). Berlin: Springer-Verlag.

Fenson, L., Dale, P., Reznick, J. S., Bates, E., Thai, D., & Pethick, S. J. (1994). Variability in early communicative development. *Monographs of the Society for Research in Child Development, 59*(5), 1–173.

Fernald, A. (2001). Hearing, listening and understanding: Auditory development in infancy. In G. Bremner & A. Fogel (Eds.), *Blackwell handbook of infant development* (pp. 35–70). Oxford: Blackwell.

Fernald, A., & Morikawa, H. (1993). Common themes and cultural variations in Japanese and American mothers' speech to infants. *Child Development, 64*, 637–656.

Gleitman, L. R., Newport, E. L., & Gleitman, H. (1984). The current status of the motherese hypothesis. *Journal of Child Language, 11*, 43–80.

Goldin-Meadow, S., & Mylander, C. (1990). Beyond the input given: The child's role in the acquisition of language. *Language, 66*(2), 323–355.

Gopnik, A., & Choi, S. (1995). Names, relational words and cognitive development in English and Korean speakers: Nouns are not always learned before verbs. In M. Tomasello & W. E. Merriman (Eds.), *Beyond names for things: Young children's acquisition of verbs* (pp. 83–90). Hillsdale, NJ: Erlbaum.

Harris, M. (1992). *Language experience and early language development: From input to uptake.* Hove: Lawrence Erlbaum.

Harris, M. (2000). Social interaction and early language development in deaf children. *Deafness and Education International, 2*, 1–11.

Harris, M. (2001). It's all a matter of timing: Sign visibility and sign reference in deaf and hearing mothers of 18 month old children. *Journal of Deaf Studies and Deaf Education, 6*, 177–185.

Harris, M., Barrett, M., Jones, D., & Brookes, S. (1988). Linguistic input and early word meaning. *Journal of Child Language, 15*, 77–94.

Harris, M., & Chasin. J. (in press). Visual attention in deaf and hearing infants: the role of auditory cues. *Journal of Child Psychology and Psychiatry*.

Harris, M., Clibbens, J., Chasin, J., & Tibbitts, R. (1989). The social context of early sign language development. *First Language, 9,* 81–97.

Harris, M., Jones, D., Brookes, S., & Grant, J. (1986). Relations between the non-verbal context of maternal speech and rate of language development. *British Journal of Developmental Psychology, 4,* 261–268.

Harris, M., & Mohay, H. (1997). Learning to look in the right place: A comparison of attentional behavior in deaf children with deaf and hearing mothers. *Journal of Deaf Studies and Deaf Education, 2,* 95–103.

Hart, B. (1991). Input frequency and children's first words. *First Language, 11,* 289–300.

Hart, B., & Risley, T. (1995). *Meaningful differences in the everyday experiences of American children.* Baltimore, MD: Paul H. Brookes.

Hoff-Ginsberg, E. (1994). Influences of mother and child on maternal talkativeness. *Discourse Processes, 18,* 105–117.

Huttenlocher, J., Haight, W., Bryk, A., Seltzer, M., & Lyons, T. (1991). Early vocabulary growth: Relation to input and gender. *Developmental Psychology, 27,* 236–248.

Kantor, R. (1982). Communicative interaction: Mother modification and child acquisition of American Sign Language. *Sign Language Studies, 36,* 233–282. (Reprinted in *The acquisition of American Sign Language by deaf children,* pp. 115–172, by M. McIntire, Ed., 1994, Burtonsville, MD: Linstok Press)

Koester, L. (1992). Intuitive parenting as a model for understanding parent-infant interactions when one partner is deaf. *American Annals of the Deaf, 137*(4), 362–369.

Koester, L., Traci, M., Brooks, L., Karkowski, A., & Smith-Gray, S. (2004). Mother-infant behaviors at 6 and 9 months: A microanalytic view. In K. Meadow-Orlans, P. Spencer, & L. Koester (Eds.), *The world of deaf infants* (pp. 40–56). New York: Oxford University Press.

Maestas y Moores, J. (1980). Early linguistic environment: Interactions of deaf parents with their infants. *Sign Language Studies, 26,* 1–13.

Marchark, M. (1993). *Psychological development of deaf children.* New York: Oxford University Press.

Masataka, N. (1992). Motherese in a signed language. *Infant Behavior and Development, 15,* 453–460.

Masataka, N. (2000). The role of modality and input in the earliest stage of language acquisition: Studies of Japanese Sign Language. In C. Chamberlain, J. Morford, & R. Mayberry (Eds.), *Language acquisition by eye* (pp. 3–24). Mahwah, NJ: Lawrence Erlbaum.

Mayne, A., Yoshinaga-Itano, C., & Sedey, A. (1999). Receptive vocabulary development of infants and toddlers who are deaf or hard of hearing. *Volta Review, 100*(5), 29–52.

Mayne, A., Yoshinaga-Itano, C., Sedey, A., & Carey, A. (2000). Expressive vocabulary development of infants and toddlers who are deaf or hard of hearing. *Volta Review, 100*(5), 1–28.

Meadow-Orlans, K., MacTurk, R., Prezioso, C., Erting, J., & [Spencer]Day, P. (1987, April). *Interactions of deaf and hearing mothers with 3 and 6 month old infants*. Paper presented at biennial meeting of the Society for Research in Child Development, Baltimore, MD.

Meadow-Orlans, K., & Spencer, P. (1996). Maternal sensitivity and the visual attentiveness of children who are deaf. *Early Development and Parenting, 5*, 213–223.

Meadow-Orlans, K., Spencer, P., & Koester, L. (2004). *The world of deaf infants*. New York: Oxford University Press.

Meier, R., & Newport, E. (1990). Out of the hands of babes: On a possible sign advantage in language acquisition. *Language, 66*, 1–23.

Mertens, D., Delk, L., & Weidekamp, L. (2003). Evaluation of early intervention programs. In B. Bodner-Johnson & M. Sass-Lehrer (Eds.), *The young deaf or hard of hearing child* (pp. 187–218). Baltimore: Paul H. Brookes.

Mitchell, R., & Karchmer, M. (2004). Chasing the mythical ten percent: Parental hearing status of deaf and hard of hearing students in the United States. *Sign Language Studies 4*, 138–163.

Mohay, H. (2000). Language in sight: Mothers' strategies for making language visually accessible to deaf children. In P. Spencer, C. Erting, & M. Marschark (Eds.), *The deaf child in the family and at school: Essays in honor of Kathryn P. Meadow-Orlans* (pp. 151–166). Mahwah, NJ: Lawrence Erlbaum.

Mohay, H., Luttrell, R., & Milton, L. (1991). How much, how often and in what form should linguistic input be given to deaf infants? In G. Lawrence (Ed.), *Pathways for the future. Proceedings of the Australian and New Zealand Conference of Educators of the Deaf* (pp. 121–131). Brisbane, Australia: the Australian Association of Teachers of the Deaf.

Mohay, H., Milton, L., Hindmarsh, G., & Ganley, K. (1998). Deaf mothers as language models for hearing families with deaf children. In A. Weisel (Ed.), *Issues unresolved: New perspectives on language and deafness* (pp. 76–87). Washington, DC: Gallaudet University Press.

Moore, V., & McConachie, H. (1994). Communication between blind and severely visually impaired children and their parents. *British Journal of Developmental Psychology, 12*, 491–502.

Morrongiello, B. A., Fenwick, K. D., Hillier, L., & Chance, G. (1994). Sound localisation in newborn human infants. *Developmental Psychobiology, 27*, 51–538.

Muir, D. W., & Field, J. (1979). Newborn infants orient to sound. *Child Development, 50*, 431–436.

Orlansky, M., & Bonvillian, J. (1985). Sign language acquisition: Language development in children of deaf parents and implications for other populations. *Merrill-Palmer Quarterly, 32*, 127–143.

Petitto, L. (1988). "Language" in the prelinguistic child. In F. S. Kessel (Ed.), *The development of language and language researchers: Essays in honor of Roger Brown* (pp. 187–221). Hillsdale, NJ: Lawrence Erlbaum.

Petitto, L., & Mareutette, P. (1991). Babbling in the manual mode: Evidence for the ontogeny of language. *Science, 251*, 1493–1496.

Pinker, S. (2002). *The blank slate*. London: Allen Lane/Penguin.

Pressman, L., Pipp-Siegel, S., Yoshinaga-Itano, C., & Deas, A. (1999). Maternal sensitivity predicts language gain in preschool children who are deaf and hard of hearing. *Journal of Deaf Studies and Deaf Education, 4*, 294–304.

Reilly, J., & Bellugi, U. (1996). Competition on the face: Affect and language in ASL motherese. *Journal of Child Language, 23*, 219–239.

Singleton, J. (1989). *Restructuring of language from impoverished input: Evidence for linguistic compensation.* Unpublished doctoral dissertation, University of Illinois, Champaign-Urbana.

Singleton, J., & Newport, E. (1987, April). *When learners surpass their models: The acquisition of American Sign Language from impoverished input.* Paper presented to biennial meeting of the Society for Research in Child Development, Baltimore, MD.

Smith, C., Adamson, L., & Bakeman, R. (1988). Interactional predictors of early language. *First Language, 8,* 143–156.

Snow, C. E. (1977). Mothers' speech research: From input to interaction. In C. E. Snow & C. A. Ferguson (Eds.), *Talking to children: Language input and acquisition* (pp. 31–49). Cambridge: Cambridge University Press.

Spelke, E., & Owsley, C. J. (1979). Intermodal exploration and knowledge in infancy. *Infant Behaviour and Development, 2,* 13–24.

Spencer, P. (1993a). Communication behaviors of infants with hearing loss and their hearing mothers. *Journal of Speech and Hearing Research, 36,* 311–321.

Spencer, P. (1993b). The expressive communication of hearing mothers and deaf infants. *American Annals of the Deaf, 138*(3), 275–283.

Spencer, P. (2000). Looking without listening: Is audition a prerequisite for normal development of visual attention during infancy? *Journal of Deaf Studies and Deaf Education, 5*(4), 291–302.

Spencer, P. (2003). Mother-child interaction. In B. Bodner-Johnson & M. Sass-Lehrer (Eds.), *The young deaf or hard of hearing child: A family-centered approach to early education* (pp. 333–371). Baltimore: Brookes.

Spencer, P. (2004). Language at 12 and 18 months: Characteristics and accessibility of linguistic models. In K. Meadow-Orlans, P. Spencer, & L. Koester, *The world of deaf infants* (pp. 147–167). New York: Oxford University Press.

Spencer, P., Bodner-Johnson, B., & Gutfreund, M. (1992). Interacting with infants with a hearing loss: What can we learn from mothers who are deaf? *Journal of Early Intervention, 16,* 64–78.

Spencer, P., & Lederberg, A. (1997). Different modes, different models: Communication and language of young deaf children and their mothers. In L. Adamson & M. Romski (Eds.), *Communication and language acquisition. Discoveries from atypical development* (pp. 203–230). Baltimore: Paul H. Brookes.

Spencer, P., Meadow-Orlans, K., Koester, L., & Ludwig, L. (2004). Relationship across developmental domains and over time. In K. Meadow-Orlans, P. Spencer, & L, Koester, *The world of deaf infants* (pp. 205–217). New York: Oxford University Press.

Spencer, P., Swisher, M. V., & Waxman, R. (2004). Visual attention: Maturation and specialization. In K. Meadow-Orlans, P. Spencer, & L. Koester, *The world of deaf infants* (pp. 168–188). New York: Oxford University Press.

Spinath, F. M., Price, T. S., Dale, P. S., & Plomin, R. (2004). The genetic and environmental origins of language disability and ability. *Child Development, 75,* 445–454.

Swisher, M. V. (2000). Learning to converse: How deaf mothers support the development of attention and conversational skills in their young deaf children. In P. Spencer, C. Erting, & M. Marschark (Eds.), *The deaf child in the family and at school* (pp. 21–37). Mahwah, NJ: Lawrence Erlbaum.

Tardif, T. (1996). Nouns are not always learned before verbs: Evidence from Mandarin speaker's early vocabularies. *Developmental Psychology, 32,* 492–504.

Todo, S. Fogel, A., & Kawai, M. (1990). Maternal speech to three-month-old infants in the United States and Japan. *Journal of Child Language, 17,* 279–294.

Tomasello, M., & Todd, J. (1983). Joint attention and lexical acquisition style. *First Language, 4,* 197–212.

Volterra, V., Beronesi, S., & Massoni, P. (1994). How does gestural communication become language? In V. Volterra & C. Erting (Eds.), *From gesture to language in hearing and deaf children* (pp. 205–218). Washington, DC: Gallaudet University Press.

Waxman, R., & Spencer, P. (1997). What mothers do to support infant visual attention: Sensitivities to age and hearing status. *Journal of Deaf Studies and Deaf Education, 2*(2), 104–114.

Wertheimer, M. (1961). Psychomotor coordination of auditory and visual space at birth. *Science, 134,* 1692.

Wilson, S., & Spencer, P. (1997, April). *Maternal topic responsiveness and child language: A cross-cultural, cross-modality replication.* Poster presented at biennial meeting of Society for Research in Child Development, Washington, DC.

Yoshinaga-Itano, C. (2003). From screening to early identification and intervention: Discovering predictors to successful outcomes for children with significant hearing losses. *Journal of Deaf Studies and Deaf Education, 8,* 11–30.

# 5

# Acquiring a Visually Motivated Language: Evidence From Diverse Learners

*Brenda Schick*

It is clear that signed languages are richly structured linguistic systems, with grammatical structures that resemble those found in spoken languages (see Emmorey, 2002; Klima & Bellugi, 1979; Stokoe, Casterline, & Croneberg, 1965). However, an interesting fact about sign languages is that they appear to be more similar typologically speaking than we see with spoken languages. For example, most, if not all, sign languages have rich morphological systems that share remarkable linguistic similarity with each other, but not with spoken languages, such as the morphological systems of verb agreement and classifiers (Schembri, 2003; T. Supalla & Webb, 1995; see also Slobin, chapter 2 this volume).

Some of these morphological systems have a strong underlying iconic motivation in that aspects of grammatical structure bear some relationship to objects and locations that occur in the real world. Many of the early studies on American Sign Language (ASL) remarked on this rich iconic potential, in comparison with spoken languages, such as Klima and Bellugi (1979), who noted that "mimetic representation is the source of many symbols used in signing" (p. 11; see also DeMatteo, 1977; Mandel, 1977; Taub, 2001). The concept that signed languages have some kind of iconic motivation is probably older than any discussion on their status as a linguistic system (see Baynton, 1996). This is not to say that signed languages are only iconic representations of the real world. There are a large number of arbitrary signs, with little connection to the referents (e.g., in ASL, MOTHER, APPLE, NAME). Sign languages are not restricted to iconic representation.

The suggestion that sign languages, such as ASL, may have iconic motivation in certain domains is not a widely accepted notion. There are many who view ASL as a system of grammatical rules that are independent of iconic motivation at the grammatical level (Liddell & Metzger, 1998; Newport & Supalla, 1980; T. Supalla, 1978). However, others see iconic motivation in various grammatical systems, such as classifier systems in ASL (DeMatteo, 1977; Emmorey, 2002; Emmorey & Herzig, 2003; Schick, 1990a; Taub, 2001) as well as other sign languages (Aronoff, Meir, Padden, & Sandler, 2003; Engberg-Pedersen, 1993; Schembri, 2003; Talmy, 2003). Several linguistic subsystems in sign languages have been proposed to have a link between form and meaning, ranging from the motivation for specific handshapes to motivation underlying linguistic systems that are integrated in complex ways across discourse. In ASL, these systems include verb agreement, discourse mapping across discourse that involves verb agreement, and what may broadly be called the classifier system in ASL. Descriptions of these systems are provided in the following sections.

It is quite possible that these typological similarities may be the result of constraints on the grammar of language imposed by the modality. There is evidence of this in the emergence of International Sign Language (ISL), which has been described by T. Supalla and Webb (1995). ISL is a contact language that has developed among deaf adults who interact at the international level (in some ways a naturally developing Esperanto). Supalla and Webb report that the verb agreement system in ISL is fairly complex and very similar to those found in fully developed signed languages. They propose that the grammatical devices of agreement transferred from the fully mature languages into ISL quite easily, resulting in a rather complex morphology in a language that is relatively young and has no native signers. What we see is a cross-linguistic similarity in an aspect of sign language grammar, in a domain where sign language is highly iconically motivated. The ease with which signed languages can incorporate iconically motivated forms may underlie these universal structural similarities.

Interestingly, acquisition of these complex morphological systems may provide insight into how the children approach learning languages that have some iconic motivation. This is hardly a new question in the field of sign language acquisition. Some of the earliest acquisition studies questioned the effects of iconic motivation, such as in the development of the lexicon (Bonvillian, Orlansky, & Novack, 1983), verb agreement (Meier, 1982), and personal pronouns (Petitto, 1987). In general, researchers have dismissed a role for iconic motivation, concluding that deaf children ignore iconic motivation in favor of a grammatical analysis (e.g., Meier, 1991; Newport & Meier, 1985; T. Supalla, 2003). However, in many studies, evidence for iconic motivation is often considered to be all or none: Either iconic motivation determines the majority of developmental patterns we observe, or development is considered driven solely by grammatical organization. In reality, the data are less straightforward, and while there is no evidence that iconic motivation dictates development, there are aspects of developmental patterns that do not rule out its role in development.

In this chapter I explore acquisition of visual, iconically motivated languages from several different perspectives. First, I describe the development of verb agreement, classifiers, and discourse mapping by deaf children who are learning sign language from their deaf parents in a manner similar to how hearing children learn language. Second, I explore language development in children who are deaf but not exposed to sign languages, who have been found to develop gesture systems that are languagelike. Third, I describe language learning in children who are learning the grammatical structure of spoken English, using a visual representation of English grammar. These children have been observed to produce grammatical structures that make sense only when sign languages are considered. Finally, I describe a unique population of learners, who quite literally have been inventing their own language, deaf children and adults in Nicaragua, who are creating a language that has aspects of linguistic organization found in other signed languages. In summary, in this chapter I explore the interesting similarities in how a variety of learners in a range of language learning environments learn visual languages, often borrowing from the real world and gestural systems to create a formal communication system.

## OVERVIEW OF ASL MORPHOLOGY

### Verb Agreement

In ASL, as in most if not all other signed languages, space can be used grammatically in order to talk about people, events, and objects. A point in signing space can become an anaphoric locus, which is associated with a particular referent, even when the referent is absent or is an abstract concept. Figure 5.1 shows an example of an anaphoric reference produced by a deaf child (with deaf parents) at age 3;10.[1] In this example, the boy establishes a location for the chimney in the story of the Three Pigs. He subsequently uses that location when he signs FIRE, to show that the fire is in the fireplace. These locations, often called loci, are often considered morphological (see Liddell, 2003, for an interesting alternative). For example, Engberg-Pedersen (1993) proposes that a locus

---

[1] Ages are expressed as, for example, 3;10, indicating 3 years 10 months. The examples come from a spontaneous retelling of the Three Pigs story. The story was obviously practiced but produced without any parental help.

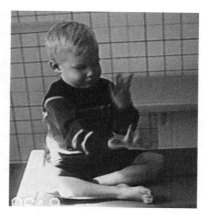

Figure 5-1. The use of a location as an anaphoric reference to a previously established reference.

is a morpheme that is expressed by how it influences the production of signs. We often see the effect on verbs, in that the beginning or end point of the verb can be changed to reference loci in space that can represent arguments of the verb, typically called verb agreement (Cokely & Baker, 1980; Meier, 1990; Wilbur, 1987). However, verb agreement is not just about single predicates being modified. Verb agreement occurs throughout discourse and its use at this level is organized in what some have called the referential framework (Bellugi, Van Hoek, Lillo-Martin, & O'Grady, 1988), the frame of reference (Lillo-Martin & Klima, 1990), or a discourse frame (Padden, 1990). Often signers will assume more than one role, shifting between speakers, and the frame of reference will also shift, termed "referential shift" (see Emmorey, 2002).

Despite its grammatical structure, there is an underlying iconic motivation in verb agreement in that verbs can also agree with objects and people in the real world, even when those people and objects are not there. If a person or object is present, verb agreement must be consistent with real world locations. But in many cases, verb agreement reflects the mental spaces of the signer, and not abstract arbitrary points in space (Emmorey & Reilly, 1995; Engberg-Pedersen, 1993; Liddell, 2003; Taub, 2001). Signers can borrow mental maps that have their bases in real space when creating a frame of reference. For example, if a mother is reporting a conversation with two children, one next to her and one some distance away, her frame of reference reflects the relative locations of the children in the original conversation. Engberg-Pedersen (1993) argues that such principles of grammatical organization rely on some elements of iconicity, even when talking about abstract references.

The form of verb agreement is not very different across sign languages, although there is still much to learn about the signed languages in the world. There are expected differences in the specific verbs that can and cannot be modified using some form of verb agreement, which is language-specific knowledge. But the underlying concepts and structuring seem to be remarkably similar across sign languages (T. Supalla & Webb, 1995).

### Classifiers, or Polycomponential Verbs in ASL

There is another large and quite productive system in sign languages, often called the classifier system. More recently, researchers have questioned the analogy to spoken language classifiers and have suggested a more theory-neutral term, polycomponential verbs (Schembri, 2003; Slobin et al., 2003). In ASL, classifiers include verbs that show the motion of objects and people, how they are located relative to each other, and how we handle objects as well as verbs that describe objects, with examples shown in figure 5.2 (Schick, 1990b; T. Supalla, 1986). As Schembri notes, polycomponential constructions have been found in more than 30 natural sign languages, and it is doubtful that any natural sign language will be found to lack them. There is some debate about regarding the number and nature of subclasses, but basically, there are three main subgroups of ASL classifiers (see Schembri, 2003). Figure 5.2 shows an example of each type as produced by a child.

(1) *Entity classifiers*: the handshape represents an agent, patient, or theme participant role. Handshape selection is somewhat categorical.
(2) *Handle classifiers*: the handshape reflects what is being handled and how the hand is handling it.
(3) *SASS classifiers*: the handshape is selected based on salient visual-geometric features of the referent.

In many sign languages, classifiers can include a wide range of different morphemic-like units[2] denoting aspects of motion, location, manner, distribution, extension, and aspect. In general, classifier systems are quite productive in sign languages, serving as the heart of word formation devices (Engberg-Pedersen, 1993; Schembri, 2003; Schick, 1990a; T. Supalla, 1982). Linguistically, descriptions that involve classifiers often involve an ordered string of predicate clauses, with each clause providing some perspective or aspect of information. There are distinct rules for ordering, for combining aspects of the referent or event that

---

[2] There is legitimate debate about the morphological status of the handshapes, movements, and locations found in classifier forms. For example, see Liddell (2003) and Schembri (2003).

(a)

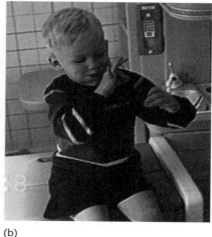

(b)

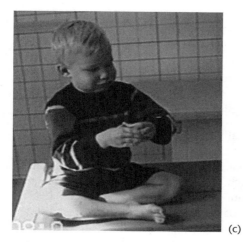

(c)

**Figure 5-2. Example (a) shows an entity classifier (right hand) and a SASS classifier (left hand). Example (b) shows a handle classifier, and example (c) shows a SASS classifier.**

represent different scales, how the handshapes and movements are combined, and so forth. It may be best to think of a classifier expression as a series of related verbs, across multiple clauses (Schembri, 2003).

Importantly, there are various forms of iconicity that underlie parts of the classifier system in ASL. Handshapes in the ASL classifier system can be iconically motivated in that the shape of the hand itself has some resemblance to the referent object, such as using a V-handshape to represent the two legs of a human, or the use of an C handshape to refer to something round, as opposed to flat or square. Despite the iconicity, these handshapes are not true analog representations, they are more like categorical morphemes, even though signers may be sensitive to the more gradient, or analogue, qualities of classifier handshapes (Emmorey & Herzig, 2003). Rather, they are categorical and schematicized representations and not an attempt to be an exact replica of what the handshape represents, using classifier constructions. However, probably even more iconic is how sign languages represent locative relationships. For example, in figure 5.2a, the position of the right hand shows that the wolf is at the top of the chimney, and the left hand shows the fireplace. The relative positioning of the hands is an iconic representation, in a schematicized miniature, of the relationship between the wolf and the base of the chimney in the real world.

There is a great deal of iconic motivation in how classifier building blocks are arranged relative to each other to resemble some aspect of the actual physical environment, such as the spatial arrangement and movement of objects. Engberg-Pedersen (1993) calls this the iconic convention. This is not to say that classifiers need be simply iconic or iconically simple; they may be neither. They are a grammaticalization or schematicization of a visual image involving an encoding into a linguistic system that has its own set of rules and constraints. In many cases, there are numerous iconic views of a scene and signers use a variety of classifier forms to change pragmatic focus and intention.

## THE DEVELOPMENT OF ASL MORPHOLOGY

Despite the fact that ASL is iconically motivated in many domains, the evidence that children take advantage of this iconic and metaphoric motivation is mixed. For example, iconicity does not seem to facilitate early lexical acquisition, which would mean that individual signs are not transparent to a very young learner (Bonvillian et al., 1983). There have been a few direct tests of the extent to which children utilize or recognize the iconic motivation of ASL, most notably Meier (1982). In this section, the acquisition of three major linguistic systems in ASL is reviewed, verb agreement, classifiers, and frames of reference, with a focus on developmental evidence for how iconic motivation may affect acquisition.

### The Development of Verb Agreement

Children learning ASL show evidence of forms that resemble verb agreement very early in acquisition. Casey (2000) found that before 2 years of age, deaf children produce what she calls "prelinguistic action gestures" that are used with spatial modifications. For example, she reports that a child, age 1;3, produced an "open" gesture near a box to mean "open the box." She found that the gestures of four children contained agreement-like forms as early as 12 months of age, when it is highly unlikely that the children had acquired much grammatical structure. Casey concludes that directionality in sign language has a gestural origin, allowing children to produce agreement even at this early age.

In terms of formal grammatical marking, children begin using some aspects of verb agreement around the time they begin to produce their first multiword utterances (Meier, 1982). Figure 5.3 shows the use of verb agreement with a spatial location by a child age 2;0. She is talking about how her juice had spilled and she articulates the verb SPILL three times. The first was produced as a citation form but by the third production, she spontaneously produced verb agreement with the real world location of where the juice had spilled. In general, the pattern of acquisition shows the use of verb agreement is variable, with omission in obligatory contexts until around age 3 years. For example, Meier, in a study of three children (ages 1;6–3;6, 2;8–3;4, and 3;1–3;9) found that at age 2;0, one child produced 27 tokens of verb agreement, producing an agreement form in 100% of the obligatory contexts. However, at age 2;2, the child used an agreement form in 50% of the obligatory contexts and 85% of the time at 2;4. By age 2;10, the child was correct greater than 90% of the time. Meier speculates that the earliest forms, produced at age 2;0, may be unanalyzed rote forms.

There is also strong evidence that real world mapping may scaffold a child's use of verb agreement. The early use of verb agreement occurs mostly with objects and people who are present in the environment, agreeing with real world locations (Casey, 2000; Lillo-Martin, 1991;

**Figure 5-3.** An example of the use of verb agreement with a real-world reference.

Meier, 1982). For example, a child might use agreement when using the verb GIVE, when the person being given an object is present in the environment. Young children in the early stages of development of verb agreement have more difficulty using agreement on verbs with the person or object is not present. For example, Casey (2000), in an investigation of five deaf children of deaf parents (ages 8 months to 2;11), found that all of the children produced significantly more verb agreement with referents that were in the environment, that than absent referents. Lillo-Martin (1991) also found that around age 3;6, when children are proficient at using verb agreement with present referents, they may not use it with nonpresent referents. She reported that children at this age often use explicit nouns as subjects and objects, rather than using verb agreement. For example, a child would produce a series of sentences in which the subject noun is repeated rather than replacing the noun with verb agreement (e.g., BOY WALK. BOY SEE A BALLOON. BOY WANT BALLOON). Lillo-Martin concluded that after children are able to use agreement with referents that are present in the environment, it takes up to 2 years more to use the agreement system with nonpresent referents.

There is also evidence that children do produce iconically motivated agreement forms. Meier's (1982) data show that two children produced a large number of verb agreement forms with verbs in which the motion and location are iconically motivated (e.g., GIVE, PUT). He shows that for one subject, from age 2;8 to 3;4, nearly all of the forms of verb agreement were these more iconic forms. The other child, from age 2;0 to 3;6 also produced mostly iconic forms even at age 3;6. The children also produced some of their most advanced verb agreement, marking both subject and object agreement, mostly with these more iconic verbs. But it is clear that while the children appeared to produce verb agreement more often with mimetic verbs, they also were producing it with verbs that are not really iconically motivated in ASL such as FALL, SEE, or KILL. Meier concludes that the children are not restricted in their use of verb agreement to verbs with a particular semiotic property or iconicity.

While children have a preference for marking verb agreement with references that are in the environment, they seem to understand the concept that a locus or point in space can refer to an abstract person or object. Research has shown that children can comprehend the meaning of a locus in space for an abstract, nonpresent referent as early as age 3, when they are fairly competent at producing verb agreement with present referents (Lillo-Martin, 1991; Lillo-Martin, Bellugi, Struxness, & O'Grady, 1985; Loew, 1984). Children must also learn verb-specific information about verb agreement in terms of which verbs require which kinds of forms. Children have been observed to make some errors that show that they are trying to figure out what forms of verb agreement a particular verb can take. For example, Meier (1982) reported that one child (3;0) produced a form, *GIVE [>plates], agreeing with the theme of the verb (plates), rather than with the person. While this type of error is interesting, it appears to be somewhat rare in that there are very few actually reported in the literature.

Children also have more difficulty explicitly marking subject argument agreement; they consistently show a preference for marking object agreement forms. As a result, children often neglect to indicate the subject, thus producing subjectless verbs (Lillo-Martin, 1991; Meier, 1982). They seem to misinterpret or not always include an agent even when adults need them for clarification. ASL allows subjectless verbs when there is sufficient pragmatic and syntactic context, but children have been observed to produce many forms where they are not sufficiently clear about who the subject is. Without properly identifying the referents, verb agreement is much like using a pronoun without knowing who you are talking about.

In general, the evidence concerning the acquisition of verb agreement indicates that children do not approach the task of learning the morphological system as a strictly iconically motivated system. There is, however, evidence that iconic motivation may scaffold development of verb agreement in that children first produce verb agreement when talking about referents that are present in the environment. The concept of using loci in space and spatially modifying verbs to agree with the physical referent appears early, before children are acquiring grammar that could later scaffold correct use of more abstract verb agreement. Although the data show that iconic motivation cannot account for all of what we know about the acquisition of verb agreement, they also show that the real world may scaffold the child's use of verb agreement or it may scaffold learning of the concept of agreement. In order to trace development from the more gestural agreement forms that Casey (2000) observed to the ability to use verb agreement more abstractly, we clearly need longitudinal data.

## The Development of Classifiers

The acquisition of the ASL classifier system is challenging for children, as evidenced by its prolonged developmental timetable: children do not seem to master the classifier system until around age 8 to 9 years (Kantor, 1980; Schick, 1990b, 2003). Even though the forms are clearly iconic, there is a great deal to learn about how they are grammatically organized, combined, and structured. In each of the three major types (entity, handle, and SASS forms), children must learn the structure and constraints for each type of classifier, as well as subtypes within each type (Slobin et al., 2003). Children must learn to select a correct handshape that can represent a semantic category (entity), a category based on how a hand interacts with an object (handle), or a category based on the visual geometric features of the referent. In addition, for some verbs of motion and location, children must be able to coordinate the hands to represent figure and ground (see Talmy, 2000, 2003). Coordinating figures and grounds can become quite complex in that in many instances, the ground is described first, and then the figure is articulated in relationship to the ground, often in a separate clause. Children also need to learn what movements may be combined with each of the classifier subsystems and how to represent scale and viewpoint. In reality, we have an inadequate linguistic understanding of how adults use the classifier system, so it is very likely that there is more to acquisition than just this.

Children do not seem to have problems with the concept of classifiers. They have been observed to produce productive classifier forms as young as age 2;5 (Lindert, 2001). For example, figure 5.4 shows examples of two early entity classifier forms produced by a child age 2;8. First, the child represents a dog using the PEOPLE-WALK handshape. Then he immediately produces a classifier in which one hand represents the building and the other hand represents the dog. Although the handshapes are incorrect in the second production—they are too generic— the relative placement of the hands is clear. Note that he produced a specific handshape in relative isolation, followed by a more complex classifier, with generic handshapes. By age 3–3;6, children have been observed to freely produce classifiers forms in tasks that obligate them (Lillo-Martin, 1988; T. Supalla, 1982). Deaf children have been found to produce productive classifier forms between age 2 and 3 years, in both ASL and Sign Language of the Netherlands, for children who have deaf parents and those who have hearing parents (Lillo-Martin, 1988;

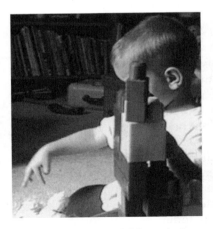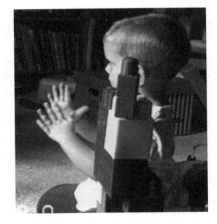

Figure 5-4. A child producing a classifier with two entity hand shapes.

Lindert, 2001; Slobin et al., 2003). Lindert found that at age 2 and 3, the number of these forms relative to all signs is relatively small (ranging from 0 to 30%), but by age 4, children were producing many more classifier forms (45–65%) when using tasks and activities designed to elicit them. It is also important to note that all of the children produced forms that appeared productive, that is there were not memorized, unanalyzed forms. In Lindert's (2001) study, very few classifier forms were observed that were unclear, where it was difficult to understand what the child intended to communicate.

In the earliest stages of development, young children have been observed to produce all three types of classifiers, but Lindert (2001) found that children produce mostly a specific type of classifiers, manipulative handle forms, which are transitive forms focusing on agentivity and a first-person report. The children also produced SASS and entity forms, but these seem to be relatively infrequent at this young age. Lindert interpreted these results as supporting a hypothesis proposed by Taub (2001), who speculated that manipulative handle forms are the earliest of classifiers because they are so transparent.

Children seem to understand the concepts of how to select a correct handshape for the various classifier types early in acquisition. Both T. Supalla (1982) and Schick (1990b) reported that 5-year-olds are able to produce entity handshapes correctly or partially correct about 85% of the time. Schick hypothesized that the kind of superordinate categorization that underlies entity handshapes is an early concept in vocabulary development and categorical organization. Children appear to have more difficulty with producing handshapes for other types of classifiers. For example, even at age 5, SASS handshapes are produced correctly less than 70% of the time (Schick, 1990b; T. Supalla, 1982).[3] The acquisition of handle classifiers is less clear. Children begin using these forms early, around age 2 (Lindert, 2001), but Schick found that handle handshapes were still produced incorrectly at around 8 years of age, when they were used as verbs of transfer (e.g., "The man moved the box to the shelf"), not the manipulative handles that have been reported as developing early. It may be that the pragmatic focus on transfer may cause children to focus less on the properties of the object and more on the verb agreement involved in transfer, affecting handshape production.

In terms of errors, children often use handshapes that are more generic than needed, or handshapes that represent some but not all of the linguistically relevant dimensions, such as in SASS forms. For example, the child in figure 5.4 correctly produced the locative

---

[3] T. Supalla (1982) used SASS handshapes in verbs of motion. Schick used them in adjectival descriptions.

relationship between two objects, but using very generic, unspecified handshapes. Children do not appear to confuse major dimensional categories, such as using a round handshape for a flat object, but they have difficulty representing all of the details of dimension. For example, T. Supalla (1982) showed that his two subjects, 3 and 4 years old, respectively, often produced a general, less marked, entity handshape (B, Z, and point) for the figure handshape about 30% of the time. For example, when representing a vehicle, the child simply pointed to the location of the vehicle rather than using a handshape that represents the category of vehicles (should be the 3 handshape). Children also use more primitive handshapes for SASS handshapes and still make errors with SASS handshapes even at age 5. The 5-year-old child he observed was correct in his SASS handshapes 67% of the time and Schick showed that children were correct about 55–60% of time. One interesting source of errors appears to be the overuse of manipulative handle forms and what Supalla terms body classifiers (e.g., "pointed ears," "sharp teeth") instead of entity or SASS forms. Supalla found that children incorrectly used manipulative handle forms when other classifiers were required nearly 10% of the time.

There is good evidence that even young children understand the iconic relationship between a figure and a ground, in that the relative placement of the hands represents the locative relationship (see figure 5.4). Even at a young age, children appear capable of understanding and producing locative forms with both a figure and ground elements. In addition to recording children's productions of classifiers, Lindert (2001) assessed the children's ability to comprehend signed descriptions of locative relationships. Even the youngest child (2;0) was able to choose the correct figure and ground from his mother's description nearly 70% of the time. By the time the children were almost 4 years of age, they were performing at ceiling. Perhaps more surprising was the fact that even the youngest children could arrange the figure and ground into the correct spatial configuration much of the time, although this did improve with age, and children with deaf mothers were generally better at this than those with hearing mothers. However, it is notable that even the deaf children of hearing parents produced these forms freely. There is other evidence that children understand the concept of representing locative relationships. At ages 3 and 4, the two younger children observed by Supalla included two handshapes in their classifier descriptions and used the correct relative placement of the hands nearly 50% of the time. By age 5, the children correctly produce the locative relationship 80% of the time. However, studies consistently show that there is a preference for producing the figure element, or the focal element, and the ground element is more frequently omitted by young children (Schick, 1990b; T. Supalla, 1982).

Children have been found to produce errors that seem to make classifier productions less iconic than an adult form would be. T. Supalla (1982) reports that children would create a classifier form in sequential constructions, rather than maintain the simultaneity between the figure and the ground referent as required in some adult classifiers. However, it is hard to interpret this as a simple reduction in iconicity. In adult classifier productions, it is common to see a string of classifier forms, each representing a different aspect of the scene, with the final form(s) indicating how all these parts are connected. Children see many examples of a visual scene that has been parsed into sequential classifier constructions. While this may make the production less iconic, it still retains the underlying spatial mapping in that the child represents the locative relationship correctly, but just by putting the pieces together sequentially, rather than simultaneously.

It is noteworthy that, with rare exceptions, researchers have not found classifiers produced with clear disregard for iconicity. Indeed, children use iconic forms early, just not with the well-formedness and sophistication one would expect in a mature grammatical production. Similarly, no study has reported that deaf children represent spatial concepts using noniconic lexical forms. It is possible to represent spatial relationships in ASL using lexical prepositions, such as IN, ON, and UNDER, and Talmy (2003) notes that spoken languages always represent space using categorical forms. Emmorey (2002) reports that deaf adults use these lexical expressions when they want to emphasize a spatial relationship or when they generalize across objects, but in general, they prefer to represent diagrammatic space using classifiers. We do not see children resorting to these lexical forms, even though we do see a preference for lexical expression in other complex grammatical domains, such as a preference for using the word IF to mark a conditional rather than a nonmanual marker, or the use of the explicit verb, SAY, to mark direct quotation rather than the nonmanual marker (see Reilly, chapter 11 this volume).

In summary, there is evidence that representing iconically based concepts using a linguistic system does not seem difficult for deaf children. Around age 2, children can produce and comprehend classifiers although they seem to have a preference for manipulative handle forms in their spontaneous productions. It seems that by age 3, children are able to select semantically appropriate handshapes and integrate these handshapes into classifier forms, combine handshapes representing figure and ground into a single sign, comprehend spatial arrangements using a figure and ground, and produce manipulative and depictive handle forms. What seems to be more difficult for children is learning all the grammatical rules on combining and constructing classifiers, not the underlying concepts.

## The Ability to Represent Role Play, Frames of Reference, and Shifted Reference

In ASL, signers can "quote" another signers, assuming a first-person role to represent the other person, sometimes termed role play, or role shift (Friedman, 1977; Padden, 1986; Taub, 2001) or surrogate space (Liddell, 2003). There is very little research on how signing children use role shift within discourse to report what others are saying. Most of what we know comes from a study conducted by Loew (1984), investigating mostly a single child (ages 3;1–4;9), with supplemental data from two other children (ages 2;11 and 4;3). What limited evidence we have suggests that that the concept of assuming the role of another character does not seem to be difficult for children to understand, children have been observed to incorporate role play into their signing rather early. For example, in British Sign Language, Morgan and Woll (2002, p. 263) observed a child age 2;1 who communicated the concept of cause and effect using a lexical verb and role play, producing the verb BITE in citation form following by a "depiction of the bitten girl's reaction (a shudder of the body and a startled facial expression)." Similarly, Loew reports the production of role play in narration in a child who was age 2;11, the youngest age she studied. Loew concluded that by age 3;1 to 3;4, children are able to use role play, and certain specific examples appear fully grammatical.

Children also need to integrate this use of space across individual sentences in discourse, requiring cohesion at the discourse level. Figure 5.5 shows an example of a child using a frame of reference consistently across sentences. In this passage, the child establishes a location for the three separate houses (brick and grass, the stick house is not shown).[4] Then the wolf blows each house down, using the locations where the houses were established. Loew (1984, p. 103) reports an example from a simple narrative report of a past event produced by her subject at age 3;4, in which the child was able to use a frame of reference, throughout the narration, most likely because she was talking about a real-world location, a door that the family cat exited and entered. The child was even able to shift the frame of reference in order to correctly show a different agreement form, from the cat's perspective, when the cat returns home and comes in from the door, rather than out of it. Loew also provided an example of a child attempting to use verb agreement within a shifted reference frame at 3;1, even though the verb agreement was incorrect (p. 104). Loew also noted that her subject was using

---

[4] The order of the figures is correct in that the wolf first blows at each house, and then each house collapses.

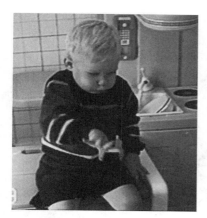

**Figure 5-5. An example of a child using a frame of reference during a story retelling.**

appropriate eye gaze, when representing the character looking at objects in the real world. However, the use of space, while sometimes correctly produced by Loew's subject, was also produced incorrectly. Figure 5.6 provides an example of a boy, age 3;10, using a spatial location anaphorically, but with an error. He establishes a location for the chimney in the story of the Three Pigs. He signs that the wolf came down the chimney twice. The first time, it is clear that the wolf landed in the fire at the base of the chimney, but the second time the boy signs it,

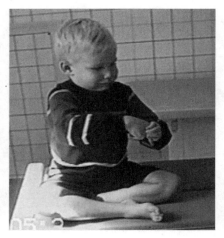

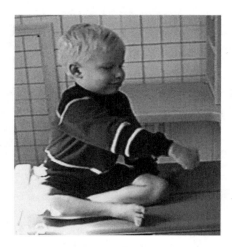

**Figure 5-6. An example of an error in anaphoric referencing.**

the wolf lands somewhere that looks like the middle of the room, not in the fireplace. However, he continues to talk about the wolf being cooked and eaten by the pigs (providing his own twist to the classic tale that his mother disputed and he insisted was the correct version).

However, using this frame of reference consistently throughout a story without real world support appears to be challenging for 3–4-year-olds. The child Loew (1984) observed, at ages 3;1–3;4, was able to use verb agreement for present referents and when telling stories about nonpresent referents, the child appeared to establish and refer to pronominal loci, but she seemed to use a similar location for many referents. Loew reports that this made her stories "extremely difficult to understand" (p. 86) in part because it was often confusing who was talking or acting. The child assumed a first-person account without indicating who was talking. This was confounded by the fact that some of the child's narratives were spontaneous stories, and possibly invented, making it difficult to know for sure who was the reference. Even for the child at an older age (3;6), Loew noted that the girl appeared to be most successful at using a frame of reference throughout the story, consistently using the same locations for an object or person, when the spatial mapping was iconically motivated, such as when representing a character looking down at a garden. The child in Loew's study was beginning to integrate the overall spatial mapping of the story at age 4;6–4;9, the last age range studied. Similarly, Lillo-Martin (1991) reported that children at age 5 were still making many errors in coordinating pronominal reference throughout a narrative. Only around age 5 do children seem to be able to consistently use a frame of reference cohesively and with proper identification, although we need more research to confirm this.

In general, it seems that using spatial locations anaphorically is not a difficult concept. Children do not have difficulty understanding the concepts that underlie the abstract use of space to represent people and events, especially when these spatial maps are richly grounded in reality. Similar to other domains, however, early evidence of the use of frames of reference and role shift during narration does not translate into early mastery. It is clear that children struggle with the complex integration of frames of reference, diagrammatic space, nonmanual marking, and discourse cohesion that is involved in producing adultlike narratives in ASL. In addition, it is likely that many of the children's difficulties and inconsistencies in using some advanced aspects of ASL in narration are due to larger issues regarding narrative construction and the types of underlying cognitive understanding that is needed to represent complicated narratives. Issues regarding a *theory of mind* may be implicated in that children seem to have particular difficulty providing the listener with sufficient information to clearly identify the referents (see Shaffer, chapter 12 this volume). In sum, children seem to acquire the concept of role play and direct quotation early in acquisition, by assuming first person in reported action and discourse. They have much more difficulty with the more abstract concepts of discourse cohesion and the use of mental space through out the discourse.

## Acquisition: Does It Reflect Iconic Motivation?

Many of the studies that attempt to test the concept of whether iconicity underlies aspects of acquisition reflect a relative simplicity in our understanding of language acquisition and of the types of iconicity that occur in sign languages. In terms of language acquisition, often researchers assume that any evidence that children approach learning sign language focusing on grammar, or that they are able to learn arbitrary signs, is

### Table 5-1: Evidence Supporting a Role for Iconic Motivation in Sign Language Development

**What we see in the development of ASL**

Early signs are both arbitrary and iconic; iconicity in single signs is often metaphoric

Verb agreement with early gestures, beginning at 12 months of age

Verb agreement better with present referents than with absent referents, until about 5 years of age

Comprehends that an abstract loci can "represent" a person by age 3

Better at using verb agreement from a first-person perspective

Somewhat protracted development of the use of verb agreement in more complex discourse environments

Young children produce novel classifier forms; when they produce classifiers, there are often many aspects that are correct, beginning during the second year

Early comprehension of classifiers representing diagrammatic space

Early use of classifiers may be predominately manipulative handle forms

In SASS forms, children tend to get at least one dimension correct, such as shape, even in the earliest handshapes

Early attempts (25 months) using role play; preference for narration from a first-person perspective

Early use of real world location as an anchor for a spatial mapping across a discourse, at 3 years 4 months of age

**What we do not see in the development of ASL**

Children do not have a preference for iconic signs

Children do not have problems connecting aspects of signing with the real world

Pronominal use in spoken language is not better for present than absent referents

Children do not have difficulty understanding the concept that a location can represent a person or thing

There are few reports of children making errors regarding which type of classifier to create, with the exception of overusing manipulative handle forms

No widespread errors that show lack of awareness that handshape can represent visual-geometric properties, how hands manipulate objects, or using hands to represent an object in space

No research reports of major violations of underlying iconicity

No preference for lexical prepositions

evidence that iconic motivation is not a factor. We should expect that any causal relationship will be somewhat complex, rather than an all-or-none effect. Researchers have used terms such as "effortlessly" and "transparent" to describe what they would expect to see if iconic motivation were a factor.

In addition, we know a great deal more about the kinds of iconicity in ASL, and the range of isomorphism with reality (see Emmorey, 2001; Liddell, 2003; Taub, 2001). In some cases, researchers have expected to see developmental effects of rather abstract forms of iconicity. For example, the ASL sign MILK is only iconic if you know something about milking a cow, a concept far more abstract than a label. It should not be surprising that rather abstract forms of iconicity do not affect development as much as the underlying cognitive complexity, grammatical complexity, and discourse skills.

We know some aspects of development argue against any simplistic role for iconic motivation, but there are also facts we know about development that may lead us to conclude that there is a role for iconic motivation in development. Table 5.1 attempts to summarize some facts of development that shed light on the role of iconic motivation. It also summarizes the types of data that have not been observed, but we might expect to see if iconic motivation played no role in acquisition, providing a form of divergent validity. There is sufficient evidence from acquisition that iconic motivation may affect acquisition, both in what we see and what we never or rarely seem to see.

## ASL-LIKE FEATURES IN THE DEVELOPMENT
## OF ENGLISH-BASED SIGN SYSTEMS

In the United States, deaf children with hearing parents are often not exposed to ASL as a first language. Many educational programs use a form of English signing, where ASL signs were borrowed and changed, and new signs were invented, in order to represent the semantic, morphological, and syntactic structures of English. What is notable about these systems is the goal to represent grammatical structures in English, such as word order and bound morphology, and the reluctance to use aspects of grammar found in ASL, such as spatial referencing. As a collection, these systems are often referred to as manually coded English (MCE; see Bornstein, 1990). When MCE systems are used with deaf children as a primary language, there is an expectation that they will learn English much like hearing children learn spoken English. It should be noted that the hearing professionals and parents who use these systems vary widely in their MCE skills, a fact not easily separated from the issue of how children learn these system. Many of these children acquire MCE with relatively restricted input, both in the numbers of people they interact with and the grammatical correctness of what they see (Moeller & Luetke-Stahlman, 1990). These facts are even more relevant because children in these educational programs also often have little opportunity to see a natural sign language or deaf adults.

It is clear that children do not learn MCE systems as easily as hearing children learn spoken languages (Livingston, 1983; Schick & Moeller, 1992; Stack, 1999; S. Supalla, 1991; Suty & Friel-Patti, 1982). Research has shown that even with consistent MCE input, many deaf children make numerous errors in English syntax and have vocabularies that are smaller than their hearing peers. In addition, there is a high degree of variability in their ability to use the bound morphology of English. Clearly, a visual system designed to mimic the grammar of English does not make the acquisition of English progress as it does in hearing children.

While children have difficulty learning English morphology by using MCE, they seem to "invent" morphology that resembles aspects of ASL grammar. Even though classifiers are pervasive in ASL, there are no linguistically similar structures in English.[5] Despite this, children learning MCE produce classifier-like forms, sometimes quite frequently, even when they seem to have little exposure to ASL (Livingston, 1983; Suty & Friel-Patti, 1982). Similarly, S. Supalla (1991) observed children learning MCE using structures that resemble the kinds of verb agreement seen in natural sign languages, even when they were known to have little exposure to ASL. Supalla concluded that the children spontaneously discovered verb agreement on their own.[6]

In summary, there is little evidence that deaf children acquire English-like signing as a natural language, even though natural signed languages are acquired similarly to spoken languages. Since the invention of these systems, researchers have speculated that children would have difficulty learning MCE specifically because it does not resemble any known natural sign language (Gee & Goodhart, 1985; Johnson, Liddell, & Erting, 1989). There may be a mismatch between the typology of the language MCE is trying to represent and the typology of sign languages in general. Because of this, even children who have never seen a natural sign language innovate structures common to sign languages yet at the same time unique to sign languages.

---

[5] Spoken languages other than English have classifiers, but in many ways classifiers, or polycomponetial verbs, are more complex in signed languages than they are in spoken languages (see Emmorey, 2003; Schembri, 2003; Talmy, 2003).

[6] Some MCE systems and some MCE advocates believe that MCE should incorporate principles of verb agreement.

## THE DEVELOPMENT OF GESTURES AND NEWLY DEVELOPING SIGN LANGUAGES

### Homesign—Gesture Systems Invented by Children

The majority of deaf children are born to hearing families and many of these families choose to exposure their children exclusively to spoken English. At least some of these children have major difficulty learning spoken language in this way, showing spoken language levels that are severely delayed compared with their hearing peers (Geers, Moog, & Schick, 1984; Geers, Nicholas, & Sedey, 2003). Research has shown that some of these children exploit gesture for communication by developing somewhat sophisticated gestural systems that assume the functions of language, albeit in a much more rudimentary form. Probably the best-studied homesign systems are those of deaf children reported by Goldin-Meadow and her colleagues (Goldin-Meadow, 2003; Goldin-Meadow & Feldman, 1975; Goldin-Meadow & Mylander, 1990; J. Morford, 1996; J. P. Morford, Singleton, & Goldin-Meadow, 1995), whose work has mostly focused on one child, David, from age 2;10 to 4;10, with some investigations of three other children (2;10–4;11). At an age when children who are typically developing are learning the grammar of their language, many of these children had developed a homesign system that displayed many functions that we see in language. Children using these homesign systems have communicated concepts involving displaced referents, generic statements about animals (e.g., "birds fly"), stories about past and future events, as well as fantasy (Goldin-Meadow, 2003).

In terms of form, most of their invented gestures had a transparent or iconic foundation (Goldin-Meadow & Mylander, 1984; Goldin-Meadow, Mylander, & Butcher, 1995). Goldin-Meadow (2003) concludes that they remain this way. She observed that without this transparency, "no one in their worlds would be able to take any meaning from the gestures they created" (p. 219). For example, in a study of four deaf children who were developing gesture systems, ages 2;10–4;11, Goldin-Meadow and Mylander (1985) reported that the gesture systems created by the children were indexical and iconic systems of representation. Most of the children's gestures were what was termed "characterizing gestures" (p. 199), which were stylized pantomimes whose iconic forms varied with the intended meaning gesture by gesture. A very small proportion of the children's gestures were considered ambiguous, ranging from 4% to 8% of the total number of gestures, meaning that most of their gestures were understandable to researchers who knew the children, the toys they played with, and the families. The children produced gestures that resembled all three major categories of classifiers in ASL: (1) manipulative handle forms, (2) entity forms, and (3) tracing SASS. They also appeared to distinguish aspects of dimension in ASL SASS handshapes (but certainly not exactly as ASL represents dimension). For example, David used three different handshapes for handling small objects, with length of object as a discriminating dimension. There were also systematic differences in handshape selection that reflected other real-world dimensions. The children used a continuum of handshapes to represent objects with increasingly larger widths, ranging from a point and thumb handshape for objects with smallest widths, followed by the fist and the O handshapes, then the C handshapes, with the palm handshape used for objects with the largest widths. Several of the handshape forms were the same for several children, including a comparable range of referents. Even the children's entity-like forms were somewhat iconically motivated, such as using a fist handshape to represent a bulky object, or using the palm to represent straight-wide objects as well as vehicles.

These children created their own systematic gestural homesign system, discovering elements in the real world and creating iconically motivated forms to represent objects, how we handle objects, and how objects look. It is also true that very few of the children's productions were arbitrary forms, with little isomorphic relationship to the target. It is important to note that their systems had little of the rich grammatical system of ASL; they are clearly not a full-blown language, but they are rich gestural systems serving some of the same functions as a rudimentary version of a true language. Their gestural systems show a level of organization that Goldin-Meadow considers morphological. Despite a lack of a language model, the children generated a system of classifiers and verb agreement. It is possible that the children used their mother's gestures as a starting point, but it is clear that they contributed a great deal of structure to their gestural systems.

Interestingly, David was also tested when he was 9;5, about 5 years after his gestural system was initially studied (Morford et al., 1995). By this age, the researchers observed that his spoken communication was still limited, although his English skills were not evaluated, and that he continued to depend on his homesign system to communicate with his parents. There was little indication that he understood ASL, even though there was some evidence that he had been exposed to it. At this time, he was given a test that predominately elicits entity and SASS forms. Somewhat surprisingly, when David's productions were compared with adult deaf ASL models, 50% of his handshapes corresponded to what an adult would use. There were productions that did not correspond to adult ASL models, but often these were iconically motivated.

In sum, children who must discover their own means of communication depend on and utilize the iconicity available in the gestural modality. Goldin-Meadow, Mylander, & Butcher (1995) conclude that the particular gestural forms used by the children may be basic to communication and cognition. They suggest that these elements might be natural to any language in the manual modality, serving as the basic framework for ASL and other signed languages.

## Emerging Sign Languages

There is also evidence for the primacy of iconic motivation in signed languages from another type of acquisition, in this case children developing a language while they are also acquiring it. In Nicaragua, until the 1970s and early 1980s, deaf children had no access to education. As a result, the majority of deaf children were isolated in rural villages, where many created idiosyncratic gestural systems to communicate with hearing people. These systems are typically called homesign, to distinguish them from true signed languages. Kegl, Senghas, and Coppola (1999) note that these idiosyncratic gestural systems were probably much like those reported by Goldin-Meadow and colleagues. Eventually, a change in governments lead to the establishment of schools for deaf children; by 1983, there were more than 400 deaf students in educational programs (Kegl & Iwata, 1989; Senghas, 1995). The deaf children all had hearing families, which means that there was no ready source of an existing sign language. The original single school and the families focused on teaching the children spoken Spanish, but with little success. However, like many reports of oral programs in the United States, the deaf children gestured with each other. Relatively soon, a rudimentary sign language emerged among the children, and its earliest form may be best considered a pidgin, because it is highly variable and has limited grammatical structures (Kegl et al., 1999).

As described by Senghas and Coppola (2001), each year more children of all ages entered the school and they were exposed to the rudimentary language of the previous "generation." With time, as children learned the current version of the emerging language, and passed it on to subsequent generations, the rudimentary gestural system has evolved to the point where it is now acknowledged as a language called *Idioma de Señas Nicaragüense* (ISN). Currently in Nicaragua, there are adults who use a range of communication systems: Late-exposed individuals continue to use homesign; others use what may be considered a "peer-group pidgin or jargon" as well as children and adults who have a full-blown sign language (Kegl et al., 1999, p. 181). The first generation of pidgin signers are in their later twenties and thirties at this time, and ISN is roughly two generations old at this time (Kegl, 2002).

There have been several studies of the emergence of grammatical structure in ISN (Kegl et al., 1999; Senghas, 1995; Senghas & Coppola, 2001; Senghas & Kegl, 1994). Kegl, Senghas, and Coppola investigated the differences between the early learners, who received homesign as an input, and later learners, who were exposed to a more language-like system. They collected narratives from 270 signers, representing the continuum from homesign to language, using nonverbal video cartoons. They found a large number of grammatical differences between the group of pidgin signers and the group of sign language users. They reported that the early homesign systems contain many gestures that are primarily action-based pantomime; both deaf and hearing Nicaraguans refer to this type of gesturing as *mimicas,* or mimetic gesture. In this type of communication, the whole body is used in gestures, and communication is heavily dependent on context and shared knowledge. Often, gesturers serve as the agent of the action, in pantomime-like forms, assuming first person. Even in the gesture systems, there is evidence of classifier forms, including handling, entity, and SASS forms. They use shifted referential space to assume the role of another referent with a first person point of view. There is also evidence that homesigners utilize verb agreement, and use space as a form of shared reference, a pronominal notion. Facial expressions are used for affect, but not for grammatical purposes.

The pidgin language users produced sign communication that look more languagelike. Individual signs were more constrained in production, and facial expression is still primarily affective, but is used for grammatical purposes, such as topic marking or questioning. However, unlike a more sophisticated language, grammatical facial expressions appear linked to a single sign and did not spread through the clause. Pidgin signers use spatial inflection in some ways, referencing things in the real world or in a shared mental space of the listener. There was some verb agreement on verbs to indicate person, but it was not consistent or frequent. Kegl et al. (1999) report that pidgin signers did not use space for abstract referencing of things that are not present, especially for people. The pidgin signers also did not seem to use space to refer anaphorically to something previously talked about, but used pointing gestures that follow the verb to show the participants who are involved. However, they did modify verbs to show where objects are moving. In contrast, ISN users used spatial modifications to indicate person agreement.

Both pidgin and language signers produce all types of classifier forms, SASS, entity, and handling forms. There are a significant number of handle forms in pidgin and ISN signing, and signers from both groups seem to favor them in production, as did homesigners. While both groups produce entity forms, the ISN group seems to have a wider range of forms and uses entity classifiers in situations where agency is not involved. In contrast, pidgin signers continue to use handle forms for nonagentive forms. One other significant difference between the groups is that pidgin signers are more likely to use mimelike whole-body signs than ISN signers (38% vs. 28%), but it is obvious that both groups use them. There is also evidence that some kind of shifted referential space was used by both the pidgin and ISN signers, the frequency of its use increased with younger exposure and exposure to a more complete language.

However, Kegl et al. (1999) point out that for many of the grammatical features, there is not a sudden shift to using new forms in ISN. Often the pidgin forms are "relatively similar to what eventually gets systematized and grammaticized in ISN" (p. 191). They report that instead, there are often more constraints, less analogic movement, and more systematic rules for combination. For example, pidgin signers produced person agreement in 9% of their signs, and ISN signers produced it 42% of the time. The one exception was the use of mimelike gestures, where the frequency of use decreased, meaning that pidgin signers resorted to pantomime more often than ISN signers.

Kegl (2002) speculated that several grammatical structures in ISN emerged from gestural origins. Her list is intriguing given some of the typical acquisition errors we see in ASL. She believes that the use of verbs without subjects (or null subjects) are common because gesturers use the whole body to act out actions, assuming an agentive role, but the agent is often not explicitly mentioned. She predicts that gesture systems will be predominately null subject. She also believes that the use of shifted referential space emerges from gesturers' tendency to use their bodies to act out events from an agentive perspective. In addition, because gesturers tend to use manipulative handle classifier forms, these handling gestures can also serve as causative markers, with the agent causing the action. Because spatial agreement exists in all signed languages, she believes that children can find evidence for these forms in gestural communication. She also argues that certain structures did not have gestural origins, such as the system of entity classifiers, which she did not observe in early gesturers.

In summary, there are notable similarities between different groups of deaf children who have been isolated from language, children in hearing families in the United States and in Nicaragua. Both groups of children discovered some of the fundamental building blocks of a mature sign language, such as aspects of classifiers, verb agreement, and first person accounts. Both groups of learners borrowed heavily from the real world in order to represent it and the structures they created are very similar to what we see in all sign languages.

## SUMMARY AND CONCLUSIONS

Unlike spoken languages, signed languages seem to utilize aspects of how the world is shaped, handled, and structured into the grammar of the languages. There are some amazing similarities in both the types of grammatical structures found across signed languages and in the physical forms of how the sign is represented (Emmorey & Casey, 1995; Engberg-Pedersen, 1993; Schick, 1990a; Taub, 2001). Research on the development of a full sign language, such as ASL, shows us that iconic motivation does not simplify a child's task. In several grammatical systems, children have been observed to use a particular grammatical structure somewhat early, yet full mastery and adult sophistication occurs at a much later age. For example, children as young as 12 months have been observed to use a type of directionality in their gestures. They have broad competence with the verb agreement system by about 3 years of age, particularly with referents that are richly grounded in discourse. The concept of using space for directionality of some type appears before the acquisition of grammar. Older children have difficulty with using agreement with abstract references, tracking those referents throughout discourse, and responding to the pragmatic obligations regarding background and shared information. In fact, it appears that the real world, or what could be called shared mental spaces, scaffolds most of the earliest uses of verb agreement.

Similarly, children have been observed to use classifier forms at a time when they are just developing grammar, particularly manipulative handle forms. Children do not seem to have problems with the underlying iconicity of handle forms, or the relative placement of hands to show locative relationships. By age 3, deaf children can freely produce novel classifiers, and to represent two different objects using different hands. However, they have difficulty mastering this system, which may be due to the fact that use of classifiers also reflects elements of pragmatic focus and informativeness. It is interesting to note that most studies of classifier development have used a design in which the examiner views the stimuli along with the child, reducing the child's need for explicitness in some aspects of the classifier construction. The use of shifted referential space also appears early, but children have considerable difficulty integrating its use with the pronominal system and nonmanual markings. In all of these grammatical subsystems, it seems that utilizing aspects of the real world into signing is not difficult, but learning the entire morphosyntactic system to grammaticalize these concepts may be the challenging part for children learning sign language.

Research has not shown that children make a significant number of errors that seem to violate iconic motivation. For example, we do not see any attempts to use lexical prepositions instead of an iconically motivated form. Similarly, when children are producing classifier handshapes that have an iconic motivation, they have been observed to use more generic handshapes or handshapes that represent some aspect of the dimension correctly, just not all dimensions. There also are no reports of children confusing handshape families such as using a round handshape when they should use a flat one. If children found the concept of iconic motivation difficult, we might see a complete lack of awareness at the earliest stages of grammar and a preference for representing these concepts using lexical items or more arbitrary forms, such as we see in other morphologically difficult domains. Instead, we see a willingness to innovate at a very young age, even though these forms are often, although not always, grammatically incorrect.

When we look at different kinds of learners, those developing their own gesture system, those learning MCE, and those in the midst of inventing a language, we see some similarities to children learning a fully developed sign language. A broad variety of learners show that incorporating aspects of the real world into a language is expected when learning through the visual modality.

In some ways, these developmental patterns may reflect a theoretical division between those aspects of sign language that are linguistic versus those that some would consider to be more gestural or borrowed from nonlinguistic domains. Talmy (2003) acknowledges that signed languages stretch the limits of any core language account, such as a Fodor-Chomsky model with universal innately specified grammar. He suggests that signed languages rely on visual parsing to an even greater extent than spoken languages, which may underlie their iconicity and gradient qualities. For Talmy, many of these motivated forms are incorporating nonlinguistic subsystems. Along similar lines, Liddell (2003) views many of the iconic and gradient properties as gestural. He believes that what we see in signing is an integration of lexical, gradient, and gestural components (see also Emmorey & Herzig, 2003; Liddell & Metzger, 1998; Singleton, Goldin-Meadow, & McNeill, 1995).

Existing developmental data are inadequate to help understand the transition from motivated forms to more grammaticalized constructions (if they are grammaticalized). It is clear that developmental patterns show early use of motivated forms by children, during the earliest stages of grammatical acquisition, and across learners in diverse environments. Engberg-Pedersen (2003) states that we should be looking at how children develop the combination of lexicalized forms, sublexical morphemelike units, and iconic forms. Similarly, Slobin (chapter 2 this volume) cautions that we should be careful of predictions that are based on spoken languages and more specifically, Indo-European languages in order to see what may be unique and common to languages that are mapped onto a visual modality.

## REFERENCES

Aronoff, M., Meir, I., Padden, C., & Sandler, W. (2003). Classifier constructions and morphology in two sign languages. In K. Emmorey (Ed.), *Perspectives on classifier constructions in sign language* (pp. 53–84). Mahwah, NJ: Lawrence Erlbaum.

Baynton, D. C. (1996). *Forbidden signs: American culture and the campaign against sign language.* Chicago: University of Chicago Press.

Bellugi, U., Van Hoek, K., Lillo-Martin, D., & O'Grady, L. (1988). The acquisition of syntax and space in young deaf signers. In D. Bishop & K. Mogford (Eds.), *Language development in exceptional circumstances* (pp. 132–149). Edinburgh: Churchill Livingstone.

Bonvillian, J. D., Orlansky, M. D., & Novack, L. L. (1983). Developmental milestones: Sign language acquisition and motor development. *Child Development, 54*, 1435–1445.

Bornstein, H. (Ed.). (1990). *Manual communication: Implications for education.* Washington, DC: Gallaudet University Press.

Casey, S. (2000). *"Agreement" in gestures and signed languages: The use of directionality to indicate referents involved in action.* Unpublished doctoral dissertation, University of California, San Diego.

Cokely, D., & Baker, C. (1980). *American Sign Language: A teacher's resource text on curriculum, methods, and evaluation.* Silver Spring, MD: T.J. Publishers.

DeMatteo, A. (1977). Visual imagery and visual analogues in American Sign Language. In L. Friedman (Ed.), *On the other hand: New perspectives in American Sign Language.* New York: Academic Press.

Emmorey, K. (2001). Space on hand: The exploitation of signing space to illustrate abstract thought. In M. Gattis (Ed.), *Spatial schemas and abstract thought* (pp. 147–174). Cambridge, MA: MIT Press.

Emmorey, K. (2002). *Language, cognition, and the brain: Insights from sign language research.* Mahwah, NJ: Lawrence Erlbaum.

Emmory, K. (2003). *Perspectives on classifier constructions in sign language.* Mahwah, NJ: Lawrence Erlbaum.

Emmorey, K., & Casey, S. (1995). A comparison of spatial language in English and American Sign Language. *Sign Language Studies, 88*, 255–288.

Emmorey, K., & Herzig, M. (2003). Categorical versus gradient properties of classifier constructions in ASL. In K. Emmorey (Ed.), *Perspectives on classifier constructions in sign languages* (pp. 221–246). Mahwah, NJ: Lawrence Erlbaum.

Emmorey, K., & Reilly, J. S. (1995). Theoretical issues relating language, gesture, and space: An overview. In K. Emmorey & J. Reilly (Eds.), *Language, gesture, and space* (pp. 1–16). Hillsdale, NJ: Lawrence Erlbaum.

Engberg-Pedersen, E. (1993). *Space in Danish Sign Language: The semantices and morphosyntax of the use of space in a visual language.* Hamburg: SIGNUM Press.

Engberg-Pedersen, E. (2003). How composite is a fall? Adults' and children's descriptions of different types of falls in Danish Sign Language. In K. Emmorey (Ed.), *Perspectives on classifier constructions in sign languages* (pp. 311–332). Mahwah, NJ: Lawrence Erlbaum.

Friedman, L. A. (1977). Formational properties of American Sign Language. In L. A. Friedman (Ed.), *On the other hand: New perspectives on American Sign Language* (pp. 13–56). New York: Academic Press.

Gee, J., & Goodhart, W. (1985). Nativization, linguistic theory, and deaf language acquisition. *Sign Language Studies, 49*, 291–342.

Geers, A. E., Moog, J., & Schick, B. (1984). Acquisition of spoken and signed English by profoundly deaf children. *Journal of Speech and Hearing Disorders, 49*, 378–388.

Geers, A. E., Nicholas, J. G., & Sedey, A. (2003). Language skills of children with early cochlear implantation. *Ear and Hearing, 24*, 46–58.

Goldin-Meadow, S. (2003). *Hearing gesture: How our hands help us think.* Cambridge, MA: Belknap Press/Harvard University Press.

Goldin-Meadow, S., & Feldman, H. (1975). The creation of a communication system: A study of deaf children of hearing parents. *Sign Language Studies, 8,* 225–234.

Goldin-Meadow, S., & Mylander, C. (1984). Gestural communication in deaf children: The effects and noneffects of parental input on early language development. *Monographs of the Society for Research in Child Development, 49,* nos. 3–4.

Goldin-Meadow, S., & Mylander, C. (1985). The development of morphology without a conventional language model. *Chicago Linguistic Society, 20,* 119–135.

Goldin-Meadow, S., & Mylander, C. (1990). Beyond the input given: The child's role in the acquisition of language. *Language, 66,* 323–355.

Goldin-Meadow, S., Mylander, C., & Butcher, C. (1995). The resilience of combinatorial structure at the word level: Morphology in self-styled gesture systems. *Cognition, 56,* 195–262.

Johnson, R. E., Liddell, S. K., & Erting, C. J. (1989). *Unlocking the curriculum: Principles for achieving access in deaf education.* Gallaudet Research Institute Working Paper 89-3. Washington, DC: Gallaudet University.

Kantor, R. (1980). The acquisition of classifiers in American Sign Language. *Sign Language Studies, 28,* 193–208.

Kegl, J. (2002). Language emergence in a language-ready brain: Acquisition. In G. Morgan & B. Woll (Eds.), *Directions in sign language acquisition* (pp. 207–254). Amsterdam: John Benjamins.

Kegl, J., & Iwata, G. (1989). *Lenguaje de Signos Necaraguense: A pidgin sheds light on the "creole?" ASL.* Paper presented at the Fourth Annual Meeting of the Pacific Linguistics Conference.

Kegl, J., Senghas, A., & Coppola, M. (1999). Creation through contact: Sign language emergence and sign language change in Nicaragua. In M. DeGraff (Ed.), *Language creation and language change: Creolization, diachrony, and development* (pp. 179–237). Cambridge, MA: MIT Press.

Klima, E., & Bellugi, U. (1979). *The signs of language.* Cambridge, MA: Harvard University Press.

Liddell, S. (2003). *Grammar, gesture, and meaning in American Sign Language.* Cambridge: Cambridge University Press.

Liddell, S., & Metzger, M. (1998). Gesture in sign language discourse. *Journal of Pragmatics, 30,* 657–697.

Lillo-Martin, D. (1988). Children's new sign creations. In M. Strong (Ed.), *Language learning and deafness* (pp. 162–183). Cambridge: Cambridge University Press.

Lillo-Martin, D. (1991). *Universal grammar and American Sign Language.* Dordrecht: Kluwer.

Lillo-Martin, D., Bellugi, U., Struxness, L., & O'Grady, M. (1985). The acquisition of spatially organized syntax. *Papers and Reported on Child Language Development, 24,* 70–80.

Lillo-Martin, D., & Klima, E. S. (1990). Pointing out differences: ASL pronouns in syntactic theory. In S. D. Fischer & P. Siple (Eds.), *Theoretical issues in sign language research* (pp. 191–210). Chicago: University of Chicago Press.

Lindert, R. (2001). *Hearing families with deaf children: Linguistic and communicative aspects of American Sign Language development.* Unpublished doctoral dissertation, University of California, Berkeley.

Livingston, S. (1983). Levels of development in the language of deaf children: ASL grammatical processes, signed English structures, and semantic features. *Sign Language Studies, 40,* 193–285.

Loew, R. (1984). *Roles and references in American Sign Language: A development perspective.* Unpublished doctoral dissertation, University of Minnesota, Minneapolis.

Mandel, M. (1977). Iconic devices in American Sign Language. In L. A. Friedman (Ed.), *On the other hand: New perspectives on American Sign Language* (pp. 57–108). New York: Academic Press.

Meier, R. P. (1982). *Icons, analogues, and morphemes: The acquisition of verb agreement in American Sign Language.* Unpublished doctoral dissertation, University of California, San Diego.

Meier, R. P. (1990). Person deixis in American Sign Language. In S. D. Fischer & P. Siple (Eds.), *Theoretical issues in sign language research* (pp. 175–190). Chicago: University of Chicago Press.

Meier, R. P. (1991). Language acquistion by deaf children. *American Scientist, 79,* 60–70.

Moeller, M. P., & Luetke-Stahlman, B. (1990). Parent's use of Signing Exact English: A descriptive analysis. *Journal of Speech and Hearing Disorders, 55,* 327–338.

Morford, J. (1996). Insights to langauge from the study of gesture: A review of research on the gestural communication of non0signing deaf people. *Language and Communication, 16,* 165–178.

Morford, J., Singleton, J. L., & Goldin-Meadow, S. (1995). The genesis of language: How much time is needed to generate arbitrary symbols in a sign system? In K. Emmorey & J. Reilly (Eds.), *Language, gesture, and space* (pp. 313–332). Hillsdale, NJ: Lawrence Erlbaum.

Morgan, G., & Woll, B. (2002). The development of complex sentences in British Sign Language. In G. Morgan & B. Woll (Eds.), *Directions in sign language acquisition* (pp. 255–275). Amsterdam: John Benjamins.

Newport, E., & Meier, R. (1985). The acquisition of American Sign Language. In D. Slobin (Ed.), *The crosslinguistic study of language acquisition: The data* (Vol. 1, pp. 881–939). Hillside, NJ: Lawrence Erlbaum.

Newport, E., & Supalla, T. (1980). The structuring of language: Clues from the acquisition of signed and spoken language. In U. Bellugi & M. Studdert-Kennedy (Eds.), *Signed and Spoken Language: Biological constraints on linguistic form* (pp. 187–212). Dahlem Konferenzen. Weinheim: Verlag Chemie.

Padden, C. (1986). Verbs and role-shifting in ASL. In C. Padden (Ed.), *Proceedings of the fourth national symposium on sign language research and teaching* (pp. 44–57). Silver Spring, MD: National Association of the Deaf.

Padden, C. (1990). The relation between space and grammar in ASL verb morphology. In C. Lucas (Ed.), *Sign language research: Theoretical issues* (pp. 118–132). Washington, DC: Gallaudet University Press.

Petitto, L. (1987). On the autonomy of language and gesture: Evidence from the acquisition of personal pronouns in American Sign Language. *Cognition, 27*, 1–52.

Schembri, A. (2003). Rethinking "classifiers" in signed languages. In K. Emmorey (Ed.), *Perspectives on classifier constructions in sign language* (pp. 3–34). Mahwah, NJ: Lawrence Erlbaum.

Schick, B. (1990a). Classifier predicates in American Sign Language. *International Journal of Sign Linguistics, 1*(1), 15–40.

Schick, B. (1990b). The effects of morphosyntactic structure on the aquisition of classifier predicates in ASL. In C. Lucas (Ed.), *Sign language research: Theoretical issues* (pp. 358–374). Washington, DC: Gallaudet University Press.

Schick, B. (2003). The development of American Sign Language and manually coded English systems. In M. Marschark & P. Spencer (Eds.), *Oxford handbook of deaf studies, language, and education* (pp. 219–231). New York: Oxford University Press.

Schick, B., & Moeller, M. P. (1992). What is learnable in manually coded English sign systems? *Applied Psycholinguistics, 13*(3), 313–340.

Senghas, A. (1995). *Children's contribution to the birth of Nicaraguan Sign Language*. Unpublished doctoral dissertation, Massachusetts Institute of Technology Cambridge, MA.

Senghas, A., & Coppola, M. (2001). Children creating language: How Nicaraguan Sign Language acquired a spatial grammar. *Psychological Science, 12*, 323–328.

Senghas, A., & Kegl, J. (1994). Social considerations in the emergence of Idioma de Signos Nicaraguense. *Signpost, 7*, 24–32.

Singleton, J. L., Goldin-Meadow, S., & McNeill, D. (1995). The cataclysmic break between gesticulation and sign: Evidence against a unified continuum of gestural communication. In K. Emmorey & J. Reilly (Eds.), *Language, gesture, and space* (pp. 287–311). Hillsdale, NJ: Lawrence Erlbaum.

Slobin, D., Hoiting, N., Kuntze, M., Lindert, R., Weinberg, A., Pyers, J., et al. (2003). A cognitive/functional perspective on the acquisition of "classifiers." In K. Emmorey (Ed.), *Perspectives on classifier constructions in sign language* (pp. 271–296). Mahwah, NJ: Lawrence Erlbaum.

Stack, K. M. (1999). *Innovation by a child acquiring Signing Exact English II*. Unpublished doctoral dissertation, University of California, Los Angeles.

Stokoe, W., Casterline, D., & Croneberg, C. (1965). *A dictionary of American Sign Language on linguistic principles*. Washington, DC: Gallaudet University Press.

Supalla, S. (1991). Manually Coded English: The modality question in signed language development. In P. Siple & S. D. Fischer (Eds.), *Theoretical issues in sign language research* (Vol. 2, pp. 85–109). Chicago: University of Chicago Press.

Supalla, T. (1978). Morphology of verbs of motion and location in American Sign Language. In F. Cacamise (Ed.), *National symposium on sign language research and training* (pp. 27–45). Silver Spring, MD: National Association of the Deaf.

Supalla, T. (1982). *Structure and acquisition of verbs of motion and location in American Sign Language*. Unpublished doctoral dissertation, University of California, San Diego.

Supalla, T. (1986). The classifier system in American Sign Language. In C. Craig (Ed.), *Noun classes and categorization* (pp. 181–214). Philadelphia: John Benjamins.

Supalla, T. (2003). Revisiting visual analogy in ASL classifier predicates. In K. Emmorey (Ed.), *Perspectives on classifier constructions in sign languages* (pp. 249–257). Mahwah, NJ: Lawrence Erlbaum.

Supalla, T., & Webb, R. (1995). The grammar of international sign: A new look at Pidgin languages. In K. Emmorey & J. Reilly (Eds.), *Language, gesture, and space* (pp. 333–352). Hillsdale, NJ: Lawrence Erlbaum.

Suty, K., & Friel-Patti, S. (1982). Looking beyond signed english to describe the language of two deaf children. *Sign Language Studies, 35*, 153–166.

Talmy, L. (2000). *Toward a cognitive semantics: Vol. 1*. Cambridge, MA: MIT Press.

Talmy, L. (2003). The representation of spatial structure in spoken and signed language. In K. Emmorey (Ed.), *Perspectives on classifier constructions in sign language* (pp. 169–195). Mahwah, NJ: Lawrence Erlbaum.

Taub, S. (2001). *Language From the Body: Iconicity and metaphor in American Sign Language*. Cambridge: Cambridge University Press.

Wilbur, R. B. (1987). *American Sign Language: Linguistic and applied dimensions*. Boston: College-Hill Press.

# 6

# Lexical Development of Deaf Children Acquiring Signed Languages

*Diane Anderson*

Over the past few years, most states in the United States have passed laws requiring newborn hearing screenings. With these screenings, many deaf children are now being identified early, typically before 6 months of age, and receiving necessary language intervention services well before their first birthdays. While many of our previous reports on the lexical acquisition of deaf children have focused on case studies and children older than 3 years, we are now in a unique position to more thoroughly evaluate young deaf children's sign language acquisition. In this chapter, I review our current understanding of the acquisition of the lexicon in American Sign Language (ASL) and manually coded English (MCE). Specifically, the acquisition of first signs, negation, and wh-questions are discussed along with vocabulary size and its early development. Where possible, the development of signed languages is considered in light of specific variables such as degree of hearing loss, parental hearing status, and age of initial exposure to a signed language that likely affect sign language acquisition.

## DEAFNESS IN THE UNITED STATES

Deafness is defined as a hearing loss that is so severe that the person, with or without amplification, is limited in processing linguistic information through hearing. Congenital hearing loss occurs in about 1–3 infants per 1,000 born in the United States. According to the American Speech-Language-Hearing Association (2004), more than 30 children will be born deaf in the United States every day. Of these births, only about 5% will be born to deaf parents (referred to as deaf children of deaf parents, DCDP). In these families, deafness presents no unusual communication challenge to the child or family. The deaf child will learn sign language from the parents, acquiring it from birth just as a hearing child might learn English from hearing parents. However, the vast majority of deaf children will be born to parents with normal hearing (referred to as deaf children of hearing parents, DCHP). In these families, hearing loss is a significant barrier to normal linguistic development, and families must make great efforts to develop effective communication between the deaf child and their hearing environment.

Prior to 1999, the average age of identification of significant hearing loss in the United States was 30 months (American Academy of Pediatrics, 1999). Fortunately, the Healthy People 2000 Initiative (Office of Disease Prevention and Health Promotion, 1990) set a goal to reduce the average age of diagnosis of deafness to be no more than 12 months of age by the year 2000. As a result, new legislation has been passed in 42 of the 50 states requiring hearing screenings for all newborns (not simply those at risk). Newborn hearing screening has been critical in the early identification of hearing loss. In New York, for example, the median age of identification has been reported to be 3 months (Dalzell et al., 2000), and in Colorado, the range was from 2.1 to 5 months (Mehl & Thompson, 1999). In many states, hospitals were required to come into compliance with the laws to conduct hearing screenings on all newborns by December 2002 in order to maintain their state funding. Thus, in the past few years, there have been a greater number of deaf children who have been identified early and received amplification and language intervention much earlier than the former 30 month mark.

With these new laws in place for the early diagnosis of hearing loss, the time has arrived for evaluating the early language acquisition in deaf children. Many of our current reports on the language acquisition of deaf children are based on those children who really did not begin to learn language until after 3 years of age, which reflects a very atypical language learning situation. We have now begun to study the language acquisition and language trajectories in children who received language exposure early, including acquisition from birth.

## FACTORS AFFECTING LEXICAL ACQUISITION

A difficulty encountered in studying the language development of children who are deaf is the number of differences that exist among important background variables that are associated with language ability. These factors include parental hearing status (deaf vs. hearing), degree of hearing loss (mild through profound), type of communication (e.g., ASL, MCE, spoken English, cued speech), age of identification of the child's hearing loss, age of language exposure, and whether the child has other conditions that may affect language development. Given the myriad of factors that can contribute to language ability, many of the studies on early language development have been descriptive or have focused only on one variable. In this chapter, I review our knowledge of each of these variables and, to the extent possible, discuss its influence on manual lexical acquisition. Because ASL and MCE are the two signed languages of interest in this chapter, a brief discussion of their properties and differences is provided in the next two sections, followed by a more thorough review of the lexical development within each sign system.

## THE BASICS OF AMERICAN SIGN LANGUAGE

ASL is the visual-gestural language used by the Deaf population in the United States. It is passed down from one generation of American Deaf to the next, and it is an independent linguistic system, not derived from any spoken language. ASL is used by members of the Deaf community for many purposes, including daily communication, poetry and theater events, protest rallies, and education. ASL exhibits both the grammatical complexity and organizational principles common to the spoken languages of the world (Klima & Bellugi, 1979; Poizner, Klima, & Bellugi, 1987). For example, unlike English, ASL is morphologically complex and has been compared in typology to polysynthetic spoken languages (Bellugi & Klima, 1982; see Slobin, chapter 2 this volume). Although the syntactic structure of ASL is subject–verb–object, as is English, it is a pro-drop language similar to Spanish where the subject is not required to be stated explicitly but rather can be indicated through morphological derivations of the verb. As such, verbs often occupy the initial position in a sentence, and verb morphology plays a salient role in the language. In addition to signs produced by the hands, nonmanual movements signaled through the eyes, face, mouth, head, shoulders, or torso also comprise an important part of the grammatical system of ASL (see Reilly, chapter 11 this volume). The use of nonmanual grammatical signals is unique to signed languages and results in a simultaneous layering of linguistic information rather than the sequential linear grammatical production in most spoken languages.

## ENGLISH-LANGUAGE–BASED SIGN SYSTEMS

While ASL is clearly the language of the Deaf population, recall that the vast majority of deaf children (~95%) are born to hearing parents where ASL is not the family's primary language. In fact, for most deaf children, ASL is a language to which they are never exposed when they are young. Rather, many hearing families, faced with complex decisions about their child's communication system, choose alternative language methods, including spoken language, cued speech, or a variety of English-based sign systems generically referred to in this chapter as manually coded English (MCE). These MCE systems include SEE-1 (Seeing Essential English; Anthony, 1972), SEE-2 (Signing Exact English; Gustason, Zawolkow, & Pfetzing, 1973), or signed English (SE; H. Bornstein, 1975). Approximately 75% of schools across the country that educate our deaf children report using some variant of an English-based sign system rather than ASL (American Annals of the Deaf, 2003).

MCE systems were initially invented to teach English to deaf children, and thus, they are based on English vocabulary, bound morphology, and syntax. Most MCE systems have signs for specific English-language–bound morphology such as plural "s" (dogs would be signed DOG + s) and past tense ("went" would be signed GO + sign for "past tense marker"), and some have signs for other prefixes and suffixes such as "-ment" (as in DEVELOP + sign for "-ment") or "-ly" (as in QUICK + sign for "-ly"). The goal of these systems is to provide a visual model of English that is often signed to the children at the same time that the spoken English is produced and spoken to them. Part of the philosophy behind the use of an English-based sign system is that it will allow the deaf child to better master the English language. Children who are exposed to ASL must essentially master written or spoken English as a second language. Children who are exposed to MCE would acquire ASL as a second signed language. Notably, there is considerable controversy about the efficacy of MCE, and there are many researchers and educators who would argue the MCE is not a viable "language" for deaf children (for discussions both for and against the viability of MCE as a natural language for deaf children, see Coryell & Holcomb, 1997; Mitchell, 1982; Strong & Charlson, 1987; Supalla, 1991; Supalla & McKee, 2002).

## LEXICAL ACQUISITION OF ASL

Thirty years of research on sign language has yielded some important knowledge about the acquisition of ASL. Overall, deaf children who acquire ASL from their deaf parents appear similar to their hearing counterparts who learn spoken languages with respect to vocabulary size, content, and onset. The general acquisition profile of manual signs in ASL begins with manual babbling, followed by a one-sign stage, and then multisign combinations (for overviews, see Newport & Meier, 1985; Schick, 2003). During the early acquisition years, children also make errors in the acquisition of ASL with respect to the formational aspects of sign hand shape (Boyes-Braem, 1990; McIntire, 1977; Siedlecki & Bonvillian, 1993, 1997), location (Bonvillian & Siedlecki, 1996; Siedlecki & Bonvillian, 1993), and movement (Bonvillian & Siedlecki, 1998; Siedlecki & Bonvillian, 1993). In the following sections, children's lexical acquisition of ASL is reviewed.

## Vocabulary Size and Trajectory

The Communicative Development Inventory (CDI) for ASL is a standardized parental report checklist for the early expressive language of ASL, based on the MacArthur CDI for English (Fenson et al., 1993). Data from 69 DCDP (deaf children of deaf parents) on the ASL-CDI have found few differences between the acquisition of ASL and that of spoken English (Anderson & Reilly, 2002). While early productive vocabularies (younger than 18 months of age) were larger for the deaf children than those reported for hearing children, by 24 months of age vocabulary size, in terms of median scores and ranges, was comparable for both ASL and English. As with spoken English, vocabulary development increases with age.

Two differences in the lexical acquisition of ASL and English were noted in the norming of the ASL-CDI and require further investigation. First, Anderson and Reilly (2002) found no evidence for a vocabulary burst in the DCDP. Overall, vocabulary growth (observed both in the cross-sectional sample and in children followed longitudinally) was steady and strikingly linear. This contrasted with the vocabulary bursts that have been noted in reports of children learning spoken languages (Bloom, 1974; Dromi, 1987; Goldfield & Reznick, 1990; Reznick & Goldfield, 1992). Second, they noted that while the early lexicons of both deaf and hearing children have a preponderance of nouns, the percentage of predicates is significantly higher among the ASL vocabularies than among the vocabularies of children acquiring spoken English (see Hoiting, chapter 7 this volume). Such a finding may reflect grammatical differences between ASL and English and has been observed in other languages such as Korean (Gopnik & Choi, 1995) and Japanese (Clancy, 1985; Ogura, Yamashita, Murase, & Mahieu, 1999) that share a grammatical organization with ASL.

## First Signs: Onset

Early research suggested that children with deaf parents demonstrated an advantage in the onset of first signs as compared to the onset of first words in hearing children (Bonvillian, Orlansky, & Novak, 1983; Orlansky & Bonvillian, 1984, 1985; Prinz & Prinz, 1979). In these studies, mostly examining hearing children with deaf parents, infants' first recognizable signs occurred around 8 months of age while most hearing children's first spoken words occurred around 12–13 months of age. Findings from a more recent report involving deaf children with deaf parents supported this perspective (Anderson & Reilly, 2002). From 8 to 11 months of age, most children were producing very little meaningful language, although they were all producing some signs. Specifically, the youngest child reported as producing signs was 8 months old, with a vocabulary of two signs (MILK, BATH). Four 10-month-old children were each reported as using two or three signs, all nouns with one iconic verb (CLAP). An 11-month-old child had a vocabulary of 17 signs. This developmental advantage for signs over spoken words suggests that children are cognitively ready for word learning prior to 1 year of age. It would appear, however, that the motor systems that control sign or speech articulators develop differentially, ultimately affecting the expression of lexical knowledge (see Meier, chapter 9 this volume).

It should also be noted that hearing children produce communicative gestures at young ages (Acredolo & Goodwyn, 1988; Petitto, 1988, 1992; Volterra & Caselli, 1985). The average number of communicative gestures for a hearing 8-month-old child is 10 (Fenson et al., 1994). Given that children gesture before they speak, it is quite likely that an early gesture may be seen as a precursor to a sign and even called a sign. However, for hearing children developing speech, a gesture would not be called a word. So, it is quite possible that both hearing and deaf children produce communicative gestures at young ages, but that only deaf children are given credit for having produced a lexical item. Moreover, as several researchers have reported, while deaf children learning ASL may demonstrate an earlier onset in language production, this advantage is not observed by the end of the second year or in future language milestones (Meier & Newport, 1990; Orlansky & Bonvillian, 1985; Prinz & Prinz, 1981).

**First Signs: Content**

Drawing again from the Anderson and Reilly (2002) data, first words and signs are remarkable similar in the ASL and English vocabularies. Table 6.1 displays the list of the first 35 words/signs in ASL and English (English list extracted from Fenson et al., 1994). These results are supported by the work of Bonvillian and his colleagues (Bonvillian & Orlansky, 1984; Folven & Bonvillian, 1991), who studied the early expressive sign language of nine children (eight hearing, one deaf) who were learning ASL from their deaf parents. Data were collected via sign diaries provided by the mothers. The content of the initial 10-item sign vocabularies of their subjects is remarkably similar to the ASL list provided in table 6.1. In fact, the signs that they found to be produced at the highest frequency across their subjects (DADDY, MILK, BALL, BEAR, EAT, MOMMY, SLEEP, BABY, DOG, DRINK, and MORE) are all listed in table 6.1, with the exception of BEAR.

Nouns, especially names for people, animals, and things to eat, far outstrip the number of verbs or predicates in early vocabularies. The significant people, especially mommy and daddy, appear early in both languages. Animal names are also a common theme, but there is a clear reflection of modality: Early lexicons from English include animal sounds

**Table 6-1: First 35 Words or Signs to Emerge in
English or ASL**

| English | ASL |
| --- | --- |
| Daddy | DADDY |
| Mommy | MOMMY |
| Baby | BABY |
| Bye | BYE |
| Ball | BALL |
| No | NO |
| Shoe | SHOE |
| Bottle | MILK |
| Cookie | COOKIE |
| Kitty | CAT |
| Dog | DOG |
| Uh oh | MORE |
| Eye | EAT/FOOD |
| Nose | DRINK |
| Bird | BIRD |
| Cracker | CRACKER |
| Banana | BANANA |
| Juice | DIAPER |
| Hi | GRANDMA |
| Baabaa | RABBIT |
| Moo | CLAP |
| Ouch | FINISH (all done) |
| Woof | COW |
| Yumyum | HAT |
| Balloon | HORSE |
| Book | BOOK |
| Bath | NAME SIGNS (including child's own name) |
| Duck | DUCK |
| Peekaboo | CRY |
| Nite-nite | BATH/WASH |
| Car | FISH |
| Cheese | TREE |
| Vroom | KISS |
| Keys | SLEEP |
| Apple | RAIN |

(English list extracted from Fenson et al., 1994)

(generally used to name the animals), but ASL includes only animal names. In fact, the range of animal names in the early sign vocabulary is somewhat broader than in English, where both the animal name and its sound are learned early, for example, "dog" and "woof," resulting in a semantic overlap among these first words.

Additional common topics are things to eat, greetings, and clothing. An interesting lexically driven difference is names for body parts. Although these appear frequently in English vocabularies, they are not part of the ASL early vocabulary because individual lexical signs for body parts do not exist. They are signaled by points on the signer's body to the appropriate body part.

Although predicates are few in these very early vocabularies, ASL has several more than English. However, many of those that do occur in ASL (e.g., SLEEP, CLAP) have a strong iconic or gestural form, making it difficult to determine if these early signs are gestures or signs. These iconic verbs may well be present in a similar form in the vocabularies of young hearing children as well.

Early vocabularies in ASL and English also include social phrases and routines, such as words or signs for "no," for leave-taking (BYE, "bye-bye"), and for quieting children, "sh!" Perhaps the most salient feature of these vocabularies is the very high degree of similarity in their content, reflecting the shared common functions of early words and the shared interests and concerns of toddlers as well as the shared culture.

## MULTISIGN COMBINATIONS

Early reports have been variable on whether an advantage exists for sign combinations from children acquiring signed languages. Using parental reports, Bonvillian et al. (1983) found that the mean age of for sign combinations was 17 months, with a range from 12.5 to 22 months. They interpreted this as advantaged compared to reports from speaking children who generally combine words at 18–21 months (Gesell & Thompson, 1934; Slobin, 1971). However, more recent reports would indicate that, in fact, no advantage exists and that both hearing and deaf children combine lexical items at about the same age (Anderson & Reilly, 2002).

As others have reported with hearing children (Bates et al., 1994; Fenson et al., 1994), age is not a good predictor of when children begin to combine words, but vocabulary size is. This is true with ASL as well. In the Anderson and Reilly (2002) study, of the 11 children with vocabulary sizes under 50 signs, only two were reported to be combining signs. Those two children had each only produced one exemplar of sign combination (WHERE BLANKET and ME DRINK). For the 14 children with vocabularies ranging between 50 and 110 words, seven were reported to be combining signs while seven were not yet doing so. Notably, all of the examples provided by the parents were two-word combinations such as MOMMY EAT, DADDY WORK, MORE CRACKER, WANT DRINK, and DOLL SLEEP. Beyond a vocabulary size of 115, every child was reported to be combining signs. Moreover, nearly every parent provided at least one exemplar of multisign combinations. When compared to English norms, these data are quite similar (Fenson et al., 1994). In English, when the vocabulary size is less than 100 words, very few children are reported to be combining words regularly. However, once the vocabulary size reaches 101–200 words, approximately 75% of parents report that their child produces multiword utterances with some regularity.

## EARLY LEXICAL CATEGORIES

Table 6.2 summarizes the early lexical categories discussed in this section. Note that table 6.2 provides a best fit between the original data and the corresponding reported ages and vocabulary sizes. Information provided below and in the original reports is more detailed, and the reader is referred to those sources for complete accuracy.

### Wh-Forms

Question signs first emerge around 12 months of age or after vocabulary size reaches 100 items (Anderson & Reilly, 2002). Without exception, the signs WHERE and WHAT are the first to appear; by age 18–21 months (and a vocabulary range of 150–200 signs), virtually every child in our sample has either WHERE or WHAT (or both) in their vocabulary. WHERE and WHAT are followed by WHO, WHICH, and FOR-FOR ("what is it for?") around 24 months and a vocabulary range of 250–300 items. HOW, WHY, and DO-DO ("what are you doing/what does it do?") emerge last around 30–35 months and a vocabulary larger than 350 signs. This sequence has been observed in English-speaking children as well as second language learners of English. In English, "what," "where," and "who" emerge between 22 and 27 months, followed by "why," "how,"

**Table 6-2: Approximate Age and Vocabulary Ranges for the Emergence of Specific Lexical Items**

| Age | Vocabulary Range | Wh-forms | Negatives | Emotion Signs | Cognitive Verbs |
|---|---|---|---|---|---|
| Younger than 18 months | <150 signs | | NO | SLEEP, HUNGRY, THIRSTY | |
| 18–21 months | 150–250 signs | WHERE, WHAT | DON'T-WANT, NONE | CRY | WANT |
| 21–24 months | 250–350 signs | WHO, WHICH, FOR-FOR | DON'T-LIKE, DON'T-KNOW, NOT-YET | SAD, HAPPY, SCARED | LIKE |
| 30–35 months | >350 signs | HOW, WHY, DO-DO | CAN'T, NOT | ANGRY | THINK |

"when," and "which," which are acquired later, around 30 months (Bloom, Merkin, & Wootten, 1982; Fenson et al., 1994).

This pattern of question acquisition has most frequently been explained as resulting from constraints on cognitive development (Ervin-Tripp, 1970; Fahey, 1942; Tyack & Ingram, 1977). That is, words acquired early in the sequence refer to concepts or ideas that are less abstract (e.g., names for things and people) than are words acquired later in the sequence (e.g., manner, causality, and time frame). In addition, linguistic constraints also appear to play a role in the sequence (Bloom et al., 1982). Specifically, more complex wh-forms require more complex, descriptive verbs, whereas simpler wh-forms could easily be used with the copula or simple verb forms such as "go" and "do."

### Emotion Signs

With respect to the development of emotion signs, signs about physical states (e.g., SLEEPY, HUNGRY, THIRSTY) emerge earliest, at around 15 months or within the first 100 signs (Anderson & Reilly, 2002). By 24 months, virtually every child is reported to be producing signs for physical states. These findings are consistent with earlier naturalistic data (Reilly, McIntire, & Bellugi, 1990). In addition, this emergence is comparable to development in English where 50% of the children are reported to be expressing physical states by 23 months. Signs that denote feelings (e.g., SAD, HAPPY, SCARED, ANGRY) are first seen around 18–20 months or when children acquire a vocabulary size of 100–200 signs. CRY usually is the earliest reported emotionally based sign, possibly because of its salient reference for young children. Signs such as SCARED and SAD also occur commonly in the vocabularies of 20 month old children. Of the emotion signs available on the ASL-CDI, ANGRY is the last to emerge around 30 months. This development of signs for emotion also maps nicely onto the development in English, in which by about 24 months, 50% of children are producing words for emotion. In English, "cry" also emerges first (around 22 months), followed by "sad," "happy," and "scared," with "mad" being acquired last around 29 months of age (Fenson et al., 1994).

### Cognitive Verbs

The emergence of three cognitive verbs, WANT, LIKE, and THINK, were examined in detail by Anderson and Reilly (2002). WANT consistently emerged first around 18 months of age or when a child's vocabulary reached 200 signs. LIKE emerged next around 24 months of age or a vocabulary size of 350 signs. THINK was last to emerge between 30 and 36 months with a vocabulary over 450 signs. While almost every older child was producing WANT and LIKE, only about half were producing the sign THINK. Again, the acquisition timeline of these cognitive verbs is consistent with that observed in English. "Wanna" emerges earliest in English (around 23 months) followed by "like" at 25 months, with "think" produced last, beyond the age of 30 months (Fenson et al., 1994).

## Negation

The sign NO is one of the first signs that children produce and represents the earliest form of manual negation (Anderson & Reilly, 1998, 2002). Of 27 children followed longitudinally by Anderson and Reilly who were reported to be producing signs for negation, every one produced NO first. The next signs to be produced consistently are DON'T-WANT and NONE, which were common in the vocabularies of children 18–24 months of age (vocabulary size between 150 and 250 signs). Between 24 and 30 months, when vocabulary sizes consistently ranged between 300 and 400 signs, DON'T-LIKE, DON'T-KNOW, and NOT-YET emerged. The last to appear are the signs CAN'T and NOT, which typically are not seen consistently until children are older than 30 months (and the vocabulary size reaches at least 350 signs). Although there are some individual variations in the acquisition of negation, the developmental sequence is remarkably consistent across samples and children.

## Pronouns

Despite the apparent similarity between prelinguistic pointing gestures and pronominal points in ASL, the acquisition of pronouns does not seem to occur earlier in ASL than in spoken languages (Petitto, 1987; Pizzuto, 1990). Points clearly referring to people emerge around 17–20 months of age. The first pronoun to emerge is ME, followed by YOU around 22–24 months of age. Pronouns for HE/SHE emerge later, often after 24 months. As has been observed with hearing children, deaf children also can make mistakes in pronoun usage including reversal errors. That is, the child will sign YOU when they really mean ME, and they often rely on proper names or other nouns as referents rather than a pronoun (Petitto, 1987).

## ACQUISITION OF MCE

We now turn our focus to the acquisition of a lexicon in MCE. Our knowledge of the specific early linguistic milestones of MCE is far less complete than the knowledge of ASL (which is also quite incomplete). Recall that MCE is primarily used with deaf children born to hearing parents, and until recently, such children were typically not identified as deaf until well after their second birthdays. However, in the past several years, some very important reports have been made available which address the influence of specific demographic variables on MCE acquisition in deaf children under the age of 5.

## VOCABULARY SIZE AND TRAJECTORY

Studies on the early vocabulary development of DCHP (deaf children of hearing parents) have shown considerable variation, but overall, DCHP appear to demonstrate delays when compared with DCDP or their hearing counterparts (Mayne, Yoshinaga-Itano, Sedey, & Carey, 1998; Moeller, 2000; Shafer & Lynch, 1981; for a thorough review, see M. Bornstein, Selmi, Hayes, Painter, & Marx, 1999; Griswold & Commings, 1974; Lederberg & Spencer, 2001). For example, although their sample size of 19 children is relatively small by current standards, Griswold and Commings (1974) used parental diaries to report a median vocabulary of 142 signed or spoken words for children 3–4 years of age and 156 words for children 5–6 years of age. More recently, using a standardized vocabulary checklist, Mayne et al. (1998) reported the average vocabulary size of a group of 113 children 2–3 years old to be 163 signs/words. When compared to hearing children who demonstrate 540 words at 30 months (Fenson et al., 1994), the linguistic delay for these deaf children is apparent.

With respect to vocabulary growth over time, deaf children using MCE have demonstrated vocabulary growth that was less than half of that for hearing children and that a typical 7-year-old deaf child had a vocabulary level comparable to a 4-year-old hearing child (H. Bornstein, Saulnier, & Hamilton, 1980). M. Bornstein et al. (1999) and Lederberg, Prezbindowski, and Spencer (2000), using a variety of standardized tests, confirm that the vocabulary development of DCHP is below that expected for hearing children of the same chronological age. In most cases, as the deaf children become older, their vocabulary deficits become even greater relative to their hearing counterparts.

There are exceptions to the findings of delayed vocabulary acquisition in DCHP. Although these are case studies, Gardner and Zorfass (1983), Howell (1984), and Lindert (2002) report that the DCHP were able to acquire a vocabulary that was typical of hearing children. All authors note that the mother's signing abilities and consistent use of sign language in the home seemed to relate to the child's linguistic success.

### First Signs: Content

Only one study has formally discussed the content of the lexicons of DCHP. Griswold and Commings (1974) studied the lexicons of 19 deaf preschool children who ranged in age from 1 year 9 months to 4 years 6 months. All were of at least average intelligence. The children were enrolled in a total communication program that utilized SE. Time enrolled in the program ranged from 2 months to 1 year 9 months. Fifteen of the children had hearing parents, and four had deaf parents. The authors specifically note that the children with deaf parents were not necessarily the best language performers in terms of overall vocabulary size and that many of the hearing families were rated comparably to the deaf families in terms of the quality of their signing environments. These are important notes because they suggest that the results are not solely due to the inclusion of DCDP with DCHP. Thus, we can have some confidence that the findings truly reflect MCE acquisition and generalizable to the larger DCHP population (within the limits of small sample size).

Griswold and Commings (1974) asked parents to keep diary records of their child's spoken or signed tokens. From these detailed reports, they compiled a composite vocabulary list of words that were used by two or more children. They reported that the proportions of nouns, verbs, types of prepositions, and question words appeared similar between DCHP and other hearing preschoolers. For example, they found that nouns averaged 55% in the expressive vocabularies of the 2-year-old children. Griswold and Commings reported that this percentage fell halfway between estimates provided by Berry (1969) and McCarthy (1954). It is also similar to the findings provided by Bates et al. (1994) for English and Anderson and Reilly (2002) for ASL, which showed that nouns tend to occupy about 50% of the tokens in children's early lexicons (the percentage is higher in smaller vocabulary sizes and levels out as vocabulary size increases). Griswold and Commings found that the proportion of verbs averaged 19%, which is slightly higher than that reported by Bates et al. (1994) for English and slightly lower that that reported by Anderson and Reilly (2002) for ASL. The differences in the proportions of noun and verbs could easily be attributed to sample size, methodological differences (parental diaries vs. standardized forms), or actual linguistic differences between MCE, English, and ASL. Further research is needed, but the initial similarities among these reports are impressive.

To investigate the actual first signs produced in MCE, I created several lists from the data provided by Griswold and Commings (1974). In order to compare these lists to those of English and ASL, I focused only on the 35 words that were produced with the highest frequency by the children. In evaluating early language content, researchers would typically focus on the youngest children to learn what words emerge first. However, for deaf children learning MCE, the amount of time exposed to MCE is also of interest because a 3-year-old child with 6 months of language exposure is also in the early stages of language learning. Her vocabulary acquisition might (or might not) resemble a younger child with a similar amount of language exposure. So, for this review, two lists were created. The first list was extracted from the Griswold and Commings's data and is based on the performance of their six youngest children, who ranged in age from 18 to 36 months. The second list was based on the performance of the six children who had been exposed to MCE for less than 6 months. Although not explicitly stated by the

**Table 6-3: First 35 Words or Signs to Emerge in English, MCE, or ASL**

| English | MCE (Age 18–36 Months) | MCE (First 6 Months of Language Exposure) | ASL |
|---|---|---|---|
| Daddy | DADDY | DADDY | DADDY |
| Mommy | MOMMY | MOMMY | MOMMY |
| Baby | BABY | BABY | BABY |
| Bye | BYE-BYE | BYE-BYE | BYE |
| Ball | BALL | BALL | BALL |
| No | AIRPLANE | AIRPLANE | NO |
| Shoe | SHOE | SHOE | SHOE |
| Bottle | MILK | MILK | MILK |
| Cookie | ICE CREAM | ICE CREAM | COOKIE |
| Kitty | CAT | CAT | CAT |
| Dog | DOG | DOG | DOG |
| Bird | BIRD | BIRD | BIRD |
| Book | BOOK | BOOK | BOOK |
| Bath | BATH | WASH | NAME SIGNS (including child's own name) |
| Uh oh | MORE | MORE | MORE |
| Eye | EAT | EAT | EAT/FOOD |
| Nose | DRINK | DRINK | DRINK |
| Cracker | HOT | HOT | CRACKER |
| Banana | COLD | COLD | BANANA |
| Juice | TREE | TREE | DIAPER |
| Hi | SOCKS | SOCKS | GRANDMA |
| Baabaa | FISH | FISH | FISH |
| Car | CAR | CAR | RABBIT |
| Moo | WHERE | WHERE | CLAP |
| Ouch | FLOWER | FLOWER | FINISH (all-done) |
| Woof | ME | ME | COW |
| Yumyum | THANK YOU | THANK YOU | HAT |
| Balloon | YOU | YOU | HORSE |
| Duck | DUCK | DUCK | DUCK |
| Peekaboo | CRY | SLEEP | CRY |
| Nite-nite | HURT | COME | BATH/WASH |
| Cheese | WATER | WATER | TREE |
| Vroom | TELEPHONE | I | KISS |
| Keys | LOVE | LOVE | SLEEP |
| Apple | RAIN | RAIN | RAIN |

English list extracted from Fenson et al. (1994); MCE list extracted from Griswold and Commings (1974); ASL list from Anderson and Reilly (2002).

authors, these groups do not contain the exact same six children, but some overlap is possible.

In selecting the items that reflected the first signs produced, the criterion for inclusion was that at least 50% of the sample must have produced that item. Table 6.3 displays the list of the first 35 words/signs produced in English, in MCE by age and by time of exposure, and in ASL. In the case of the age-related column for MCE, all signs that were produced by five or six children were included (27 signs); the remaining eight signs were produced by at least 67% of the children (i.e., four of the six children) and reflect only a subset of the signs that were produced by 67% of the children. In the time-exposed column, all of the signs that were produced by four, five, or six children are included (24 signs); the remaining 11 signs were produced by at least 50% of the children and reflect only a subset of the signs that at least 50% of the children produced. Thus, it must be emphasized that not all of the possible signs are included on these lists and that these lists reflect an interpretation made by the author.

With respect to that actual first signs produced by children learning MCE, there is great similarity across the columns in table 6.3. Thus, children learning English, ASL, or MCE appear to learn the same first signs. Most common are names for people, animals, and things to eat, followed by clothing and social phrases.

## EARLY LEXICAL CATEGORIES

Unlike the beginning investigations that have been made in ASL, there have been no formal studies on the emergence of specific lexical categories in MCE. Theoretically, the emergence of particular signs, such as signs for emotional words, negation, or wh-questions, should occur in a pattern similar to that of spoken English. However, no such studies have yet tested this theory. This will be an important area of focus in the future in order to better understand whether deaf children are able to master English via MCE.

## FACTORS AFFECTING LEXICAL ACQUISITION

Several factors seem to significantly affect vocabulary size and overall lexical development in the DCHP population, including age of identification of deafness, age of intervention, parental involvement, and nonverbal intelligence. While these variables may well influence language acquisition in the DCDP population as well, they are suspected to be more influential in the DCHP population where parents are just learning to sign. We turn now to research that addresses the relation between lexical development and these influential factors.

## Age of Diagnosis/Intervention and MCE Vocabulary Size

With the introduction of universal newborn hearing screening programs, several investigators have begun to examine the effects of early identification and intervention on language acquisition. Yoshinaga-Itano, Sedey, Coulter, and Mehl (1998) reported that when cognitive abilities were controlled, children identified with a hearing loss prior to the age of 6 months (and who received appropriate intervention) displayed significantly better receptive and expressive communication and language skills as compared to those children whose hearing losses were identified after 6 months of age. In fact, many of these early-identified children performed within the normal range on global measures of receptive and expressive language, and this finding held true regardless of gender, socioeconomic status, ethnicity, degree of hearing loss, mode of communication, or presence or absence of other disabling conditions. However, it should be noted that, as a group, the median vocabulary scores of these early-identified children fell around the 20th percentile for children with normal hearing at 30 months relative to the normative data presented by Fenson et al. (1994). Similarly, Calderon and Naidu (1998) reported that the age of entry into an intervention program was significantly related to receptive language scores. At 36 months, children who began intervention before 12 months demonstrated receptive scores at or near their chronological age. Children who began interventions between 12 and 24 months showed a 6–12 month receptive language delay, while those who began between 24 and 36 months demonstrated a 12–16 month delay. These findings of the significant benefit of early diagnosis and intervention were important both educationally and politically to help motivate the necessity of newborn hearing screenings and early identification and intervention for deaf children.

In one of the larger and more comprehensive studies to date, Mayne et al. (1998) formally tested the expressive vocabulary development of DCHP between 8 and 37 months. All of the children were enrolled in an early intervention program that delivered approximately 1 hour of services per week. Although not all the children in their study were learning MCE, in many cases the authors provided separate results for those who were primarily educated orally versus those who were learning MCE. Using a modified version of the English CDI (Fenson et al., 1994), they collected signed and spoken vocabulary data and then explored a number of demographic variables related to vocabulary development including age of diagnosis. Mayne et al. (1998) found that children who were identified by 6 months of age and who received prompt intervention demonstrated vocabulary scores that were significantly better than their peers who were identified after 6 months of age. Similar to the Yoshinaga-Itano et al. (1998) report, children with higher cognitive scores and those without additional disabling conditions also demonstrated higher vocabulary scores. When compared to normally developing hearing children, the early-identified deaf children performed well, with on average no more than a 6-month delay in their expressive vocabulary. Many children attained vocabulary scores that were comparable to their hearing peers (but in the lowest quartile), and in general, the children displayed a linear growth pattern indicating steady vocabulary acquisition. For children who were identified after 6 months of age, their expressive vocabulary scores were delayed relative to the early-identified deaf children and to normally developing hearing peers. On average, a 36-month-old deaf child who was identified after 6 months of age demonstrated a vocabulary score similar to a 28-month-old early-identified deaf child and similar to a 24-month-old hearing child. Additionally, the children's vocabulary growth patterns were relatively flat, only accelerating in the final ages tested. Overall, the pattern of their reported scores suggested that a delay in language acquisition increases with a delay in diagnosis. While all the children were clearly acquiring language, the benefit of early identification and intervention of deafness was apparent.

Moeller (2000) also studied the relationship between age of enrollment in intervention services and language measures at 5 years of age. She evaluated 110 DCHP who had bilateral, sensorineural hearing loss and no evidence of major secondary disabilities. All the children attended an early intervention program where they were either exposed to MCE or to spoken English. Her analyses revealed no differences between the children learning MCE and the children learning spoken English only, and she combined the groups for further analyses. The reader is therefore cautioned that Moeller's results about language performance include children who were not learning MCE and thus may reflect performance simply for all DCHP rather than only to those learning MCE. Nonetheless, Moeller found a negative correlation between the age of enrollment in intervention services and vocabulary skills as measured by the Peabody Picture Vocabulary Test. Thus, earlier enrollment in intervention (e.g., before 11 months of age) was associated with significantly better vocabulary skills at age 5. In fact, there was a very systematic decline in vocabulary performance for every 12-month delay in the onset of services.

## Degree of Hearing Loss and MCE Vocabulary Abilities

For decades, differences in the spoken language acquisition and receptive or expressive vocabulary levels based on degree of hearing loss have been reported (Brannon, 1968; Davis, 1974; Davis, Shepard, Stelmachowicz, & Gorga, 1981; Musselman, Wilson, & Lindsay, 1988). Intuitively, such findings make sense: The more difficult it is to hear the language around you, the more difficult it should be to acquire speech. One suspects that degree of hearing loss makes no difference in the acquisition of ASL by deaf children who are learning language from their deaf parents, although this author knows of no studies that have actually tested such a hypothesis. Interestingly, Calderon and Naidu (1998) found that pure tone hearing loss accounted for only 1% of the variance in receptive vocabulary scores beyond the variance explained by the age at which the child began an intervention. However, is there any evidence to suggest that degree of hearing loss influences MCE acquisition given that a primary communicative channel is visual? The findings by Mayne et al. (1998) help to address this question.

To assess the influence of hearing loss on expressive vocabulary, the children in Mayne et al.'s (1998) study were divided into the four categories commonly used in studies of deaf children, based on the degree of their hearing losses: mild (26–40 dB loss), moderate (41–55 dB loss), moderate-severe (56–70 dB loss), and severe-profound (71–>90 dB loss). No differences in expressive vocabulary size were identified based on these categories. However, the authors noted that they used both spoken and signed tokens in their vocabulary scores. Had they only used spoken vocabulary items, differences in expressive vocabulary sizes based on degree of hearing loss might have emerged. Additionally, their findings to do not rule out the possibility that degree of hearing loss may exert its influence at a different threshold. That is, differences might have been observed between children with less than 70 dB loss versus greater than 70 dB loss rather than the artificial four-category system they imposed or by using degree of hearing loss as a continuous variable and correlating it with vocabulary performance.

Moeller (2000) also failed to find a relationship between degree of hearing loss and vocabulary skills at 5 years of age. As with the Mayne et al. (1998) study, children were allowed to respond in either signed or spoken English. If she had only scored spoken vocabulary items, differences in vocabulary skills based on degree of hearing loss might have been observed. Thus, these initial findings converge to suggest that the degree of hearing loss may not be a variable of significance in the early stages of vocabulary acquisition of children learning a signed language. Additional research is needed to better clarify the relationship between degree of hearing loss and language acquisition (especially if it means altering intervention strategies or communication patterns in order to maximize later success).

## Amount of Signing Exposure/Family Involvement and MCE Acquisition

The amount of language input and exposure that a DCHP receives is one of the greatest areas of variability in this population because hearing parents vary a great deal in how well they can sign. When children are first diagnosed and parents decide to use a sign language with their child, the parents must ultimately learn the sign system along with their child. Communication is far from complete or comfortable. However, the parent is the primary source of language for their child, and the primary importance of parental communication remains strong throughout the first 5 years (and beyond). For example, although intervention services vary greatly from state to state, a typical deaf child who is 1–18 months of age might receive 1 hour per week of in-home services from a speech therapist or special education teacher. During that visit, the parent might be taught some new signs or some strategies to communicate with their child. From 18 months through 5 years, a typical deaf child might be enrolled in a school for deaf children. She or he might attend between 6 and 15 hours per week. It is clear that the child must receive other sources of language input beyond the services provided in order to develop communication skills. Unlike hearing children, who can easily pick up language and vocabulary through their communications with other children and adults, television, and the general world around them, the deaf child must be constantly and intentionally exposed to language in order to maximize communication and linguistic growth. In sum, the environment for the deaf child is very different than that for the hearing child, and this difference is magnified for DCHP, who often have very few people with whom they can sign.

Vocabulary development is clearly linked to word use in the child's environment. During early vocabulary development, the rate of vocabulary growth of hearing children is related to the amount of language their mothers use with them (Huttenlocher, Haight, Bryk, Sletzer, & Lyons, 1991). A similar relationship is found for deaf children acquiring signs from their hearing parents. However, the signing ability of hearing parents varies greatly, with many parents (typically mothers) signing only a small percentage of their utterances (Lederberg & Everhart, 1998; Spencer, 1993). Lederberg and Everhart (1998) and Spencer (1993) reported that the number of signs used by hearing mothers predicts the number of signs used by their deaf child. Over time, many parents demonstrate very little growth in the sign language ability such that even after 3 years of MCE exposure, parents do not advance beyond a beginning level of proficiency (H. Bornstein et al., 1980), and this lack of proficiency may well be the primary source of delay in the parent–child communication (Greenberg & Marvin, 1979). Thus, one explanation for the small vocabulary sizes of young deaf children may well be the impoverished signing environment to which they are exposed.

In an effort to better understand parental use of MCE, Moeller and Luetke-Stahlman (1990) studied five parent–child dyads. All parents were hearing and all children were deaf. The children ranged in age from 3 years 6 months to 4 years 9 months. The families had been using SEE-2 for at least 3 years and were involved in a preschool program where signing and speaking simultaneously was encouraged. The authors calculated the mean length of utterance (MLU) for each parent and for their child. In all five cases, the parent's signed MLU was shorter than their spoken MLU. Additionally, the parent's MLU was shorter than that of their child.

Swisher and Thompson (1985), studying six parent–child dyads similar to those described in Moeller and Luetke-Stahlman (1990), reported that the average MLU for the parents in the group was 3.89 morphemes. Thus, parents appeared to confine their communication to grammatically simple, short utterances. The shortness of their utterances may have been due to an underestimation of their child's linguistic ability, the difficulty in signing and speaking simultaneously, or a lack of knowledge of complex signs. In any case, it would appear that much of the language provided by the parent would be considered nonfacilitative because when sentences are short, the quality and quantity of linguistic information available to the child are limited. Unfortunately, the authors did not measure or assess the child's language and relate child performance to parental performance. Additional studies that look at this relationship will be critical to understanding the influence of parental input and child performance.

In the report by Mayne et al. (1998), mode of communication (e.g., does vs. does not use sign language) was used as a variable to predict differences in expressive vocabulary size in deaf children under 37 months of age. Surprisingly, they found no difference in vocabulary size between families that signed and families that did not sign. Two factors likely influence this finding. First, whether or not a family was categorized as a signing family or not was based on a 25-minute videotaped session. If a family member used *any* sign, the family was categorized as "uses signs." This global categorization system resulted in including families who rarely use sign language with those who regularly do so thus possibly obscuring any real effects. Second, this categorization method only looks at the family at one discrete moment in time rather than over a period of time. Thus, a more accurate measure might be a test of a family's proficiency in MCE or a percentage of utterances signed over a given period.

The importance of family involvement on the vocabulary development of DCHP is made clear in the study by Moeller (2000). Using the Peabody Picture Vocabulary Test, she assessed the vocabulary skills of 110 DCHP at age 5. She also rated family involvement on a 5-point scale, with 5 indicating high involvement (e.g., family has made a good adjustment to the child's deafness, family members have become fluent users of the child's mode of communication, extended family members are involved, parents attend school meetings, etc.) to a score of 1 indicating low involvement (e.g., family faces significant life stresses, parent–child communication is limited to very basic needs, participation

is sporadic, family has little understanding of deafness and its consequences for the child). She found that high levels of family involvement
correlated with higher vocabulary scores (as well as higher verbal reasoning abilities as assessed by the Preschool Language Assessment Instrument). In fact, all children, regardless of the age at which they were
enrolled in intervention services, showed at least average vocabulary
scores if their family demonstrated a high level of involvement. In
contrast, low family involvement was correlated with lower vocabulary
scores such that even early enrollment in intervention services was not
sufficient buffer the child's linguistic development. Children who enrolled early but had low family involvement had below average vocabulary scores. Thus, high family involvement appears to be critically
important in the early language development of deaf children born to
hearing parents.

## SUMMARY AND CONCLUSIONS

Progress is being made in the realm of early sign language acquisition
research. With respect to the acquisition of ASL, we have a good beginning understanding of the emergence of first signs, the emergence of
multisign combinations, and the development of early lexical categories.
In general, children acquiring ASL do so in a fashion very similar to their
hearing counterparts. With the exception of productive language onset,
which appears to happen at an earlier age than children acquiring spoken
language, all other linguistic areas seem comparable. Specifically, the
content of their early vocabularies are similar to children learning English,
and the order of acquisition of specific lexical categories also parallels that
seen in English.

In the future, additional studies are needed to answer basic questions about how children acquire ASL and what affects its acquisition.
For example, what variables, such as gender, socioeconomic status, or
birth order, influence early acquisition? With an increase in sample size,
we may be able to finally develop normative data such that it would
be possible to identify children who demonstrate gifted as well as impaired sign language abilities. Eventually, a standardized test is needed
that assesses ASL proficiency such that the skills of young deaf children
can be thoroughly evaluated and assigned a percentile score, and they
can begin receiving intervention services if they are identified as language impaired.

Our knowledge of the early acquisition of MCE is quite incomplete.
At this time, we can only state with marginal confidence that children
who are identified before 6–12 months of age seem to be attain a vocabulary size of MCE that is similar to hearing children acquiring English. As the number of early-identified deaf children increases, we will
be in a better position to more thoroughly evaluate the early language

profiles of this group. Basic studies are needed to chart the acquisition process and delineate how children are learning MCE. Specifically, do the early linguistic milestones of onset of first signs and sign combinations resemble those of their hearing counterparts (or deaf counterparts learning ASL)? Is the content of their early vocabulary similar? Extremely important in this line of research will be attention to the myriad of variables (e.g., age of diagnosis, amount of family involvement, age of intervention, amount of intervention, etc.) that can influence the findings. The heterogeneity of the DCHP population is one of the greatest challenges facing researchers in this field, and yet tackling this challenge and synthesizing the findings stand to be the greatest contributions to this population for long-term educational success.

## REFERENCES

Acredolo, L., & Goodwyn, S. (1988). Symbolic gesturing in language development: A case study. *Human Development, 28,* 40–49.

American Academy of Pediatrics. (1999). Newborn and infant hearing loss: Detection and intervention (RE9846). *Pediatrics, 103,* 527–530.

American Annals of the Deaf. (2003). Educational programs for deaf students. *American Annals of the Deaf, 148,* 75–146.

American Speech-Language-Hearing Association. (1997–2005). Home page. Retrieved (March 10, 2004) from http://www.asha.com.

Anderson, D., & Reilly, J. (1998). The puzzle of negation: How children move from communicative to grammatical negation in ASL. *Applied Psycholinguistics, 18,* 411–429.

Anderson, D., & Reilly, J. S. (2002). The MacArthur Communicative Development Inventory: Normative data for American Sign Language. *Journal of Deaf Studies and Deaf Education, 7,* 83–106.

Anthony, D. A. (Ed.). (1972). *Seeing Essential English* (2 vols.). Anaheim, CA: Educational Services Division, Anaheim Union High School District.

Bates, E., Marchman, V., Thal, D., Fenson, L., Dale, P., Reznick, S., Reilly, J., & Hartung, J. (1994). Developmental and stylistic variation in the composition of early vocabulary. *Journal of Child Language, 21,* 85–123.

Bellugi, U., & Klima, E. (1982). The acquisition of three morphological systems in American Sign Language. *Papers and Reports on Child Language Development, 21,* 135.

Berry, M. (1969). *Language disorders of children: The bases and diagnoses.* New York: Appleton-Century-Crofts.

Bloom, L. (1974). Talking, understanding, and thinking: Developmental relationships between receptive and expressive language. In R. L. Schiefelbusch & L. L. Lloyd (Eds.), *Language perspectives: Acquisition, retardation and intervention* (pp. 285–311). Baltimore, MD: University Park Press.

Bloom, L., Merkin, S., & Wootten, J. (1982). Wh-questions: Linguistic factors that contribute to the sequence of acquisition. *Child Development, 53,* 1084–1092.

Bonvillian, J., & Orlansky, M. (1984). The role of iconicity in early sign language acquisition. *Journal of Hearing and Speech Disorders, 49,* 287–292.

Bonvillian, J. D., Orlansky, M. D., & Novak, L. L. (1983). Developmental Milestones: Sign language acquisition and motor development. *Child Development, 54,* 1435–1445.

Bonvillian, J. D., & Siedlecki, T. (1996). Young children's acquisition of the location aspect of American Sign Language: Parental report findings. *Journal of Communication Disorders, 29,* 13–35.

Bonvillian, J. D., & Siedlecki, T. (1998). Young children's acquisition of the movement aspect in American Sign Language: Parental report findings. *Journal of Speech, Language and Hearing Research, 41,* 588–602.

Bornstein, H. (1975). *The Signed English dictionary for preschool and elementary levels.* Washington, DC: Gallaudet College Press.

Bornstein, H., Saulnier, K., & Hamilton, L. (1980). Signed English: A first evaluation. *American Annals of the Deaf, 125,* 467–481.

Bornstein, M., Selmi, A., Hayes, O., Painter, K., & Marx, E. (1999). Representational abilities and the hearing status of child/mother dyads. *Child Development, 70,* 833–852.

Boyes-Braem, P. (1990). Acquisition of the handshape in American Sign Language: A preliminary analysis. In V. Volterra & C. Erting (Eds.), *From gesture to language in hearing and deaf children* (pp. 107–127). Heidelberg: Springer-Verlag.

Brannon, J. B., Jr. (1968). Linguistic word classes in the spoken language of normal, hard of hearing and deaf children. *Journal of Speech and Hearing Research, 11,* 279–287.

Calderon, R., & Naidu, S. (1998). Further support for the benefits of early identification and intervention for children with hearing loss. *The Volta Review* 100(5), 53–84.

Clancy, P. M. (1985). The acquisition if Japanese. In D. I. Slobin (Ed.), *The crosslinguistic study of language acquisition* (Vol. 1). Hillsdale, NJ: Lawrence Erlbaum.

Coryell, J., & Holcomb, T. (1997). The use of sign language and sign systems in facilitating the language acquisition and communication of deaf students. *Language, Speech, and Hearing Services in Schools, 28,* 384–394.

Dalzell, L., Orlando, M., MacDonald, M., Berg, A., Cacace, A., Campbell. D., et al. (2000). The New York State universal newborn hearing screening demonstration project: Ages of hearing loss identification, hearing aid fitting, and enrollment in early intervention. *Ear Hear, 21*(2), 118–130.

Davis, J. (1974). Performance of young hearing-impaired children on a test of basic concepts. *Journal of Speech and Hearing Research, 17,* 342–351.

Davis, J. M., Shepard, N. T., Stelmachowicz, P. G., & Gorga, M. P. (1981). Characteristics of hearing-impaired children in public schools: Part II. Psycho-educational data. *Journal of Speech and Hearing Disorders, 46,* 130–137.

Dromi, E. (1987). *Early lexical development.* New York: Cambridge University Press.

Ervin-Tripp, S. (1970). Discourse agreement: How children answer questions. In J. R. Hayes (Ed.), *Cognition and the development of language* (pp. 79–107). New York: Wiley

Fahey, G. (1942). The questioning activity of children. *Journal of Genetic Psychology, 60,* 337–357.

Fenson, L., Dale, P., Reznick, E., Thal, D., Bates, E., Hartung, J., et al. (1993). *The MacArthur Communicative Development Inventories: User's Guide and Technical Manual*. San Diego: Singular Publishing Group.

Fenson, L., Dale, P., Reznick, E., Thal, D., Bates, E., & Pethick, S. (1994). Variability in early communicative development. *Monographs of the Society for Research in Child Development, 59*(5), 1–189.

Folven, R., & Bonvillian, J. (1991). The transition from nonreferential to referential language in children acquiring American Sign Language. *Develomental Psychology, 27*, 806–816.

Gardner, J., & Zorfass, J. (1983). From sign to speech: The language development of a hearing-impaired child. *American Annals of the Deaf, 128*, 20–24.

Gesell, A., & Thompson, H. (1934). *Infant behavior: Its genesis and growth*. New York: McGraw-Hill.

Goldfield, R., & Reznick, S. (1990). Early lexical acquisition: Rate, content, and vocabulary spurt. *Journal of Child Language, 17*, 171–183.

Gopnik, A., & Choi, S. (1995). Names, relational words, and cognitive development in English and Korean speakers: Nouns are not always learned before verbs. In M. Tomasello & W. Merrimen (Eds.), *Beyond names for things: Young children's acquisition of verbs* (pp. 63–80). Hillsdale, NJ: Lawrence Erlbaum.

Greenberg, M. T., & Marvin, R. S. (1979). Attachment patterns in profoundly deaf preschool children. *Merrill*-Palmer Quarterly, 25(4), 265–279.

Griswold, L., & Commings, J. (1974). The expressive vocabulary of preschool deaf children. *American Annals of the Deaf, 119*, 16–29.

Gustason, G., Zawolkow, E., & Pfetzing, C. (1973). *Signing Exact English*. Los Alamitos, CA: Modern Sign.

Howell, R. (1984). Maternal reports of vocabulary development in four-year-old deaf children. *American Annals of the Deaf, 129*, 459–465.

Huttenlocher, J., Haight, W., Bryk, A., Sletzer, M., & Lyons, T. (1991). Early vocabulary growth: Relation to input and gender. *Developmental Psychology, 27*, 236–248.

Klima, E., & Bellugi, U. (1979). *The signs of language*. Cambridge, MA: Harvard University Press.

Lederberg, A., & Everhart, V. (1998). Communication between deaf children and their hearing mothers: The role of language, gesture, and vocalization. *Journal of Speech, Language and Hearing Research, 41*, 887–899.

Lederberg, A., Prezbindowski, A., & Spencer, P. (2000). Word learning skills of deaf preschoolers: The development of novel mapping and rapid word learning strategies. *Child Development, 71*, 1571–1585.

Lederberg, A., & Spencer, P. (2001). Vocabulary development of deaf and hard of hearing children. In M. Clark, M. Marschark, & M. Karchmer (Eds.), *Context, cognition and deafness* (pp. 88–112). Washington, DC: Gallaudet University Press.

Lindert, R. (2002). Hearing families with deaf children: Linguistic and communicative aspects of American Sign Language development. *Dissertation Abstracts International, 63*, 1066-B.

Mayne, A., Yoshinaga-Itano, C., Sedey, A., & Carey, S. (1998). Expressive vocabulary development of infants and toddlers who are deaf or hard of hearing. *The Volta Review, 100*, 1–28.

McCarthy, D. (1954). Language development in children. In L. Carmichael (Ed.), *Manual of child psychology* (pp. 492–630). New York: John Wiley & Sons.

McIntire, M. (1977). The acquisition of American Sign Language hand configurations. *Sign Language Studies, 16,* 247–266.

Mehl, A. L., & Thompson, V. (1999). The Colorado Newborn Hearing Screening Project, 1992–1999: On the threshold of effective population-based universal newborn hearing screening. *Pediatrics, 109,* e7.

Meier, R. P., & Newport, E. L. (1990). Out of the hands of babes: On a possible sign advantage in language acquisition. *Language, 66,* 1–23.

Mitchell, G. (1982). Can deaf children acquire English? An evaluation of manually coded English systems in terms of the principles of language acquisition. *American Annals of the Deaf, 127,* 331–336.

Moeller, M. (2000). Early intervention and language development in children who are deaf and hard of hearing. *Pediatrics, 106,* e43.

Moeller, M., & Luetke-Stahlman, B. (1990). Parent's use of Signing Exact English: A descriptive analysis. *Journal of Speech and Hearing Disorders, 55,* 327–338.

Musselman, C. R., Wilson, A. K., & Lindsay, P. H. (1988). Effects of early intervention on hearing impaired children. *Exceptional Children, 55,* 222–228.

Newport, E. L., & Meier, R. (1985). The acquisition of American Sign Language. In D. Slobin (Ed.), *The crosslinguistic study of language acquisition: Vol. 1. The data* (pp. 881–939). Hillside, NJ: Lawrence Erlbaum.

Office of Disease Prevention and Health Promotion. (1990). *Healthy People 2000* (DHHS Publication No. 017-001-00473-1). Washington. DC: U.S. Government Printing Office.

Ogura, T., Yamashita, Y., Murase, T., & Mahieu, A. (1999, July). *Acquisition of nouns and verbs in Japanese children.* Paper presented at the International Congress for the Study of Child Language, San Sebastian, Spain.

Orlansky, M., & Bonvillian, J. (1984). The role of iconicity in early sign language acquisition. *Journal of Speech and Hearing Disorders, 49,* 287–292.

Orlansky, M., & Bonvillian, J. (1985). Sign language acquisition: Language development in children of deaf parents and implications for other populations. *Merrill-Palmer Quarterly, 31,* 127–143.

Petitto, L. (1987). On the autonomy of language and gestures: Evidence from the acquisition of personal pronouns in American Sign Language. *Cognition, 27,* 1–52.

Petitto, L. (1988). "Language" in the prelinguistic child. In Frank S. Kessel (Ed.), *The development of language and language researchers: Essays in honor of Roger Brown* (pp. 187–221). Hillsdale, NJ: Lawrence Erlbaum.

Petitto, L. (1992). Modularity and constraints in early lexical acquisition: Evidence form children's early language and gesture. In M. R. Gunner & M. Maratsos (Eds.), *Modularity and constraints in language and cognition* (pp. 25–58). Hillsdale, NJ: Lawrence Erlbaum.

Pizzuto, E. (1990). The early development of deixis in American Sign Language: What is the point? In V. Volterra & C. J. Erting (Eds.), *From gesture to language in hearing and deaf children* (pp. 142–161). New York: Springer-Verlag.

Poizner, H., Klima, E., & Bellugi, U. (1987). *What the hands reveal about the brain.* Cambridge, MA: MIT Press.

Prinz, P. M., & Prinz, E. A. (1979). Simultaneous acquisition of ASL and spoken English (In a hearing child of a deaf mother and a hearing father). Phase I: Early lexical development. *Sign Language Studies, 25,* 283–296.

Prinz, P., & Prinz, E. (1981). Acquisition of ASL and spoken English by a hearing child of a deaf mother and a hearing father. Phase II: Early combinatorial patterns. *Sign Language Studies, 30,* 78–88.

Reilly, J. S., McIntire, M., & Bellugi, U. (1990). Faces: The relationship between language and affect. In V. Volterra & C. Erting (Eds.), *From gesture to language in hearing and deaf children* (pp. 9–30). New York: Springer-Verlag.

Reznick, S., & Goldfield, L. (1992). Rapid change in lexical development in comphension and production. *Developmental Psychology, 28,* 406–413.

Schick, B. (2003). The development of American Sign Language and manually coded English systems. In M. Marschark & P. Spencer (Eds.), *Oxford handbook of deaf studies, language, and education* (pp. 219–231). New York: Oxford University Press.

Shafer, D., & Lynch, J. (1981). Emergent language of six prelingually deaf children. *Journal of the British Association of Teachers of the Deaf, 5,* 94–111.

Siedlecki, T., & Bonvillian, J. (1993). Location, handshape & movement: Young children's acquisition of the formational aspects of American Sign Language. *Sign Language Studies, 78,* 31–52.

Siedlecki, T., & Bonvillian, J. (1997). Young children's acquisition of the handshape aspect of American Sign Language signs: Parental report findings. *Applied Psycholinguistics, 18,* 17–39.

Slobin, D. (1971). *Psycholinguistics.* Glenview, IL: Scott, Foresmann.

Spencer, P. (1993). The expressive communication of hearing mothers and deaf infants. *American Annals of the Deaf, 138,* 275–283.

Strong, M., & Charlson, E. (1987). Simultaneous communication: Are teachers attempting an impossible task? *American Annals of the Deaf, 132,* 376–382.

Supalla, S. (1991). Manually coded English: The modality question in signed language development. In P. Siple & S. Fischer (Eds.), *Theoretical issues in sign language research* (pp. 85–109). Chicago: University of Chicago Press.

Supalla, S., & McKee, C. (2002). The role of manually coded English in language development of deaf children. In R. Meier, K. Cormier, & D. Quinto-Pozos (Eds.), *Modality and structure in signed and spoken languages* (pp. 143–165). Cambridge University Press: New York.

Swisher, V. M., & Thompson, M. (1985). Mothers learning simultaneous communication: The dimensions of the task. *American Annals of the Deaf, 130*(3), 212–217.

Tyack, D., & Ingram, D. (1977). Children's production and comprehension of questions. *Journal of Psycholinguistic Research, 8*(4), 333–341.

Volterra, V., & Caselli, C. (1985). From gestures and vocalizations to signs and words. In W. Stokoe & V. Volterra (Eds.), *Sign language research '83* (pp. 263–277). Silver Spring, MD: Linstock.

Yoshinaga-Itano, C., Sedey, A. L., Coulter, D. K., & Mehl, A. L. (1998). The language of early- and later-identified children with hearing loss. *Pediatrics, 102,* 1161–1171.

# 7

# Deaf Children Are Verb Attenders: Early Sign Vocabulary Development in Dutch Toddlers

*Nini Hoiting*

## MEASURING SIGN VOCABULARY

As we say in Dutch, *meten is weten* ("measuring is knowing"). This is a twentieth-century claim that might well be true for physical objects and events but is certainly less sure for living systems such as languages and their users. In that respect, the MacArthur Communicative Development Inventory (MCDI) has proven itself to be a useful tool for assessing early vocabulary growth in many spoken languages (Fenson et al., 1993, 1994); however, it needs to be refined for use with children learning a sign language. In this chapter I explain how the MCDI has been adapted for use in Sign Language of the Netherlands (SLN), with applications to the diagnostic process as well as the selection and categorization of lexical items in research. In the process of applying this instrument of early language assessment, it became clear that important theoretical issues were involved. The age of detection of deafness, ranging from 6 to 30 months, indicates later onset of learning compared with samples of hearing children learning spoken languages. In addition, deaf babies with hearing parents seem to be exposed to "imperfect input" from parents who are themselves early second-language learners of SLN. This later onset of language learning is indeed revealed in vocabulary size and rate of growth—but not to the extent one would expect.

In interpreting the data, one is confronted with categories that divide nouns and verbs, but are these traditional linguistic categorizations for words of spoken languages comparable to lexical categories of a sign language? I will illustrate how these issues add new dimensions to what may be called the "noun–verb controversy" in child language research. The growth curves of the sign vocabularies from a sample of 30 Dutch deaf children—of both Deaf and hearing parents, in the age range of 16–36 months—clearly demonstrate that sign acquisition, as assessed by the MCDI, is qualitatively and quantitatively different from patterns of acquisition of spoken languages by hearing children. As I will argue, these differences are not simply due to later onset and diminished language exposure; rather, they reflect deep-seated differences in language *typology*. Using the MCDI for the purpose of sign assessment is clearly an important tool for discovering many aspects of acquisition, as has proven to be the case for spoken languages; in addition, the tool proves to be useful in comparative linguistic analysis.

## DATA COLLECTION

The data presented here were collected within the procedures of the Family Support Program introduced in 1989 at the Royal Institute of the Deaf "H. D. Guyot" in Haren, in the northeast part of the Netherlands. This program provides weekly preschool experience for young deaf children, parental meetings along with social services, a testing program for psychological development, and five years of sign languages courses for parents—initially in their homes and subsequently at the institute. The institute's starting program for language development combined three goals: to design diagnostic instruments for evaluating language development of deaf toddlers, to set up an intervention model for deaf and hearing parents, and to conduct research in the field of sign language acquisition. These goals were combined in a program of twice-yearly visits to family homes for gathering as well as providing information, videotaping family interaction, discussing parental reports of vocabulary development, and reviewing the child's performance. The videotapes were analyzed for communicative patterns in the family and grammatical complexity of both child and parental signing; at the same time, the parental checklists of vocabulary growth were analyzed and summarized in quantitative and qualitative form. All of these types of information, including social reports and psychological test results, serve as input for a final linguistic diagnostic report on each child at age 36 months, when the child enters a special education school in Holland. These data are part of a larger set of data collected, including children in the United States. A selection of all the data gained from these reports was used in an investigation supported by the National Science Foundation entitled "Can a Deaf Child Learn to Sign From Hearing Parents?" (Slobin & Hoiting, 2002). A summary of the data of this research project, carried out at the University of California, Berkeley, is shown in table 7.1.

**Table 7-1: Research Sample**

| Language | Parents | Age Range | N |
|----------|---------|-----------|---|
| SLN | Deaf | 1;3–3;0 | 4 |
| SLN | Hearing | 1;4–3;0 | 13 |
| SSD | Hearing | 1;5–3;0 | 13 |

## Participants

The sample of 30 children (see Table 7.1), selected from a diagnostic pool of about 350 children, includes deaf children with both Deaf and hearing parents. In the Netherlands we have been able to compare children learning two different kinds of manual communication systems: a natural sign language, SLN, and an artificial sign system, Sign Supported Dutch (SSD). SSD was originally designed for educational purposes in the early eighteenth century in Holland by the founder of the institute, Henri Daniel Guyot, where the system was known as the "mixed method," later referred to as the "Old Dutch Method." After the formal introduction of bilingual education in 1995, SSD has no longer been used in programs of early language training, but the rise of the use of cochlear implantation has brought SSD back into attention.[1] In the last part of the analysis provided here, the results of the SSD group are compared with the data of both SLN groups.

## The Input Languages: SLN and SSD

SLN was the natural language of the Dutch Deaf, dating back to 1790, when Guyot started to teach deaf children in the north of Holland (for a history of deaf education in the Netherlands, see Hoiting, 1983; Hoiting, Menke, & Kuik, 1990). At that time, in the period of the Enlightenment, sign languages were a topic of intense discussion and debate. In 1784, the famous religious Zurich Convention favored *La Méthode des Signes,* as presented by the French Abbé de l'Epée, in preference to the Oral Method, presented by the German pastor Samuel Heinicke, as a linguistic tool to introduce the deaf to the Bible. Guyot, a student of de l'Epée, favored the bilingual approach *avant la lettre,* and indeed, deaf teachers were part of the educational system back then. Guyot and his colleagues pragmatically designed the "mixed method" as a language tool for those who were able to speak, possibly hard of hearing, in times when audiologists did not yet exist. Central to his language teaching method was a pragmatic approach not to bother pupils with visualized

---

[1] Deaf schools in Holland require a loss of 90 dB or more for selecting a child for deaf education, whereas a child with a loss less than 90 dB would be selected for a school for hard-of-hearing children, provided there are no additional handicaps at the time.

Dutch grammar. Instead, early educators used SLN to explain spoken and written Dutch, so as not to *lose pupils in the translation*. This "Old Dutch Method" as a teaching model underlies the present-day SSD as a flexible system following Dutch word order and a borrowed SLN lexicon, primarily adding fingerspelling for Dutch grammar excursions and proper names. SLN itself went underground—unfortunately—from the middle of the eighteenth century until the 1970s. On the basis of research on SLN, we know that the language is strongly related to Old French Sign Language, and—like all sign languages—functions as a living, natural language, displaying semantic and grammatical complexity and organizational principles of its own.

SLN made its public comeback around 1980. Because it became evident that SSD was failing for natural discourse and language learning, bilingual education was formally reintroduced in 1995, and from then on SLN flourished in the schools, fed by intense SLN training for hearing parents and teachers, including the contributions of many Deaf teachers. In this growing bilingual context, the demand for teaching and testing materials—in particular, for assessment of the language acquisition of young deaf children—led to endeavors to develop an SLN version of the MCDI. This task became a true linguistic journey of discovery, as I describe below.

## ADAPTATION OF THE MCDI FOR SLN

The MCDI is a standardized parental report tool that has been successfully used in the study of vocabulary development in a number of languages (Caselli et al., 1995; Fenson et al., 1993, 1994). The format is a systematic checklist of vocabulary items that can be used by a parent to indicate forms used by the child, including preverbal communication and symbolic skills, lexical items, morphology, and syntax. Anderson (chapter 6 this volume) discusses an American Sign Language (ASL) adaptation of the MCDI.

In order to modify the MCDI for use as a diagnostic tool in SLN, a list of possible words was developed. An initial list of 250 glosses, serving as a preliminary inventory, was based on three sources: (1) the *Groninger Gebaren Woordenboek* (Groningen Sign Dictionary, 1979), (2) a collection of preschool signs and expressions collected by Deaf and hearing preschool teachers, and (3) signs and communicative gestures used in sign language courses for parents. This list was then compared to the Kohnstamm list of frequent Dutch words in the vocabularies of hearing preschool children (Kohnstamm, Schaerlaekens, Vries, de Akkerhuis, & Frooninncksx, 1981). The resulting inventory provided a useful preparation for the first MCDI version, which I designed in 1990 and adapted in 1991, adding topic groupings and additional sections for the use of voice/sound and the use of hand configurations. The current inventory is shown in the appendix to this chapter. Unlike the early ASL version of Reilly (1992), the Dutch MCDI did not contain written questions for parents concerning their child's grammatical constructions, since the Dutch parents were personally interviewed. The interviews made it possible to maintain the section on comprehension in the original ASL-MCDI adaptation, later excluded for practical reasons in research on ASL vocabulary acquisition with a larger population of deaf children of Deaf parents (Anderson & Reilly, 2002). The parental answers concerning the child's productivity were recorded by the clinician and compared to analyses of the video materials in home and preschool settings, as well as to the parent's checklists. For clinical purposes, the division of the English MCDI into separate infant and toddler versions was kept in the Dutch sign language variant, but without mentioning particular age-related factors. The second SLN list applies only to advanced signers and can be used when it is clear that a particular child can manage basic signing. The initial version consists of 150 lexical items in 20 conceptual categories, and the advanced version contains 560 lexical items in 23 additional conceptual categories. The starter's version of the SLN-MCDI does not contain the category of "connecting signs" or "helping signs" that are included in the ASL version. This starter's list is currently being used for all incoming deaf children, with hearing or deaf parents. The advanced version contains the starter categories but with additional words; for example, the category "toys" is expanded to include "vacation" and "play," and the category "family" is expanded to include "pronouns" and "professions." Both versions contain a category of idiomatic expressions in SLN, with some signs reflecting particular Deaf culture and experiences. Signs that Anderson and Reilly (2002) label in the ASL version as having "virtually the same form" (p. 86), such as EAT and FOOD, SIT, and CHAIR, are kept as separate signs in the SLN version, precisely because SLN acquisition shows considerable changes in the verbal forms between the ages of 2 and 3 years, for deaf children with deaf or hearing parents, provided they receive SLN language models. In addition, in both SLN-MCDI versions, the comprehension/production distinction was kept for all lexical items in the parental forms. Because of this, it was possible to keep the category "body parts," because it turned out that comprehension of this particular category often appeared early, and some of these signs were produced like the actual SLN signs for body parts of people or animals. To summarize, the ASL and the SLN versions of the MCDI differ on the following dimensions:

- Administration of the SLN-MCDI to Deaf and hearing parents via personal contact
- The use of two lists in SLN: a "starter's" version and an "advanced" version

- Preservation of the comprehension/production distinction in the SLN adaptation
- Replacing the written "grammar" questions of the ASL version by personal interview of the parents in the SLN version on sign production, supported by video analysis
- Addition of questions about handshape configuration in the starter's list
- Addition of questions concerning the use of sound, speech, or mouthing in the starter's list
- Addition of an advanced list of 560 lexical items in 23 semantic categories
- Deletion of the category of "early understanding" in the advanced list

## CRITERIA FOR SIGN COMPREHENSION AND PRODUCTION

For hearing parents—generally learning sign language at the same time as their child—it is not an easy job to recognize the child's phonologically "incorrect" signing as conventional signs. For the SLN-MCDI, parents are asked to fill the circles for comprehension only if their child responded at least three times in different contexts to the signing of a parent by responding to a question or request, following an instruction, or acting with or on objects. For the child's sign production, again the parent had to be sure of having observed the same gesture or sign at least three times on different occasions with a stable referent—with or without pointing— and a stable but not necessarily correct phonological form. Distinctions as to whether a production appeared to be an action, a gesture, or a sign were not part of the parental task. This criterion for observational frequency may seem to be fairly strict, but it helped the parent to be alert and to distinguish between productive and purely imitated forms.

## CATEGORIZATION OF LEXICAL ITEMS

Categorization of lexical items in many spoken languages is often a battlefield of acquisitional linguistics. An early noun dominance has been claimed for spoken languages by Gentner (1982), whereas Merriman and Tomasello (1995) and others hypothesize that early language use centralizes the role of verbs. A mini literature has sprung up in this debate, presenting evidence for both noun and verb dominance, depending on language and methodology (see, e.g., Choi, 1998; Choi & Gopnik, 1995; Gelman & Tardif, 1997; Tardif, 1996; Tardif, Shatz, & Naigles, 1997).

In applying traditional form classes such noun, verb, adverb, and the like to sign languages, one is faced with several challenges. For many conceptual categories, nouns and verb forms use the same handshape but differ in movement patterns. The noun form is restricted in movement and comes to a noticeable stop, whereas the verb form shows a continuous sweeping movement. The noun/verb distinction appeared to be difficult to distinguish for hearing parents, but also for Deaf parents, who struggled, for example, with the minimal perceptual distinctions between such items as "to comb" and "a comb." Such pairs might differ in SLN in repetition of hand movement versus a hold or direction; sometimes just a minimal change in orientation occurs.

Another challenging issue was posed by the special verbal construction type in sign languages, traditionally known as "classifiers," here referred to as "polycomponential verbs" (following Slobin et al., 2003). In this type of construction, meaning elements cooccur neatly packed into what seem to be single units with compositional structure. Contrary to earlier research claims, some of these forms do appear early in signing children, and again, these early constructions seem to be best looked upon as verbs with incorporated information about nominal arguments. In example 7.1, the child is simultaneously providing information about an object—a balloon—and its movement (Slobin et al., 2003, p. 283). (For the sake of the reader, a reduced transcription is presented; the interested reader can find an elaborated analysis in Slobin and Hoiting et al. 2003)

(7.1) *Situation*: child describes hot-air balloon seen on earlier occasion.

*Utterance*: two curved vertical 5-hands, palms facing, arms extended wide and drifting about, puffed mouth and pursed lips

*Translation*: "A very big balloon (was) floating about in the air."

*(Reduced) Transcription*: (float)—spherical object(2H)—wander-(movement)—augmented modification

## INPUT FACTORS

The data presented here must be considered in the light of Dutch practices with regard to deaf infants. With regard to age of detection, note that the time window of the children in the Dutch sample is small: 14–36 months of age. Age of detection for children of hearing parents is within this time frame in the Netherlands. Second, we used computations based on both chronological age and exposure age, the latter varying with the age of detection of deafness. And last but not least, the hearing parents of these children are divided into two different "input groups" (SSD and SLN), whereas the deaf children of deaf parents form a group apart (native SLN input), allowing for three-way comparisons:

- Children of SLN-using Deaf parents (SLN-D), who shared their SLN as a native language with their deaf child

- Children of SLN-using hearing parents (SLN-H) who were taught SLN, rather than speech-driven sign systems, and consequently provided their child with SLN
- Children of SSD-using hearing parents (SSD-H), who were taught a speech-driven sign system, offering their child speech and sign simultaneously

The quality of SLN input provided by the hearing parents does not equal that of native SLN-using parents. Due to age of detection and consequent delayed input of a perceivable language for deaf children of hearing parents, many authors have suggested that deaf children have impoverished language exposure. In reality, hearing parents may be only months ahead of their child's sign language skills. However, in this respect it is important to stress that it is not necessarily the case that all deaf parents can provide fully native sign language input language to their children. Many deaf adults were themselves raised by hearing parents and were surrounded by many hearing people who cannot sign well. In addition, as Maxwell, Bernstein, and Mear (1991) have pointed out with regard to ASL, "the sign language used in the United States is not a single homogeneous language code" and "it is worthwhile to open our minds and direct our attention to the varieties of sign language and the combinations of speech and sign modes that we can see around us" (p. 190). According to Anderson and Reilly (2002, p. 86), we should define all hearing parents as late learners of a sign language *simply because* they are hearing. However, in an earlier study of sign complexity in the Dutch 2–3-year-olds (Hoiting & Slobin, 2002), the deaf children with hearing parents who were learning SLN were not delayed as much in their language development as the deaf children with hearing parents who were learning SSD. Thus, the parental group exposing their children to SSD was closer to the label of "impoverished input," since none of the SSD children or their parents showed early growth in complexity of verbal constructions. The MCDI allows us to ask whether this situation is different with regard to vocabulary, since counts of signs as lexical items alone may not show the same deficits as seen in language production in situated use. According to expectations based on claims of "imperfect" or "impoverished input," I expected that the SLN-D children would present the highest vocabulary counts, followed by both groups of children of hearing parents, SLN-H and SSD-H. However, the SSD group proved to be considerably behind both SLN groups.

## WHEN DOES SIGNING BEGIN: BABBLING SEQUENCE, GESTURE, OR SIGN?

Another issue related to assessing the onset of signing is when to call the early movement of the hands a sign. Deaf babies have been repeatedly observed to produce their first signs at around 8 months of age (e.g., Anderson & Reilly, 2002; Bonvillian & Folven, 1987; Conlin, Mirus, Mauk, & Meier, 2000; Newport & Meier, 1985). Is this precocity due to the relative ease of motor production by the hand as compared to the more difficult task of fine motor control in the speech channel? Other explanations of these early productions consider them "communicative gestures" that are similar to gestural precursors to spoken language, as defined by Bates and her colleagues (1979). Accordingly, the suggestion for acquisition of a signed language would be that conventional signs spring from these early gestures, allowing the deaf infant to profit from the iconic features of gestures. Indeed, in sign language research this topic is even more complex than it is in spoken languages, since there are convincing similarities in the form of early gestures when compared to conventional signs (for extensive literature review and discussion, see Casey, 2003). Anderson and Reilly (2002, p. 89) raise a doubt with regard to early onset in their data, suggesting that maybe "only deaf children are given credit for having produced a lexical item" when they gesture. It is interesting to note in this regard that two of the Dutch Deaf parents claimed, literally, that their babies were communicating and "trying to sign"; however, they concluded that "real signs" did not come until several months later. An intriguing aspect of the data of the current project is that all deaf children of hearing parents, after being exposed to signs—at whatever age—started using "communicative gestures," and indeed before their parents could identify their gestures as conventional SLN forms. That is, the children were using the manual modality for communicative purposes.

It remains an open question whether children profit from potentially iconic features of early gesture (see Schick, chapter 5 this volume). Research on homesign by Goldin-Meadow and her colleagues seems to suggest an affirmative answer, since the children they have observed make use of dimensions of sublexical information, such as movement and hand configuration, for systematic referential contrasts (Goldin-Meadow, 2003; Goldin-Meadow, Mylander, & Butcher, 1995).

## EARLY SIGNS AS LEXICAL TYPES

The topic of gesture and iconicity brings us back to the issue of categorizing the vocabulary data. Videos of spontaneous signing by the children clearly showed that many signs were realized as action signs, even when referring to an entity, such as CUT (opening and closing of index and middle fingers while moving the hand forward) instead of SCISSORS (opening and closing of index and middle fingers in place). Surprisingly, the ASL data come close to the vocabulary data reported for the English MCDI, even in terms of distribution of the categories (however, Anderson and Reilly [2002] point to some changes in the ASL adaptation, as well as cautioning about interpretations of their ASL categorization). The ASL and English patterns, however, are unlike the SLN and SSD vocabularies, as described below. The young Dutch signers seem to be extremely attentive to movement and produce their early signs as if they are over-extending this phonetic feature across lexical items. This is particularly true of early verbs such as DRINK, CUT, COMB, and GLUE. All of the children, whatever their input group, express these first signs first as verb forms— that is, with an extended movement component—and only later as nouns. Note that in most cases the phonetic realization of these Dutch verb signs is easier to produce than the noun versions, which require either an abrupt hold or some more limited and less perceptible perceptual feature. According to principles of both ease of production and perceptual saliency, the verb form of these paired lexical items seems to be more accessible to the beginning signer. In addition, for some items in this group of paired signs one might claim a more transparent and/or iconic meaning as part of the explanation. For example, some of the verb signs depict components of actual movements involved in their referent situations, such as EAT, HAMMER, COMB, and CUT.

## SLN VOCABULARY GROWTH

### Development by Chronological Age

To begin with, consider what the growth curves tell us about the development of sign vocabulary in the two SLN groups. Figure 7.1 presents vocabulary growth by chronological age ("birth age") for SLN-D and SLN-H children. The mean number of signs refers to the average number of different *types* of signs on the vocabulary checklist.

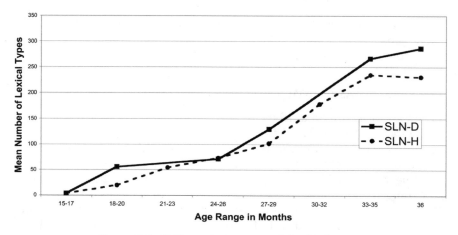

Figure 7-1. SLN vocabulary growth by birth age.

The vocabulary growth by birth age for both groups is remarkably parallel. But, in addition, the SLN-D curve is marginally but consistently higher than the SLN-H curve, with increasing divergence after about 33 months. This is what we might expect: deaf children of Deaf parents have an overall advantage, because they have been seeing a great deal of signing from the very start, and their parents are fluent signers. So it is reasonable that these children tend to have bigger vocabularies than their peers with hearing parents. However, this gap may be illusory, as discussed below, when children are compared with regard to their age of exposure to sign language.

When we compare the SLN results to the published data from native ASL-learning children (Anderson & Reilly, 2002), we see a considerable difference in total numbers. The ASL vocabularies reach 550 signs at 36 months, whereas the SLN-D group shows an average of about 300 items at the age of 35 months. This difference can at least partly be explained by criteria used in the SLN adaptation of the MCDI, as discussed above. Note that the current analysis excludes early communicative gestures, proper names, body parts, most prepositions, and locations, as well as any fingerspelling for words, numbers, or letters. Reports about the development of these items will appear in the overall study of early linguistic development in SLN at a later point in time. At any rate, the strict criteria observed here obviously influence the totals in the SLN list.

Turning back to figure 7.1, one is struck by a relatively high and rapid growth curve in the SLN-H group; this is remarkable, given that these children are supposedly dependent on "impoverished" input. Maybe this is only a matter of vocabulary counts of types of lexical items, but, in addition, our data show that most of the children in this group also use SLN grammatical structures in their early signing (Hoiting & Slobin, 2002). The biggest difference in comparison with the SLN-D group seems to lie in speed and fluency of signing, rather than in early acquisition of lexicon and grammar.

## Development by Age of Exposure

However, with regard to developmental patterns, it is necessary to take account of the age of detection of deafness. Deaf children with Deaf parents are exposed to signing from the start, whereas those with hearing parents do not begin to receive sign input until deafness is detected. Therefore, it is helpful to control for this factor, grouping children by "starting age" rather than "birth age," thereby giving all of the children roughly comparable starting points. The SLN-D children represented in figure 7.1 have received sign input from early infancy; by contrast, SLN-H children at a particular age point on the graph vary in the age at which they were exposed to sign. Figure 7.2 attempts to make the two groups comparable. The "starting age" for children with hearing parents can be taken as the point

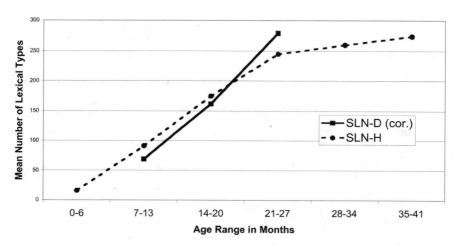

**Figure 7-2. SLN vocabulary growth by starting age. SLN-D (cor.): the "starting age" for SLN-D children set at 10 months, because deaf-of-deaf infants begin to use signlike gestures communicatively at about age 10 months.**

at which these children begin to be exposed to signs—in this case, because it is the first time they were presented with signs (generally later than 10 months or so of age). Although SLN-D children were born into signing environments, one cannot assume that they initially differentiate signed communication from gestural and affective movement. Because deaf-of-deaf infants begin to use sign like gestures communicatively at about age 10 months, an arbitrary, but not unreasonable, decision was made to set the "starting age" for SLN-D children at 10 months.[2] This corrected adjustment is indicated in figure 7.2 as SLN-D (cor.). For example, an SLN-H infant whose parents began to sign when the infant was 15 months old is equated with an SLN-D child of 10 months. Using this correction, the growth curves of the two SLN groups are virtually identical for each starting age at which comparable data are available.

Looking back at figure 7.1, both the "birth age" and "starting age" curves suggest some advantage for the SLN-D group toward the end of the period under study, but the striking parallels in the second graph indicate that children with hearing parents have the potential of catching up—at least if the input is SLN. Before considering the SSD-H group, it will be useful to analyze vocabulary development in terms of *categories* of lexical items, particularly with regard to verb-like signs.

---

[2] I am grateful to the late Elizabeth Bates (personal communication, April 7, 2003) for advice in devising this procedure for defining a comparable starting point for deaf-of-deaf and deaf-of-hearing infants.

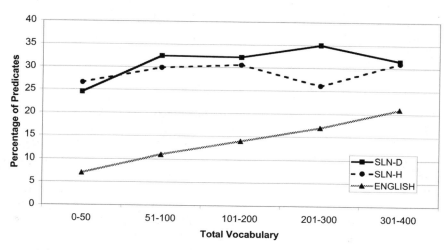

Figure 7-3. Percentage of predicates out of total vocabulary: SLN-D, SLN-H, English.

## Development of Predicate Forms

Lexical items in the SLN-MCDI have been grouped into categories of terms that designate *entities* (roughly, nouns), *predicates* (including verbal and adjectival notions), and *operators* (such elements as question words, negation, temporal expressions—i.e., forms that have propositional scope). Counts of the proportions of predicates make it possible to address the "noun/verb" issue in vocabulary acquisition. Using data for English presented by Bates et al. (1994, p. 95), figure 7.3 presents the percentage of predicates out of total vocabulary for successive stages of vocabulary growth for the SLN groups compared with English-speaking children. Plotting predicates against vocabulary size makes it possible to relate lexicon and grammar in development, as well as providing a precise comparison with a spoken language—English. The typical pattern for English is a slow but steady increase in proportion of predicates, indicating changes in the organization of grammar as lexical items are accumulated. The SLN development is strikingly different. The percentage of predicates is consistently higher in SLN than in English: five times as large at the start and still twice as large at end of the period. Clearly, there are significant differences in the organization of SLN and English, probably reflecting general differences between types of languages, as discussed below.

The two groups of SLN children are comparable except for a slight decline later in development. For the SLN-H group the decline occurs after reaching a vocabulary of 100 items, and for the SLN-D group at the 200-item level. These later declines may reflect encounters with more demanding complex utterances that may temporarily slow down the ongoing intake of new signs. This issue calls for a more detailed discussion of linguistic issues, which I address before returning to a comparison of the role of predicates in signed and spoken versions of the MCDI.

## DEAF CHILDREN AS VERB ATTENDERS

The manual-visual modality of sign languages differs considerably from the vocal-auditory modality of spoken languages—in perception as well as production. In spite of similarities in strategies and stages in language acquisition in the two modalities, most research exhibits consensus in recognizing sign languages as representing a special typological group. In the early research stages they were grouped with American Indian languages, such as Navajo, due to the use of something like sign language "classifiers" as grammatical markers (Frishberg, 1972). More recently, this particular salient property of sign languages has been reconsidered, starting with Engberg-Pedersen's (1993) innovative analyses of "polymorphemic verbs," and, most recently, insightfully debated in Emmorey (2003). Those reports discuss many classifier phenomena in both spoken and signed languages, resulting in the view that many of the classifier phenomena described for spoken languages are rather different from those in sign languages. Slobin et al. (2003) propose a polycomponential analysis of the development of verbs in young deaf children acquiring SLN and ASL, demonstrating increasing conventionalization of integrated verbal-referential forms. That is, signed predicates contain more explicit referential information than verbs in the standard spoken comparison languages.

These considerations return us to the "noun/verb controversy" in the child language literature. Clearly, the Dutch deaf children are far ahead from the very beginning in predicate acquisition compared to English-speaking children. Furthermore, as discussed below, the same is true of the SSD-H children. Why should this be the case? The most simple explanation would be to refer to some lexical items in SLN that do have a very slight phonological difference between noun and verb forms, such as COMB (noun)—COMB (verb), SWING (noun)—SWING (verb), and SCISSORS—CUT-WITH-SCISSORS. The "verb" forms may well be more salient in perception, as well as more active in production. We have already noted that sign languages have rich verbs that are full of information about entities in combination with movement of various sorts. Deaf children are very focused on movement, and this is apparently a linguistic place where they can determine the referential intent of parental signing. (Consider, e.g., verbs of handling, in which the combination of handshape and movement indicates both type of object and action.) However, this would still not explain the considerable quantitative differences reflected in figure 7.3. I suggest that the answer lies in a basic typological difference between languages like English and Dutch on the one hand, and sign languages on the other.

## A Revision in Typology

In all of the languages spoken by the surrounding communities where sign languages have been studied in depth—Indo-European as well as Japanese, Turkish, and Chinese—the basic verb argument structure of the clause locates information about argument roles *outside of the verb*. That is, one must look to the nouns—either their word-order arrangement in relation to the verb, or their case marking—in order to determine their roles with regard to the verb. Nominal arguments are dependents of the verb, and these are all *dependent-marked* languages. By contrast, a large group of spoken languages provide information about the roles of nominal arguments in elements located as part of the verb—that is, on the head of the clause. These are *head-marked languages* (Nichols, 1986, 1992). Examples are found, for example, in the Americas (Blackfoot, Cree, Lakhota, Nootka, and others) and in the Caucasus (Abkhaz and others). Such languages have not provided the point of comparison for sign language grammars, but it is apparent that all of the sign languages that have been described are head-marked rather than dependent-marked languages (Hoiting & Slobin, 2003; see also Slobin, chapter 2 this volume).

Consider the following two examples provided by Nichols (1986, p. 61). Japanese is a dependent-marking language. The role of each noun argument is marked by a particle following the noun, and the verb is bare, as shown in example 7.2:

(7.2) *boku ga tomodati ni hana o ageta*
1st PERSON SUBJECT friend DATIVE flowers OBJECT gave
"I gave flowers to (my) friend."

We are familiar with such arrangements in the case-marking suffixes of Latin or Russian or Turkish, the case-marking articles of German, and the case-marked pronouns of Indo-European languages such as Dutch, English, and Spanish, which also rely on fixed word-order patterns of dependents to identify their roles when case marking is not available. By contrast, example 7.3 is an example from Abkhaz, a head-marked language of the Caucasus. The verb is italicized.

(7.3) *a- xàc'a a- pħ°ɜs a- š°' ɜ Ø- l ɜ - y- te- yt'*
the- man the- woman the- book *it- to her- he- gave- FINITE*
"The man gave the woman the book."

Note that in example 7.3 there are no markings on any of the dependent nouns: the-man, the-woman, the-book. All of the relations between the nouns are marked by affixes of the verb.

It will be evident to readers of this volume that example 7.3 is parallel to sign languages, although relying on spoken phonetic material to indicate argument roles on the verb, whereas sign languages do the same by means of movement between loci, often associated with gaze direction and body shift as well. Because of this, it is incorrect to treat the loci as dependents whose roles are marked independent of the directional movement of the verb. Rather, the verb's movement, in itself, identifies those roles. In other words, sign languages are head marked, using spatiotemporal means to mark the argument roles of dependents. The widespread use of terms such as "pronoun" and "agreement" masks the obvious deep typological difference between head-marked languages and the dependent-marked languages from which the prevailing grammatical descriptions are drawn. Once we recognize this essential typological characteristic of sign languages, it is evident why children pay more attention to verbs in acquiring such languages. The nouns are simply much less frequent, and much less salient, in signed utterances, and the verbs are informationally rich with regard to both predicates and their argument relations.

When we consider the lexicon as the starting point for the child to derive morphological and syntactic structure, then it seems that verbs serve as the main "carriers" for deaf children. In order to know how to "package" an event for encoding, deaf children have to learn where types of *carriers* (verbs—"float, drive") *move* (adverbs—"to, in, from around") *particular* types (adjectives—big/round, thin, long) of *nominals* (nouns—balloon, car, pencil). Indeed, the predicates in the "adult" language—the input—carry most nouns, adverbs, and adjectives to locations/goals. This is unlike Dutch or English, because those languages take all these linguistic categories apart to put them in strict sequential order, but the predicate expressions of SLN are convergent with structures that have been documented for head-marked languages (e.g., Bohnemeyer, 1998; Nichols, 1986, 2001; Pye, 1992).

Thus, natural sign languages guide deaf children into a type of language, with typologically specific constructions, from the earliest stages. Not only must the child select the appropriate meaningful elements, but those elements must also be categorized and constructed according to the typological grammar of the exposure language. As a consequence, the typological characteristics of the language come into focus. This, of course, makes us wonder what we will see in the process of lexical acquisition when SSD serves as the input language.

## ACQUIRING VOCABULARY WITH SSD AS THE INPUT LANGUAGE

### The Structure of SSD

In the historical overview presented above, I characterized SSD as a flexible system that follows Dutch word order and a borrowed SLN lexicon, primarily adding fingerspelling for Dutch grammatical elements and proper names. This sort of hybrid sign system qualitatively approaches the designation of "impoverished input." In the pre-1995 clinical setting, SSD functioned in the Dutch educational system as a system comparable to manually coded English (MCE) in the United States—that is, a speech-driven system, in which signs are used in citation form with speech accompanying most of the signing and following the word order of the spoken language. In many European countries, sign systems are still the norm as the educational and communicative tool for language teaching and learning of deaf children. The recent medical technique of improving hearing by means of cochlear implantation has brought SSD back into attention in Holland, challenging the prevailing bilingual approaches. Although hearing parents are encouraged to use SLN as the visual language for young implanted children, many parents understand the bilingual educational policies but respond by signing and speaking at the same time to their implanted children. (At the time of writing, in spring 2004, implantation begins as early as age 6 months.) As a consequence, the picture may be changing back to the use of a speech-driven sign system, which may not be the optimal linguistic answer for all deaf children. At any rate, the current situation suggests a potential return of SSD, making our earlier assessment data on SSD relevant at this time.

A brief discussion of predicate expression in SSD is necessary to set the stage for the analysis. Verbs are produced as citation forms in SSD—that is, they are not directed in space to indicate their arguments. Rather, the arguments are established by the use of nouns and points. For example, a child might be presented with the citation form of GO, followed by a point to the goal along with a noun labeling the goal, using Dutch word order, as shown in example 7.4a, where the spoken sentence means "I go to school", accompanied by signing.

(7.4a) *spoken Dutch:* Ik ga naar school
       *simultaneous SSD:* POINT-TO-SELF GO
       POINT-TO-LOCATION SCHOOL

By contrast, example 7.4b presents the SLN equivalent of the same proposition:

(7.4b) *SLN:* SCHOOL POINT-TO-LOCATION POINT-TO-SELF
       $_{me}$MOVE-TO$_{school-locus}$

Note that in the SLN version, SCHOOL is signed as the first lexical item and is then located, allowing the directional sign MOVE-TO to move from the signer's body—identifying the actor—to a locus that has already been identified as the school. In brief, this is a typical head-marked construction, in contrast to the dependent-marked construction in example 7.4a, where a preposition associated with a noun indicates the noun's role as goal. Note, too, the difference in sign order between example 7.4a and example 7.4b, along with the different status of the pointing gesture. In SSD, the points identify source and goal but do not explicitly encode the motion event; in SLN the points identify the arguments that then serve as source and goal when the verb is anchored by those two points. In this regard, it is significant that the video analyses of the SSD children's utterances at around the age of 3 years start to show remarkable changes. Some of the children sign the citation form first and then start to trace the directional path with their index toward the located sign SCHOOL. That is, they are in the process of creating a "dynamic auxiliary" for SSD, such as has been documented as a support for "plain verbs" in SLN (Bos, 1994; Hoiting & Slobin, 2001) and Taiwan Sign Language (Smith, 1990). It seems that the naturalness of movement for the manual/visual modality cannot be avoided, resulting in the use of directional pointing as a kind of "auxiliary" to identify the relevant arguments of the verb. These findings are comparable to spontaneous uses of directionality that have been documented at length by Casey (2003) for children's early productions in both ASL and homesign, echoing findings by Supalla (1991) that children learning MCE begin to move verbs through space to indicate source and goal, actor and recipient, and so forth.

### Vocabulary Growth in SSD

Children acquiring SSD do acquire a lexicon, although at a much slower rate than children exposed to SLN. Figure 7.4 presents vocabulary growth by birth age for the three groups of Dutch deaf children. The SSD children have smaller vocabulary than both groups of SLN children and show a much longer period before they begin to acquire

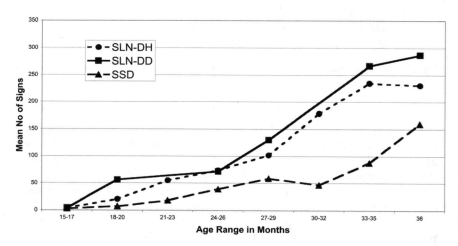

Figure 7-4. SLN and SSD vocabulary growth by birth age.

vocabulary more rapidly. This salient starting delay is unlike both SLN curves, with the SLN-H group continuing to grow steadily in vocabulary size, comparable to the SLN-D group. Although the SSD group increases the rate of acquisition after the age of 30–32 months, it does not reach the SLN levels by the end of the age range under study.

The SSD developmental pattern is quite likely due to factors involved in the use of simultaneous streams of speech and sign (for an analysis of SSD as a non-natural sign system, with negative implications for communication and acquisition, see Hoiting & Slobin, 2002). The child receiving SSD input has to divide visual attention between the hand and the mouth and, as a consequence, misses parts of the signed input. In addition, parents often repeat the same signs without any variation in form or order, often demanding vocalization from the child. Because SSD is modeled on Dutch, the parents do not have recourse to the normal use of sign order variation in a natural sign language such as SLN. Consequently, there is limited variety in the input, often resulting in loss of interest from the child's side. Note, too, that lack of variation deprives the child of essential cues to meaning. Young language learners benefit from receiving various versions of utterances conveying the same essential meaning. Such "variation sets" (Küntay & Slobin, 1996; Slobin, Hoiting, & Küntay, 2000) allow the learner to focus both on lexical items and the constructions in which they can occur. A natural language, such as SLN, facilitates parental use of variation sets, whereas a speech-supported system, such as SSD, predisposes parents to repeat stereotyped patterns. This is due to at least two factors: (1) Parents desire to focus on vocalization and lip-reading and so put more attention on exact utterance repetition, and (2) variation sets in spoken Dutch often rely on a range of discourse particles that have no signed equivalents. It may be that the resulting stereotypy is the most serious obstacle for the SSD-learning child, since this causes difficulty in inferring meanings of new lexical items.

### Development of Predicate Forms in SSD

Figure 7.5 combines the two SLN curves of figure 7.3, adding the percentage of predicates out of total vocabulary for the SSD group. In light of the features of SSD discussed above, it is remarkable that the lower vocabulary growth of the SSD group in comparison with the SLN groups does not alter the preponderance of predicates.

Video analyses of the SSD children show that they realize many early signs as verbs, as do the SLN children. Their accuracy in discriminating nouns and verbs generally also seems to rise after the age of 3 years. Both the MCDI and video data indicate that action signs are more salient to deaf children than are verbs for hearing learners of English.

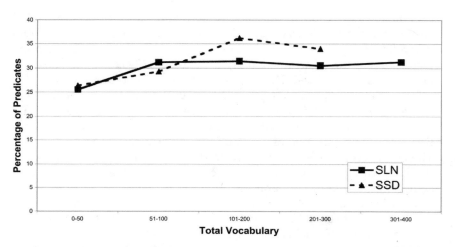

Figure 7-5.  Percentage of predicates out of total vocabulary: SLN (D + H) and SSD.

## PREDICATE USE IN DUTCH DEAF AND
## ENGLISH HEARING CHILDREN

The SLN and SSD predicate curves are close enough to be combined, as shown in figure 7.6, which collapses the data from the three Dutch deaf groups into a single curve that can be compared with published English data on the MCDI. The graph shows the percentage of predicates in relationship to vocabulary size, in order to make the sign and speech data comparable. We are now confronted with a considerable and remarkable difference: The deaf as a group, including those acquiring

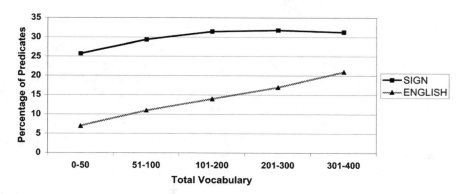

Figure 7-6.  Percentage of predicates out of total vocabulary: comparing Dutch Sign Language (SLN + SSD) and English.

SSD, are far ahead in predicate acquisition at every age, with no apparent change in development after reaching a vocabulary level of 100 words. By contrast, the English group shows a steady and linear growth trend, ending the sample period with 20% in comparison to 30% for the deaf children. The fact that the pattern for the deaf children is essentially similar whether they have deaf or hearing parents, and whether they are exposed to SLN or SSD, indicates that the quality of input may not be important as far as predicate acquisition is concerned. What counts is the salient role of predicates in sign language, that is, language in the visual-manual modality—even if supported by speech. SLN and SSD children are all verb attenders. Verb attending is clearly a deaf child's job since it is primarily verbs that satisfy the child's demand for meaning in a sign language.

## CONCLUSIONS

The data gathered by means of both the SLN-MCDI and video analyses of natural interaction demonstrate that deaf children with hearing parents can have normal early vocabulary growth, when parents are trained to use a natural sign language such as SLN. The comparison of the three groups of learners according to their input makes it clear that the notion of "impoverished input" has to be specified more carefully. Although the SSD learners show the expected relatively high use of predicates, they lag behind in overall vocabulary size and rate of growth. Sign systems—as has been known for so long—do not empower all the linguistic capacities that these children potentially possess.

With regard to the acquisition of predicates, I have proposed that the modality of sign languages makes action and motion salient, drawing attention to verbs. This is also true for SSD, where even the use of citation forms of SLN verbs often display action components, and where points that move toward goals or away from sources come to serve as analogues for the grammaticized use of motion in SLN predicates. Accordingly, early sign vocabularies show relatively high proportions of predicates in comparison with spoken languages such as English.

Treating sign languages as head marked in typology underlines the salience of verbs, since nominal arguments do not need separate expression once their identities have been established. This is clear in the videos of SLN discourse—with both Deaf and hearing parents. The verb-oriented patterns of early vocabulary reported here are similar to those found in the acquisition of spoken head-marked languages, such as Mayan (de León, 1999, for Tzotzil; Pye, 1992, for K'iche') and Inuktitut (Allen, 1996; Fortescue & Lennert Olsen, 1992). In a paper appropriately titled "Why Tzotzil (Mayan) children prefer verbs over nouns," de León (1999) points out that "the patterns of verb semantics orient the learner to refer both to objects and actions by a single semantic packet contained in the verb root" (p. 3). She presents data for two children "beyond the 50-word level": verbs made up 52% of the vocabulary for a child 1 year 8 months (1;8) of age, and 58% for a child of 1;9. A K'iche' Mayan child studied by Pye (1992) had a vocabulary made up of 45% predicates at age 2;1. Predicate statistics derived from MCDI vocabulary assessments have been useful in drawing attention to this major typological issue, leading to the need for more in-depth linguistic and discourse analysis.

Last but not least, the MCDI has proven to be a fruitful tool to fit this less familiar language type. The process of adapting the measure for SLN made clear that the instrument must attend to language-specific lexical categories. The division into entities, predicates, and operators has been a useful first pass, but finer grained and typologically sensitive analyses will be necessary. A major problem with all current versions of the MCDI for use with sign languages is the fact that the actual lexical items are presented to the parents in the written form of their spoken language. This inevitably distorts the data. For example, if a Dutch-speaking parent reports that a child uses a sign meaning *eten* ("eat"), we do not know precisely what SLN form is used by the child. Indeed, the child may actually use several different signs, with handshape indicating the type of object being eaten, and/or mouth movement indicating the manner of eating. By simply checking off "eat," therefore, we miss information about possible lexical diversity. Similarly, checking off the verb "give" fails to provide information about possible variability in handshape for different types of object transfer, as well as the range of source–goal relations commanded by the child. The fact that the MCDI was designed for a dependent-marked and minimally inflecting language—English—has thus obscured issues of lexical development that are critical to other types of languages. Future versions of the MCDI should present parents with video clips of signs rather than written words in the spoken language. For example, it would be unacceptable to assess the vocabulary of Turkish-speaking children in the Netherlands by presenting their parents with checklists of Dutch words, asking them to indicate which words their children used in Turkish. The same attention to the actual language being assessed should now be turned to the assessment of sign language competence, using easily available video technology.

Nonetheless, the present endeavor to assess the vocabularies of Dutch deaf children using an adaptation of the MCDI has yielded valuable data, with suggestions for theory, methodology, and application. And modeling the measure after versions of the MCDI for spoken languages allows for cross-linguistic and cross-typological comparisons of the sort carried out here. In conclusion, then, this study has aimed at fulfilling the ideal that Elizabeth Bates presented in designing the MCDI as an assessment tool for all types of languages. There is no better way to thank her—in memoriam—for her model and for her advice and efforts in the last spring of her life (April 2003) to contribute to this same but different MCDI endeavor.

## APPENDIX: MACARTHUR DEVELOPMENTAL INVENTORY (REILLY, 1992) ADAPTED FOR SLN

### Parental Checklist to Be Used by Parents of Children Acquiring SLN

A brief English summary of the main points is provided here. The original Dutch version of the parental checklist is available from N. Hoiting, Royal Effatha Guyot Group, Rijksstraatweg 63, 9752 AC Haren, Netherlands.

The form begins with an explanation of the goals and procedures. The checklist is divided into the following categories, with examples of the first few items in each category. *Actions, Pointing, and Games.* When children begin to communicate, they use many body expressions to make their wishes clear. Which of these does your child use? Check: *not yet / sometimes / often.*

- offers and gives you something
- points to something with an outstretched arm
- lifts both arms to be picked up
- . . .

Does your child play the games listed below? Check: *yes /no.*

- plays "peek-a-boo"
- plays "catch me"
- dances
- . . .

*Comprehension of Gestures and Words.* Before children use signs and/ or words, they show people that they understand simple expressions. A few examples are given below. Does your child understand any of these expressions? Check: *yes/ no.*

- your child reacts to his/her name
- your child reacts to "don't"
- . . .

Below is a list of frequently used expressions. Does your child understand any of these expressions. Check: *understands.*

- are you hungry?
- are you tired?
- be quiet!
- look there

- does mama/papa get a kiss?
- ...

On the next page a list of concepts begins. There you will find signs/ words that children use frequently. The concepts are grouped by topics, as in the sign-language dictionary. Some signs or words are understood by a child; others can be used by the child by himself or herself. If your child understands and uses the signs, put a check in the space. If your child also understands the words, add +W in the space. Check: *understands /uses.*

- Animal names: cat, dog...
- Food: apple, banana...
- Body: hands, feet...
- Question word: what, where...
- Vehicles: car, bike...
- Clothing: pants, sweater...
- Toys: ball, blocks...
- Time: now, right away...
- People: mama, papa...
- Place: away, back...
- Action words: walk, go, give...
- Home: living room, kitchen, sleep, bed...
- Quantity: all, more, a lot...
- Descriptive word: gone, broken, soft, wet...
- Objects of use: blanket, bottle, box...
- Outside: outside, grass, sun, school...

*Use of Voice and Sound.* Some children enjoy imitating. Sometimes they imitate sounds in words or expressions, sometimes mouth movements. How often does your child do this? Check: *never / sometimes / often.*

- imitates sounds
- imitates mouth movements
- ...

Some children like making sounds; others rarely do so. What sounds does your child make? Check: *never / sometimes / often.*

- aaa and ooo
- eee and iii
- mmmmm and bbbb
- ...

Some children have residual hearing and make use of it. What sounds does your child react to? Check: *never / sometimes / often.*

- the doorbell
- the telephone

- the door of a room
- ...

Can you list other sounds that your child reacts to?
Some children have a monotonous voice; other children have clearly audible changes of voice. What voice distinctions do you notice? Check: *never / sometimes / often.*

- high voice
- low deep voice
- questioning voice
- demanding voice
- ...

*Use of handshape.* Below are a few questions about the way in which signs are made. Just like the first words of a child, the first signs are also not yet "complete." At first a child may call a horse [*paard*] "pa" or "paat." We find these kinds of simplifications in signs, too: "a house might be signed as if it had a completely open roof; the signs for "cat" and "lion" may look the same for a while. This is because the handshapes aren't complete yet: Signs often are made bigger and float about in space. Pictures of a number of handshape are given below. Can you indicate which handshape your child can produce well?
[pictures of handshapes]
  In conclusion, there is some space for your own questions or observations.

Many thanks for your cooperation.
Nini Hoiting
Diny Visch

## REFERENCES

Allen, S. E. M. (1996). *Aspects of argument structure acquisition in Inuktitut.* Amsterdam: John Benjamins.

Anderson, D. E., & Reilly, J. S. (2002). The MacArthur Communicative Development Inventory for American Sign Language: The normative data. *Journal of Deaf Studies and Deaf Education 7,* 83–106.

Bates, E. (with Benigni, L., Bretherton, I., Camaioni, L., & Volterra, V.) (1979). *The emergence of symbols: Cognition and communication in infancy.* New York: Academic Press.

Bates, E. Marchman, V. A., Thal, D., Fenson, L., Dale, P., Reznick, J. S., et al. (1994). Development and stylistic variation in the composition of early vocabulary. *Journal of Child Language, 21,* 85–123.

Bohnemeyer, J. (1998). *Time relations in discourse: Evidence from a comparative approach to Yukatek Maya.* Unpublished doctoral dissertation, Katholieke Universiteit Brabant, Tilburg, The Netherlands.

Bonvillian, J. D., & Folven, R. D. (1987). The onset of signing in young children. In W. H. Edmondson & F. Karlsson (Eds.), *SLR '87: Papers from the Fourth International Symposium on Sign Language Research*. Hamburg: Signum.

Bos, H. F. (1994). An auxiliary verb in Sign Language of the Netherlands. In I. Ahlgren, B. Bergman, & M. Brennan (Eds.), *Perspectives on sign language structure* (pp. 37–53). Durham, UK: International Sign Linguistics Association.

Caselli, M. C., Bates, E., Casadio, P., Fenson, J., Fenson, L., Sanders, L., & Weir, J. (1995). A crosslinguistic study of early lexical development. *Cognitive Development, 10,* 159–199.

Casey, S. K. (2003). *"Agreement" in gestures and signed languages: The use of directionality to indicate referents involved in actions.* Unpublished doctoral dissertation, University of California, San Diego.

Choi, S. (1998). Verbs in early lexical and syntactic development in Korean. *Linguistics, 36,* 755–780.

Choi, S., & Gopnik, A. (1995). Early acquisition of verbs in Korean: A cross-linguistic study. *Journal of Child Language, 22,* 497–531.

Conlin, K., Mirus, G. R., Mauk, C., & Meier, R. P. (2000). Acquisition of first signs: Place, handshape, and movement. In C. Chamberlain, J. P. Morford, & R. I. Mayberry (Eds.), *Language acquisition by eye* (pp. 51–70). Mahwah, NJ: Lawrence Erlbaum

de León, L. (1999, July). *Why Tzotzil (Mayan) children prefer verbs over nouns: Input and interaction vs. cognitive constraints.* Paper presented to conference of the International Association for the Study of Child Language (IASCL), Donostia, Spain.

Emmorey, K. (Ed.) (2003). *Perspectives on classifier constructions in sign languages.* Mahwah, NJ: Lawrence, Erlbaum.

Engberg-Pedersen, E. (1993). *Space in Danish Sign Language: The semantics and morphosyntax of the use of space in a visual language.* Hamburg: Signum.

Fenson, L., Dale, P. S., Reznick, J. S., Bates, E., Thal, D. J., & Pethick, S. J. (1994). Variability in early communicative development. *Monographs of the Society for Research in Child Development, 59*(5, Serial No. 242).

Fenson, L., Dale, P. S., Reznick, J. S., Bates, E., Thal, D. J., Bates, E., Hartung, J. P., et al. (1993). *MacArthur Communicative Development Inventories: User's guide and technical manual.* San Diego, CA: Singular Publishing Group.

Fenson, L., Dale, P. S., Reznick, J. S., Bates, E., Thal, D. J., & Pethick, S. J. (1994). Variability in early communicative development. *Monographs of the Society for Research in Child Development, 59* (5, Serial No. 242).

Fortescue, M., & Lennert Olsen, L. (1992). The acquisition of West Greenlandic. In D. I. Slobin (Ed.), *The crosslinguistic study of language acquisition: Vol. 3* (pp. 111–220). Hillsdale, NJ: Lawrence Erlbaum.

Frishberg, N. (1972). Navajo object markers and the Great Chain of Being. In J. Kimball (Ed.), *Syntax and semantics: Vol. 1.* New York: Seminar Press.

Gelman, S., & Tardif, T. (1997). Acquisition of nouns and verbs in Mandarin and English. In E. Clark (Ed.), *The proceedings of the Twenty-ninth Annual Child Language Research Forum* (pp. 73–81). Stanford: Center for the Study of Language and Information.

Gentner, D. (1982). Why nouns are learned before verbs: Linguistic relativity versus natural partitioning. In S. A. Kuczaj (Ed.), *Language development: Vol. 2. Language, thought, and culture* (pp. 301–334). Hillsdale, NJ: Lawrence Erlbaum.

Goldin-Meadow, S. (2003). *The resilience of language: What gesture creation in deaf children can tell us about how all children learn language.* New York: Psychology Press.

Goldin-Meadow, S., Mylander, C., & Butcher, C. (1995). The resilience of combinatorial structure at the word level: Morphology in self-styled gesture systems. *Cognition, 56,* 195–262.

*Groningen gebaren woorden boek* [Groningen Sign dictionary]. (1979). Groningen: Royal Institute for the Deaf "H.D. Guyot."

Hoiting, N. (1983). *'Guyot en God's uitgestootenen'. De plaats van het Koninklijk Instituut voor Doven te Groningen in de geschiedenis van het dovenonderwijs in the 19e eeuw.* ["Guyot and those excluded by God". The role of the Royal Institute for the Deaf in Groningen in the history of deaf education in the 19th century]. Haren, The Netherlands: Royal Institute for the Deaf "H. D. Guyot."

Hoiting, N., Menke, R., & Kuik, E. (1990). Notities bij 200 jaar dovenonderwijs. *Tijdschrift voor Orthopedagogiek, 29*(12), 608–626.

Hoiting, N., & Slobin, D. I. (2001). Typological and modality constraints on borrowing: Examples from the Sign Language of the Netherlands. In D. Brentari (Ed.), *Foreign vocabulary in sign languages* (pp. 121–137). Mahwah, NJ: Lawrence Erlbaum.

Hoiting, N, & Slobin, D. I. (2002). What a deaf child needs to see: Advantages of a natural sign language over a sign system. In R. Schulmeister & H. Reinitzer (Eds.), *Progress in sign language research. In honor of Siegmund Prillwitz / Fortschritte in der Gebärdensprachforschung. Festschrift für Siegmund Prillwitz* (pp. 267–277). Hamburg: Signum.

Hoiting, N., & Slobin, D. I. (2003, November). *Motion and space in sign languages.* Colloquium, Max Planck Institute for Psycholinguistics, Nijmegen.

Kohnstamm, G. A., Schaerlaekens, A. M., Vries, A. D. de, Akkerhuis, G. W., & Froonincksx, M. (1981). *Nieuwe streeflijst woordenschat zes-jarigen.* Lisse: Swets & Zeitlinger.

Küntay, A., & Slobin, D. I. (1996). Listening to a Turkish mother: Some puzzles for acquisition. In D. I. Slobin, J. Gerhardt, A. Kyratzis, & J. Guo (Eds.), *Social interaction, social context, and language: Essays in honor of Susan Ervin-Tripp* (pp. 265–287). Hillsdale, NJ: Lawrence Erlbaum.

Maxwell, M., Bernstein, M. E., & Mear, K. M. (1991). In P. Siple & S. D. Fischer (Eds.), *Theoretical issues in sign language research: Vol. 2. Psychology* (pp. 171–190). Chicago: University of Chicago Press.

Merriman, W., & Tomasello, M. (1995). Introduction: Verbs are words too. In M. Tomasello & W. Merriman (Eds.), *Beyond names for things: Young children's acquisition of verbs* (pp. 1–21). Hillsdale, NJ: Lawrence Erlbaum.

Newport, E. L., & Meier, R. P. (1985). The acquisition of American Sign Language. In D. I. Slobin (Ed.), *The crosslinguistic study of language acquisition: Vol. 1. The data* (pp. 881–938). Hillsdale, NJ: Lawrence Erlbaum.

Nichols, J. (1986). Head-marking and dependent-marking grammar. *Language, 62,* 56–119.

Nichols, J. (1992). *Linguistic diversity in space and time.* Chicago: University of Chicago Press.

Pye, C. (1992). The acquisition of K'iche' Maya. In D. I. Slobin (Ed.), *The crosslinguistic study of language acquisition: Vol. 3* (pp. 221–308). Hillsdale, NJ: Lawrence Erlbaum.

Reilly, J. S. (1992). *The MacArthur Communicative Developmental Inventory for American Sign Language for children 8 to 36 months*. Unpublished document, San Diego, CA.

Slobin, D. I., & Hoiting, J. F. A. (2002). *Can a deaf child learn to sign from hearing parents?* Final Report, NSF Grant #No. SBR-97-27050. http://ihd.berkeley.edu/slobin.htm.

Slobin, D. I., Hoiting, N., & Küntay, A. (2000, May). *Variations in child-directed speech as a guide to language form and use*. Paper presented at conference, "Building Linguistic Structure in Ontogeny," Max Planck Institute for Evolutionary Anthropology, Leipzig.

Slobin, D. I., Hoiting, N., Kuntze, M., Lindert, R., Weinberg, A., Pyers, J., Anthony, M., Biederman, Y., & Thumann, H. (2003). A cognitive/functional perspective on the acquisition of "classifiers." In K. Emmorey (Ed.), *Perspectives on classifier constructions in sign languages* (pp. 271–296). Mahwah, NJ: Lawrence Erlbaum.

Smith, W. H. (1990). Evidence for auxiliaries in Taiwan Sign Language. In S. D. Fischer & P. Siple (Eds.), *Theoretical issues in sign language research: Vol. 1. Linguistics* (pp. 211–228). Chicago: University of Chicago Press.

Supalla, S. (1991). Manually coded English: The modality question in signed language development. In P. Siple & S. D. Fischer (Eds.), *Theoretical issues in sign language research* (pp. 85–109). Chicago: University of Chicago Press.

Tardif, T. (1996). Nouns are not always learned before verbs: Evidence from Mandarin speakers' early vocabularies. *Developmental Psychology, 32*, 492–504.

Tardif, T., Shatz, M., & Naigles, L. (1997). Caregiver speech and children's use of nouns vs. verbs: A comparison of English, Italian, and Mandarin. *Journal of Child Language, 24*, 535–566.

# 8

# Learning to Fingerspell Twice: Young Signing Children's Acquisition of Fingerspelling

*Carol A. Padden*

We tend to think of fingerspelling as a simple manual system for representing the alphabet. When adult second-language learners of American Sign Language (ASL) are first taught the system, they are often told that a fingerspelled word is made up of a sequence of hand shapes and that fingerspelling involves transitioning each hand shape into the next in an efficient way. Though some hand shapes are similar and are easily confused, adults can learn the system in a few lessons. For the young sign language learner, however, learning to fingerspell is a different task altogether.

This chapter reviews recent studies of fingerspelling in ASL, including those that discuss how young signers begin to construct fingerspelled words. As I will explain, these descriptions of early fingerspelling show that acquiring fingerspelling in ASL involves two sets of skills: first, the child learns to recognize fingerspelled words as whole units, and then, when reading and writing English become more prominent in the child's life, the child begins to understand fingerspelled words as made up of hand shapes that correspond to the letters of the alphabet. In the latter sense, the child learns fingerspelling a second time—this time in terms of its internal composition and its link to English words in their written form. I conclude by addressing implications of this pattern of acquisition of fingerspelling for early education of young deaf children.

## FINGERSPELLING IN ASL

### The ASL Lexicon: Frequency

Compared to many other sign languages of the world, ASL uses finger-spelling more often and more prominently. As a measure of frequency of fingerspelling in ASL, my colleagues and I counted the number of times fingerspelled words appeared in short narratives of 18 native signers (Padden & Gunsauls, 2003). We selected a 150-sign segment from each signer during a narrative and counted the number of fingerspelled words as a percentage of the total vocabulary. We found an average of 18% finger-spelled words in our group of native signers of different ages and back-grounds, with some signers fingerspelling more (at 30%) and less (at 12%).

When we took an inventory of 2,164 fingerspelled words culled from group conversations among 14 signers, we found that nearly 70% of their fingerspelled words were nouns (Padden & Gunsauls, 2003). Next in frequency were adjectives. Verbs were comparatively much reduced in frequency, at about 6% of the total. Adverbs, conjunctions, and pro-nouns each constituted between 2% and 3% of the total. It is clear from these data that fingerspelled words are overwhelmingly nouns and dis-proportionately not verbs.

When we looked at fingerspelled loan signs, a category of adapted fingerspelled words that add prominent movement (Battison, 1978; Brentari and Padden, 2001), we found many more verbs represented among them than among fingerspelled words. The main distinction between the two types—fingerspelled words and fingerspelled loan signs—is that the latter vocabulary is nativized; that is, they often have a reduced number of just two hand shapes and an added move-ment such as path, for example, the verb #TO-FAX. Fingerspelled words can stand in pairs with fingerspelled loan signs: the fingerspelled word F-A-X can be used to refer to the sheet of paper that is faxed, and the loan sign #TO-FAX is used for the act of faxing.

Other sign languages use fingerspelling very little or not at all. Boyes-Braem (2001) reports that Swiss German Sign Language relies on mouth-ing as a system of representing German words. Italian Sign Language and many other sign languages likewise use more on mouthing for words from the spoken language, resorting to fingerspelling largely for foreign names (S. Corrazza, personal communication, October 1989). British Sign Lan-guage, on the other hand, joins ASL in its prominent use of fingerspelling (Brennan, 2001), with an average of 10% fingerspelled words of total vo-cabulary appearing in a signed segment (Sutton-Spence, 1994).

### The ASL Lexicon: Grammatical Distinctions

The frequency of and regularity of fingerspelled words in ASL is related to the fact that fingerspelling is deeply entrenched in the lexicon (Brentari &

Padden, 2001). ASL signers use fingerspelling to represent not only personal names but also many other English words, including names of cities, areas, regions, names of companies, car manufacturers, and brand names. Fingerspelling is an active means of borrowing English words into ASL, and unlike other sign languages that quickly translate spoken words into native signs of equivalent meaning, ASL has a large lexicon of stable fingerspelled words. Words like "rice," "broccoli," and "flour" are reliably always fingerspelled and have no signed counterparts. With respect to other English vocabulary, ASL fingerspells most brand names and manufacturers: "Gateway," "Dell," "Compaq" (computers), "Ford," "Toyota," "Honda," (car manufacturers), where in other sign languages these names would be translated. For example, many European sign languages refer to the lion symbol in their signs for "Peugeot" or to the famous three-triangle hood ornament when signing "Mercedes-Benz."

In addition to fingerspelling entire words, ASL has fingerspelled words derived from abbreviations or shortened words. Fingerspelled abbreviations can be short or long, such as "IBM," "post office" (P-O), "vice president," (V-P), and "Chevrolet" (C-H-E-V). Abbreviations may overlap with those used in English but not always; when the U.S. Postal Service moved to two letter abbreviations for all states, ASL abbreviations did not change, and to this day, the longer abbreviations are still commonly used, for example, FLA, "Florida," MISS, "Mississippi," MICH, "Michigan."

A large subcategory of ASL signs are initialized signs where the hand shape corresponds to the first letter of the word such as CITIZEN or UNIVERSITY. (Rarely, the hand shape corresponds to the last letter of the word, as in SEX.) Days of the week as well as many colors are initialized signs. Initialized signs are commonly used for personal name signs in ASL, unlike in other sign languages that tend to use noninitialized descriptive name signs, referring to some physical or psychological characteristic of the individual. As a variation on the single hand shape found in initialized signs, abbreviations can be incorporated in two-syllable signs: SENIOR-CITIZEN, SOCIAL-WORK, DOWN-SYNDROME.

There are a number of sign-fingerspelled pairs that contrast in meaning and grammatical class. For example, the sign LOVE (verb) can be paired with the fingerspelled word L-O-V-E (noun) to contrast the grammatical class of the former with the latter. The sign RENT means "to rent," but the fingerspelled R-E-N-T refers to the rental payment. In another pair, the sign DRIVE (verb) refers to driving a car but the fingerspelled word D-R-I-V-E (noun) is used for a computer hard drive. In a third-grade science class, a deaf teacher explained to her students that she was going to demonstrate the idea of a scientific "problem," a word that she fingerspelled, then added that it was not the same as the meaning of the sign PROBLEM, which is typically used to refer to a personal problem or dilemma (Padden & Gunsauls, 2003).

To further illustrate, there are a large number of sign-fingerspelled compounds, where usually, but not always, the first segment of a compound is signed while the second is fingerspelled, for example, RED T-A-P-E ("red tape"), BLACK + M-A-I-L ("blackmail"), WATER + F-A-L-L ("waterfall"), PLAY + O-F-F ("playoff game"), SOFT + W-A-R-E, and HARD + W-A-R-E ("computer software and hardware"). In all these cases, the second part of the compound or phrase is fingerspelled, even though there are signs for "tape," "mail," and "water flowing." There seem to be two reasons why the second segment is fingerspelled: (1) to distinguish literal from metaphorical meaning, and (2) to identify the compound as a noun. The compound "blackmail" does not literally involve the mail, nor does "red tape" involve scotch tape. The noun "waterfall" is distinguished from the verb, "water flowing," by the fact that the second segment is fingerspelled, not signed. There are many more such examples, including further contrasts within compounds: Computer "hardware" can be a sign-fingerspelled compound, HARD + W-A-R-E, but a "hardware" store must be completely fingerspelled: H-A-R-D-W-A-R-E. Fluent and native signers know these distinctions, though they are rarely reported in ASL dictionaries. Young children, in time, also pick up these distinctions.

Fingerspelled words are conventionally regarded as a means of representing English words for which there are no equivalent signs. This is a misleading characterization for three reasons: (1) it incorrectly assumes that fingerspelled words exist in place of signs, when in fact, they can co-exist with already existing signs. (2) It describes fingerspelled words as English words. A more accurate description is one which recognizes fingerspelled words as existing within the ASL lexicon as a category of borrowed or "foreign" vocabulary (Brentari, 2001; Brentari & Padden, 2001; Padden, 1998). And (3) it incorrectly views fingerspelling primarily as a means of translation. ASL signers could translate words into signs; instead, they maintain an active lexicon of fingerspelled words that exist stably in that category. For example, "diglossia" has a signed translation in British Sign Language (Brennan, 2001), but in ASL it is always fingerspelled.

To sum up, fingerspelled words are both frequent and pervasive and are deeply entrenched in the grammar of ASL.

## The Phonology of Fingerspelling

ASL signers fingerspell rapidly, which is yet another characteristic unique to those sign languages that use fingerspelling extensively such as British Sign Language and Swedish Sign Language. To the adult second-language learner, fingerspelled words seem like a blur of rapidly executed hand shapes, frustrating those who are learning ASL. Comparatively speaking, signs are easier to perceive: They are larger in physical shape and can sweep across the broad space in front of the signer's body. New signers can pick up clues to a sign's meaning from its representative or iconic qualities. Fingerspelled words, on the other hand, have no iconic qualities and involve many more hand shapes than in a single sign. Unlike signs, in which the units of hand shape, location, and movement are layered and executed at once, fingerspelled words are linearly expressed, with units sequenced over time.

In a seminal description of the phonetics of fingerspelling, Wilcox (1992) observes that though fingerspelling is popularly conceived of as an act of stringing together hand shapes in a sequence, the psychological reality is otherwise: The most salient aspect of a fingerspelled word is not its hand shapes, but the combination of small movements that link the hand shapes together and the overall "contour" or movement shape of the fingerspelled word. This idea of contour was also developed by Akamatsu (1982), who studied fingerspelling used by preschool hearing children of deaf parents.

When an ASL signer fingerspells, the hand is positioned in neutral space, often to one side. The hand usually does not move to one side as the hand shapes are executed in sequence. When a word is fingerspelled at normal speed, which is quite rapid for the adult second-language learner of ASL, the hand shifts slightly downward, to the sides and upward, but mostly remains in the same position. The shifts of the hands reflect transitions from one hand shape to another. For example, in the slower version of the fingerspelled word B-A-N-K, the hand moves slightly downward during the transition from B to A, and then only the fingers move during the transition from A to N; finally the hand sweeps upward as it transitions from N to K. When the word is fingerspelled at normal speed, hand shapes are clustered together in a movement unit: the three hand shapes, B-A-N are positioned slightly downward, and then the hand moves slightly upward in for the last hand shape: K. Crucially, there are two elements in the movement contour of this particular fingerspelled word: the first involves three hand shapes, and the second involves the transition to the last hand shape.

Because movement shifts do not coincide with individual hand shapes but instead involve units of more than one hand shape, future analyses of fingerspelling will likely consider the notion of syllable a useful means of accounting for when and where movement shifts occur in a fingerspelled word. Returning to the example of B-A-N-K, it may be that the fingerspelled word is made up of two movement peaks, or possibly, two syllables despite the fact that the spoken word, "bank," is a single-syllable word.

## FINGERSPELLING IN CHILD LANGUAGE

Studies of ASL acquisition rarely include descriptions of a child's use of fingerspelling since it is believed that fingerspelled words are English words and thus are not part of a description of how children learn ASL. However, as I have argued in the preceding section, fingerspelling is frequent and pervasive in signed discourse, and a very young signer cannot avoid learning fingerspelled forms used by parents or others in the signing environment. In their home studies with deaf families Erting et al. (2000) find numerous examples of very young deaf children attempting to fingerspell as early as 2 years old. In this section, I review studies about fingerspelling and acquisition of fingerspelling. Akamatsu (1982) studied the acquisition of fingerspelling in hearing children of deaf parents who use ASL extensively in the family, and, not unexpectedly, many of her findings are similar to those described in the literature regarding how deaf children learn ASL and fingerspelling. In recent years increasing numbers of hearing parents are using ASL in the home, and like deaf parents, many try to use fingerspelling. Signing hearing parents often consult with deaf parents for advice about literacy; as a result, ideas about fingerspelling and other language practices circulate through the community.

Some signing parents say they try to avoid using fingerspelled words around very young children because they believe they are not yet capable of understanding the words. But in videotaped interactions between parents and children using ASL, it can be seen that parents cannot entirely avoid fingerspelling to their children (Akamatsu, 1982; Erting et al., 2000; Kelly, 1995; Padden, 1991). Kelly found an instance on videotape of a parent fingerspelling to her 2-month-old infant, again in another videotape at 14 weeks, and in subsequent videotaped interactions. Before the end of the first year, the parents added more fingerspelled words, for example, C-E-I-L-I-N-G, when describing it to the child. Some of the most common vocabulary items in a young signer's language environment are fingerspelled, for example, B-U-S and I-C-E. Moreover, Kelly found numerous instances of parents fingerspelling to older children or to other adults; as such, fingerspelled words are plentiful in the ambient signing environment.

Much like hearing parents who read aloud to infants, some parents will insist on fingerspelling to their very young children because they believe that early exposure to fingerspelling is good preparation for literacy. They view fingerspelling as intimately linked to the alphabet that is itself the centerpiece of English literacy. As such, signing parents' ideas about fingerspelling are a mix of beliefs about sign language, English literacy, schooling, and even social class. One middle-class deaf mother described less advantaged deaf children as those who use little or no fingerspelling. The absence of such forms is seen as an indication of poor early education, or poor sign language environments. Fingerspelling is both about representing English words as well as representing bilingualism in signing children's lives. The act of fingerspelling signals and communicates: In this sense, it both *signifies* and is a *signifier*; that is, it makes a symbolic statement as well (Padden & Gunsauls, 2003).

## Learning Fingerspelling Twice

I describe the acquisition of fingerspelling as involving mastery of two different kinds of skills: the skill of fingerspelling, on the one hand, and the skill of connecting fingerspelled words to their English alphabetic counterparts, on the other. The former skill involves understanding how fingerspelling is used in ASL, including what types of words are likely to be fingerspelled. This skill also involves recognizing shapes of fingerspelled words and knowing the meanings of commonly used fingerspelled words.

The second skill, of linking fingerspelling to English words, develops when the child begins to acquire English literacy. In this sense, the child learns fingerspelling a second time, that is, comes to understand the words as having internal linguistic patterning, as made up of hand shapes that correspond to alphabetic letters. The timing of the acquisition of the two kinds of acquisition can vary from child to child; typically signing children can use fingerspelled words before they are able to identify their internal structure. Some children move smoothly into both skills and others struggle, particularly those who are also struggling to read and write. I will describe the first and second skills in terms of a child's knowledge of different kinds of language and literacy practices and how this knowledge changes over the course of childhood. As children leave home and begin school, their attention is oriented toward reading and writing behaviors, and they begin to link fingerspelling to those contexts.

## First Skill of Fingerspelling

Because fingerspelling is described as representing the alphabetic structure of English words, it is almost automatic to think of fingerspelling as intimately linked to reading and writing. In fact, many young signers cannot yet read when they begin to understand and use fingerspelled words. Young children commonly see fingerspelled words outside of literacy contexts in everyday discourse. Their parents may be reading aloud to them, signing stories from books, and making a point of using fingerspelled names and words while reading from books (Erting et al., 2000), but the connection between reading, writing, and fingerspelling is not an obvious one to the young child. As I have discussed previously (Padden, 1991), the child has a sense of the interaction of fingerspelling, signing, reading, and writing, but that relationship takes time to develop, and it crucially involves the developing skill of reading and writing.

Fingerspelled words can appear early in a child's productive vocabulary; a young child in Kelly's (1995) study was videotaped trying to fingerspell C-H-I-P ("potato chip") at age 24 months. The child's productions involved clusters of movement, in which a salient component of the movement is preserved in the production of the fingerspelled word, and hand shapes are deleted in medial position: C-H-P. A colleague, Tom Holcomb (personal communication, April 1987) once described his child at this age as making a movement distinction between I-C-E and R-I-C-E, which are identical except for one extra letter in "rice." The child produced I-C-E with opening and closing movement but R-I-C-E with a circular movement, deriving from the letter R, which in turn influences the movement of the remaining three letters. At this young age, these children cannot read or write and have little or no realization of the alphabetic distinction of similarly spelled words. Instead, the children are able to detect small movement components of fingerspelled words, and they strive to replicate them in their use of the forms.

Akamatsu (1982) in her description of fingerspelling in young hearing preschool children who use ASL finds similar attempts in which the children try to replicate what she calls the "movement contour" of the fingerspelled word. In such clusters of movement, the hand shapes are barely discernible. The salient features of fingerspelled words are their movement shapes, and the children produce those shapes when they replicate the word.

Aside from Wilcox's (1992) work on phonetics of fingerspelling, there has been little work on the phonology of fingerspelling. Such work would shed light on what young children learn about movement in fingerspelling. We know from studying errors in young signers' fingerspelled attempts that certain movement components are salient to them, particularly movement associated with doubled letters in words, for example, doubled vowels or doubled consonants as in "Lee, "zoo," or "cattle." In one such error reported in Padden (1991), the child was trying to fingerspell the name of a relative, Dee. Instead of fingerspelling D, the child substituted L but preserved the bouncing movement for the doubled vowel, ee. In ASL doubled letters can involve either reiterating the hand shape, bouncing the hand shape or sliding the hand shape to the side. Signing children pick up all these possible small internal movements and use them in their earliest attempts. There are likely to be other similar correspondences between frequently appearing letter sequences and movements that go with them, for example, the suffix -ion or the prefix ex-, but these are not well described in either the fingerspelling or acquisition literature.

More broadly, children begin to recognize and replicate fingerspelled words that frequently appear in their everyday language: names of family members and friends, brand names such as grocery stores (e.g., S-A-F-E-W-A-Y), place names, as well as fingerspelled words of common nouns (e.g., ice and rice). They often can replicate the general movement shape of the words if they don't yet get the internal sequence of letters correct.

## Second Skill of Fingerspelling

The second skill is being able to link the internal sequence of hand shapes of a fingerspelled word to an English word. The first and second skills are not always linearly ordered with respect to one another, and young signers can be seen making errors involving both types of skills. A very young signer can be seen trying to create a sequence of hand shapes, particularly if their parents have been teaching them the letters of the alphabet both in print and in fingerspelling. Often, though, when they try to fingerspell words by their letters, they get the sequence wrong. A young child at age 2 years 9 months (2;9) could only spell her name as E-U-B when asked what her name was (without revealing the child's name, only the letter E appears in her name). When asked the name of her dog, Sasha, she switched around the letters she knew and fingerspelled U-B-A (Padden & LeMaster, 1985). The struggle to construct a correct sequence of letters will continue through most of the child's early literacy years. Parents are greatly pleased when their signing child can finally produce their name with the correct sequence of letters, but spelling in a certain sequence requires a great deal of practice, as well as the awareness that the correct sequence is important.

In other examples from Padden and LeMaster (1985), a father teased his daughter, age 4;11, and told her that E.T. the extraterrestrial from the popular movie at that time had taken her candy. The daughter shook her head and insisted it could not have been the alien, fingerspelling the name as T-E. She seemed unperturbed at her attempt, apparently focusing more on which letters appeared in the word rather than what sequence was correct. Another child, age 4;9, has several spellings for "cat," which include correct as well as incorrect sequences: C-R-I, C-N-I.

As the signing child's literacy education begins in earnest, then attention is focused on developing the ability to link different literacy skills with different fingerspelling skills. Kelly (1995) describes an interaction between a deaf mother and her deaf daughter where the mother holds up index cards with written words on them and encourages the daughter to try and fingerspell the words. The daughter, at age 3;4, could match hand shapes to letters but then couldn't say what the words represented. When her mother fingerspelled the words "rice" and "seed" back to her daughter, the daughter then recognized what they were.

## Convergence of Skills

I have described these early literacy attempts as pushing toward a *convergence of skills*, where the skill of fingerspelling is aligned to the skill of reading and written spelling (Padden, 1991). There are several skills that need to be aligned together in the signing literate child: writing a word, fingerspelling it as well as understanding the same word as fingerspelled by someone else. The move toward convergence can take a number of years, from the first year of school through even second or third grade, until the child moves effortlessly between the skill domains of finger-spelling, spelling, writing, and reading. Some signing children, however, struggle to accomplish convergence even by third grade: They may be able to recognize a fingerspelled word but not be able to write the same word correctly on a page. Other children may be able to recognize a word on a page but stumble when they try to fingerspell the same word without being able to see it in written form. Difficulty at convergence is often seen in those children who are struggling at the task of learning to read.

My colleague Claire Ramsey and I carried out a series of studies ex-amining the development of reading ability in young signing deaf chil-dren (Padden & Hanson, 2000; Padden & Ramsey, 1998). In one study, we developed a fingerspelling test in which the children were asked to view a list of signed sentences on videotape, each containing a single finger-spelled word. After viewing each sentence, the child was asked to write down the fingerspelled word contained in it. We wanted to know whe-ther skill in correctly writing down the fingerspelled word had a rela-tionship to reading ability. Indeed it does: We found that accuracy in correctly spelling the word in written form correlated with reading comprehension skill as measured by their Stanford Achievement Test score ($n = 22$; $r = 0.43$, $p < 0.05$). In other words, correctly writing a word as it was fingerspelled is not simply being able to see the sequence of hand shapes and then writing down that sequence; the child must also possess reading ability. The child might be able to understand the fingerspelled word in a signed sentence, but the skill of writing it down in English is related to reading ability.

Knowing the sequence of letters in a written word is a literate skill, acquired in the course of learning to read and write. For children who are struggling to read and write, they are also struggling to write down words they have just seen fingerspelled. Ramsey and Padden (1998) describe deaf children who require that each letter be fingerspelled to them one at a time in order for them to write words down. In fact, the children often require the fingerspeller to tell them that they have reached the end of the word. Unlike more skilled deaf children, they cannot watch a fingerspelled word in its entirety and then write the word. Their difficulty is a complex one: It involves memory—being able to remember the word as it was fingerspelled, but equally, it in-volves literate ability in English—knowing what types of spellings English words tend to have, and using this knowledge to predict the likely spelling of the target English word.

## SUMMARY AND CONCLUSION: IMPLICATIONS FOR EDUCATION

In a report about use of fingerspelling during simultaneous commu-nication, Akamatsu and Stewart (1989) found that preschool teachers of deaf children fingerspell much less than do teachers of older children. Furthermore, if they use fingerspelling, they often confine their vocabulary to a small set of words, used repeatedly. They express concerns that preschool and elementary teachers may have misconceptions about the nature of fingerspelling and how it should be used with young children. Based on the body of research currently available, there are a number of implications for early education of deaf children.

Very young deaf children can be exposed to commonly used fingerspelled words while interacting with language models. These include words that are meaningful in their lives: ice, rice, bus, okay, chips, flour. Most of these words are short, and refer to objects familiar to the child. These fingerspelled words are often found in the home language environment of children who are not yet reading or writing, demonstrating that use of fingerspelling by teachers should not be delayed until literacy education begins. Instead, fingerspelling should be a part of a child's early preschool language as well.

In ASL, personal names, place names, and brand names (or proper nouns) are often fingerspelled. The young child can learn a great deal from seeing these words used in a teacher's language. First, they learn about the category of vocabulary that is routinely fingerspelled in the language, and second, they learn distinctions between common and proper nouns.

Kelly (1995) and Humphries and MacDougall (2000) report that deaf parents and deaf elementary level teachers often embed fingerspelled words in "sandwiched" or "chained" structures where the word is immediately followed by a sign of related or close definition. This provides immediate context for the child. Kelly gives two examples: DUCK DUCK Q-U-A-C-K, to show that quacking is what ducks do, and another where the father uses sandwiching to show that a chapstick is a special kind of lipstick: LIPSTICK C-H-A-P-S-T-I-C-K. Humphries and MacDougall report from their studies of teacher talk that chaining is prevalent in the elementary years among deaf teachers but not in later years where other strategies are used for word definition. Such strategies seem "childlike" when used repeatedly with older children. Hearing teachers, in contrast, use little or no chaining at any level, most likely because they are unaware of such techniques. Teacher training programs can benefit from learning more about such "indigenous" strategies and incorporating them in courses that train signing elementary-level teachers.

When signing deaf children begin literacy education, teachers should expect to see a transition in use of fingerspelling, from more global units to more analytical spelling, where the child is more aware of the internal composition of fingerspelled words. Spelling correctly in fingerspelling as well as writing is a developmental task, and teachers should have expectations that as the child's literacy skills increase, the components of these skills, including fingerspelling, will change.

Fingerspelling should not be viewed—as it often is—as a system for supplying words to ideas, concepts, and objects that "have no signs." This undermines the status of both signs and fingerspelling as rich sources of vocabulary within the language. Fingerspelled words and their relatives, initialized signs, abbreviations, and sign-fingerspelled compounds, form a robust and active component of the lexicon.

Fingerspelled vocabulary can be used productively both as signifiers, that is, as words within the sign stream, and to signify, to make a symbolic distinction, as when a teacher explains that she is illustrating not a personal PROBLEM but a computational P-R-O-B-L-E-M (Padden & Gunsauls, 2003).

To paraphrase Akamatsu slightly, what these suggestions indicate is that fingerspelling is more than the "sum of its parts." It is not merely a linear means of representing the orthography but has taken on rich symbolic content above and beyond the words themselves. Fingerspelled words occupy a place in the ASL lexicon and carry grammatical content as well as semantic contrasts with other vocabulary in the language. In the future, when studies of child language acquisition of ASL routinely include fingerspelled tokens, we will learn more about how young children learn complex and rich vocabularies in sign languages.

## REFERENCES

Akamatsu, C. (1982). *The acquisition of fingerspelling in pre-school children.* Unpublished doctoral dissertation, University of Rochester, Rochester, NY.

Akamatsu, C. T., & Stewart, D. (1989). The role of fingerspelling in simultaneous communication. *Sign Language Studies, 65,* 361–374.

Battison, R. (1978). *Lexical borrowing in American Sign Language.* Silver Spring, MD: Linstok Press.

Boyes-Braem, P. (2001). Functions of the mouthing component in the signing of deaf early and late learners of Swiss German Sign Language. In D. Brentari (Ed.), *Foreign vocabulary in sign languages: A cross-linguistic investigation of word formation* (pp. 1–47). Mahwah, NJ: Lawrence Erlbaum.

Brennan, M. (2001). Making borrowing work in British Sign Language. In D. Brentari (Ed.), *Foreign vocabulary in sign languages: A cross-linguistic investigation of word formation* (pp. 49–85). Mahwah, NJ: Lawrence Erlbaum.

Brentari, D. (Ed.) (2001). *Foreign vocabulary in sign languages: A cross-linguistic investigation of word formation.* Mahwah, NJ: Lawrence Erlbaum.

Brentari, D., & Padden, C. (2001). Native and foreign vocabulary in American Sign Language: A lexicon with multiple origins. In D. Brentari (Ed.), *Foreign vocabulary in sign languages: A cross-linguistic investigation of word formation* (pp. 49–85). Mahwah, NJ: Lawrence Erlbaum.

Erting, C., Thumann-Prezioso, C., & Benedict, B. (2000). Bilingualism in a deaf family: Fingerspelling in early childhood. In P. Spencer, C. Erting, & M. Marschark (Eds.) *The deaf child in the family and the school: Essays in honor of Kathryu P. Meadow-Orlans* (pp. 41–54). Mahwah, NJ: Lawrence Erbaum.

Humphries, T., & MacDougall, F. (2000). "Chaining" and other links: Making connections between American Sign Language and English in two types of school settings. *Visual Anthropology Review, 15*(2), 84–94.

Kelly, A. (1995). Fingerspelling interaction: A set of deaf parents and their deaf daughter. In C. Lucas (Ed.), *Sociolinguistics in deaf communities* (Vol. I, pp. 62–73). Washington, DC: Gallaudet University Press.

Padden, C. (1991). The acquisition of fingerspelling by deaf children. In P. Siple & S. Fischer (Eds.), *Theoretical issues in sign language research:* Vol. 2. Psychology (pp. 191–210). Chicago: University of Chicago Press.

Padden, C. (1998). The ASL lexicon. *Sign Language and Linguistics, 1*(1), 39–64.

Padden, C., & Gunsauls, D. (2003). How the alphabet came to be used in a sign language. *Sign Language Studies, 4*(1), 1–33.

Padden, C., & Hanson, V. (2000). Search for the missing link: The development of skilled reading in deaf children. In K. Emmorey & H. Lane (Eds.), *The signs of language revisited: An anthology to honor Ursula Bellugi and Edward Klima* (pp. 435–447). Mahwah, NJ: Lawrence Erlbaum.

Padden, C., & LeMaster, B. (1985). An alphabet on hand: The acquisition of fingerspelling in deaf children. *Sign Language Studies, 47*, 161–172.

Padden, C., & Ramsey, C. (1998). Reading ability in signing deaf children. *Topics in Language Disorders, 18*, 30–46.

Ramsey, C., & Padden, C. (1998). Natives & newcomers: Literacy education for deaf children. *Anthropology and Education Quarterly, 29*(1), 5–24.

Sutton-Spence, R. (1994). *The role of the manual alphabet and fingerspelling in British Sign Language.* Unpublished doctoral dissertation, University of Bristol.

Wilcox, S. (1992). *The phonetics of fingerspelling.* Philadelphia: J. Benjamins.

# 9

# The Form of Early Signs: Explaining Signing Children's Articulatory Development

*Richard P. Meier*

Studies of early language development, whether in speech or sign, look to articulatory, perceptual, and grammatical factors to account for which words and signs children learn earliest and for how children form early words and signs (see Vihman, 1996, for an overview of phonological development in speech). Signs, like words, are structured, rule-governed, and learned. In the articulation of words and signs, the child's motor behavior is guided by his or her mental representation of those lexical units.

Although the acquisition literature on American Sign Language (ASL) and other signed languages is relatively large (for reviews of the literature on ASL, see Meier, 1991; Newport & Meier, 1985), the literature on the form of early signs is rather fragmented. Research on how children acquire their first signs has been animated by such issues as whether first signs appear earlier than first words and whether early signs are distinct from nonlinguistic gesture (e.g., Anderson & Reilly, 2002; Meier & Newport, 1990; Orlansky & Bonvillian, 1985; Petitto, 1988; Volterra & Iverson, 1995). There has also been attention to manual babbling, that is, to the prelinguistic precursors to children's first signs (Cheek, Cormier, Repp, & Meier, 2001; Meier & Willerman, 1995; Petitto, Holowka, Sergio, Levy, & Ostry, 2004; Petitto & Marentette, 1991). Now, however, increasing attention is being paid to describing the form of children's early signs and to proposing explanations for why children articulate signs in the way that they do.

As we seek to account for the ways in which young children produce signs, we can build predictions on several types of foundations: (1) The literature on motor development in children suggests extralinguistic factors that may determine the articulation of linguistic forms. (2) Developmental models may base predictions about the form of early signs on the hypothesized persistence of articulatory patterns found in prelinguistic gesture. (3) Perceptual factors may be another source of prediction; particularly in the acquisition of handshape, perceptual confusions may lead children to substitute incorrect handshapes for adult targets. Lastly, (4) input factors may offer explanations for patterns identified in children's production. Such input factors might include the characteristic properties of child-directed signing (as opposed to adult-directed signing). Other relevant input properties may arise from phonological differences between distinct sign languages.

To date, most work on the form of children's signs has been informed by an understanding of sign articulation. There has, in contrast, been little work on children's perception of signs. Consequently, the focus of much of this chapter is on articulatory (or motoric) explanations for why children articulate signs as they do. One advantage of looking at motor control issues in the acquisition of sign is that, unlike the speech articulators, the sign articulators (i.e., the shoulder, the segments of the arm, and the hand) are large and externally observable.

This chapter begins with an overview of the methods that have been used in research on phonetic and phonological development in signing children. It then turns to a consideration of certain properties of signs that are key to an understanding of the phonetics of signs and that will also prove important to an understanding of the current literature on articulatory development in signing children.

## METHODS OF STUDYING PHONOLOGICAL DEVELOPMENT IN SIGN

### Participants

Most studies discussed here report data gathered from deaf children raised in deaf, signing families. However, some studies—notably the diary studies authored by Bonvillian and his colleagues (e.g., Orlansky & Bonvillian, 1984)—report data from hearing children. The subject of Marentette and Mayberry's (2000) case study was likewise the hearing daughter of deaf parents. In studies of articulatory development in very young children, the child's own hearing status may not be crucial. However, the child's hearing status may be of greater significance to studies of other aspects of language acquisition. Although there may be little prospect of interference from English phonology on phonological development in ASL, the same is not true for the acquisition of ASL syntax.

There is one way in which the form of early signs may be affected by the child's hearing status. Specifically, there could be interesting differences in the input environments of the deaf and hearing children born to deaf parents. Consider one possible effect: deaf parents may sometimes use their voices to attract their hearing children's attention. In contrast, deaf parents are likely to use visually-salient means to attract, and maintain, their deaf children's attention. Some of those visual mechanisms (e.g., enlarging a sign) have consequences for the form of the signs that parents present to their children (see Holzrichter & Meier, 2000). It is possible that, by comparing articulatory development in the deaf and hearing offspring of deaf parents, we may discover whether or not these parental strategies for gaining and maintaining a child's visual attention have any effect on how children themselves produce signs.

Research on the acquisition of sign phonology in late-learning children or in hearing adult learners is of independent interest. By examining phonological development in late-learning deaf children we may identify effects of delayed exposure. Inasmuch as most deaf children are born to hearing parents and most such children experience some delay in their exposure to a sign language, studies of phonological development in late-learning children may also be of immediate practical value for deaf children. Research on phonological learning in hearing adults has obvious potential implications for the design of high school and college sign language curricula. Such research might also help us to separate maturational effects on articulatory development in sign from the effects of skill acquisition (Mirus, Rathmann, & Meier, 2000). For the adult learner, producing signs requires the acquisition of new motor skills, but—unlike the child—the adult produces those signs using a fully mature motor system.

## Diary Studies

In a diary study, the researcher typically asks parents to make written observations of the language development of their children; for example, a mother might be asked to make daily records of what new words or signs her child has used. Diary studies allow researchers to avoid certain well-known pitfalls of working with young children; for example, when parents collect data, we worry less about the fact that children in the earliest stages of language acquisition may speak or sign only occasionally, and perhaps not at all in the presence of an observer. Diary studies may in some instances allow data collection from larger numbers of children than would be possible with more labor-intensive data collection procedures. The fact that the manual articulators are visible could mean that, compared to hearing parents of hearing, speaking children, signing parents might be relatively reliable reporters of the form of children's errors (although this has not been demonstrated).

Bonvillian and his colleagues have published a number of studies of early sign development that are based largely on parental reports (e.g., Bonvillian, Orlansky, & Novack, 1983; Orlansky & Bonvillian, 1985). In recent years, parental report methods have been augmented by checklist procedures such as those used in the MacArthur Communicative Development Inventory (MCDI). This inventory has been adapted for many languages, including ASL (Anderson & Reilly, 2002).

Notwithstanding the advantages of diary studies, a detailed understanding of early sign development demands access to videotaped data of children's productions. Only with careful transcription of video recordings can we be confident that our account of the acquisition of sign is not unduly biased by parental observers. Signing parents, like speaking parents, want their child to be the first kid on the block to produce a true sign. Like the father who hears himself being called every time his kid babbles "dada," signing parents may erroneously judge gestures or manual babbles to be meaningful signs (Petitto, 1988).

## Naturalistic, Observational Studies

Most studies of early sign production are based on videotaped observations of children interacting in a spontaneous fashion with a parent or signing experimenter. To date a number of different signed languages have been examined including ASL, Quebec Sign Language (LSQ), the Sign Language of Spain (LSE), Brazilian Sign Language (LIBRAS), the Sign Language of the Netherlands, Finnish Sign Language (FinSL), and others.

A summary table included in Karnopp (2002, p. 32) makes it clear that many published studies have been based on limited corpora of signs. Most observational studies report a small number of children; many reports are case studies. Interestingly, one case study (Marentette & Mayberry, 2000) reports one of the larger data sets analyzed to date.

There are several factors that may depress the size of sign corpora that are gleaned from videotaped observations: (1) It is possible that insufficient attention to nonmanual signals may lead to underrepresentation of functional categories and of adverbials. However, research on the acquisition of nonmanual signals suggests that children use few nonmanuals before 2 years of age (Reilly & Anderson, 2002). (2) Many studies exclude all pointing signs from their analyses; this means that, in contrast to analyses of speech development, most pronouns and body-part signs do not contribute to the corpora (see Karnopp, 2002, p. 36). (3) The constraints of videotaping mean that when children wander off camera their signing is not captured on videotape. And (4) the availability of attractive toys for children to manipulate may depress their signing.

Importantly, however, we can be confident that these small sample sizes are not reflective of signing children's total vocabularies—Anderson and Reilly (2002) have found, using the MCDI, that early sign vocabularies of deaf children with deaf parents may perhaps even exceed the spoken vocabularies of hearing children. In general, researchers studying early phonological development in signing children should seek to address this apparent problem of sample size. More structured data collection procedures may be necessary, ones in which the child's attention is not engaged by toys that occupy the child's hands. In longitudinal studies, larger sample sizes will permit a better understanding of developmental change.

## Experimental Studies

Experimental studies of early sign production have been sparse. In work with adult participants, there has been intermittent work on the kinematics of sign production. Movement analysis systems often involve the analysis of optical information collected in the infrared portion of the spectrum. Markers are placed on landmarks on the signer's arms; these markers may be either light-emitting diodes or highly reflective spheres. If an individual marker is in view of two or more cameras, the information from those cameras permits a computer to determine the precise location of each marker in space and to track its movement. In this way, very detailed analyses of sign movement are possible. Such systems have allowed analyses of the dynamic movement patterns that mark temporal aspect on verbs (Poizner, Newkirk, & Bellugi, 1983) as well as analyses of sign stress (Wilbur, 1990) and of coarticulation in fingerspelling (Wilcox, 1992). More recently, kinematic analyses have probed coarticulation in signing (Cheek, 2001), the spatial locations used by agreeing verbs (Cormier, 2002), and the phenomenon of undershoot in rapid signing (Mauk, 2003). All this work has examined ASL. Petitto et al. (2004) have recently reported kinematic work on patterns of cyclicity in the prelinguistic gesture of hearing infants, with and without early sign exposure.

## ARTICULATING SIGNS

The articulatory systems in speech and sign differ in impressive ways. In speech, the sound source is internal to the speaker, whereas in sign the light source is external to the signer. Supraglottal articulation in speech may alter the size of resonance chambers, add an additional chamber (through lowering of the velum), or create audible turbulence. In sign, the movements and postures of the manual articulators create patterns in the reflected light that falls upon the addressee's retina. There are other differences: The oral articulators are largely hidden from view, whereas the manual articulators must be largely visible to the addressee if communication is to take place. Consider now some articulatory properties of signs that may be important to an understanding of early sign development:

(1) The manual articulators are paired. Some signs of ASL are one-handed whereas others are two-handed. Among the two-handed signs, the two hands may execute identical movements (albeit the hands may be in or out of phase with each other), or the dominant hand may act upon a static nondominant hand (see Battison, 1978).

(2) The articulation of signs entails the coordination of the shoulder, elbow, forearm, wrist, and fingers within each arm, as well as the co-ordination of the two arms for those signs that require both. Production of a single sign may require coordinated articulation at different joints with the arm, whether to bring the arms and hands into the signing space that stretches from the waist to the top of the head or to perform the lexically specified movement of a sign. Some of the joints involved in sign articulation are proximal to the torso, whereas others are rela-tively distal from it, as shown below:

Proximal to Torso                                                    Distal from Torso

←―――――――――――――――――――――――――――――――――――――――→

shoulder ... elbow ... radioulnar ... wrist ... 1st-knuckles ... 2nd-knuckles

It is unclear whether the phonological representations of signs specify a particular joint or joints as the articulator(s) of a given sign (Brentari, 1998; Crasborn, 2001); it is possible that a default joint is specified pho-nologically. Proximalization of sign movement may contribute to the enlargement of signs, when shouting or when signing to an infant (Holzrichter & Meier, 2000). For example, the ASL signs WARN and YES are both articulated with a repeated nodding movement at the wrist. Both signs may be enlarged by executing that movement at the shoul-der, specifically though an inward rotation of the arm along its longi-tudinal axis. As a consequence of enlargement, signs are likely more readily perceived. Signs may also be distalized, for example, when whispering. The sign WARN, but not the sign YES, can be distalized such that the sign is executed at the first knuckles. The fisted handshape (S-hand) of YES, unlike the open handshape (B-hand) of WARN, blocks distalization.

(3) Accurate production of the large number of contrastive hand-shapes in ASL requires considerable fine motor control of the fingers, the most distal segments of the arm. Ann (1996) has described anatomical and physiological factors that predict the relative difficulty of hand-shapes. A particularly striking example of the import—and potential difficulty—of handshape contrasts comes from the ASL number name system: The sign SIX requires opposition of the thumb and little finger, SEVEN requires opposition of the thumb and ring finger, EIGHT requires opposition of the thumb and middle finger, and NINE requires opposi-tion of the thumb and first finger. As any late learner of ASL knows,

these handshapes are also perceptually confusable—novice learners have difficulty distinguishing the signs SIX and NINE, or SEVEN and EIGHT.

(4) Many signs have repeated movements. Monomorphemic words such as "papa" or "mama," with repeated identical syllables, are relatively few in spoken languages. But they are common in signed languages (Channon, 2002). Patterns of repetition are also crucial in the morphology of signed languages; one crucial difference between SIT and CHAIR lies in the repeated movement of the derived noun. In the noun–verb pairs that Supalla and Newport (1978) investigated, repetition was characteristic of the nouns. Patterns of repeated movement also characterize verbs inflected for temporal aspect in ASL and other languages (Fischer, 1973; Klima & Bellugi, 1979).

(5) Sign articulation is relatively slow. In contrast to the oral articulators, the manual articulators are relatively massive and often must execute large movement excursions. Perhaps as a consequence, the articulation of ASL signs appears to be substantially slower than the production of English words, although the rate at which propositions are transmitted is equivalent across the two language modalities (Bellugi & Fischer, 1972; Klima & Bellugi, 1979). This seeming paradox may be resolved in the following way: The slow rate of sign articulation may push sign languages toward more simultaneous linguistic organization, in phonology, morphology, and syntax. The slow rate of sign articulation may also pull signed languages away from the sequential morphology that is characteristic of spoken languages.

Why are these and other articulatory properties of sign languages important? First, as already suggested, certain articulatory factors—like the slow rate of sign articulation—may promote particular kinds of linguistic organization. Articulatory factors are likely to be particularly exigent early in development. For example, rate factors might particularly limit children's elaboration of sequential morphological structures in the visual-gestural modality (whether those children are innovating home sign systems or emergent signed languages such as Nicaraguan Sign Language). Thus, modality-specific motoric factors that might have little impact on the adult may have more profound effects on the child. Second, in comparisons of early milestones of speech and sign development, there have been controversial claims of an early sign advantage, or perhaps a disadvantage for speech (Meier & Newport, 1990). One explanation might lie in motor factors; infants may show better motor control over the sign articulators than of the speech articulators. Third, by examining the extent to which motoric factors explain early sign development, we make progress toward identifying those phenomena of early sign development that cannot be explained in this way. Instead, what phenomena must be explained in terms of perceptual, grammatical, or input factors?

## AN OVERVIEW OF THE FORM OF EARLY SIGNS

### What Does a Typical Early Sign Look Like?

Data reported in Conlin, Mirus, Mauk, and Meier (2000) on the signing of 8- to 17-month old deaf children raised in Deaf, signing families suggest that an early ASL sign will likely be articulated in neutral space or on the face. Although a plurality of early signs in their corpus were articulated in neutral space, almost 38% were articulated on the face or head. By raising the hands to the head, such signs were displaced far from the resting position of child's arms. Apparently, this displacement is not costly for the child. Similar results have been reported for older children acquiring LSQ (Lavoie & Villeneuve, 1999): In data from three 3year-old children, 43% of their signs were produced in neutral space and 37% on the face. Signs on the trunk or arms were very sparsely represented.

The handshape of an early sign will likely be a 5-hand (all fingers extended and spread) or its lax variant, although other handshapes—particularly, fisted handshapes and handshapes with an extended index finger—will occur.[1] Interestingly, the 5-hand, especially when lax, may approximate the neutral hand configuration. Recent work (Cheek et al., 2001) suggests that palm orientation will be downward or mid (where mid is either toward or away from the midline).[2]

The typical early sign may be one- or two-handed, although one-handed forms predominate in children's productions (Cheek et al., 2001). Base hand signs may be later to emerge than one-handed or two-handed symmetrical signs; see evidence to this effect from LIBRAS (Karnopp, 2002), Norwegian Sign Language (von Tetzchner, 1994), and FinSL (Takkinen, 2003). The error rate on base hand signs may be relatively high: In about 60% of the tokens reported in Cheek et al. (2001), the base hand was omitted or the sign movement became inappropriately symmetrical, with both hands executing the same movement. However the data on children's production of base hand signs are sparse, perhaps because base hand target signs may be underrepresented vis-à-vis their frequency amongst dictionary entries (Cheek et al., 2001).

---

[1] Clibbens (1998) reports on the acquisition of British Sign Language by a child named Anne. Her first recognizable sign appeared at 14 months. From 14 to 19 months of age, the only handshapes she produced were a fisted hand and a spread hand. At 19 months she began producing signs with an extended index finger (other fingers fisted). Also see the results reported in Karnopp (2002) on the acquisition of handshape in LIBRAS-signing children.

[2] See Juncos et al. (1997) for a similar characterization of the early signs of three infants, 12–16 months of age, who were acquiring LSE.

The typical early sign may involve articulation at the relatively proximal articulators of the arm, the elbow, and the shoulder; movement at the first knuckles is also well controlled (Meier, Mauk, Cheek, & Moreland, 2004). Articulation at the wrist and forearm is not well controlled by infant signers. Articulation at the second knuckles appears to be strongly linked to articulation at the first knuckles, consistent with the observation that simple open–close movements of the hand may be frequent in early signing (Petitto, 1988). A consequence of this apparent linkage between the first and second knuckles is that target signs, such as PIG, that have movement restricted to the first knuckles may be articulated using a closing movement of the hand executed at both sets of knuckles. Lastly, the typical early sign has repeated movement, and children may substitute repeated movement in signs that have just a single movement in the adult language.

Some of these characteristics of very early signing may persist in older children. For example, Karnopp (1994) reports data on four children (ages, in years;months: 2;8, 2;8, 4;9, and 5;9) who were acquiring LIBRAS as their first language. All four children were deaf and were born into Deaf families. Even for these older children, a fully open handshape (all fingers extended and spread, i.e., a 5-hand) and a fisted handshape (an A-hand) were most common in one-handed target signs that do not have handshape change in the adult language. Takkinen (2003) reports data on the acquisition of FinSL handshapes by deaf children who have deaf, signing parents and whose ages ranged from 2 to 7 years over the course of the study. At age 5, there were still errors in handshape articulation (e.g., in the number of selected fingers, in the extension of the fingers, and in the handshape of the nondominant hand). Handshape errors had largely disappeared by age 7.

## The Three Major Parameters of Sign Formation

As a first step toward understanding how children articulate signs, let's consider children's overall accuracy on the three major parameters of sign formation. Figure 9.1 displays data reported in Cheek et al. (2001). The movement data summarized in figure 9.1 are data on path movements only; hand-internal movements (e.g., opening and closing movements of the hands, finger wiggling, etc.) are not included. The key result here is the low error rate on place of articulation, especially by comparison to the high rate of error on handshape. (The movement results are more difficult to interpret at this juncture.) For ASL, the low frequency of errors on place has also been reported in a diary study of nine children (Siedlecki & Bonvillian, 1993), in analyses of longitudinally collected video data from four children (Cheek et al., 2001; Conlin et al., 2000), and in a case study using videotaped data (Marentette & Mayberry, 2000). This same result has also been reported for children learning LSE (Juncos et al., 1997) and LIBRAS (Karnopp, 1994, 2002). Thus, this phenomenon may be

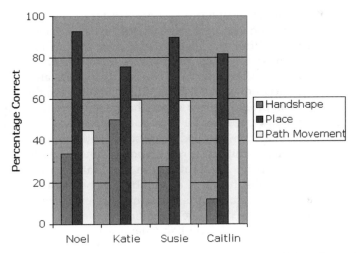

Figure 9-1. Overall accuracy on three major parameters of sign formation in the spontaneous signing of four deaf children of deaf parents (ages 8–17 months); see Cheek et al. (2001) for details.

characteristic of the acquisition of sign languages in general, not just of ASL.

The contrasting error rates on place and handshape can be interpreted by reference to the developmental functions for gross and fine motor development (see Conlin et al., 2000; Siedlecki & Bonvillian, 1993): Young children may lack the fine motor control to produce the array of distinct handshapes that occur in ASL, whereas the gross motor control required to reach a location, whether a toy or an anatomical landmark on the child's own body, is firmly in place before the first year. In essence, achieving correct place of articulation requires the child to reach to a location on his or her upper body. Such reaching movements can be accomplished using proximal articulators of the arm. Perceptual factors may also promote higher error rates on handshape than on place: Handshape distinctions may be less perceptible to the child than place distinctions.

Infants appear to be more variable in their production of handshape than in the production of place. Conlin et al. (2000) reported that, with respect to those signs on which one or more of the three children they studied (8–17 months of age) erred in place or handshape, the children produced more distinct handshapes (mean = 2.53 per sign type) than places (mean = 1.47 per sign type). In other words, these three children tended to be relatively consistent in how they erred on place; for example, one child (Susie at 14 and 15 months) consistently erred in her production of the ASL sign DOLL; she produced it at the upper lip instead of at the nose. In contrast, children's handshape errors tended to be quite variable from one production of a target sign to the next. Conlin et al. speculated that their data on children's place errors are not consistent with a motoric explanation, but may instead indicate that the children had misrepresented the place value of certain signs.

Marentette and Mayberry (2000) likewise argue that, although motoric factors may account for the overarching differences in the accuracy with which infants produce place versus handshape, motoric explanations cannot readily account for the particular place substitutions present in their data. They instead suggest the child's emerging body schema—that is, her cognitive representation of landmarks on her own body—may explain place substitutions. In their data, place errors typically involved the substitution of a neighboring, but more prominent, location for the target location. As an example, their subject produced the sign TELEPHONE at the ear rather than on the cheek.

Children's overall accuracy on handshape is low, but their production of handshape is nonetheless patterned. As reviewed in Marentette and Mayberry (2000), children's earliest handshapes are largely limited to a rather small set: 5 (all fingers extended and spread), A (a fisted handshape), 1 (index only extended from the fist), B (fingers extended but together), and baby-O (index and thumb opposed, other fingers fisted). The early use of these handshapes can be explained largely by the anatomy and physiology of the hand (Ann, 1996; Boyes-Braem, 1990). When young children erroneously substitute a handshape for an adult target, they tend to draw from this same small set (again, see Marentette and Mayberry's, 2000, review of the pertinent literature). On Boyes-Braem's (1990) model, the determinants of handshape substitution include linguistic complexity (e.g., the complexity of the sign's movement), the availability or not of visual feedback during the child's production of the sign, and a bias toward fingertip contact, among other considerations. Marentette and Mayberry's case study of SF (1;0 to 2;1) showed that handshapes substitutions occurred within families of similar handshapes, so that the 5-hand replaced B, bent-B, clawed-5, and C-handshapes, whereas the fistlike A-hand replaced other fisted handshapes (S) and the baby-O. Knapp (2000) identified this same phenomenon in the data set that she examined (i.e., the same corpus of data reported in Cheek et al., 2001; Meier et al., 2004).

Interestingly, high error rates on handshape have been found in two types of errors encountered in adult populations. In slips of the hand, handshape-only slips are much more frequent than place-only or movement-only slips. This is true for the two signed languages on which we have slips data: ASL (Klima & Bellugi, 1979) and German Sign Language (Hohenberger, Happ, & Leuninger, 2002). Slips data in speech also show that contain phonological units are particularly susceptible to being slipped; for example, syllable–initial consonants are more likely to be slipped than are syllable–final ones. The data on sign slips find an echo in the small body of data on paraphasias produced by aphasic signers: The preponderance of paraphasias are handshape errors (Corina, 2000). Handshape may also be an important source of dialect variation in signed languages; in analyses of data on Mexican Sign Language collected in Mexico City and Aguascalientes, Guerra Currie (1999) found that most variation across her adult consultants was in handshape. Further research may reveal whether a unified account is possible for the seeming fragility of handshape in development, in slips, in aphasia, and in dialect variation. For example, is there a grammatical explanation for this phenomenon? Sandler (1989) sought to explain the frequency of handshape slips, as well as a variety of phonological facts about handshape in ASL, by arguing that handshape is located on a separate "autosegmental" tier in the phonological representation of signs.

## ICONICITY AS A PREDICTOR OF CHILDREN'S ERRORS

Following Saussure (1916/1959), we can define a word, or a sign, as a conventional form-meaning pair. To learn a word or sign, the child must know the concept that is signified, the linguistic form that signifies that concept, and the mapping between concept and form. As Saussure observed, the mapping between form and meaning is typically arbitrary in spoken languages, notwithstanding the existence of onomatopoeia. In signed languages, nonarbitrary signs are more frequent than are nonarbitrary words in spoken languages. Do signing children seek to enhance the transparency of form-meaning mappings in signed languages? If so, is this urge a source of errors in their production of first signs?

### Iconicity and Input

Do parents enhance the iconicity of the signs that they address to infants or do they seek to explicate the iconic basis of those signs? Launer (1982) examined early sign development in two deaf children of deaf parents, aged 1;0,9 to 1;11,16 (Corinne) and 1;5,20 to 2;0,6 (Sally). (Ages are expressed as years; months, days; e.g. 1;11,16 indicates 1 year, 11 months, 16 days.) She reports that 8% of the sign tokens addressed to these children before age 2;0 showed some kind of elaboration of the iconic basis of those signs. For example, in articulating the sign DRIVE, one mother accompanied the manual gesture with rhythmic movements of the head and torso (Launer, 1982, p. 143). However, other maternal productions submerged the iconicity of signs, as when one mother (Sally's at 1;6) imitated her daughter's production of CAR. In the child's form, the alternating movement of the adult form was replaced by a simultaneous, in-phase, up-and-down movement of the two hands. Neither the child's form—nor the mother's imitation—matched the movement of turning a steering wheel.

## Iconicity as a Determinant of Which Signs Children Learn?

One might predict that iconic signs would be overrepresented in children's early vocabularies because iconicity in the adult target sign would make it easier for the child to form the association between a particular form and its meaning. Orlansky and Bonvillian (1984) examined parental reports of 9 children; they found no evidence that iconic signs were overrepresented in these children's earliest ASL vocabularies. Although recent work has argued for effects of iconicity on the emergence of classifier constructions (Slobin et al., 2003) and of verb agreement (Casey, 2003) in older ASL-exposed children, there is little evidence of iconic effects on the set of frozen, morphologically simplex signs that generally form children's earliest vocabularies.

## Iconicity as a Determinant of the Form of Children's Errors?

The results from Orlansky and Bonvillian (1984) cast doubt on whether iconicity is an important determinant of the composition of children's earliest sign vocabularies. An alternative hypothesis would hold that effects of iconicity might be revealed not in the composition of children's vocabularies but in the form of their errors. As noted, Launer (1982) examined early sign production in two deaf children of deaf parents, ages 1;0,9 to 1;11,16 and 1;5,20 to 2;0,6. In approximately 15% of the tokens, children's productions enhanced the iconicity of the adult target sign. So, in one instance, the child (1;6) produced the verb EAT-ICE-CREAM by licking the back of her hand. However, in Launer's data, such proiconic errors were exceeded by a larger proportion of errors that reduced the iconicity of the adult target.

Recently, Meier et al. (2002, 2004) examined how infant sign production affected the judged iconicity of the signs that four infants (8–17 months of age) attempted. All four children showed significantly more countericonic errors (approximately one-third of the data set) than proiconic errors (substantially less than 10% of the data). In sum, the preponderance of children's productions in this study either were neutral with respect to iconicity (i.e., the child's form was judged to be no more or no less iconic than the adult target) or were actually less iconic than the adult target. We speculate that the slightly older age of Launer's two children and the seemingly higher proportion of verbs in her sample may account for the somewhat more frequent effects of iconicity that she encountered.

The results reported by Launer (1982) and by Meier et al. (2004) make it clear that iconicity cannot account for the preponderance of signing children's error forms. Errors that reduce the iconicity of adult signs are not restricted to ASL; for example, Clibbens (1998, p. 12) reports an instance in which a child acquiring British Sign Language (BSL) substituted an S-handshape for the Y-hand target of the BSL sign COW, thus obscuring the image of the animal's horns. The finding that iconicity is not a major factor in determining which signs children produce or how they produce those signs is consistent with research on older children's acquisition of deixis (Petitto, 1987), verb agreement (Meier, 1982, 1987), and classifiers (Supalla, 1982) in ASL. This pattern of results suggest that we must seek other explanations for the errors that children make in the production of their first signs. The crucial effect of iconicity in language development may lie not in the acquisition of conventional signed languages such as ASL but in children's contribution to the invention of home sign systems and other emerging communication systems (Goldin-Meadow, 2003; Goldin-Meadow & Mylander, 1990). The pictorial resources of the visual-gestural modality may allow children to invent iconic gestures that can be readily understood by their nonsigning parents.

## MOTOR CONTROL FACTORS AS PREDICTORS OF CHILDREN'S ERRORS IN MOVEMENT

In two recent publications, my colleagues and I have discussed three properties of general motor development that may predict the kinds of errors that children make in the formation of signs (Cheek et al., 2001; Meier et al., 2002, 2004). These factors may contribute particularly to our understanding of the kinds of errors encountered in children's production of sign movement.

### Repetition

In many aspects of their motor development, children frequently display repeated movements. This is true of the stereotypies such as repeated kicking or arm waving that children show early in development (Thelen, 1979), and is also characteristic of vocal and manual babbling. Deaf and hearing children, with and without sign exposure, produce meaningless prelinguistic gestures characterized by repeated movements. This infant bias toward repeated movement patterns may also underlie the kinds of place harmony errors that children show in speech development (e.g., [gag] for "dog"). In dynamic systems theory, repetitive cyclic movements are considered to be an "attractor" for the developing motor system (Thelen, 1991).

Given this background, Meier et al. (2004) reasoned that signing infants might show highly accurate production of signs with repeated movement in the adult languages. Moreover, they suggested, children might tend to add repetition to adult signs that have a single movement cycle. These predictions were confirmed by an analysis of their data from 8- to 17-month old infants. Interestingly, Juncos et al. (1997, p. 179) have suggested that repetition is well controlled in infants (12–16 months of age) acquiring LSE.

## Sympathy

Through much of the first year, children may have some difficulty inhibiting the action of one hand when the other hand is active (Wiesendanger, Wicki, & Rouiller, 1994); this phenomenon is apparent in early reaching (Fagard, 1994). In older, language-delayed children, the action of the active hand may sometimes be mirrored by movements of the other hand (Trauner, Wulfeck, Tallal, & Hesselink, 2000; also see McDowell & Wolff, 1997, for a review). In our work, we have referred to such movements as sympathetic movements. Even in the adult, control over movements in which both arms execute identical movements appears to be more robust than is the control of movements in which the two arms act independently; thus, the latter type of movements may be more affected by damage to the brain (Wiesendanger et al., 1994). Mirror movements can be elicited even from normal adults under appropriate task conditions (McDowell & Wolff, 1997).

Although infants do not have difficulty inhibiting the nondominant hand in the production of one-handed signs such as ASL YELLOW, children experience considerable difficulty in the production of adult signs in which the nondominant hand is a static base hand on which the dominant hand acts.[3] Cheek et al. (2001) report that the four children in their study (8 to 17 months of age) made 62 attempts to produce such signs. The infants correctly produced the static base hand in 25 instances (40%), omitted the nondominant hand entirely in 12 instances (19%), and in the remaining 25 instances (40%) produced a sign in which both hands executed identical movements. Thus, in this last kind of error, the nondominant hand moved sympathetically to the dominant. As an example, Katie (1;4,3) produced the sign COOKIE with identical, twisting rotations of the two hands. Another child (Noel at 1;4,25) produced a version of FALL in which both hands moved up and then down. Marentette and Mayberry (2000, p. 83) also report instances of this type of error. Like our subject Katie, the subject in their case study (SJ) erred in the production of the ASL sign COOKIE; SJ's form showed identical movements on both hands.[4]

A related problem appears in the production of handshape in base-hand signs. Signs in which both hands are active must have the same handshape. However, base-hand signs may have distinct handshapes on the dominant and nondominant hands (Battison, 1978). Handshape

---

[3] Children do make occasional errors in the production of one-handed target signs; in the corpus reported by Cheek et al. (2001), approximately 7% of the 444 tokens of one-handed target signs were produced as two-handed symmetrical signs.

[4] This error type was infrequent in the data reported by Siedlecki and Bonvillian (1993). However, their methods are different inasmuch as they rely primarily on parental reports.

errors appear to be particularly frequent and persistent in children's production of such signs (ASL: Siedlecki & Bonvillian, 1997; FinSL: Takkinen, 2003). In the just-cited example from Katie, the handshape of the nondominant hand assimilated to that of the dominant hand in her production of COOKIE. In sum, these results suggest that motor factors, likely in concert with the cognitive demands attendant upon producing a lexical item, yield sympathetic movements in the production of base hand signs. There is little evidence of input factors that would promote these error types.

The relative infrequency of base-hand signs in samples of early signing raises the possibility that children might be avoiding these signs. For example, Cheek et al. (2001) note that just 10% of their data had a base hand sign as the target sign, whereas 25% of the entries in the *Dictionary of American Sign Language* (Stokoe, Casterline, & Croneberg, 1965) are base hand signs (Klima & Bellugi, 1979). Other studies of other languages have also remarked on the infrequency of base hand signs in the signing of 2–3-year-olds (FinSL: Takkinen, 2003; LIBRAS: Karnopp, 1994). However, evaluation of the hypothesis the children are actively avoiding base-hand signs depends on comparisons of the frequency of such signs in children's signing as compared to the incidence of such signs in the input available to these children.

## Proximalization

Since Gesell and Thompson (1934), it has been suggested that the development of motor control in infants proceeds from joints that are relatively proximal to the torso (e.g., the shoulder or elbow) to articulators that are distal from the torso (e.g., the wrist and fingers). As reviewed in Meier et al. (2004), this pattern of development may be evident in infant kicking and in the development of writing in older children. Even adults proximalize movement when asked to write with their nondominant hand. Lastly, certain brain-damaged populations (e.g., ideomotor apraxics) show proximalization of movement in their gesturing (Poizner, Mack, Verfaellie, Gonzalez Rothi, & Heilman, 1990).

Meier et al. (2004) examined whether infants show proximalization of movement in early signing. Joint usage was coded qualitatively for every sign token in their corpus; children's productions were then compared to those of an adult model. An analysis of children's errors (i.e., an analysis of all tokens in which the child form did not match the adult model) revealed that, when children substituted (i.e., replaced) action at one joint with action at another joint, children reliably used a joint that was proximal to the target joint. For example, one child (0;11,23) produced the ASL sign HORSE with a nodding movement of the wrist, rather than with the repeated bending at the first knuckles that is characteristic of the adult target. A similar pattern was uncovered for omission errors: When an adult target sign required action at two (or more) joints, the child was more likely to omit action at the more distal target joint. An analysis of additions errors—that is, errors in which children added action articulated at a joint not present in the adult target—revealed that proximalization of movement was not the only factor at work in these data. Specifically, an apparent coupling of the first and second knuckles yielded a class of distalization errors. When the adult target demanded articulation at just the first knuckles, children frequently added articulation at the second knuckles, as in one child's (0;9,0) articulation of the sign DOG. Coupling of articulation at the first and second knuckles may be consistent with early infant grasping abilities.

Proximalization errors appear to occur in the acquisition of other signed languages as well; for example, Takkinen's (2003, p. 84) report of the acquisition of handshape in FinSL indicates that flexion of the wrist sometimes substituted for flexion at the first knuckles. Interestingly, the data for her analysis came, as noted above, from older children than those examined in Meier et al. (2004). Lavoie and Villeneuve (1999) have also reported proximalization errors in the acquisition of LSQ.

Proximalization of movement also occurs in parental input to children; parents frequently enlarge sign movement (e.g., Masataka, 2000), and as a result, they may articulate signs at more proximal joints of the arm whose use would not be expected in adult-directed renditions of the same sign (Holzrichter & Meier, 2000). However, the finding that hearing adult learners of signed languages (ASL and German Sign Language) also produced proximalization errors in an elicited imitation task (Mirus et al., 2000) suggests that perceptual and/or input factors cannot be a complete explanation. Instead, proximalization of movement may be common in the acquisition of new motor skills. Moreover, proximalization may be a particularly frequent outcome in immature mature systems.

## THE BABBLE–SIGN TRANSITION

It is possible that the motoric factors discussed in this chapter most directly constrain the prelinguistic infant. Gestural forms that are characteristic of the babbling period may persist into the early sign period because those forms are entrenched and well-controlled. The cognitive load of producing lexical items may lead the child to produce sign forms that are articulatorily simpler than would be otherwise expected given his or her nonlinguistic motor skills.

In sign, as in speech, there appears to be a babbling stage that precedes the production of true signs (Meier & Willerman, 1995; Petitto & Marentette, 1991). What is the relationship between children's babbles and their first signs? In speech, there is a smooth transition between babbling and first words. The phonetics of babbling predicts the phonetics of children's first words. During the babbling period, children are much more likely to produce [d] than [m] and, to the dismay of mothers, children are likely to say *dada* well before they first utter *mama* (Locke, 1985). When we turn to manual babbles and other prelinguistic gestures, the following questions arise: Does the form of prelinguistic gesturing in deaf children reared in signing families predict the form of their first signs? The answer appears to be yes (Petitto & Marentette, 1991). For example, Meier, Mauk, Mirus, and Conlin (1998) suggested that the repetitive character of manual babbling carries over into children's early sign productions.

To the extent that manual babbling also occurs in hearing children with no sign exposure, then the form of such babbling is likely to reflect motoric constraints operating on the child. Cheek et al. (2001) considered data from both deaf and hearing babies. The babbling data came from five deaf and five hearing babies. The early sign observations came from four deaf infants, the same infants considered in Meier et al. (2004). All deaf children had deaf parents, and all hearing children had hearing non-signing parents. Between the ages of 7 and 17 months, children were videotaped biweekly while interacting at home with a parent and/or an experimenter. Gestures were coded as signs only if recognizably related to an adult sign in form and if used in an appropriate context for that adult sign. All gestures—whether signs or not—were coded for an array of articulatory properties; interested readers should see the article for a detailed description of their coding system. For the analyses reviewed below, all prelinguistic gestures—whether babbles or communicative gestures—are considered together.

The data yielded interesting similarities between prelinguistic gestures and first signs. The analysis of articulatory properties of prelinguistic gestures and signs showed the following: (1) For handshape, all infants produced a relaxed hand with all fingers extended more often than any other handshape in their prelinguistic gesturing; the same held for deaf infants in their first signs (see also Conlin et al., 2000). (2) For movement, infants displayed downward movements more often for prelinguistic gestures and signs than any other movement category. (3) Babies demonstrated a preference for one-handed prelinguistic gestures over two-handed ones. For first signs, deaf babies maintained this preference by producing more one-handed signs than two-handed ones. (4) For palm orientation, children predominately gestured or signed with palms down. An error analysis of the early sign data provides further evidence that features of prelinguistic gesture persist into early signing. For example, the most frequent handshape in prelinguistic gesture is a spread handshape made with all fingers spread and either fully extended (the 5-hand of ASL) or partially extended (the lax version of the 5-hand). These spread handshapes were, much more frequently than any other handshape, substituted for adult target handshapes when deaf children erred in their production of signs.

The shared features (e.g., downward movement, relaxed handshape and downward palm orientation) suggest that prelinguistic gestures in deaf and hearing babies may be similarly constrained by their particular level of motor development. And these constraints may carry over into the deaf child's early sign production. However, the transition between prelinguistic gesture and first signs is not entirely seamless. As observed in Conlin et al. (2000), signs articulated on the head are frequent in children's early vocabularies, constituting 38% of their productions. However, we rarely saw prelinguistic gestures, even from deaf children, that were articulated on the head (but see Petitto & Marentette, 1991, for a report of one deaf child who produced such babbles frequently).

## PERCEIVING THE FORMS OF SIGNS

The literature on infant speech perception demonstrates that young hearing infants discriminate phonetic contrasts that are not exemplified in the language (or languages) to which they are exposed; this ability declines by 10–12-months of age, likely because these contrasts are not part of the phonological systems of the language(s) they are learning (Werker & Tees, 1984). Likewise, hearing infants with no sign exposure may be well-prepared to perceive the phonetic distinctions that are important in signed languages. Studies using habituation procedures have demonstrated that 4-month-old hearing infants are sensitive to contrasts in movement (Carroll & Gibson, 1986) and handshape (Baker, Sootsman, Golinkoff, & Petitto, 2003) that are important in the phonology of ASL.

Despite evidence of impressive infant abilities to discriminate speech sounds, children seem slower to discriminate phonemic contrasts within words. Within-subjects comparisons of speaking children's production and perception of phonemic contrasts in words suggest that children even at age 3 and older may have difficulty discriminating certain English consonants (e.g., θ/f and r/w) and that this difficulty may account for lingering errors in production. In contrast, other production errors, such as distorted productions of /s/, are not associated with any difficulty in discrimination (see Vihman, 1996, for a review).

Perceptual factors may likewise contribute to children's errors in their production of signs. It would not seem surprising if children found it difficult to discriminate pairs of signs that differ only in the presence of an 1-hand (index finger extended; other fingers fisted, as in ASL MOUSE) versus an R-hand (index and middle fingers extended and crossed; other fingers fisted, as in RAT). Consequently, children might represent such signs incorrectly and might subsequently manifest errors in production. Currently, there is very limited evidence that for older children—at least for deaf children of hearing parents—recognition of place values may be more robust than their recognition of handshape and movement values: Hamilton (1986) tested 36 deaf children, ages 6;0–9;1, all of whom had hearing parents and attended a day school for deaf children. On each trial, Hamilton placed two pictures in front of the child. The child then had to pick the picture that matched a sign stimulus; the sign names for the target and distracter pictures were minimal pairs that differed only in place of articulation, handshape, or movement. Children made significantly fewer errors on stimuli testing place of articulation than on stimuli that tested either movement or handshape.

An important goal for future research should be to tease apart perceptual and articulatory explanations of children's errors in sign formation, particularly children's errors in the production of handshape. Lane, Boyes-Braem, and Bellugi (1976) reported data on the perceptual confusability of 20 ASL handshapes; among the handshape pairs that were highly confusable were (1) W (thumb and little finger opposed, others extended) and F (thumb and index finger opposed, others extended), and (2) H and R (both handshapes have the index and middle finger extended, with the others fisted; however, in the R-hand the index and middle fingers are crossed). Substitutions of H for R could readily be explained on articulatory grounds; that is, the uncrossed H-hand is presumably easier to articulate than the R-hand. However, if children were shown to substitute R for H, this substitution would presumably arise only from the perceptual confusability of the two handshapes and the consequent misrepresentation of an H-hand sign as having an R-handshape.

## INPUT FACTORS

By emphasizing motoric, and to a lesser extent perceptual, explanations for why children articulate signs as they do, I have focused on factors that are largely internal to the child. Yet, children clearly acquire signs in linguistic and social environments. There are three potential classes of effects that the linguistic environment may have on children's gestural and sign development: (1) effects of early sign exposure, (2) effects of specific signed languages, and (3) effects of child-directed signing (i.e., effects of the particular register that parents use with children).

### Effects of Early Sign Exposure

Whether an adult has prior linguistic experience with a signed language affects the way in which signs are perceived. For example, linguistic experience affects perception of movement, such that signers and non-signers provide different judgments of the relative similarity of sign movements in point-light displays (Poizner, Bellugi, & Lutes-Driscoll, 1981). In addition, signers—but, not nonsigners—show evidence of categorical perception of handshape (Emmorey, McCullough, & Brentari, 2003). Interestingly, neither signers nor nonsigners perceive place of articulation in a categorical fashion.

Obviously infants also differ in whether or not they have early exposure to a conventional signed language such as ASL or BSL. Unless their
parents are deaf, hearing children rarely have early exposure to a signed
language. Hearing children born to hearing parents uniformly have early
access to a spoken language; in contrast, deaf infants reared in hearing
families may have limited linguistic exposure of any sort. Those hearing
parents who learn some sign after the birth of a deaf infant are also likely
to be highly variable in the quality of the input that they provide their
deaf children. In sum, comparisons of children with and without early
exposure to a signed language afford unique opportunities to examine
the effects of the early linguistic environment on subsequent language
development.

Can we identify effects of sign exposure early in infant development?
In particular, can we identify effects on early articulatory development?
Clearly we cannot investigate sign articulation in children who have no
sign exposure. But we can investigate the prelinguistic gestures of deaf
and hearing infants who differ in whether or not they have early sign
exposure. Meier and Willerman (1995) looked at the manual babbles of
such infants. Although these authors generally reported considerable
similarity in the prelinguistic gestures of deaf and hearing infants, they
did report a tendency for the nonreferential gestures of deaf, sign-
exposed infants to be more repetitious than the gestures of their hearing
counterparts; that is, the deaf infants produced a higher proportion of
nonreferential gestures (manual babbles) that were multicyclic. The
greater proportion of multicyclic prelinguistic gestures produced by
the deaf infants may reflect the fact that repeated movement is such a
frequent characteristic of the signs that these children see in their linguistic input.

More recently, Petitto et al. (2004) have used a movement analysis
system (Optotrak) to examine the rhythmic properties of prelinguistic
gesture in hearing infants who varied in whether or not they had exposure only to speech or only to sign. Speech-exposed and sign-exposed
babies were alike in producing prelinguistic gestures that have a cyclicity of 2.5–3.0 Hz; however, the sign-exposed infants produced another class of gestures with a cyclicity of approximately 1 Hz. Petitto et al.
found these slower gestures were more signlike (and therefore more
babblelike) in other articulatory dimensions, such as being produced
within the sign space.

## Effects of Specific Signed Languages

There currently is too little information on cross-linguistic differences in
sign phonology. They certainly exist: There are well-known differences in
handshape inventory (Woodward, 1982); thus, some signed languages
have a handshape in which just the middle finger is extended, a handshape
that is obscene in American culture and that is absent from ASL. Klima and

Bellugi (1979) report differences between ASL and Chinese Sign Language (CSL) in permissible hand-internal movements, in permissible contacting regions for F-hands, and in place inventory (e.g., the CSL sign WEDNESDAY begins at the underarm, a location not allowed in ASL). ASL and CSL may also show phonetic differences in the form of the A-handshape. Cross-linguistic differences between sign phonologies might also be sought in loan sign vocabularies, inasmuch as signed languages differ considerably in how they represent the written words of spoken languages; compare, for example, the one-handed fingerspelling system of ASL with its two-handed counterpart in BSL.

It is unclear, however, that any of the just-cited differences are of sufficient magnitude to have much effect on early sign production. Language-specific effects can be hard to detect even in early speech development; for example, early differences in vocal babbling may be largely of a statistical nature (e.g., de Boysson-Bardies & Vihman, 1991), not differences in the repertoire of babbled sounds. Aside from effects of phonological inventory or structure, language-specific effects on early sign development might also arise from differences in the relative frequency of, say, specific handshape or place values in the vocabularies of two signed languages. Future research might seek to identify such effects.

## Effects of Child-Directed Signing

The properties of child-directed signing may promote some of the phenomena noted in this chapter (for recent overviews of the literature, see Holzrichter & Meier, 2000; particularly, for discussion of motherese in Japanese Sign Language, see Masataka, 2000).[5]

Many characteristics of child-directed signing may arise from the demands of gaining and maintaining the child's visual attention to the parent. Enlarging signs, repeating them, and displacing them into the child's visual field may help to ensure that those signs are noticed by the child (Holzrichter & Meier, 2000). The enlargement of signs is sometimes achieved by using more proximal articulators of the arm than would be expected in adult-to-adult signing.

Although these properties of child-directed signing may contribute to some trends in early sign articulation noted in this chapter, there is little reason now to think that the properties of child-directed signing are the only precipitating factors. Even adults with no sign experience show evidence of proximalization of movement when asked to imitate signs (Mirus et al., 2000). Moreover, to date there is no evidence suggesting that, in child-directed signing, parents systematically modify signs with a static nondominant hand (e.g., ASL FALL) so that both hands would

---

[5] It is certainly possible that the properties of child-directed signing are specific to a given culture—or language. However, we have no evidence of this now.

execute identical movements or that the handshape of the nondominant hand would assimilate to that of the dominant hand.

## SUMMARY AND CONCLUSIONS

This chapter has discussed typical patterns of early sign production that emerge from a review of the literature on articulatory development in signing children. For example, an analysis of children's accuracy on three major parameters of sign formation (handshape, place of articulation, and movement) reveals very low error rates on place of articulation, as compared to the much higher error rates on handshape (Cheek et al., 2001; Conlin et al., 2000; Marentette & Mayberry, 2000; Siedlecki & Bonvillian, 1993). Motoric factors (e.g., differences between the gross motor control required to attain a place of articulation vs. the fine motor control required for correct handshape production) may account for this overarching difference between children's acquisition of place and handshape. Yet even on place of articulation, children do make errors. The particular place errors encountered in the literature cannot be readily explained on motoric grounds; instead, nonmotoric explanations must be sought. For example, the relative salience of body landmarks may offer an explanation for place substitutions that have been reported in the literature (Marentette & Mayberry, 2000).

This review has revealed a number of trends in early sign articulation that, despite the somewhat fragmented literature on the form of children's early signs, have been reported by different groups, using different methods, working on different signed languages. For example, children's apparent early success on place, as compared to the persistence of handshape errors, has been found not only for ASL, but also for LSE (Juncos et al., 1997) and for LIBRAS (Karnopp, 1994, 2002). Other phenomena discussed here (e.g., the smooth transition between prelinguistic gesture and first signs, children's tendency to proximalize sign movement) are also likely to reflect normative patterns of development in signing children across languages and cultures. But much more research is needed in order to document those normative patterns fully.

Studies of early articulatory development in signing children can also be of very broad interest to researchers on first language acquisition. Such studies allow us to examine the effects that properties unique, respectively, to the visual-gestural or oral-aural modalities have on the ways in which children learn and articulate their first signs or words. For example, the two major language modalities differ in their capacities for iconic representation. Iconic form-meaning mappings appear to be much more frequent in the vocabularies of signed languages than in the vocabularies of spoken languages. Even so, few of children's early errors in sign articulation are driven by iconicity; instead, far more of children's earliest errors can be explained by the constraints on the infant motor system. Those motoric constraints may in some instances be common to the two language modalities—an infant tendency toward repeated movement patterns is one example. In other instances, those motoric constraints may be modality-specific; infant tendencies to proximalize movement or to perform sympathetic movements of the nondominant hand are unique to the visual-gestural modality.

The demographic context in which the signing communities are situated also affords unique opportunities to psycholinguistics. It is unfortunately the case that, within the population of deaf children, there are many who have very limited or no early exposure to any conventional language, whether signed or spoken. It will be very useful to compare the ways in which native-signing children and late-learning children articulate their first signs. Such comparisons may help us to identify the extent to which native-signing children's errors are due to the constraints of an immature motor system as opposed to the difficulties attendant upon the acquisition of a new motor skill. Comparisons of sign acquisition by deaf children and hearing adults may also be useful here. As Mirus et al. (2000) found, naive hearing adults show evidence of proximalization of movement, suggesting that this motoric tendency is, in part, an effect of skill acquisition.

There are pressing needs for future research. To date, most early work on early sign development has been founded in naturalistic observation. Experimental work is necessary, with more controlled procedures and larger numbers of children. Such experimental work should seek to tease apart perceptual versus articulatory explanations of the kinds of errors that children make. Additionally, much more cross-linguistic work is necessary; such work should seek to isolate the effects of specific signed languages on early sign development in deaf and hearing children.

## ACKNOWLEDGMENT

I thank Heather Knapp for her very helpful comments on a draft of this chapter.

## REFERENCES

Anderson, D., & Reilly, J. (2002). The MacArthur Communicative Development Inventory: Normative data for American Sign Language. *Journal of Deaf Studies and Deaf Education, 7*, 83–106.

Ann, J. (1996). On the relation between ease of articulation and frequency of occurrence of handshapes in two sign languages. *Lingua, 98*, 19–41.

Baker, S., Sootsman, J., Golinkoff, R., & Petitto, L. (2003, April). *Hearing four-month olds perception of handshapes in American Sign Language: No experience required.* Paper presented at the biennial meeting of the Society for Research in Child Development, Tampa, FL.

Battison, R. (1978). *Lexical borrowing in American Sign Language.* Silver Spring, MD: Linstok Press.

Bellugi, U., & Fischer, S. (1972). A comparison of sign language and spoken language. *Cognition, 1,* 173–200.

Bonvillian, J. D., Orlansky, M. D., & Novack, L. L. (1983). Developmental milestones: Sign language acquisition and motor development. *Child Development, 54,* 1435–1445.

Boyes-Braem, P. (1990). Acquisition of the handshape in American Sign Language: A preliminary analysis. In V. Volterra & C. J. Erting (Eds.), *From gesture to language in hearing and deaf children* (pp. 107–127). Heidelberg: Springer-Verlag.

de Boysson Bardies, B. de, & Vihman, M. M. (1991). Adaptation to language: evidence from babbling and first words in four languages. *Language, 67,* 297–319.

Brentari, D. (1998). *A prosodic model of sign language phonology.* Cambridge, MA: MIT Press.

Carroll, J, J., & Gibson, E. J. (1986). Infant perception of gestural contrasts: Prerequisites for the acquisition of a visually specified language. *Journal of Child Language, 13,* 31–49.

Casey, S. K. (2003). *"Agreement" in gestures and signed languages: The use of directionality to indicate referents involved in actions.* Unpublished doctoral dissertation, University of California, San Diego.

Channon, R. (2002). Beads on a string? Representations of repetition in spoken and signed languages. In R. P. Meier, K. Cormier, & D. Quinto-Pozos (Eds.), *Modality and structure in signed and spoken languages* (pp. 65–87). Cambridge: Cambridge University Press.

Cheek, A. (2001). *The phonetics and phonology of handshape in American Sign Language.* Unpublished doctoral dissertation, University of Texas at Austin.

Cheek, A., Cormier, K., Repp, A., & Meier, R. P. (2001). Prelinguistic gesture predicts mastery and error in the production of first signs. *Language, 77,* 292–323.

Clibbens, J. (1998). Research on the acquisition of British Sign Language: Current issues. *Deafness and Education, 22,* 10–15.

Conlin, K. E., Mirus, G. R., Mauk, C., & Meier, R. P. (2000). The acquisition of first signs: Place, handshape, and movement. In C. Chamberlain, J. P. Morford, & R. I. Mayberry (Eds.), *Language acquisition by eye* (pp. 51–69). Mahwah, NJ: Erlbaum.

Corina, D. P. (2000). Some observations regarding paraphasia in American Sign Language. In K. Emmorey & H. Lane (Eds.), *The signs of language revisited* (pp. 493–507). Mahwah, NJ: Erlbaum.

Cormier, K. A. (2002). *Grammaticization of index signs: How American Sign Language expresses numerosity.* Unpublished doctoral dissertation, University of Texas, Austin.

Crasborn, O. (2001). *Phonetic implementation of phonological categories in Sign Language of the Netherlands.* Utrecht: LOT.

Emmorey, K., McCullough, S., & Brentari, D. 2003. Categorical perception in American Sign Language. *Language and Cognitive Processes, 18,* 21–45

Fagard, J. (1994). Manual strategies and interlimb coordination during reaching, grasping, and manipulating throughout the first year of life. In S. Swinnen,

H. H. Heuer, J. Massion, & P. Casaer (Eds.), *Interlimb coordination: Neural, dynamical, and cognitive constraints* (pp. 439–460). San Diego: Academic Press.

Fischer, S. (1973). Two processes of reduplication in American Sign Language. *Foundations of Language, 9,* 469–480.

Gesell, A., & Thompson, H. (1934). *Infant behavior.* New York: McGraw-Hill.

Goldin-Meadow, S. (2003). *The resilience of language.* New York: Psychology Press.

Goldin-Meadow, S., & Mylander, C. (1990). Beyond the input given: The child's role in the acquisition of language. *Language, 66,* 323–355.

Guerra Currie, A.-M. P. (1999). *A Mexican Sign Language lexicon: Internal and cross-linguistic similarities and variations.* Unpublished doctoral dissertation, University of Texas at, Austin.

Hamilton, H. (1986). Perception of sign features by deaf children. *Sign Language Studies, 50,* 73–77.

Hohenberger, A., Happ, D., & Leuninger, H. (2002). Modality-dependent aspects of sign language production: Evidence from slips of the hands and their repairs in German Sign Language (Deutsche Gebaerdensprache). In R. P. Meier, K. Cormier, & D. Quinto-Pozos (Eds.), *Modality and structure in signed and spoken languages* (pp. 112–142). Cambridge: Cambridge University Press.

Holzrichter, A. S., & Meier, R. P. (2000). Child-directed signing in American Sign Language. In C. Chamberlain, J. P. Morford, & R. I. Mayberry (Eds.), *Language acquisition by eye* (pp. 25–40). Mahwah, NJ: Erlbaum.

Juncos, O., Caamaño, A., Justo, M. J., López, E., Rivas, R. M., López, M. T., & Sola, F. (1997). Primeras palabras en la Lengua de Signos Española (LSE). Estructura formal, semántica y contextual. *Revista de Logopedia, Foniatría y Audiología, 17,* 170–181.

Karnopp, L. B. (1994). *Aquisição do parametro configuração de mão na Língua Brasileira dos Sinais (LIBRAS).* Unpublished master's thesis, Pontifícia Universidade Católica do Rio Grande do Sul, Porto Alegre, Brasil.

Karnopp, L. B. (2002). Phonology acquisition in Brazilian Sign Language. In G. Morgan & B. Woll (Eds.), *Directions in sign language acquisition* (pp. 29–53). Amsterdam: John Benjamins.

Klima, E. S., & Bellugi, U. (1979). *The signs of language.* Cambridge, MA: Harvard University Press.

Knapp, H. (2000). *Acquisition of hand configuration and place of articulation in American Sign Language.* Unpublished master's thesis, University of Texas at, Austin.

Lane, H., Boyes-Braem, P., & Bellugi, U. (1976). Preliminaries to a distinctive feature analysis of American Sign Language. *Cognitive Psychology, 8,* 263–289.

Launer, P. B. (1982). *"A plane" is not "to fly": Acquiring the distinction between related nouns and verbs in American Sign Language.* Unpublished doctoral dissertation, City University of New York.

Lavoie, C., & Villeneuve, S. (1999). Acquisition du lieu d'articulation en Langue des Signes Québécoise: Étude de cas. *Variations: le langage en théorie et en pratique. Actes du colloque: Le colloque des étudiants et étudiantes en sciences du langage.* Montreal: University of Quebec at Montreal.

Locke, J. (1985). The role of phonetic factors in parent reference. *Journal of Child Language, 12,* 215–220.

Marentette, P. F., & Mayberry, R. I. (2000). Principles for an emerging phonological system: A case study of acquisition of American Sign Language. In

C. Chamberlain, J. P. Morford, & R. I. Mayberry (Eds.), *Language acquisition by eye* (pp. 71–90). Mahwah, NJ: Erlbaum.

Masataka, N. (2000). The role of modality and input in the earliest stage of language acquisition: Studies of Japanese Sign Language. In C. Chamberlain, J. P. Morford, & R. I. Mayberry (Eds.), *Language acquisition by eye* (pp. 3–24). Mahwah, NJ: Erlbaum.

Mauk, C. E. (2003). *Undershoot in two modalities: Evidence from fast speech and fast signing.* Unpublished doctoral dissertation, University of Texas, at Austin.

McDowell, M. J., & Wolff, P. H. (1997). A functional analysis of human mirror movements. *Journal of Motor Behavior, 29,* 85–96.

Meier, R. P. (1982). *Icons, analogues, and morphemes: The acquisition of verb agreement in American Sign Language.* Unpublished doctoral dissertation, University of California, San Diego.

Meier, R. P. (1987). Elicited imitation of verb agreement in American Sign Language: Iconically or morphologically determined? *Journal of Memory and Language, 26,* 362–376.

Meier, R. P. (1991). Language acquisition by deaf children. *American Scientist, 79,* 60–70.

Meier, R. P., Cheek, A., & Moreland, C. J. (2002). Iconic versus motoric determinants of the form of children's early signs. In B. Skarabela, S. Fish, & A. H.-J. Do (Eds.), *BUCLD 26: Proceedings of the 26th annual Boston University Conference on Language Development* (pp. 393–405). Somerville, MA: Cascadilla Press.

Meier, R. P., Mauk, C., Cheek, A., & Moreland, C. J. (2004). *The form of children's early signs: Iconic or motoric determinants?* Manuscript submitted for publication.

Meier, R. P., Mauk, C., Mirus, G., & Conlin, K. E. (1998). Motoric constraints on early sign acquisition. In E. Clark (Ed.), *Papers and reports in child language development* (Vol. 29, pp. 63–72). Stanford, CA: CSLI Press.

Meier, R. P., & Newport, E. L. (1990). Out of the hands of babes: On a possible sign advantage in language acquisition. *Language, 66,* 1–23.

Meier, R. P., & Willerman, R. (1995). Prelinguistic gesture in deaf and hearing children. In K. Emmorey & J. Reilly (Eds.), *Language, gesture, and space* (pp. 391–409). Hillsdale, NJ: Erlbaum.

Mirus, G. R., Rathmann, C., & Meier, R. P. (2001). Proximalization and distalization of sign movement in adult learners. In V. Dively, M. Metzger, S. Taub, & A. M. Baer (Eds.), *Signed languages: Discoveries from international research* (pp. 103–119). Washington, DC: Gallaudet University Press.

Newport, E. L., & Meier, R. P. (1985). The acquisition of American Sign Language. In D. I. Slobin (Ed.), *The crosslinguistic study of language acquisition: Vol. 1. The data* (pp. 881–938). Hillsdale, NJ: Erlbaum.

Orlansky, M. D., & Bonvillian, J. D. (1984). The role of iconicity in early sign language acquisition. *Journal of Speech and Hearing Disorders, 49,* 287–292.

Orlansky, M. D., & Bonvillian, J. D. (1985). Sign language acquisition: Language development in children of deaf parents and implications for other populations. *Merrill-Palmer Quarterly, 31,* 127–143.

Petitto, L. A. (1987). On the autonomy of language and gesture: Evidence from the acquisition of personal pronouns in American Sign Language. *Cognition, 27,* 1–52.

Petitto, L. A. (1988). "Language" in the pre-linguistic child. In F. S. Kessel (Ed.), *The development of language and language researchers* (pp. 187–221). Hillsdale, NJ: Erlbaum.

Petitto, L. A., Holowka, S., Sergio, L. E., Levy, B., & Ostry, D. J. (2004). Baby hands that move to the rhythm of language: Hearing babies acquiring sign languages babble silently on the hands. *Cognition, 93*, 43–73.

Petitto, L. A., & Marentette, P. (1991). Babbling in the manual mode: Evidence from the ontogeny of language. *Science, 251*, 1493–1496.

Poizner, H., Bellugi, U., & Lutes-Driscoll, V. (1981). Perception of American Sign Language in dynamic point-light displays. *Journal of Experimental Psychology: Human Perception and Performance, 7*, 430–440.

Poizner, H., Newkirk, D., & Bellugi, U. (1983). Processes controlling human movement: Neuromotor constraints on American Sign Language. *Journal of Motor Behavior, 15*, 2–18.

Poizner, H., Mack, L., Verfaellie, M., Gonzalez Rothi, L. J., & Heilman, K. M. (1990). Three-dimensional computergraphic analysis of apraxia. *Brain, 113*, 85–101.

Reilly, J., & Anderson, D. (2002). FACES: The acquisition of nonmanual morphology in ASL. In G. Morgan & B. Woll (Eds.). *Directions in sign language acquisition* (pp. 159–181). Amsterdam: Benjamins.

Sandler, W. (1989). *Phonological representation of the sign: Linearity and nonlinearity in American Sign Language.* Dordrecht: Foris.

Saussure, F. de. (1959). *Course in general linguistics.* New York: Philosophical Library, translated by Wade Baskin (English edition of *Cours de linguistic générale*, 1916, Paris: Payot).

Siedlecki, T., Jr., & Bonvillian, J. D. (1993). Location, handshape & movement: Young children's acquisition of the formational aspects of American Sign Language. *Sign Language Studies, 78*, 31–52.

Siedlecki, T., Jr., & Bonvillian, J. D. (1997). Young children's acquisition of the handshape aspect of American Sign Language signs: Parental report findings. *Applied Psycholinguistics, 18*, 17–39.

Slobin, D. I., Hoiting, N., Kuntze, M., Lindert, R., Weinberg, A., Pyers, J. et al. (2003). A cognitive/functional perspective on the acquisition of "classifiers." In K. Emmorey (Ed.), *Perspectives on classifier constructions in sign languages* (pp. 271–296). Mahwah, NJ: Erlbaum.

Stokoe, W. C., Casterline, D. C., & Croneberg, C. G. (1965). *A dictionary of American Sign Language on linguistic principles.* Washington, DC: Gallaudet University Press.

Supalla, T. (1982). *Structure and acquisition of verbs of motion and location in American Sign Language.* Unpublished doctoral dissertation, University of California San Diego.

Supalla, T., & Newport, E. L. (1978). How many seats in a chair? The derivation of nouns and verbs in American Sign Language. In P. Siple (Ed.), *Understanding language through sign language research* (pp. 91–133). New York: Academic Press.

Takkinen, R. (2003). Variations of handshape features in the acquisition process. In A. Baker, B. van den Bogaerde, & O. Crasborn (Eds.), *Cross-linguistic perspectives in sign language research: Selected papers from TISLR 2000* (pp. 81–91). Hamburg: Signum.

von Tetzchner, S. (1994). First signs acquired by a Norwegian deaf child with hearing parents. *Sign Language Studies, 44*, 225–257.

Thelen, E. (1979). Rhythmical stereotypies in normal hearing infants. *Animal Behaviour, 27*, 699–715.

Thelen, E. (1991). Motor aspects of emergent speech: A dynamic approach. In N. A. Krasnegor, D. M. Rumbaugh, R. L. Schiefelbusch, & M. Studdert-Kennedy (Eds.), *Biological and behavioral determinants of language development* (pp. 339–362). Hillsdale, NJ: Erlbaum.

Trauner, D., Wulfeck, B., Tallal, P., & Hesselink, J. (2000). Neurological and MRI profiles of children with developmental language impairment. *Developmental Medicine and Child Neurology, 42*, 470–475.

Vihman, M. M. (1996). *Phonological development: The origins of language in the child*. Cambridge, MA: Blackwell.

Volterra, V., & Iverson, J. M. (1995). When do modality factors affect the course of language acquisition? In K. Emmorey & J. Reilly (Eds.), *Language, gesture, and space* (pp. 371–390). Hillsdale, NJ: Erlbaum.

Werker, J. F., & Tees, R. C. (1984). Cross-language speech perception: Evidence for perceptual reorganization during the first year of life. *Infant Behavior and Development, 7*, 49–63.

Wiesendanger, M., Wicki, U., & Rouiller, E. (1994). Are there unifying structures in the brain responsible for interlimb coordination? In S. Swinnen, H. Heuer, J. Massion, & P. Casaer (Eds.), *Interlimb coordination: Neural, dynamical, and cognitive constraints* (pp. 179–207). San Diego: Academic Press.

Wilbur, R. (1990). An experimental investigation of stressed sign production. *International Journal of Sign Linguistics, 1*, 41–59.

Wilcox, S. (1992). *The phonetics of fingerspelling*. Amsterdam: John Benjamins.

Woodward, J. (1982). Single finger extension: Toward a theory of naturalness in sign language phonology. *Sign Language Studies, 37*, 289–304.

# 10

# Acquisition of Syntax in Signed Languages

*Diane Lillo-Martin & Deborah Chen Pichler*

There are at least two reasons to be interested in the acquisition of syntax in sign languages. One is in order to see the development of language in the deaf child—the process by which deaf children come to determine how their language operates. A second is to learn about the nature of language, thereby informing linguistic theory. By studying how deaf children acquire the syntactic structure of their language, we can test theories of language and language acquisition. We concentrate on the latter goal in the present chapter.

It is important for linguistic theory to consider data from the acquisition of sign languages. Generally, linguistic theory is developed on the basis of data from spoken languages only—and often, primarily on the basis of English and other Indo-European languages. Languages with distinct structures—particularly, languages employing a distinct modality—are crucial testing grounds for such theories. When linguistic theory is concerned with those properties that hold across all languages, its proposals should hold for sign languages as well as spoken languages. If some proposed universal does not hold for sign languages, the question should be asked whether there is an explanation for this gap as a modality effect. That is, is there some characteristic of the manual-visual modality as opposed to the oral-aural modality that explains why one group of languages, but not the other, displays this property (i.e., modality effect)? If not, the status of the purported universal as a true linguistic universal is threatened (Sandler & Lillo-Martin, 2005).

As an example, let us consider the tendency for signs to be monosyllabic yet multimorphemic (Brentari, 1995). What this means is that signs can convey a lot of information in a small unit. For example, many verbs with agreement (discussed in some detail below) convey information about the verb root, the subject, and the object, all within a sign with one simple movement path—the typical shape of a mono-morphemic sign. Even more dramatically, classifier signs (discussed in several other chapters of this book) may convey multiple types of information about a moving entity, its path, and manner of movement, also within a single syllable. Unlike many familiar spoken languages, sign languages primarily employ nonconcatenative morphology—that is, they add morphemes without adding affixes. There are some spoken languages that employ this kind of nonconcatenative morphology (e.g., Semitic languages), but many do not. Similarly, while some spoken languages have a largely monosyllabic lexicon, others have rampant multisyllabicity. Sign languages, quite generally, as far as we know, do both: Both lexical and derived forms tend to be monosyllabic, due to the common use of nonconcatenative morphology (Brentari, 1998; Liddell, 1984; Sandler, 1989).

This is a true modality effect. The availability of simultaneous en-coding is taken advantage of in sign languages. Sign languages make use of mechanisms generally available to language (spoken and signed), but particularly those that are most compatible with the manual-visual modality. Theories of language should take these observations into account.

Although additional variables come into play when considering lan-guage acquisition, the point is still vital. There might even be more op-portunities for modality effects to appear in language acquisition, due to physiological aspects of the articulatory system. For example, sup-pose that the articulators for sign language develop at an earlier age than the articulators for spoken language. Then, the first words might occur at an earlier age in sign languages as compared with spo-ken languages. This, in fact, seems to be the case. Meier and Newport (1990) have argued that the observed development of first signs about 2 months earlier than first words can be attributed, at least in part, to the earlier development of control over the articulators needed to produce recognizable signs. This would be an example of a modality effect that holds for acquisition without holding for the mature grammar—there is no consequence in the mature grammar of this effect. But a theory of the development of first words must take into account the observa-tion that words are acquired differently (i.e., earlier) in sign languages. Thus, linguistic theorists need to be aware of the areas of sign language, and sign language acquisition, which do and do not exhibit modality effects (Lillo-Martin, 1999).

In this chapter, we review studies of the acquisition of two areas of sign language morphology and syntax. For each of these areas, we ask whether the theories developed on the basis of spoken languages make the right predictions for sign language. If there are differences between sign languages and spoken languages, what would the reasons be? In neither of these areas is the work completed, and we suggest areas for further study in both.

## THE ACQUISITION OF VERB AGREEMENT

Quite a few studies have examined the acquisition of verb agreement in American Sign Language (ASL) and other sign languages. Most of the questions these studies have addressed are sign-language specific; that is, they concern issues that do not arise in the study of spoken languages. Some, however, relate to proposals that apply to the acquisition of verbal morphology in both signed and spoken languages. Sign language verb agreement in itself has properties that are unusual, from the point of view of spoken language agreement systems. Thus, study of sign language verb agreement systems is important for theories of agreement more generally, and the study of the development of sign language verb agreement should be of broad interest.

### Verb Agreement in Sign Languages

Agreement can be described as a system by which a "target" element changes its form based on characteristics of a "controller," which is the item whose inherent features are matched. So, for example, the form of a verb—the target—may reflect the person, number, and gender characteristics of its subject—the controller. As another example, the form of an adjective (target) may reflect the gender and number of the noun it modifies (controller).

In sign languages, there is a class of verbs that is modified depending on aspects of the subject and object; this is the phenomenon generally considered verb agreement.[1] Verbs show agreement with their subject and object by sharing a spatial locus with them, and this is generally taken to mean that the verb agrees with its arguments in person and number (though not gender).

Before discussing verb agreement in more detail, a few words must be said about the spatial loci. Many referents can be associated with locations in signing space. People who are actually present in a discourse situation, for example, are associated with the locations they actually occupy. People who are not present, but referred to in the conversation, may be "imagined" as occupying various spatial locations, or "associated" with loci. These loci are used by pronouns, which point to them, and by agreeing verbs, which move with respect to them.

---

[1] Not all verbs can be modified in this way. Verbs that do not indicate subject and object agreement are known as "plain" verbs.

To illustrate, consider the verb "ask." When the signer wants to convey, "I ask John," the sign moves from the location associated with the signer (the signer's own trunk) to the location associated with John, with the palm facing John. To convey, "John asks me," the sign moves from the location associated with John to the location associated with the signer, with the palm facing the signer.

When John is not actually present in the discourse, but the signer wants to refer to him, one of a number of devices may be used to associate him with some location (or imagine him at a location; see Liddell 1990). Then, the agreeing verbs are used in the same way. The use of agreement with nonpresent referents is illustrated in figures 10.1 and 10.2.

**Figure 10-1.** I-ASK-JOHN.

**Figure 10-2.** JOHN-ASK-ME.

The description just given is the standard one assumed for many years (e.g. Fischer & Gough, 1978; Klima & Bellugi, 1979; Padden, 1988). In recent years, however, various aspects of this analysis have been questioned (for discussion, see Liddell, 1995, 2000; Lillo-Martin, 2002; Meir, 2002; Rathmann & Mathur, 2002). For the purposes of the present chapter, we assume the description given; at the end of this section, we discuss some areas for future research based on some of the new concerns. We now turn to an examination of the role of iconicity in the development of verb agreement.

## Iconicity and Verb Agreement

Brown (1980) thought that the acquisition of sign languages by hearing people would be facilitated because of the iconicity of signs. He suggested that "iconic signs, when the iconicity can be recognized, will be more easily learned and remembered than arbitrary signs" (p. 14). There are reasons to think he did not make the right prediction even for second language learners, but let's consider whether his argument would hold for young deaf children acquiring sign language as a first language. Does the iconicity of some signs make them easier to learn?

This question was addressed explicitly in Meier's (1981, 1982, 1987) study of the acquisition of verb agreement in ASL. While iconicity of verb agreement is not blatant in an example like "ask" given above, other verbs do bear a resemblance to the actions they denote. For example, when a signer produces the sign I-GIVE-YOU (figure 10.3), it is very similar to the action the signer would use to hand something over to the addressee.

**Figure 10-3.** I-GIVE-YOU.

Meier asked whether this iconicity might make it easier for deaf children to acquire verb agreement than it is for children learning spoken languages to acquire their systems of verbal or other inflectional morphology. Does the spatial analogy between the sign and the event facilitate acquisition of verb agreement?

Before addressing this main question, let us first consider how the acquisition of inflectional morphology in spoken languages takes place. Drawing on the work of Slobin (1982), Meier identified three kinds of spoken languages with respect to inflectional morphology (including verb agreement and nominal case). In one kind, exemplified by Turkish and Hungarian, inflectional morphemes are syllabic, stressed, and acquired quite early—before 2 years of age. In the second kind, which includes English, inflectional morphology is unstressed and unreliable, so comprehension of grammatical roles requires attention to word order. Acquisition is slower in such languages (around 3 years to 3 years 6 months [3;6]). In the third, including Serbo-Croatian, inflection is fusional, which means that multiple meanings may be expressed in a single unstressed affix, with the same form sometimes conveying different kinds of information. According to Slobin, acquisition is even slower in such languages, because the child must attend to both inflection and word order for appropriate comprehension.

Meier studied the acquisition of verb agreement by three deaf children who were exposed to ASL by their deaf parents from birth. One child was studied from the age of 1;6 through 3;6, and the other two were studied for shorter periods: 3;1 though 3;9, and 2;7 through 3;3. The percent use of agreement in obligatory contexts at each session is given in figure 10.4.

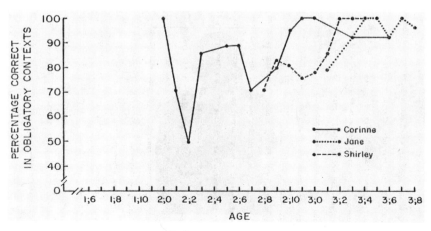

**Figure 10-4. Production of verb agreement in obligatory contexts. Reproduced with permission from Meier (1982).**

Meier set as his criterion for acquisition the correct use of agreement in at least 90% of obligatory contexts in each of three successive samples (following Cazden, 1968). Using this strict criterion, he found that the three children acquired ASL verb agreement at the ages of 3;0, 3;4, and 3;6. This is clearly not "early," particularly in comparison with the acquisition of Turkish. Rather, it is more in line with the acquisition of verbal morphology in English.

Meier's study showed that deaf children acquiring ASL treat it just like any other language. Children see words as things that must be analyzed, decomposed, broken down into their component parts. They resist what might be seen as a temptation to treat words holistically. Rather, the nature of ASL verb agreement as a morphological system means that it is acquired much like other similar morphological systems. In particular, since the agreement inflections are not stressed syllables, they are acquired around the age that inflection is acquired in languages like English. The iconicity of some signs seems to play no role in their acquisition—a conclusion reached on independent grounds by Supalla (1982).

The role of iconicity in the development of verb agreement has been addressed again more recently by Casey (2003). Casey observed "directionality" in the signs and gestures of six deaf children, ages 0;8 to 2;11, exposed to ASL by their deaf parents.[2] These children were observed longitudinally in 41 free-play and structured sessions. In her detailed study, she compared the age of first use of directional and nondirectional literal versus metaphorical verbs. All of the children produced literal verbs prior to their production of metaphorical verbs. While two of the children produced directional and nondirectional metaphorical verbs for the first time at the same session (ages 1;11 and 2;3), two others were delayed in their production of directional metaphorical verbs. Casey suggested that the delay in these two children, at least, likely indicated that they were attending to iconicity. If they were treating directionality as purely morphemic, there would be no explanation for their later use of directionality with metaphorical verbs.

Meier's (1982) study concerned the acquisition of verb agreement with present referents. He did not include in his analysis children's use of verb agreement with nonpresent referents. Is there a difference in the use of verb agreement between these two contexts? If so, to what would such a difference be attributed? We now turn to several studies that address this question.

---

[2] Casey uses the term "directionality" rather than agreement in order to be neutral concerning whether the child's uses should be considered agreement or not. This also allows her to make direct comparisons with directionality in gesture, a major component of her study.

## Verb Agreement With Present and Nonpresent Referents

Very young children generally talk about the here-and-now. However, there are various reasons for them to talk about nonpresent referents. For example, they may ask about a missing parent, friend, or toy. They may also engage in storytelling, telling about a past event or one that exists only in the imagination.

How do young children use verb agreement when discussing nonpresent referents? According to several studies, children use verb agreement with present referents before doing so with nonpresent referents.

Loew (1984) studied children's use of aspects of grammar and discourse involving space, including verb agreement (part of what she called "indexing") and role play. She focused on the association of referents with locations in space, and later reference to these locations through pronouns, verb agreement, and role play, in children's storytelling. She studied one child from the age of 3;1 to 4;9, with some additional information from two other children at 2;11 and 4;3.

Loew found that children produce verb agreement with nonpresent referents much later than the age at which Meier observed verb agreement with present referents. During the first stage she investigated (3;1–3;4), the child she observed frequently produced verb agreement with present referents but generally used the "citation" (uninflected) form with nonpresent referents. Agreement is used with some consistency during the second period (3;6–3;11), but the location for a referent does not remain consistent across sentences within a narrative. Multiple referents may also be "stacked" in the same location. By the age of 4;6–4;9, Loew reports frequent and often consistent use of agreement with nonpresent referents. However, a quantitative analysis is not provided, so it is not clear at what point this child would pass a stringent criterion such as 90% correct use in three consecutive sessions.

Further support for Loew's observations come from experimental studies of children's development of verb agreement and spatial mechanisms. Bellugi, Lillo-Martin, O'Grady, and vanHoek (1990) asked children to tell a story associated with wordless picture books (the "balloon" and "paint" stories).[3] They found that 2–3-year-old children may produce the signs of the story on the book, using the pictures as "present referents" for agreeing verbs. However, the children did not set up and use abstract loci and verb agreement with nonpresent referents until around four, making errors of the same types that Loew reported until around five.

---

[3] For more information on the results of these story elicitations, see Bellugi, vanHoek, Lillo-Martin, and O'Grady (1988), Lillo-Martin (1991), and vanHoek, O'Grady, Bellugi, and Norman (1987, 1989, 1990).

Lillo-Martin, Bellugi, Struxness, and O'Grady (1985) conducted experimental studies of 5- to 10-year-old children's comprehension of verb agreement with nonpresent referents. They found that children's performance on picture-choice and act-out tests of agreement for nonpresent referents did not reach ceiling until 6 years of age.

In summarizing the results of studies such as Meier's and Loew's, Newport and Meier (1985) argued that the verb agreement system is acquired around 3 years of age, and the later observation of verb agreement with nonpresent referents is due to the difficulties of establishing and maintaining abstract loci. This proposal contrasts with one that attributes the acquisition of agreement with nonpresent referents to a system separate from the one used with present referents.

Lillo-Martin et al. (1985) tested one part of this hypothesis by examining children's ability to understand the association of a referent with a location in space. The experimenter begins by associating two or three referents with points in space. Then the experimenter asks where a particular referent is located, or what is in a particular location.

The results showed that very young children do indeed have difficulty with abstractly associating referents with locations in space. After associating a doll with one location, for example, when the experimenter asked a 2-year-old, "Where's the doll?" the child ran to her bedroom to find her own favorite toy.

However, this problem was only found for the youngest children, the 2-year-olds. Three-year-olds were able to answer the questions indicating an understanding of abstract association. They did show effects of limited memory, as their results were higher when they only had to remember where two items were located. But the concept was already in place.

Thus, it is unlikely that failure to understand the relationship between nonpresent referents and abstract locations in space fully explains the failure of 3- and 4-year-old children to consistently produce and understand verb agreement with nonpresent referents. But does this mean that the child acquires verb agreement with nonpresent referents as a completely separate system?

Lillo-Martin (1991, 1999) argues against this extreme, noting that the experiment by Lillo-Martin et al. (1985) only required children to recognize the relationship between a potential referent and a location in signing space, not to set it up themselves or remember it across a discourse. She presented children's failure to use verb agreement with nonpresent referents as a performance problem rather than an indication of a lack of grammatical competence.

The use of directionality with present versus absent referents in the acquisition of ASL was also studied by Casey (2003). In her study, children spontaneously produced directionality with nonpresent referents at much younger ages than those reported by the earlier studies.

Although three children exhibited a delay of 3 months to 1 year between the production of directionality with present versus nonpresent referents, four children did produce directionality with nonpresent referents by the age of 2;7. The youngest productions of directionality with absent referents used real locations of unseen referents, and the latest ones used abstract spatial loci. This observation fits with the notion that the complexity of establishing and remembering locations for nonpresent referents is behind the later acquisition.

This conclusion is bolstered by the study of Hänel (2004), who studied the acquisition of verb agreement with present and nonpresent referents in two deaf children, ages 2;2–3;4, learning German Sign Language (*Deutsche Gebärdensprache*, DGS). She studied monthly recordings of the children's spontaneous productions, and coded verbs for the presence or absence of agreement (as well as additional aspects of syntactic development).

Hänel found an early stage (until 2;3 for one child and 2;7 for the other) during which the children did not productively use verb agreement with either present or nonpresent referents. The children used the "citation" form of agreeing verbs during this period, just like what has been reported for ASL. During phase II, however, both children productively used verb agreement with present referents and with nonpresent referents. That is, Hänel did not find the same kind of delay in the use of agreement with nonpresent referents reported by other researchers working on ASL.

During phase II, then, verb agreement is productive with both present and nonpresent referents. This does not mean, however, that there are no cases of verb agreement errors during this time. In fact, Hänel illustrates an interesting commission error made by both children, in which the verb is signed twice—once moving toward the location associated with the subject, and then toward the location associated with the object. How many errors of commission or omission are made during phase II is not reported.

Overall, Hänel concludes that the mechanisms underlying verb agreement with both present and nonpresent referents are acquired simultaneously. The apparent difference in their use is attributed to performance, not competence.

We have seen a variety of results regarding the earliest appearance of verb agreement with present and nonpresent referents. In part, the variability of these results reflect the different foci of the studies, as well as different criteria used. Meier observed overall usage of agreement, but did not consider it acquired until it was used in 90% of obligatory contexts across three successive sessions—a very strict requirement. Hänel considers verb agreement to be productive if the form appears with more than one agreement verb, and is shown in several subsequent recordings. This is not as strict as the criterion used by Meier, but more strict than simple first usage. In Hänel's early stage, then, agreement with present referents might have been used, although not productively. Other researchers report overall descriptions without figures (Loew), or present figures without a strict criterion of acquisition (Casey). Comparing across studies can thus only be tentative. However, there is general consensus that although agreement with nonpresent referents may be somewhat delayed with respect to that with present referents, this difference is attributable to the abstract performance demands of the latter (particularly, memory for spatial locations).

## Omissions of Verb Agreement

All of the studies summarized thus far have in common the observation that children acquiring sign languages omit verb agreement in a sizable number of the obligatory contexts at an early age. This might be comparable to the observation in the spoken language literature that 2-year-old children frequently use a nonfinite (or uninflected) form where a finite form is called for. In English, this results in the use of bare forms such as "Mommy work," where an inflected form ("Mommy works/ worked/ is working") is called for. In languages with a morphological marker on the verb for the infinitive form, children's productions use this infinitive, such as the German *du das haben* (you that have-inf), and so this period has come to be known as an "optional infinitive stage"[4] (Poeppel & Wexler, 1993; Rizzi, 1993/94; Wexler, 1994, 1998).

Studies of the acquisition of spoken languages have determined that the languages that most convincingly display such a stage are those that do not productively allow syntactic subjects to be omitted (i.e., nonnull subject languages such as English and German). Children acquiring languages with rich verbal morphology, which do allow subjects to be omitted (e.g., Italian), do not produce optional infinitive forms at anywhere near the same rate.

Are children acquiring sign languages going through an optional infinitive stage? Since sign languages are like Italian in allowing subjects to be omitted (in fact, objects may be omitted as well; see Lillo-Martin, 1986), it might be expected that children would not go through such a stage. Yet the studies cited above seem to indicate that they do.

To investigate this further, Lillo-Martin, Quadros, and Mathur (1998) took another look at young children's use of verb agreement in the

---

[4] In English, the infinitive form of the verb is simply bare: "run" ("to run" vs. "I run," "he runs"). In German, however, the infinitive (*laufen* "to run"), and the inflected forms (*er lauft*, "he runs") employ distinct morphological affixes.

development of ASL and Brazilian Sign Language (*Língua de Sinais Brasileira*, LSB). They wanted to see if the pattern of agreement omission and null argument use was unlike that found for spoken languages. They examined nine sessions from two children ages 1;9–2;3 learning ASL, and 10 sessions from one child age 1;8–2;10 learning LSB. Each verb was categorized as to verb type (agreeing or not) and the agreement morphology used. They also categorized the subject and object as overt or omitted, in order to check these children's use of null arguments.

Lillo-Martin et al. (1998) found a surprising result. Unlike the previous studies, they found virtually *no* instances of verb agreement omission, even in the 2-year-old age range. That is, the children they studied consistently used verb agreement where it was required.

What can explain the different results found by Lillo-Martin et al. (1998) as compared with the other studies? Of course, it is possible that Lillo-Martin et al. might have miscoded children's use of agreement in some way. However, there is support for their conclusion from one other recent study. Berk (2003) examined the acquisition of verb agreement by children whose exposure to sign language began only after the age of 6 years. She found that these children had many errors of omission and commission in their verb agreement. As a comparison, Berk also coded verb agreement in one native signer, at the ages of 2;0, 2;6, and 2;9. Like Lillo-Martin et al., Berk found that agreeing verbs were used with virtually no errors during this time.

Another possibility is that Lillo-Martin et al. (1998) had a different standard for coding forms as agreeing. In particular, they observed the use of eye gaze during verb production, noting Bahan's (Bahan, 1996; Neidle, Kegl, MacLaughlin, Bahan, & Lee, 2000) argument that eye gaze is a nonmanual marker of agreement. If the child's manual form displayed some minimal movement in the agreeing direction, a more conservative coding might not count this as agreement. However, as long as eye gaze also marked the object, Lillo-Martin et al. counted such forms as displaying agreement. (There were not cases, however, where eye gaze would have been the only possible marker of agreement.)

Finally, there could be a difference in terms of which verbs are considered agreeing. In recent years, it has become clearer how to assign verbs to the category of agreeing or plain (Janis, 1995; Meir, 2002). In particular, only verbs that have [human] controllers can be marked for person agreement. Verbs with [location] controllers can be marked for spatial agreement. For some plain verbs, location can optionally be marked. Thus, these verbs might have been considered agreeing verbs in earlier studies, but would not be considered agreeing now. If the verb agreement omissions previously reported were primarily from verbs of this type, this would account for the much lower attribution of omissions in the recent studies. Interestingly, Meier (1982) reports that in the earliest sessions of one of the children he investigated, she frequently used agreement with the verb TELL-NO, using it in two different agreeing forms at 2;2. Agreement was missing from verbs including POUR and DROP, which would not be considered agreeing verbs under many current classifications. Removing such verbs would bring the proportion of required agreement omissions down, although not to zero, since verbs including GIVE, TAKE, and GET are also reported by Meier as missing agreement. Also, Casey (2003) found many instances of obligatory agreement missing, although her classification of agreeing verbs is quite similar to that of Lillo-Martin et al. (1998).

The difference in results from these studies remains to be fully explained. All examined native signing children of about the same ages, yet some find many more errors of agreement omission than others. Studies of the acquisition of verbal morphology with children learning spoken languages have in general found relative consistency across speakers within languages, with wider cross-language differences. Are there wider differences across children learning a sign language? Or is there another reason for these different results?

## Topics for Future Study

The conflicting findings regarding missing obligatory agreement call for more extensive research. Verb classification does vary from study to study and could account for an important portion of the differential results observed. However, it is clear that more work must be done to understand the different patterns of results just reviewed. Are the differences all due to different criteria used in coding? Do some children omit obligatory agreement while others progress without errors? Are there certain verbs or verb types that are more susceptible to agreement errors than others? These and related questions concerning the "optionality" of agreement in sign languages are of interest for understanding both how sign languages are acquired and more general questions about the acquisition of verbal morphology.

Studies of the acquisition of verbal morphology in spoken languages also suggest additional paths of inquiry. Researchers have attempted to account for children's problems with verbal morphology in different ways. Some researchers have suggested that children's early grammars allow tense to be omitted, while others claim that the uninflected forms used by children reflect nonadult understanding of temporal aspect rather than tense (Hoekstra & Hyams, 1998; Wexler, 1994). Both tense and aspect relate to the time of an event, but tense conveys its relation to the utterance time, while aspect conveys its duration (among other things). Previous research on sign language verbal morphology has not examined aspect, which could be a confound in the apparent different results on agreement. Examination of the development of verbal aspect in sign languages would contribute to this discussion.

As in many areas, further examination of the acquisition of verb agreement across sign languages would be especially appealing. Since sign languages seem to universally employ very similar agreement systems, they might be expected to display similar paths of development. However, sign languages do vary in their use of an auxiliary-like element with plain verbs; auxiliaries are found, for example, in Sign Language of the Netherlands (*Nederlandse Gebarentaal*, NGT), LSB, and DGS but not ASL. This auxiliary seems to take the place of agreement in signs that fail to mark it for phonological reasons. It is well known that in spoken languages, the acquisition of verbal morphology is related to the acquisition of auxiliaries. Lillo-Martin et al. (1998) did not observe the use of an auxiliary in the child acquiring LSB they studied. How does the acquisition of agreement relate to the acquisition of the auxiliary system in sign languages?

Finally, there are many aspects of the relationship between agreement and sentence structure that call for additional study. Lillo-Martin (1991), Quadros (1995), and Hänel (2004) have all examined the acquisition of null arguments and verb agreement. These studies can be compared with each other and also should be re-examined under the more recent classifications of agreeing verbs. The relationship between agreement and word order is another area of great interest. In the next section, we examine several studies of the acquisition of word order.

## THE ACQUISITION OF WORD ORDER

Around the age of 2 years, most children begin producing their first word combinations, or early "sentences." The word order of these first sentences or, more specifically, the order in which subject, object, and verb (S, O, V) appear has long been an area of interest to language acquisition researchers. In his highly influential book, Brown (1973) reported that children learning English exhibit mastery of the canonical (typical) order of their target language (SVO) from their earliest multiword combinations. Other researchers studying languages with greater word order variability than English (e.g., Park, 1970, for Korean; Slobin, 1966, for Russian) reported a similar pattern among children acquiring these languages. Some researchers proposed that this over-reliance on a single word order (typically the canonical order of the language) was an early strategy for distinguishing subjects from objects until more advanced grammatical devices (e.g., case morphology) developed.

More recently, researchers working within the popular Principles and Parameters theory (Chomsky, 1981)—according to which children must discover the right "settings" for a variety of features (parameters) of their language—concluded that the parameters controlling canonical word order must be especially easy for children to set (e.g., Clahsen &

Muysken, 1986; Wexler, 1998). Specifically, they proposed that the spec(ifier)-head parameter (responsible for the order of subjects with respect to the rest of the sentence) and the head-complement parameter (responsible for the order of the verb and object with respect to each other) are among the earliest parameters to be set. If this is true of all children, it would explain why even those acquiring languages with high word order variability initially adopt a fixed order strategy.

The investigation of word order acquisition in ASL is of great interest because ASL exhibits variable word order, thus providing a good test for the hypothesis that the word order parameters are set early, and the claim that children exhibit overreliance on the canonical order of their target language. It is all the more compelling because studies on the topic have come to contradictory conclusions. In early reviews of sign language acquisition (e.g., Newport & Meier, 1985), Hoffmeister (1978) is credited with discovering an overdependence on canonical SVO word order by his deaf subjects, confirming the patterns described above for English, Korean, and Russian. The apparent rigidity with which deaf children maintained canonical order, even once they had acquired morphological means for marking grammatical relations, led Newport and Meier to categorize word order as the only aspect of ASL grammar to be "acquired early and without error (if acquiring and consistently using the canonical order of a language with great order flexibility can be considered a nonerror)" (1985, p. 912).

The portrayal of early ASL word order as reliably canonical stands in stark contrast to the findings of more recent studies conducted by Schick and Gale (1996; Schick, 2002), Chen(2001), and Chen Pichler (2001), as well as Coerts and Mills (1994; Coerts, 2000) for NGT. All of these studies emphasize the frequently noncanonical order of early sign combinations, presenting a potential challenge to the notion of universally early setting of the word order parameters. In the following sections, we take a careful look at the relevant literature and conclude that the data reported so far are not necessarily contradictory. In fact, they are consistent with one conclusion: Deaf children acquiring ASL not only set the word order parameters early but also learn early on to modify the resulting canonical order in grammatical ways.

## Word Order in ASL

Investigation of the acquisition of word order in ASL began at a time when sign language linguists were debating the properties of word order variability found in adult signing. While some claimed that ASL had no basic word order scheme (e.g., Friedman, 1977), Fischer (1975) and Liddell (1977) had argued convincingly that the basic word order for the language was SVO, and that departures from this order occurred as a result of various grammatical mechanisms such as object topicalization or "modulation" of the verb.

Topicalization refers to syntactic structures in which the grammatical topic (presupposed information) appears in sentence-initial position (Fischer, 1974; Liddell, 1980). Objects are very frequently topicalized in ASL (although other constituents can also be topicalized), resulting in structures with the order O[topic], SV. In sign languages, topics are generally accompanied by a particular non-manual marker; the typical ASL topicalization nonmanual includes raised eyebrows and lengthening of the duration of the topicalized sign(s).

"Modulation" is described by Hoffmeister (1978), citing Kegl (1976), as the process by which verbs are made to indicate subject and object through spatial means, referred to as verbal agreement in modern terminology.[5] Kegl noted flexibility in word order with "modulated" verbs, or verbs modified to move from the subject to the object, reinforcing earlier observations of word order variation associated with certain syntactic properties of the language. Additional contexts resulting in word order flexibility have since been identified and are discussed in greater detail below.

## Is Early Word Order Strict?

Interestingly, the conclusion for which Hoffmeister (1978) is remembered and cited is not completely accurate. Although Hoffmeister did conclude that deaf children show strong preference for canonical word order in their early production, he also acknowledged variation and "error" in word order, particularly when verbal inflection is involved. His stated goal was not to document whether or not young deaf children display the same fixed word order strategy observed for hearing children, but rather how they transition from such a stage to one in which they can use adultlike verbal inflection and corresponding word order variation. Unfortunately, because Hoffmeister (1978) said so little about the many noncanonically ordered utterances produced by his subjects *prior* to their mastery of verbal inflection, he is remembered as claiming that noncanonical orders do not occur in the early sign combinations of deaf children.

Hoffmeister followed three deaf children acquiring ASL from deaf, signing parents. Two deaf sisters, Alice and Anne, were filmed beginning at 24 months of age and continuing until 4;6 for Anne and 3;0 for Alice. A third child, Thomas, was filmed from 43 months of age to 5;7. All three children were filmed at home as they interacted naturally with their parents. The data were arbitrarily divided into four stages of development based loosely on age, and comparisons were made

---

[5] "Modulation" may also have included certain types of spatial or locative inflection. However, in this chapter we will substitute the current term "verbal agreement" for "modulation" and assume that it refers to subject and object features marked on the verb.

Table 10-1: Percentages of Utterances Following Canonical Order in the Hoffmeister (1978) Data

| Child, Stage | Total Subject–Verb Utterances | % Subject–Verb Order | Total Verb–Object Utterances | % Verb–Object Order |
|---|---|---|---|---|
| Anne, stage I | 72 | 67% | 26 | 58% |
| Alice, stage I | 36 | 83% | 15 | 60% |
| Anne, stage II | 53 | 83% | 34 | 62% |
| Alice, stage II | 79 | 90% | 57 | 88% |
| Thomas, stage II | 189 | 87% | 134 | 81% |
| Alice, stage III | 181 | 86% | 100 | 88% |
| Thomas, stage III | 90 | 92% | 75 | 87% |
| Alice, stage IV | 541 | 92% | 259 | 86% |
| Thomas, stage IV | 251 | 87% | 171 | 80% |

between children at comparable levels of production (as determined by mean length of utterance, MLU).

Although Hoffmeister did not include a list of the actual utterances used for his analysis, he did specify that his analysis included only sentences containing an overt verb, and focused only on S, V, O, and locations (L; including either a phrase or a point [notated by Hoffmeister as PT]). For each child at each stage, Hoffmeister reported the frequency of eighteen possible ordering combinations. To answer the broader question of how often the children produced canonical ordering (in terms of preverbal subjects and postverbal objects), we have reorganized Hoffmeister's data by collapsing the counts.[6] Table 10.1 summarizes percentage counts for each child at each stage.

At stage I, Anne and Alice followed canonical patterns (preverbal subjects and postverbal objects) for most of their recorded utterances. However, noncanonical sequences were also frequent. Of her utterances containing a verb and object, Anne produced preverbal objects 42% of the time (11 of 26 utterances), and Alice 40% of the time (6 of 15 utterances). Postverbal subjects, also exhibiting noncanonical order, appeared in 33% of Anne's utterances containing a subject and a verb (24 of 72 utterances) and 17% of the time (6 of 36 utterances) in Alice's. Interestingly, nearly all of the girls' postverbal subjects in this stage occurred in two-sign VS strings, as illustrated by examples CRY PT (this/doll) and

---

[6] To arrive at the total percentage of preverbal subjects used by each child at each stage, we counted all utterances in which the subject appears before the verb and then divided by the total of all utterances containing both a subject and verb in any order, with or without additional constituents. Figures for the percentage of postverbal objects were similarly calculated.

FALL-DOWN PT (this/clown). It is worth noting that both example sentences are acceptable in adult ASL, suggesting that the girls' VS utterances are *grammatical* instances of noncanonical order.

Hoffmeister also noted that Anne in stage I occasionally produced utterances such as example (10.1), in which a verb that allows inflection appears in citation form, without any change in space to indicate subject or object. Grammatical relations are made clear by the addition of indexes (points) to subject and object.

(10.1) PT(this picture) HIT PT(me/Alice)
"He/she (the person in the picture) hit me."[7]

At this stage, noted Hoffmeister, the children appeared to be oblivious to the word order altering potential of inflecting verbs and used them in canonical order, just like any ordinary verb.

At stage II, use of canonical preverbal subjects and postverbal objects increased and Hoffmeister reported that the sisters "have developed distinct preferences for basic sentence orders, either S-V or S-V-O." Although Alice and Anne now correctly inflected some verbs for subject and object, they continued to use overt arguments in canonical order with such utterances. Hoffmeister interpreted this redundancy as a learning strategy designed to ensure clear communication of grammatical relations while the children worked out the function and formation of verbal inflection. In addition to redundantly marking subject and object with inflected verbs, Hoffmeister's children also produced non adult-like OV sequences with verbs that do not allow inflection. Both types of errors persisted into stages III and IV, during which the percentage of canonically ordered subjects and objects remained similar to that found in stage II. Thus the overall characterization of word order during stages II–IV is strong preference for canonical order, even in conjunction with verb inflection that would normally permit the use of noncanonical order or null arguments.

The main conclusion of Hoffmeister (1978) was that deaf children acquire noncanonical orders gradually, discovering that verbal inflection is associated with word order variation after progressing through a stage where grammatical relations are redundantly specified. By the end of the study, all three children continued to favor canonical order, despite being able to use verbal inflection correctly. This is the conclusion for which Hoffmeister is widely cited in later work. In contrast, the early use by Anne and Alice of grammatical noncanonical orders independent of verbal inflection (viz., VS order) has escaped notice, but is also an important finding.

---

[7] We have modified Hoffmeister's notation somewhat to be consistent with current notational standards. Also, Hoffmeister does not include a translation, so we have provided one that we assume fits the gloss.

A more recent study reported in Schick and Gale (1996) and Schick (2002), investigating the way(s) in which deaf children specify grammatical relations in their early sign combinations, came to the conclusion that early word order is anything but strict. Schick (2002), the more comprehensive of the two reports, considered three possible ways in which deaf children might mark grammatical relations: (1) via canonical word order, as concluded by Hoffmeister, (2) via positional patterns specific to individual verbs, and (3) via context or pragmatics.

Whereas the Hoffmeister study followed a small set of children over the course of many months, the Schick study included data for 12 children carefully controlled for age and parental deafness, but filmed at a single point in their language development. Each child was filmed within two weeks of his second birthday, interacting naturally with a parent. A total of five hours of data was recorded for each child, spread over two to three days. All multi-word utterances including a verb were coded for agent—the one doing an action—and theme—the entity that moves in an action (to avoid any grammatical bias inherent in identifying subjects and objects).

Like Hoffmeister, Schick (2002) reported little use of ASL verbal morphology by her subjects at this stage. She noted that this is consistent with the general consensus that "children do not have mastery of the complex morphological system that accompanies alterations from SVO order" (p. 147) in ASL. However, whereas Hoffmeister emphasized a strong canonical word order strategy for marking grammatical relations, Schick found no evidence for this strategy in her data. Of the multisign utterances including an overt theme argument, anywhere from 43% to 68% (mean, 56%) displayed canonical verb—theme order. Thus, with respect to verbs and themes (objects), children only appeared to choose canonical order roughly half the time, far less often than found by Hoffmeister (1978).

Overt agent arguments were considerably less frequent in Schick's data than overt themes, occurring on average in only 7% of the children's multisign utterances. With the exception of two children who used canonical agent–verb order in 100% of their multisign utterances containing an agent, no child used this order more than 78% of the time (mean, 66%). Furthermore, the two children who used agent–verb order 100% of the time only actually produced one and four utterances with an agent, respectively. Thus, once again, Schick's findings departed dramatically from those of Hoffmeister (1978).

Having ruled out canonical order as a strategy for specifying grammatical relations, Schick next explored the possibility that children follow positional preferences based on individual verbs. This concept was inspired by the Verb Island Hypothesis advanced by Tomasello (1992), by which children assign grammatical properties to verbs on an individual basis, rather than generalizing across the entire class of verbs in the target language. Thus, Schick investigated the possibility that children might have consistently used verb—theme order with one verb (e.g., EAT COOKIE, EAT SANDWICH), but theme—verb order with another (e.g., BALL WANT, DOLL WANT). Particular patterns would also presumably vary across different children, giving the initial impression of randomness.

The three children with the highest mean length of utterance in words (MLW) were selected for detailed examination of their multisign utterances. The results indicated that no child showed strict positional patterns for specific verbs, although in several cases positional *tendencies* were observed. For example, subject 1 showed almost exclusive use of theme–verb order for the verbs LOOK-FOR and PUT-IN, and verb–theme order for the verbs EAT, SEE, and DRINK. However, the same subject produced some verbs such as WANT and LIKE in both canonical and noncanonical orders, with roughly equal frequency. Table 10.2, extracted from Schick (2002), lists all verbs used a minimum of four times in multisign utterances by child 1, as well as the number of times each verb appeared in verb–theme and theme–verb order, respectively.

Due to the general paucity of verb + agent combinations, these were not included in the analysis. Schick noted that the limited data available did not appear to indicate any positional patterns. Subject 1 produced a fair number of agents (42 in all), but used both preverbal and postverbal order for the same verb, as illustrated by the examples with WANT and EAT in table 10.3.

Schick (2002) concluded that although her subjects did not demonstrate any overall word order pattern used for disambiguating grammatical relations, there was some evidence that word order patterns existed on a verb-to-verb basis. However, positional patterns alone clearly do not account for all the word order variation in the data. Schick proposed two additional factors that could plausibly contribute to word order variability. First, she noted the frequency of topicalized objects in typical ASL. This might have led children to

**Table 10-2: Positional Patterns With Individual Verbs From Schick (2002)**

| Verb | Verb–Theme | Theme–Verb |
|------|------------|------------|
| WANT | 5 | 9 |
| EAT | 9 | 1 |
| SEE | 5 | 1 |
| DRINK | 4 | 0 |
| LIKE | 2 | 2 |
| PUT-IN | 1 | 5 |
| LOOK-FOR | 0 | 4 |

**Table 10-3: Positional Variability
with Sample Verbs
From Schick (2002)**

| Examples with AGENT + WANT AGENT + EAT |
| --- |
| WANT ME |
| ME WANT POINT-object |
| ME WANT GRAPES |
| EAT ME |
| DADDY EAT |

associate topic noun phrases (NPs) (i.e., presupposed information) with preverbal position. However, topicalization in children's production may have been obscured by the absence of the adult nonmanual marker, reported to emerge around 3;0 (Reilly, McIntire, & Bellugi, 1990). A related possibility is that deaf children view word order variation as encoding pragmatic distinctions (e.g., old vs. new information). Studies of Turkish, a language with highly variable word order, indicate that children manipulate order in pragmatically appropriate ways from around age 2;0 (Aksu-Koc & Slobin, 1985).

Schick's study demonstrates that deaf children use a variety of word orders, "[reflecting] the diversity of word orders that they see in their input" (Schick 2002, p. 157). Thus they are aware that certain noncanonical orders are permitted in their language and produce preverbal objects associated with topicalization and verbal agreement, for example, despite lacking control of the nonmanual marker and inflectional system required to correctly mark these departures from canonical order.

## Is Early Word Order Grammatical?

Both Hoffmeister (1978) and Schick (2002) repeatedly mentioned that certain aspects of ASL grammar associated with word order change, such as topicalization and verb agreement, reportedly emerge late in deaf children. While these particular aspects of ASL grammar may be beyond the capacity of 2-year-old children, there may be other order-modifying processes that are already acquired by this age. Chen (2001) and Chen Pichler (2001) investigated early multisign productions with respect to two syntactic devices observed to trigger noncanonical order in adult ASL: subject pronoun copy and nonagreement verbal morphology[8] (handling, spatial, and aspectual inflections).

---

[8] It has been argued elsewhere (recently, as well as at the time that the Hoffmeister study was conducted) that agreement morphology also licenses noncanonical word order, but Chen Pichler does not discuss this.

Subject-pronoun copy (Padden, 1988) produces a sentence-final index coreferenced with the subject, as shown in example 10.2. As Padden notes, the preverbal subject itself may be implied rather than explicit, as indicated by the parentheses. The pronominal index is glossed IX, with the object being pointed to following in parentheses.

(10.2) (BABY) SLEEP IX(baby)
"(The baby) is sleeping (he is)."

Crucially, the subject copy must be a pronoun; full NPs in this position are ungrammatical. Postverbal subjects of this kind are extremely common in adult signing and have been described by Padden (1988) as having a pragmatic function of adding emphasis or confirmation.

Nontopicalized, preverbal objects are normally considered ungrammatical in ASL, but grammatical preverbal objects occur when the verb is inflected with aspectual, spatial or handling morphology, as illustrated in examples 10.3–10.5, respectively.

(10.3) PAPER TYPE$_{asp}$[9]
"(She was) typing (and typing) her paper."

(10.4) MONEY PUT-ON-TABLE
"Just put the money on the table."

(10.5) . . . SHOES TAKE-OFF-shoes
"(In Japan, before entering a house, people) take off their shoes."

In light of their similar effects on word order, Chen Pichler grouped aspectual, spatial, and handling morphology together as a class in ASL, collectively referred to as *reordering morphology*. Following a derivation for preverbal objects of aspectual verbs proposed by Braze (2004), she proposed that the syntactic tree for ASL includes a functional projection for encoding features such as aspect, location, and instrument. Chen Pichler labeled this projection "manner phrase" and proposed (in line with theories of spoken language morphology) that all verbs with reordering morphology must move to this projection to "check" their aspectual, spatial, and/or handling features. Chen Pichler further proposed that manner phrase branches out to the right, such that checked reordering verbs appear to the right of their object. This is consistent with the OV order observed in sentences with reordering verbs.

Chen Pichler (2001) followed four deaf children of deaf, signing parents, acquiring ASL as their native language between the ages of roughly 20–30 months. The children, referred to by their pseudonyms Ned, Sal, Jil, and Aby, were videotaped on a weekly/biweekly basis at

---

[9] The subscript *asp* indicates that the verb is produced with durative or continuative aspect.

normal play. All multisign utterances that included a verb plus a subject and/or object were counted for analysis, excluding any utterances judged to be imitation of a prior adult utterance.

Chen Pichler's analysis revealed that the children used canonical word order inconsistently, similarly to the children in the Schick (2002) report. They used predominantly canonical orders one session and then noncanonical orders the next, giving the overall impression of random word order choice. Table 10.4 summarizes the children's use of canonical preverbal subjects and canonical postverbal objects during the period of study.

At first glance, the children's inconsistent reliance on canonical order would appear to indicate failure to set the basic word order parameters by 20–30 months of age. Such a finding would be in stark contrast to those reported for spoken language acquisition, where the word order parameters are reportedly set extremely early (Clahsen & Muysken, 1986; Wexler, 1998). However, Chen Pichler (2001) reasoned that the apparent randomness of the data need not indicate failure to set the word order parameters, but might indicate instead that the children were using grammatical noncanonical orders *in addition* to canonical order. To test for this possibility, she inspected all instances of postverbal subjects and preverbal objects for evidence of subject pronoun copy and reordering morphology, respectively. Chen Pichler adopted the following criteria for identifying reordering operations: for subject-pronoun copy, the presence of a sentence-final subject in pronoun (index) form (i.e., a point); for aspectual OV, repetition of the verb in large movements with extended duration; for spatial OV, articulation of the verb toward or at a specific location, with corresponding eye gaze; and for handling OV, use of a handling classifier in articulation of the verb.

In their SV combinations, all four children favored pronoun subjects over full NPs in postverbal position, consistent with subject-pronoun copy. Samples of postverbal subjects counted as subject-pronoun copy are given in example 10.6.

(10.6a) I SEARCH$_{asp}$ I (Aby, 29.5 months)
"I'm looking and looking (for my shoes)."

**Table 10-4: Use of Canonical Word Orders From Chen Pichler (2001)**

| Child | Total Utterances with Overt Subject | Percentage Preverbal Subject | Total Utterances with Overt Object | Percentage Postverbal Object |
|-------|-------------------------------------|------------------------------|------------------------------------|------------------------------|
| Ned | 68 | 72% | 25 | 52% |
| Sal | 50 | 54% | 44 | 32% |
| Jil | 33 | 73% | 50 | 50% |
| Aby | 98 | 57% | 76 | 50% |

(10.6b) BOY MUST IX(page) (Ned, 29 months)
"The boy (in the picture) must (do it)."

When considered together with instances of canonical preverbal subjects (all of which were counted as grammatical), the total percentage of
grammatical combinations of subject and verb over all sessions rose to
97% for Ned, 96% for Sal, 97% for Jil, and 96% for Aby. Chen Pichler
added that this high rate of grammatical subject ordering was already
evident within the first few sessions for each child and was largely
sustained throughout the entire period of observation, indicating that
knowledge of subject and verb SV ordering becomes adultlike early,
usually before 22 months.

Grammatical preverbal objects due to reordering morphology were
also present in the data of all four children, as illustrated by example 10.7.

(10.7a) YELLOW THROW-INTO-CORNER (Sal, 20.75 months)
"I threw the yellow one (ball) into the corner."

(10.7b) CAT SEARCH$_{asp}$ (Jil, 26.0 months)
"I'm looking and looking for the cat."

(10.7c) IX(picture) BOAT ROW (Ned, 27.5 months)
"He (boy in picture) is rowing a boat."

Chen Pichler (2001) reported that, in general, spatial and handling
verbs were more common in the data than aspectual verbs and occurred with both preverbal and postverbal objects. This variability is
not inconsistent with the adult grammar, which allows flexible word
order with many spatial and handling verbs. In contrast, OV order is
obligatory with aspectual verbs for some signers, while optional for
others. This difference appears to be dialectal (Braze, 2004).

Once preverbal objects with reordering verbs were taken into account, the overall percentage of grammatical object ordering rose to 80%
for Ned, 86% for Sal, 76% for Jil, and 63% for Aby. These percentages are
somewhat lower than those for grammatical subject and verb SV combinations. Chen Pichler (2001) noted a relatively high percentage of
unaccountable preverbal objects in the earliest transcripts, and speculated that the head-complement parameter may be set later than the
spec-head parameter. Alternatively, particularly in the case of Aby, she
noted there are likely to be other sources of preverbal objects not identified in her initial study, such as early object topicalization.

Chen Pichler (2001) concluded that her data were compatible with
the cross-linguistic generalization that the word order parameters are
set early, but that the effects of parameter setting are obscured by early
use of syntactic devices that generate noncanonical orders. It is worth
noting that there are some indications such an analysis might apply to
at least some of the Schick (2002) data as well. For example, the verbs

LOOK-FOR and PUT-IN from table 10.2 are excellent candidates for verbs with reordering morphology (aspectual and spatial, respectively) and, as such, could be expected to appear with preverbal objects. Also, the alternations in subject position shown in table 10.3 conform to adultlike instances of subject-pronoun copy, rendering a positional pattern analysis unnecessary. Evaluation of Chen Pichler's analysis with respect to the Hoffmeister (1978) data is not possible, due to the limited number of examples provided in the latter study. However, since Hoffmeister made no mention of verbal inflection beyond person agreement, it is certainly possible that the effects of other reordering morphology were simply not yet recognized at the time of his study.

The proposal that deaf children master certain syntactically driven noncanonical orders has also been made by Coerts (2000) in her investigation of subject placement in early NGT (Sign Language of the Netherlands), a language with SOV canonical word order. Coerts reanalyzed spontaneous production data from two deaf twins, Mark and Laura, children of a deaf and signing mother, between the ages of 1;6 and 2;6. The data were originally reported by Coerts and Mills (1994) in the context of an investigation of early word order and null arguments in NGT. In that study, high variability in subject and verb ordering appeared to constitute evidence against early setting of the word order parameters. With the subsequent identification of subject-pronoun copy as a productive process in NGT (Bos, 1995), Coerts (2000) proposed that Mark and Laura had mastered this aspect of NGT grammar at an early age, resulting in the noncanonical subject placement observed by Coerts and Mills (1994).

Coerts (2000) applied the same criteria for sentence-final subjects as Chen Pichler, with one added requirement: VS sequences were counted only if they occurred after the child had produced at least one SVS sequence. This requirement was adopted as a conservative measure, on the premise that the clearest possible instance of subject-pronoun copy is that in which the subject appears twice: once preverbally and once postverbally. By these criteria, 93% (13 of 14) of Laura's sentence-final subjects qualified as subject-pronoun copies, as did 79% (27 of 34 total) of Mark's. In light of this reanalysis, the NGT data become consistent with the generalization of early setting of the word order parameters. They also provide important cross-linguistic support for the claims of early mastery of syntactic devices affecting word order proposed by Chen Pichler (2001) for ASL.

## Topics for Future Study

Investigation of word order acquisition in ASL began more than 25 years ago, yet the topics addressed in this summary represent only a sample of the many sign language word order phenomena that have yet to be formally investigated. To begin with, we still have a relatively poor understanding of word order phenomena in adult ASL. Non-topicalized preverbal objects, in particular, seem to occur frequently in ASL and may be the result of object shift, movement of the verb to the sentence-final position, or both. Verbs presumably move syntactically for morphological reasons, as briefly described above, but there is no consensus on the types of morphology that trigger movement, or on the functional projection(s) targeted by such movement (the proposal for manner phrase by Chen Pichler being only a working proposal with few details of the derivation worked out).

Once we have a better idea of the patterns of word order variation that occur in normal adult ASL, we can address the question of whether these patterns are altered in child-directed signing and, if so, what effects these changes have on children's word order choices. It is likely that many aspects of ASL development are susceptible to input patterns. To date, very few studies have focused on word order in child-directed ASL and corresponding effects on children's word order choice (but see van den Bogaerde & Mills, 1994, for NGT).

Another area that requires further research is the development of topicalization. Object topicalization is a noted source of preverbal objects in adult ASL, yet the status of this construction in children's early production has not yet been seriously investigated (but for preliminary discussion, see Chen Pichler, 2001; Reilly, McIntire, & Bellugi, 1991). The emergence of topics, in turn, is linked to children's development of pragmatic distinctions such as old versus new information and the knowledge that only old information can function as topics.

Finally, there is always a need for more research conducted using disparate methodologies and focusing on different sign languages. All the word order studies cited in this summary rely on spontaneous production data. This is due to the fact that children begin producing multisign combinations at 2;0 or younger, an age at which few children have the attention span required for experimental tasks. As the focus of early word order research broadens to include older children, experimental techniques such as elicited production and acceptability judgments become appropriate. Experimental methodologies will allow researchers to conduct studies on specific word order phenomena that may occur with low frequency in spontaneous signing. More studies focusing on sign languages other than ASL are also sorely needed, particularly non-SVO sign languages. Only via cross-linguistic comparison can we determine whether patterns observed for ASL are representative of sign languages more broadly, or simply language-specific artifacts.

## SUMMARY AND CONCLUSIONS

We have examined in some detail the acquisition of two aspects of sign language morphosyntax: verb agreement and word order. We have concentrated on these two areas because there has been sufficient research on them that interesting theoretical questions have been raised and addressed. We find tying studies of the acquisition of sign languages to theoretical issues in language development and linguistics to be of utmost interest and importance. Only by the examination of data from all language types can truly explanatory theories be developed.

Our overview has only scratched the surface of "acquisition of syntax." Studies of other areas of syntax have been conducted or are in progress. As an illustration, consider Morgan (chapter 13 this volume) on morphosyntax in British Sign Language, Reilly (chapter 11 this volume) on nonmanuals (an important part of the syntax of sign languages), Schick (chapter 5 this volume) on classifiers (prevalent across sign languages), and Shaffer (chapter 12 this volume) on modality (an issue not yet well studied). We are involved in additional studies of the acquisition of syntax as well, including studies of wh-questions (Lillo-Martin, 2000, Lillo-Martin and Quadros 2004a) and focus (Lillo-Martin & Quadros, 2004b).

We look forward to the outcomes of these and additional studies on the acquisition of syntax in sign languages.

## ACKNOWLEDGMENTS

The preparation of this chapter was supported in part by National Institutes of Health grant NIDCD 00183 to D.L.-M. We thank our sign models, Brenda Schertz and Doreen Simons-Marques.

## REFERENCES

Aksu-Koc, A. A., & Slobin, D. I. (1985). The acquisition of Turkish. In D. I. Slobin (Ed.), *The crosslinguistic study of language acquisition* (Vol. 1, pp. 839–878). Hillsdale, NJ: Lawrence Erlbaum.

Bahan, B. (1996). *Non-manual realization of agreement in American Sign Language.* Unpublished doctoral dissertation, Boston University.

Bellugi, U., Lillo-Martin, D., O'Grady, L., & VanHoek, K. (1990). The Development of spatialized syntactic mechanisms in American Sign Language. In W. H. Edmondson & F. Karlsson (Eds.), *SLR '87: Papers from the Fourth International Symposium on Sign Language Research* (Vol. 10, pp. 183–189). Hamburg: Signum-Verlag.

Bellugi, U., vanHoek, K., Lillo-Martin, D., & O'Grady, L. (1988). The acquisition of syntax and space in young deaf signers. In D. Bishop & K. Mogford (Eds.), *Language development in exceptional circumstances* (pp. 132–149). Edinburgh: Churchill Livingstone.

Berk, S. (2003). *Sensitive period effects on the acquisition of language: A study of language development.* Unpublished doctoral dissertation, University of Connecticut, Storrs.

Bos, H. (1995). Pronoun copy in Sign Language of the Netherlands. In H. Bos & T. Schermer (Eds.), *Sign language research 1994: Proceedings of the 4th European Congress on Sign Language Research* (pp. 121–147). Hamburg: Signum.

Braze, F. D. (2004). Aspectual inflection, verb raising, and object fronting in American Sign Language. *Lingua, 114,* 29–58.

Brentari, D. (1995). Sign language phonology: ASL. In J. Goldsmith (Ed.), *A handbook of phonological theory* (pp. 615–639). New York: Basil Blackwell.

Brentari, D. (1998). *A prosodic model of sign language phonology.* Cambridge, MA: MIT Press.

Brown, R. (1973). *A first language: The early stages.* Cambridge, MA: Harvard University Press.

Brown, R. (1980). Why are signed languages easier to learn than spoken languages? In W. C. Stokoe (Ed.), *Proceedings of the First National Symposium on Sign Language Research and Teaching* (pp. 9–24). Washington, DC: National Association of the Deaf.

Casey, S. (2003). *"Agreement" in gestures and signed languages: The use of directionality to indicate referents involved in actions.* Unpublished doctoral dissertation, University of California, San Diego.

Cazden, C. (1968). The acquisition of noun and verb inflections. *Child Development, 39,* 433–438.

Chen, D. (2001). Evidence for early word order acquisition in a variable word order language. In A. H.-J. Do, L. Dominguez, & A. Johansen (Eds.), *Proceedings of the 25th Boston University Conference on Language Development* (pp. 145–156). Sommerville, MA: Cascadilla Press.

Chen Pichler, D. (2001). *Word order variability and acquisition in American Sign Language.* Unpublished doctoral dissertation, University of Connecticut, Storrs.

Chomsky, N. (1981). *Lectures on government and binding.* Dordrecht: Foris.

Clahsen, H., & Muysken, P. (1986). The availability of universal grammar to adult and child learners—a study of the acquisition of German word order. *Second Language Research, 2,* 93–119.

Coerts, J. (2000). Early sign combinations in the acquisition of Sign Language of the Netherlands: Evidence for language-specific features. In C. Chamberlain, J. Morford, & R. Mayberry (Eds.), *Language acquisition by eye* (pp. 91–109). Mahwah, NJ: Lawrence Erlbaum.

Coerts, J., & Mills, A. E. (1994). Early sign combinations of deaf children in Sign Language of the Netherlands. In I. Ahlgren, B. Bergman, & M. Brennan (Eds.), *Perspectives on sign language usage: Papers from the Fifth International Symposium on Sign Language Research* (Vol. 2, pp. 319–331). Durham, UK: ISLA.

Fischer, S. D. (1974). Sign language and linguistic universals. In C. Rohrer & N. Ruwet (Eds.), *Actes du Colloque Franco-Allemand de Grammaire Transformationelle, Band II; Études de Sémantique et Autres* (pp. 187–204). Tübingen: Max Niemeyer Verlag.

Fischer, S. D. (1975). Influences on word order change in American Sign Language. In C. Li (Ed.), *Word order and word order change* (pp. 1–25). Austin: University of Texas Press.

Fischer, S. D., & Gough, B. (1978). Verbs in American Sign Language. *Sign Language Studies, 7*(18), 17–48.

Friedman, L. (1977). Formational properties of American Sign Language. In L. Friedman (Ed.), *On the other hand* (pp. 13–56). New York: Academic Press.

Hänel, B. (2004). The acquisition of DGS: early steps into a spatially expressed syntax. *Linguistische Berichte.*

Hoekstra, T., & Hyams, N. (1998). Aspects of root infinitives. *Lingua, 106*, 81–112.

Hoffmeister, R. J. (1978). Word order in the acquisition of ASL. Unpublished ms, Boston Univ.

Janis, W. (1995). A crosslinguistic perspective on ASL verb agreement. In K. Emmorey & J. Reilly (Eds.), *Language, gesture, and space* (pp. 195–223). Hillsdale, NJ: Lawrence Erlbaum.

Kegl, J. (1976). *Relational grammar and American Sign Language.* Unpublished manuscript.

Klima, E. S., & Bellugi, U. (1979). *The signs of language.* Cambridge, MA: Harvard University Press.

Liddell, S. K. (1977). *An investigation into the syntax of American Sign Language.* Unpublished doctoral dissertation, University of California, San Diego.

Liddell, S. K. (1980). *American Sign Language syntax.* The Hague: Mouton.

Liddell, S. K. (1984). Unrealized-inceptive aspect in America Sign Language. *Papers from the Chicago Linguistic Society, 20*(1), 257–270.

Liddell, S. K. (1990). Four functions of a locus: Reexamining the structure of space in ASL. In C. Lucas (Ed.), *Sign language research: Theoretical issues* (pp. 176–198). Washington, DC: Gallaudet University Press.

Liddell, S. K. (1995). Real, surrogate, and token space: Grammatical consequences in ASL. In K. Emmorey & J. Reilly (Eds.), *Language, gesture, and space* (pp. 19–41). Hillsdale, NJ: Lawrence Erlbaum.

Liddell, S. K. (2000). Indicating verbs and pronouns: Pointing away from agreement. In K. Emmorey & H. Lane (Eds.), *The signs of language revisited: An anthology to honor Ursula Bellugi and Edward Klima* (pp. 303–320). Mahwah, NJ: Lawrence Erlbaum.

Lillo-Martin, D. (1986). Two kinds of null arguments in American Sign Language. *Natural Language and Linguistic Theory, 4*, 415–444.

Lillo-Martin, D. (1991). *Universal grammar and American Sign Language: Setting the null argument parameters.* Dordrecht: Kluwer.

Lillo-Martin, D. (1999). Modality effects and modularity in language acquisition: The acquisition of American Sign Language. In W. C. Ritchie & T. K. Bhatia (Eds.), *Handbook of language acquisition* (pp. 531–567). San Diego, CA: Academic Press.

Lillo-Martin, D. (2000). Aspects of the syntax and acquisition of wh-questions in American Sign Language. In K. Emmorey & H. Lane (Eds.), *The signs of language revisited: An anthology in honor of Ursula Bellugi and Edward Klima* (pp.401–413). Mahwah, NJ: Lawrence Erlbaum.

Lillo-Martin, D. (2002). Where are all the modality effects? In R. Meier, K. Cormier, & D. Quinto-Pozos (Eds.), *Modality and structure in signed language and spoken language* (pp. 241–262). Cambridge: Cambridge University Press.

Lillo-Martin, D., Bellugi, U., Struxness, L., & O'Grady, M. (1985). The acquisition of spatially organized syntax. *Papers and Reports on Child Language Development, 24*, 70–78.

Lillo-Martin, D. & Quadros, R. M. (2004a). The position of early WH-elements in American Sign Language and Brazilian Sign Language. Paper presented at Generative Approaches to Language Acquisition-North America, Honolulu, Hawaii, December 2004.

Lillo-Martin, D. & Quadros, R. M. (2004b). The acquisition of focus constructions in American Sign Language and Lingua de Sinais Brasiliera. Presented at the 29th Boston University Conference on Language Development, Boston, November 2004.

Lillo-Martin, D., Quadros, R. M. D., & Mathur, G. (1998, November). *Acquisition of verb agreement in ASL and LIBRAS: A cross-linguistic study.* Poster presented at the Sixth International Conference on Theoretical Issues in Sign Language Research, Gallaudet University, Washington, DC.

Loew, R. (1984). *Roles and reference in American Sign Language: A developmental Perspective.* Unpublished doctoral dissertation, University of Minnesota.

Meier, R. P. (1981). Icons and morphemes: Models of the acquisition of verb agreement in ASL. *Papers and Reports on Child Language Development, 20*, 92–99.

Meier, R. P. (1982). *Icons, analogues, and morphemes: The acquisition of verb agreement in ASL.* Unpublished doctoral dissertation, University of California, San Diego.

Meier, R. P. (1987). Elicited Imitation of Verb Agreement in American Sign Language: Iconically or morphologically determined? *Journal of Memory and Language, 26*, 362–376.

Meier, R. P., & Newport, E. L. (1990). Out of the hands of babes: On a possible sign advantage in language acquisition. *Language, 66*, 1–23.

Meir, I. (2002). A cross-modality perspective on verb agreement. *Natural Language and Linguistic Theory, 20*, 413–450.

Neidle, C., Kegl, J., MacLaughlin, D., Bahan, B., & Lee, R. G. (2000). *The syntax of American Sign Language: Functional categories and hierarchical structure.* Cambridge, MA: MIT Press.

Newport, E. L., & Meier, R. P. (1985). The acquisition of American Sign Language. In D. I. Slobin (Ed.), *The cross-linguistic study of language acquisition* (Vol. 1, pp. 881–938). Hillsdale, NJ: Lawrence Erlbaum.

Padden, C. A. (1988). *Interaction of morphology and syntax in American Sign Language.* New York: Garland.

Park, T.-Z. (1970). *Language acquisition in a Korean child.* Unpublished manuscript. Psychological Institute, University of Bern, Switzerland.

Poeppel, D., & Wexler, K. (1993). The full competence hypothesis of clause structure in early German. *Language, 69*, 1–33.

Quadros, R. M. d. (1995). *As categorias vazias pronominais: Uma análise alternativa com base na lingua de sinais brasileira e reflexos no processo de acquisição.* Unpublished master's thesis, PUCRS, Porto Alegre, Brazil.

Rathmann, C., & Mathur, G. (2002). Is verb agreement the same cross-modally? In R. P. Meier, K. Cormier, & D. Quinto-Pozos (Eds.), *Modality and structure in signed and spoken languages* (pp. 370–404). Cambridge: Cambridge University Press.

Reilly, J. S., McIntire, M. L., & Bellugi, U. (1990). Faces: The relationship between language and affect. In V. Volterra & C. J. Erting (Eds.), *From gesture to language in hearing and deaf children* (Vol. 27, pp. 128–141). Berlin: Springer-Verlag.

Reilly, J. S., McIntire, M. L., & Bellugi, U. (1991). Baby face: A new perspective on universals in language acquisition. In P. Siple & S. D. Fischer (Eds.), *Theoretical issues in sign language research: Vol. 2. Psychology* (pp. 9–23). Chicago: University of Chicago Press.

Rizzi, L. (1993/94). Some notes on linguistic theory and language development: The case of root infinitives. *Language Acquisition, 3,* 371–393.

Sandler, W. (1989). *Phonological representation of the sign: linearity and nonlinearity in American Sign Language.* Dordrecht: Foris.

Sandler, W., & Lillo-Martin, D. (2005). *Sign language and linguistic universals.* Cambridge: Cambridge University Press.

Schick, B. S. (2002). The expression of grammatical relations by deaf toddlers learning ASL. In G. Morgan & B. Woll (Eds.), *Directions in sign language acquisition* (pp. 143–158). Amsterdam: John Benjamins.

Schick, B. S., & Gale, E. (1996). The development of syntax in deaf toddlers learning ASL. Paper presented at the 5th International Conference on Theoretical Issues in Sign Language Research, Montreal, Canada, September 19–22.

Slobin, D. I. (1966). The acquisition of Russian as a native language. In F. Smith & G. A. Miller (Eds.), *The genesis of language: A psycholinguistic approach* (pp. 129–148). Cambridge, MA: MIT Press.

Slobin, D. I. (1982). Universal and particular in the acquisition of langauge. In E. Wanner & L. R. Gleitman (Eds.), *Language acquisition: The state of the art* (pp. 128–172). New York: Cambridge University Press.

Supalla, T. (1982). *Structure and acquisition of verbs of motion and location in American Sign Language.* Unpublished doctoral dissertation, University of California, San Diego.

Tomasello, M. (1992). *First verbs: A case study of early grammatical development.* Cambridge: Cambridge University Press.

van den Bogaerde, B., & Mills, A. E. (1994). Word order in language input: SLN or Dutch. In M. Brennan & G. H. Turner (Eds.), *Word-order issues in sign language* (pp. 133–157). Durham, UK: University of Durham.

vanHoek, K., O'Grady, L., Bellugi, U., & Norman, F. (1987, April). *Innovative spatial morphology in deaf children's signing.* Paper presented at the Stanford Child Language Research Forum, Stanford, CA.

vanHoek, K., O'Grady, L., Bellugi, U., & Norman, F. (1989, April). *The acquisition of perspective shift and serial verbs.* Paper presented at the Stanford Child Language Research Forum, Stanford, CA.

vanHoek, K., O'Grady, L., Bellugi, U., & Norman, F. (1990, April). *Spatial and nonspatial referential cohesion.* Paper presented at the Stanford Child Language Research Forum, Stanford, CA.

Wexler, K. (1994). Optional infinitives, head movement and the economy of derivations. In D. Lightfoot & N. Hornstein (Eds.), *Verb movement* (pp. 305–350). Cambridge: Cambridge University Press.

Wexler, K. (1998). Very early parameter setting and the unique checking constraint: A new explanation of the optional infinitive stage. *Lingua, 106,* 23–79.

# 11

# How Faces Come to Serve Grammar: The Development of Nonmanual Morphology in American Sign Language

*Judy Reilly*

Research concerning the development of signed languages has overwhelmingly found that children acquiring a signed language from their signing parents follow the same steps and overall sequence of development as do hearing children learning a spoken language (Bellugi & Klima, 1982; Lillo-Martin, 1999; Newport & Meier, 1985). Similar to hearing babies, deaf infants babble (Pettito & Martenette, 1991), and Deaf parents use a special "motherese" when signing to their deaf infants and toddlers (Erting, Prezioso, & O'Grady-Hines, 1990; Reilly & Bellugi, 1996; Spencer & Harris, chapter 4 this volume). In acquiring the phonology of American Sign Language (ASL), deaf children make the same type of "errors" as to children learning a spoken language; for example, signs may have the wrong handshape or movement (Schick, chapter 5 this volume) simplifying the sign, just as children learning English may say "sketti" rather than the more phonologically complex "spaghetti." Both hearing and deaf children begin producing gestures during the second half of their first year, giving rise to extensive discussion regarding a developmental advantage for the emergence of first signs over first words (see Meier & Newport, 1990; see also Volterra, Iverson, & Castrataro, chapter 3 this volume). However, the first true symbolic use of signs appears during the same developmental period as the first symbolic words (Pettito, 2000; see also Anderson, chapter 6 this volume), and researchers generally agree that there is an early "one-sign stage" followed by the onset of syntax, that is, utterances that combine multiple manual signs, beginning at about 20–24 months of age. From then on, for children acquiring signed languages, their utterances increase in length and complexity as they slowly master the complex manually incorporated morphology (Bellugi, Lillo-Martin, O'Grady, & van Hoek, 1990; Lillo-Martin, 1999; Newport & Meier, 1985).

In spite of the commonalities found across children learning signed and spoken languages, the visual-gestural modality of signed languages presents special challenges to the young language learner that differ from those faced by children acquiring spoken languages. This chapter investigates one such aspect of sign language development that is special to signed languages, linguistic facial expression. An unusual feature of ASL and other sign languages, relative to spoken languages, is that facial expression is multifunctional: It conveys emotion, just as it does accompanying spoken discourse (Ekman, 1972, 1979), but it also constitutes part of the grammar of the language. Particular constellations of facial behaviors function as the morphological markers for such structures as conditional clauses, topics, negation, and relative clauses. In fact, facial signals are frequently the only morphological marker signaling a grammatical structure (Baker-Shenk, 1983). Moreover, an emerging literature indicates that nonmanual behaviors, including eye gaze, facial behaviors, and head and shoulder movements, are used grammatically in a number of signed languages (Baker, 1977; Baker & Cokely, 1980; Baker & Padden, 1978; Baker-Shenk, 1983; Coulter, 1980; Liddell, 1978; and see also Engberg-Pedersen, 1995, in Danish Sign Language; Poulin & Miller, 1995, in Quebec Sign Language; Rossini, Reilly, Febbretti, & Volterra, 2000, in Italian Sign Language).

The focus of this chapter is the acquisition of nonmanual behaviors in ASL by deaf children of deaf parents who are acquiring ASL as their native language. Chronicling the development of such grammatical behaviors permits us to address basic issues in development, such as the relations of language and affect as they emerge and co-develop. Because sign language, unlike spoken languages, exploits multiple channels simultaneously, we can also investigate how children acquire linguistic structures that are signaled across two channels: hands and faces. Because there are few, if any, studies in other sign languages addressing the acquisition of grammatical facial behaviors in children, this chapter is limited to data from ASL. However, it is anticipated that children acquiring other sign languages will use similar strategies and follow a similar developmental path. The first section begins with a brief overview of nonmanual morphology in adult ASL, followed by a statement of issues to be addressed. The second section chronicles the development of grammatical facial behaviors in deaf children of deaf parents acquiring ASL, from the appearance of first signs (at about 1 year of age) through the acquisition of facial expression for discourse purposes (about age 7).

## Nonmanual Morphology in ASL

Nonmanual behaviors in ASL occur on the upper face, the lower face, or both and can also include head and shoulder movements as well as eye blinks or gaze change as part of the grammatical signal. Grammatical facial morphology can occur with single manual, lexical items, that is, single signs, or with multisigned predicates (verbs, verb phrases, or adjectival predicates), or they can co-occur with an entire clause. To contextualize the developmental discussion of nonmanual morphology in ASL, below is brief overview of the adult facial grammar.

### *Lexical Behaviors*

Single lexical signs can be accompanied by nonmanual behaviors. In some cases (see example 11.2), the nonmanual behavior actually changes the meaning of a manual sign that has an alternative meaning when signed alone. In contrast, example 11.1 is a case in which the statement includes a manual sign and a nonmanual signal that express the same meaning.

(11.1)  _____ gaze + head (head and eye movement mirroring
          SEARCH                       a "search" behavior)

(11.2)  _____th (slightly open mouth, tongue slightly
          LATE NOT-YET      protruding between teeth)

Above, LATE and NOT-YET share the same manual form; that is, the physical sign is the same. They are distinguished by the "th," which accompanies NOT-YET but not LATE.

### *Adverbial Facial Behaviors*

Nonmanual adverbials can co-occur with a range of manual predicates; these adverbs tend to be on the lower face and semantically modify the manually signed predicate with which they co-occur. For example, the adverbial "mm" (which is shown by the signer pursing and extending closed lips) is glossed as "regularly, easily, or pleasurably," whereas the adverbial "th" is often glossed as "awkwardly or carelessly." The following set of examples presents the identical string of manual signs, initially bare and then co-occurring with two different nonmanual adverbials that modify the meaning of the signed predicate (WRITE LETTER):

(11.3a) BOY WRITE LETTER  "The boy is writing/wrote a letter."

                            _____mm
(11.3b) BOY WRITE LETTER          "The boy writes/wrote letters regu-
                                   larly or easily."

                            _____th
(11.3c) BOY WRITE LETTER    "The boy writes/wrote letters carelessly."

*Syntactic Facial Behaviors*

Sentential or clausal structures can also be signaled by nonmanual morphology in ASL. In example 11.4, a WH-question is indicated by a specific set of facial behaviors and head posture as well as a manual sign. Similarly, in example 11.5, both a head shake and the manual sign NOT redundantly express the negative meaning.

> _____wh-q    (furrowed brow, head tilt back)
> (11.4)  WHO STEAL MY CANDY WHO   "Who stole my candy?"
> _____neg
> (11.5)  ME NOT GO SCHOOL        "I'm not going to school."

Even though examples 11.4 and 11.5 above include a wh-question and negative sign, respectively, the redundant nonmanual component is required in each case. Additionally, negation can be conveyed by just the nonmanual signal, as in examples 11.6a and 11.6b, where the headshake is the only negative marker and renders example 11.6b a negative utterance:

> (11.6a)  ME LIKE CHOCOLATE    "I like chocolate."

> _____neg
> (11.6b)  ME LIKE CHOCOLATE    "I don't like chocolate."

Conditional sentences, as in example 11.7a, are similar in that the nonmanual behavior is the only indication that the utterance is a conditional sentence. Without the nonmanual signal (example 11.7b), the utterance is interpreted as a sequence of two conjoined declarative statements.

> _____cond (brow raise, head tilt + nod, blink)
> (11.7a)  EAT BUG      SICK YOU   "If you eat bugs, you'll get sick."

> (11.7b)  EAT BUG      SICK YOU   "You ate bugs and got sick."

In sum, in the adult grammar of ASL, nonmanual grammatical behaviors differ in length and complexity; they can be redundant with the manual signs, or they can serve as the sole grammatical marker. In all cases, they represent an obligatory aspect of the morphology of the linguistic structure.

*Nonmanual Behaviors in Discourse: Direct Quote*

An additional context in which nonmanual behaviors carry linguistic significance in adult ASL is in discourse. Perspective marking, or what has been commonly known in the literature as "referential shift" or "role shift" (e.g., Bahan & Supalla, 1995; Padden, 1986; Smith, Lentz, & Mikos, 1988) or point of view (Emmorey & Reilly, 1998; Engberg-Pedersen, 1995; Poulin & Miller, 1995) also include nonmanual behaviors. Referential shift recruits emotional facial expression, to linguistically delineate the scope, that is, the beginning, duration, and end, of a direct quote or reported action. Such facial expressions often reflect the character's emotion or response in a story. Example 11.8 comes from an adult telling the story of the Three Bears. In this utterance, the adult signals the character's identity (BABY BEAR) with a nonmanual topic marker (raised brows) and eye contact (+K) with the addressee. The beginning of the quote itself is then signaled by a break in gaze contact (−K) and a slight head turn beginning with the sign LOOK-AT; the narrator then assumes the Baby Bear's emotional facial expression, in this case, surprise, as he discovers that his soup is gone followed by distress beginning with the sign SOMEONE and then a pout reflecting his response to the empty bowl.

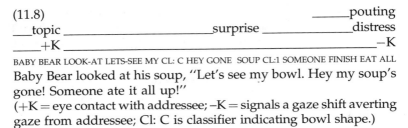

(11.8) _____pouting
___topic _____surprise _____distress
____+K _____−K

BABY BEAR LOOK-AT LETS-SEE MY CL: C HEY GONE  SOUP CL:1 SOMEONE FINISH EAT ALL

Baby Bear looked at his soup, "Let's see my bowl. Hey my soup's gone! Someone ate it all up!"

(+K = eye contact with addressee; −K = signals a gaze shift averting gaze from addressee; Cl: C is classifier indicating bowl shape.)

Unlike the morphological and syntactic nonmanual signals described above, direct quotation in ASL directly recruits affective expressions into the service of language. These affective expressions, plus the change in gaze, signal that the utterance is a direct quote or reported action; they also indicate the role the narrator is taking (or "who is speaking") as the story is recounted. Narrators may display different emotions for various characters in a given story. Nonetheless, gaze and emotional expression delineate the scope, that is, the beginning, duration, and end of the direct quote.

### Affective and Linguistic Facial Signals

Although grammatical facial morphology uses the same muscles as those that are recruited for emotional expression, their timing, scope (onset, offset, and duration), and context often differ. First, whereas facial expression for emotion can be used independently of language (e.g., we smile as a child runs to greet us), grammatical facial behaviors invariably co-occur with a manually signed utterance. Second, the timing of grammatical facial expression is linguistically constrained. It begins milliseconds before the initiation of the manually signed string over which it has scope, and immediately attains apex intensity that is maintained until the termination of the manual string (Baker-Schenk, 1983). In contrast, emotional expression is variable in intensity, and its timing is inconsistent

(Scherer, 1986). For example, we can frown slightly, in disapproval, or intensely, when very angry, and these expressions can last a fleeting second or for minutes on end. Moreover, these emotional expressions can co-occur with an utterance or they can exist independently of any linguistic behaviors. Overall, grammatical nonmanual signals are governed by specific linguistic rules whereas the production of emotional expressions is variable and not linguistically dependent. Below the two are graphically contrasted. In example 11.9, the adverbial expression begins just before the manually signed predicate (WRITE LETTER), reaches apex intensity immediately and this level of intensity is maintained until just before the end of the manual sign LETTER. In example 11.10, the expression of anger begins before the signed utterance and terminates sometime after the utterance is completed; its curvilinear form representing changes in intensity as the utterance progresses, is just one possible shape for expressing anger.

(11.9) Grammatical facial expression

BOY WRITE LETTER

(11.10) Affective facial expression (one of many possible shapes)

ME HATE HOMEWORK

## Development: Affect and Language

Similar to hearing babies, deaf infants are using emotional expression to communicate by the end of their first year (Campos, Barret, Lamb, Goldsmith, & Stenberg, 1983; de Haan, 2001; Hiatt, Campos, & Emde, 1979; Nelson, 1987; Nelson & de Haan, 1997; Reilly, Mcintire, & Bellugi, 1986/1990). Thus, at this age when first signs emerge, deaf infants face an interesting developmental problem: how to use affective/communicative behaviors for both emotion and language, and how to distinguish the different functions of these apparently isomorphic behaviors. Charting this transition and the development of nonmanual morphology in deaf children of deaf parents, children who are acquiring ASL as their first language, permits us to address some basic questions in developmental cognitive science:

(1) What are the developmental relations between affect, communication, and language? Can the infant use her affective/

communicative prowess to bootstrap herself into the linguistic system?

(2) What is the underlying functional organization of these communicative systems?

(3) How do children acquire these unusual linguistic structures that are expressed across channels?

First, from the adult neuropsychological literature, we know that for adults affective expression is primarily mediated by the right hemisphere (e.g., Borod, 2000) whereas core aspects of language, for example, morphology and syntax, are mediated by the left hemisphere in signed as well as spoken languages (Goodglass, 1993; Poizner, Klima, & Bellugi, 1987). However, we do not yet know how this specialization develops. Since both deaf and hearing infants use emotional facial expression during the first year of life, and children acquiring a sign language must subsequently use faces for grammar, tracking the acquisition of grammatical facial behaviors will provide insight into how the brain becomes specialized for language.

Second, an ongoing discussion in language development involves the degree to which language is an innately specified independent cognitive function (for differing perspectives, see Elman, 1996; Pinker, 1999). A hypothesis supporting a general cognitive model for language acquisition in which language is viewed as one of several symbolic systems that develop during the toddler and preschool years would predict that, with the acquisition of each new linguistic structure, infants would recruit their prelinguistic affective and communicative abilities and generalize them directly to the appropriate linguistic contexts. A more modular approach stemming from the view that the principles and parameters of universal grammar are innately specified would predict that children would not access these apparently pertinent affective behaviors; rather, children would approach each linguistic structure and its morphology de novo. Examining how children acquire structures where the grammatical and communicative signals are similar, as in negation, will address this issue.

Third, because signed languages recruit multiple channels (the hands, face, head, shoulders, and eyes), charting the acquisition of these unusual linguistic structures expressed across channels, provides us new insights into aspects of language development that are unique, thus broadening our understanding of the language acquisition process itself.

## THE DATA

In the mid-1980s my colleagues and I began to investigate the acquisition of grammatical facial expression in deaf children growing up with ASL; our goal was to address the three questions above. Thus, the data presented here come from more than 15 years of studies of deaf children of deaf parents where ASL is the language of the home and thus the children's native language. Over the years, we have seen and videotaped more than 60 deaf children who were acquiring ASL (1–10 years of age), often longitudinally, over a span of several years. The data set includes naturalistic conversations with parents and experimenters, storytelling, and experimental tasks designed to assess both production and comprehension of targeted linguistic structures. Finally, parental report data (MacArthur Communicative Developmental Inventory for ASL; Anderson & Reilly, 2002) are used to supplement the videotapes when appropriate. Together, these data reveal a profile of the developmental course of nonmanual morphology in ASL, the strategies children are using to acquire them, and some answers to the questions posed above.

The complexities of transcribing manual signing are well-known (see Baker & Cokely, 1980, for a detailed exposition). Acquisition data present another layer of issues that have recently been discussed by Slobin et al. (2001). The transcription and coding of facial and other nonmanual behaviors raise additional problems. To address these latter issues, the Facial Action Coding System (FACS; Ekman & Freisen, 1978) was used to transcribe the nonmanual behaviors. FACS was originally designed to code facial behaviors relating to emotion. Before FACS was available, facial behaviors were often described subjectively in terms of expressions, such as an "angry scowl." While this label conveys an idea of the expression, it is imprecise; scowls may differ in intensity and components from person to person. Ekman and Friesen created FACS in response to this imprecision. FACS distinguishes more than 40 individual muscle movements of the face, head, and eyes. Each individual muscle contraction is represented by a numbered action unit (AU). For example, in a "scowl" one might have furrowed brows (AU4) and contracted lower eyelids (AU7). One also might have tightened lips (AU23) that are down turned (AU15). As such, FACS offers an objective method to transcribe all kinds of facial behaviors, in this case, linguistic facial movements.

## Beginnings

As noted above, by their first birthday, deaf infants are competent affective communicators, using emotional facial expression both productively and receptively. However, it is not until about 18 months of age that children begin to produce emotional signs, such as HAPPY and SAD, and it is in this context that deaf children are first using a facial behavior, in this case a smile and pout/frown, to co-occur with the sign as in the adult model (Reilly, McIntire, & Bellugi, 1986/1990). At first glance, it appears that the facial configuration has "spread" to the appropriate linguistic context (examples 11.11 and 11.12). That is, the child appears to be directly using her prelinguistic knowledge to serve language. An alternative interpretation is that the child is merely expressing her own "felt" emotion:

(11.11) MAD ___(AU4: brow furrow)

(11.12) CRY ___(AU17 + AU22b: lip pout)

During the child's second year, while still at the one-sign stage, additional evidence appeared supporting the notion that children could indeed combine their communicative facial behaviors with single signs. Signs that had no relation to emotions occurred with facial behaviors. For example, children imitated parental facial expressions as in example 11.13, and they used the communicative brow furrowing for puzzlement with WH-signs as in example 11.14.

(11.13) SCADS (imitating her mother's sign and facial behaviors) ___(AU18 + AU44: puckered lips + squint)

(11.14) WHAT ___(AU4: brow furrow) "puzzled"

In other instances children accompanied signs with mouthings. In example 11.15, the child opened and then closed her mouth mimicking the vowel and final consonant of "home" as she signs HOME.

(11.15) HOME ___(AU25, 0) "om"

Given that the child does not use the English word "home," it appears that she has seen these two behaviors (the mouthing of "home" and the manual sign HOME) co-occurring in those signing to her, and that she, in turn, has encoded both the facial movements and the manual sign as one unanalyzed package. The hypothesis is that this is also the case for the other single sign utterances with facial behaviors, including the emotion signs. These holistic constructions are similar to the "amalgams" or "gestalts" noted in the spoken language acquisition literature (MacWhinney, 1975) when children regularly produce multimorphemic utterances before having mastered the individual components.

Let us return now to the question regarding the relation between affective and linguistic facial expression. The initial productions suggest that children are acquiring the individual lexical items with co-occurring nonmanual morphology as gestalts, that is, single packages that include components from multiple channels. As such, the data from the single sign stage (up until about the child's second birthday) suggest that emotional and linguistic facial behaviors may well be mediated by one underlying system and that children's early prelinguistic emotional facility has helped bootstrap them into using their faces linguistically.

## The Onset of Syntax

The onset of multisign utterances provides additional confirmation of the "gestalt" hypothesis. Many of the single signs that the children had been using with facial markers, for example, WH-signs, are subsequently produced in utterances with blank faces. After about 2 years of age, with the onset of syntax, it appears that the children have separately analyzed the two channels (hands and faces) as independent components, no longer relying on their earlier abilities with facial expression. Another type of evidence occurs after the child has begun to combine signs and begins to explicitly manipulate the facial morphology, independently of the manual signs. Unlike earlier utterances as in example 11.16 the child signs CRY with no co-occurring facial behavior; rather, the facial behaviors precede and follow the manual sign:

(11.16) age (2;3):

‾‾‾‾‾(AU17 + AU22b: lip pout)     ‾‾‾‾‾(AU17 + AU22b: lip pout)
                  CRY

By pouting and then signing CRY with a blank face and then reassuming a pout, this child demonstrates that at this point in development the manual and facial channels have become separate and distinct; that is, she has analyzed them as independent signals. They are no longer a "fixed" package. To further explore these developments, the next section presents data from two complementary studies by Anderson and Reilly (1997, 1999). These studies examine the acquisition of negation and facial adverbials, two nonmanual structures that co-occur with manually signed predicates (verbs, verb phrases, and adjectives).

As mentioned briefly above, negation in ASL is signaled by a negative headshake that co-occurs with the predicate of the manually signed utterance. Even if a sentence includes a negative sign, such as DON'T, CANT, or NO, the headshake is obligatory. This grammatical headshake is similar in both form and meaning to the communicative headshake that both deaf and hearing children and adults use to convey a negative response. In contrast, facial adverbs in ASL, which occur on the lower face, are unique to ASL. They have no communicative counterpart. By comparing the acquisition sequences for these two types of functionally similar structures (they both co-occur with and modify predicates), we can test the hypothesis that the onset of syntax modifies how children approach nonmanual morphology; will they continue to use their affective/communicative capabilities as a road into the facial grammar? Or will language follow its own individual course?

*Grammatical Negation in ASL*

Two common types of negation that occur in child discourse are the following:

Negative headshake co-occurring with a negative sign:

      \_\_\_\_t              \_\_\_\_neg
(11.17)  BOOK READ ME     CAN'T
      "I can't read the book."

negative headshake with predicates with incorporated negation:

       _____t          _____neg
(11.18)  ICE-CREAM ME    DON'T-LIKE
      "I don't like ice cream."

And a negative headshake with a neutral predicate:

              _____neg
(11.19)  ME    EAT ICE-CREAM
      "I don't eat ice cream."

As noted above, the grammatical headshake for negation is semantically and formally similar to the early communicative headshake, and whereas the communicative negative headshake often occurs alone as a response, that is, without any words or signs, the grammatical negative headshake co-occurs with a signed utterance. If the child can recruit her earlier communicative abilities (as she did during the one-sign stage) and bring them directly into the service of language, we would expect that nonmanual negation would emerge spontaneously with the production of negative manual utterances.

To chart the developmental sequence of negation in ASL we looked at all instances of negative utterances in the naturalistic data from 51 deaf children (ages 1;0 to 4;11; see Anderson & Reilly, 1997). The children were videotaped in their homes or at preschool and were interacting with either a family member or a deaf experimenter. These free-play data were supplemented by parental reports of language development, the MacArthur Communicative Developmental Inventory for ASL (Anderson & Reilly, 2002) from 68 deaf children (ages 0;8 to 3;0) of deaf parents. Together, these data demonstrate that similar to hearing children, the communicative negative headshake appears about 12 months of age in deaf children, and the earliest negative manual signs emerge at 18–20 months; these are NO and DON'T-WANT. Interestingly, during the one-sign stage, we saw one or two examples in which the negative headshake was produced with N-O (fingerspelled sign NO). As the child approaches her second birthday, her repertoire of negative signs increases and multisigned utterances become more frequent. However, as each new negative sign comes online, it first appears in the videotapes without the required co-occurring headshake. Then, several months following its emergence, these same negative lexical signs are accompanied by the required headshake. Figure 11.1 shows the acquisition sequence for negative signs with and without the negative headshake.

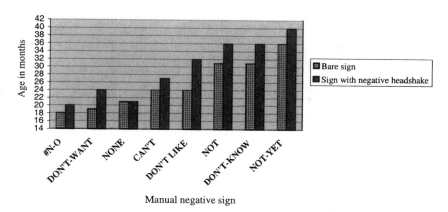

Figure 11-1. The acquisition of negation. Modified from Anderson and Reilly (1997).

These data are striking, and the pattern is consistent across negative signs. Even though the child already signals negation with a headshake, when she begins to use a negative sign, she invariably does not recruit this headshake to the required linguistic context. Rather than the negative headshake, which she already commands, it is the *manual* signs that take developmental precedence in signed utterances. These data suggest that children are analyzing the manual and nonmanual signals independently, and that they no longer directly recruit prelinguistic communicative abilities to the appropriate linguistic context even when the forms are apparently identical, both formally and semantically.

*Facial Adverbials*

These grammatical facial behaviors offer an interesting contrast in that they too modify predicates, but unlike negation, they have no communicative correlate; they are unique to ASL. Their acquisition then provides a contrastive context to investigate how children acquire nonmanual morphology in which there is no competition from a formally and semantically isomorphic communicative form. Facial adverbs represent a finite set of facial behaviors that occur on the lower face (see table 11.1 for a description of facial adverbs appearing in the children's discourse). They invariably accompany a manually signed predicate (adjectives or verbs, individual, serial, or classifier verbs). They can scope multisigned predicates; however, in the discourse of young children, single-sign predicates are most common. The onset and offset of the adverb are coterminous with the manual predicate, and they may be required with certain lexical items (e.g., FAT, NOT-YET) or when manual predicates are modulated for aspect (e.g., SICK "repeatedly"; see Anderson & Reilly, 1999, for a more extensive discussion of the nonmanual adverbs and their development).

Table 11-1:  Common Adverbials in Children's Discourse

| Adverbial | Significance (Baker & Cokely, 1980) | Description |
|---|---|---|
| puff | A large amount, too much | AU 13: cheeks filled with air |
| mm | Normally/regularly or with pleasure | AU 15 + 22: lips pressed together and protruding |
| pah | Finally/exactly | AU 24, 27: lips open suddenly to mouthe PAH |
| th | Carelessly, wrong | AU 19 + 26: lips parted, tongue slightly protruding |
| int | Surprisingly large | AU 20 + 25: lips are drawn back and parted |
| cha | Relatively large | AU 22 + 25, 27: lips slightly open, teeth clenched, jaw drops suddenly |
| pow | Meaning still being investigated | AU 24 + 27, 18 + 26: lips closed, open suddenly |
| ps | Just missed, very thin, smooth | AU 23 + 25: lips pressed together, drawn slightly |

Initially, in the one-sign stage, as noted above (examples 11.13–11.15), children produce single predicates with an unanalyzed co-occurring facial adverb. To follow their development, we coded their occurrence in naturalistic videotaped data from 38 children ages 2;0 to 4;11 (Anderson & Reilly, 1999). We found the first productive nonmanual adverbials co-occurring with a single sign predicate at age 2;0, and multisigned predicates with nonmanual adverbs emerged at 2;3. Children were using a range of adverbials by 42 months (3;6), as shown in figure 11.2.

Interestingly, in any individual videotaping session, children used specific adverbials with different predicates and also used those same manually signed predicates without any adverbial, for example a child (age 3;3) signed the verb FALL with no facial adverb and also produced the following:

                       ___th
(11.20)  FALL     FALL
          (instructing mother to fall down)

                       __pah
(11.21)  YOU    FALL   YOU
          "You fell down!"

Consonant with the findings on negation, these developmental data on facial adverbs suggest that after the one-sign stage, children are acquiring manual predicates separately from the nonmanual behaviors. Overall, a particular manual predicate, such as DRIVE, would emerge, and

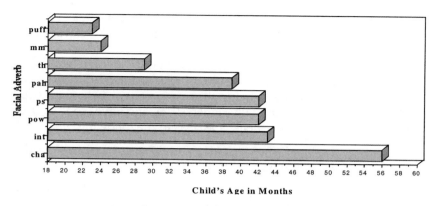

**Figure 11-2. The development of facial adverbs. Modified from Anderson and Reilly (1999).**

then, months later, the child would use it with a nonmanual adverbial. It is worth noting that before a child produced a particular facial adverbial, a semantically similar manual sign had been produced. For example, before producing "mm," or "th," the children already had the signs GOOD, BAD, or YUCKY in their lexicon.

Comparing the acquisition of adverbials to that of negation, we see similar patterns: Nonmanual morphology (facial adverbs and negation) is acquired independently from the manual predicates they modify. As in spoken language acquisition (Brown, 1973), free lexical signs (GOOD, YUCKY) precede the acquisition of bound, in this case, nonmanual, morphology ("mm," "th"). Thus, it appears that with competition from an isomorphic communicative form (as in negation where the grammatical signal headshake resembles a communicative headshake) or without a similar communicative form (as in adverbials where there is no communicative correlate), children approach nonmanual morphology with the same strategy: hands before faces. Moreover, after the one-sign stage, children no longer recruit their prelinguistic communicative abilities to serve language. In fact, they ignore apparently pertinent information.

## Nonmanual Morphology in Clausal Structures

### WH-*Sign Questions*

We now turn to the acquisition of facial morphology in the more complex structures: WH-questions and conditional sentences. Here, too, there is an interesting contrast between wh-questions and conditionals: WH-questions are signaled by a furrowed brow, which bears a remarkable resemblance to the communicative gesture of "puzzlement" (children, both hearing and deaf, are using this expression communicatively by 1 year of age), and conditional sentences are signaled by a nonmanual signal that has no semantically relevant communicative or affective correlate.

For adults, WH-sign questions in ASL include a WH-sign (e.g., WHAT, HOW, WHERE, etc.) as well as a furrowed brow and head tilt, and sometimes an abbreviated headshake; these nonmanual behaviors begin immediately before the manually signed string and have scope over the entire wh-question (Baker-Shenk, 1983), as in the following:

(11.22) WHERE SHOE WHERE    (AU4 + AU57: brow furrow + head forward)

As noted above, children's questions before the age of 2 years or so frequently were accompanied by aspects of the adult nonmanual behavior (Reilly & McIntire, 1991; Reilly, McIntire, & Bellugi, 1986/1990). However, the timing, scope, and individual components often did not match the adults'. In example 11.23, the child uses a furrowed brow without the head tilt, and in example 11.24 she shakes her head slowly as if looking for the melon. In fact, in viewing the tape, we noticed that when the mother signed WHERE questions, she, too, often turned her head from side to side, as if looking for the item. It is quite possible that the child is doing the same.

(11.23) Age 1;6:
  ____(AU4: brow furrow)
  WHAT                "what?"

(11.24) Age 1;9:
  ____(AU51 AU52: headshake)
  WHERE MELON   "Where's the melon?"

By age 30 months, the children's productive discourse included frequent manually signed questions, however similar to negation and emotional expressions, their faces were now neutral; they omitted the obligatory nonmanual behaviors:

(11.25) Age 2;3:
  WHERE "WHAT"
  "Where is it?"

From figure 11.3, we can see that before 4 years of age, children's questions lack the appropriate facial morphology, although they do use some aspects of the adult form; for example, they sometimes use a head shake but are less likely to use the brow movement.

It is not until about 5 years of age that children accompany the manually signed WH-questions with the required facial behaviors, but the facial behaviors first have scope only over the WH-signs, rather than the

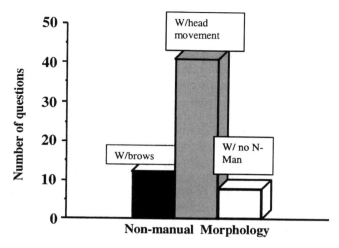

**Figure 11-3. Nonmanual marking in wh-questions from 3-year-old children. Modified from Reilly and McIntire (1991).**

entire wh-question (for more detail, see Reilly & McIntire, 1991; for complementary data, see Lillo-Martin, 1997; Lillo-Martin, 2000 Lillo-Martin & Pichler, chapter 10 this volume). By 6 or 7 years of age, children are using a variety of wh-questions, and they are producing the appropriate nonmanual morphology.

Overall, the pattern of acquisition we see for the nonmanual morphology of wh-questions appears to be very similar to that of both negation and facial adverbials: During the one-sign stage, WH-signs co-occur with the communicative brow furrow, signaling puzzlement. Then as syntax emerges, wh-questions are manually signed with predominantly blank faces, and yet again, children do not recruit their prelinguistic communicative abilities to signal wh-questions. Rather, they approach questions with a lexical strategy. Even when they begin to use the nonmanual marker, its scope or duration is limited to the WH-sign, confirming the strength of this lexical, manual approach. Thus, whether or not the children have in their repertoire a prelinguistic communicative behavior that is similar to the grammatical facial behavior in form and function (as in negatives and wh-questions), they do not immediately draw upon these behaviors to produce the required morphology. Rather, they first express these linguistic functions, such as negation and wh-questions, using manual lexical signs. This consistent pattern of results across structures suggests that once the children are producing sentences, language development is guided by its own rules; it ignores apparently relevant communicative behaviors and follows its own independent course.

same children are at the same time using nonmanual morphology for other structures, such as adverbials. It suggests that children approach each new linguistic structure somewhat independently, and the entry route for each is via the manual lexical marker.

To sum up so far, we have seen that initially, at the one-sign stage, children acquiring ASL produce utterances that include both a manual sign and an apparently appropriate nonmanual marker suggesting that facial behaviors stem from one broadly based symbolic system that serves affect and language. Then with the onset of syntax, there is a dramatic shift in the child's approach: For all the constructions we have reviewed, children do not recruit their prelinguistic affective and communicative abilities directly into the appropriate linguistic contexts. Rather, a lexical manual strategy is persistently preferable and invariably occurs without the requisite nonmanual behaviors. This is true for both phrasal and clausal structures, and for structures that have a communicative counterpart as well as those that are unique to ASL. It is not until after the lexical marker has emerged that children begin to acquire the nonmanual components and that occurs in a slow and analytic manner. Table 11.2 provides a developmental overview.

## Emotional Expression in the Service of Language

With these data in mind, we now turn to the use of nonmanual behaviors to signal point of view in discourse. In this context, particular constellations of facial behaviors, particularly emotional expressions, can span any where from one sign to multiple sentences. Whereas spoken languages may signal changes in discourse perspective prosodically, the visual-gestural modality of signed languages offers different possibilities for conveying alternate points of view, phenomena that have been widely discussed (see Engberg-Pedersen, 1993, 1995; Padden, 1986; Poulin & Miller, 1995; Smith, Lentz, & Mikos, 1988) and often referred to as role shift. This section focuses particularly on children's development of direct quote, a common instance of role shift that will provide another perspective on the developing relation between affective expression and language.

The insightful analysis by Engberg-Pedersen (1993, 1995) on Danish Sign Language proposes different "shifters," two of which are relevant to our discussion: shifted reference and shifted attribution of expressive elements. Shifted reference occurs in direct quotes or reported speech, and in each case, the first person pronoun represents the character in the story or a quoted individual rather than the signer herself. Shifted attribution of expressive elements is a strategy frequently used in reporting a dialogue or telling a story; the narrator assumes the emotion or attitude of the quoted individual. As Engberg-Pedersen (1995) notes, "shifted attribution of expressive elements contributes to the impression that the events of the narrative are presented through the psyche of

**Table 11-2: The Developmental Sequence of Facial Morphology in ASL**

| Structure | 1 Year | 2 Years | 3 Years | 4 Years | 5+ Years |
|---|---|---|---|---|---|
| Negation | neg / #NO | DON'T-WANT | neg / DON'T-WANT | neg / DON'T-WANT | |
| | Holistic | Lexical only | Asynchronous | Coordinated timing | |
| Adverbials | | mm / WALK | mm / WALK | mm / WALK | |
| | | cheek puff / WOMAN FAT | cheek puff / WOMAN FAT | cheek puff / WOMAN FAT | |
| | | | th / FALL | th / FALL | |
| | | | nose wrinkle / DIAPER STINKY | nose wrinkle / DIAPER STINKY | |
| | | | | ee / CLOSE-CALL | |
| | | | | pow / FINALLY | |
| | | | | pursed lips / WOMAN THIN | |
| | | Holistic | Asynchronous | Coordinated timing | |
| Conditionals | | Unmarked propositions | #IF, SUPPOSE | 1 + 2 / SUPPOSE... | 1 + 2 / #IF, SUPPOSE... |
| | | No nonmanuals | Lexical only | Incomplete scope | Coordinated timing |
| WH-q | | 4 / WHAT... | WHAT... | 4 + headshake / WHAT WHERE | 4 + headshake / WHERE SHOE |
| | | Holistic | Lexical only | Incomplete scope | Coordinated timing |

one of the characters" (p. 145). These "expressive elements" invariably consist of facial expressions reflecting the character or quoted individual's current emotion. In concert with other nonmanual and manual components, these behaviors span the entire piece of quoted discourse, and they constitute the linguistic signal defining the scope of the quote. In this instance, emotional expression is truly recruited to serve linguistic purposes.

To understand the development of perspective marking, this next section is devoted to a study that examined the development of direct quotes in children's narratives (Reilly, 2000; Reilly, McIntire, & Anderson, 1994). The data include the videotaped stories of the Three Bears from 28 deaf children of deaf parents (ages 3;0–7;5) and five adult native signers. Because this story offers numerous opportunities for shifts in point of view and adult storytellers frequently exploit this device (Emmorey & Reilly, 1998), this well-known children's story presents a rich context to chronicle the acquisition of referential shift. Look again at example 11.8:

(11.8 [repeated from above]) Adult:

```
                                                          _____pouting
___topic _____surprise _____distress
____+K _____−K
```
BABY BEAR LOOK-AT LETS-SEE MY CL: C HEY GONE  SOUP CL:1 SOMEONE FINISH EAT ALL
Baby Bear looked at his soup, "Let's see my bowl. Hey my soup's gone! Someone ate it all up!"

We see that in the adult model, to produce a direct quote a signer will: label the character (BABY BEAR) or point to the locus of that character in space; break eye gaze with the addressee (−K), and look in the direction that the character would look (or use "undirected" gaze); assume the facial expression of the character (surprise, then distress) as the quoted signed utterance begins; and shift head, and frequently shoulders/body, to reflect the physical perspective of the character or quoted individual. These nonmanual behaviors begin with the quoted utterance and terminate with its conclusion, similar to the other types of nonmanual signals discussed above. An interesting difference in this case is that it is facial expression conveying *emotion* that is linguistically constrained; that is, the scope or duration of the facial behaviors indicates the duration of the direct quote.

Looking at the children's data in figure 11.4, it is clear that even the 3-year-olds include direct quotes in their stories. And for both 3- and 4-year-olds, quotes are signaled by a break in eye contact, and emotional facial expression is used frequently as they sign the character's utterances. However, the presence, timing and scope of these facial behaviors

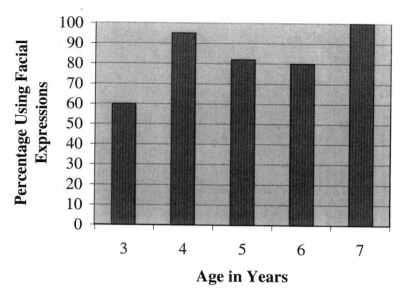

**Figure 11-4. Frequency of facial expression in children's direct quotes. Modified from Reilly (2000).**

are erratic and inconsistent; it is not until age 6 or 7 that children use facial expression consistently with appropriate timing in direct quote. This profile is apparent in figure 11.5.

For the manual aspects of signaling point of view, the youngest children often fail to indicate "who" is talking; however, by age 6, children label the character to introduce the quote 80% of the time (adults, 95%) as seen in figure 11.6. Some children also used the verb SAY, as shown in figure 11.7), a manual strategy that we did not see in any of the adult stories, as in the following example:

(11.32) Age 5;0:

| | disgust | | disgust | | disgust |

    _____+K \_\_\_–K    _____+K \_\_\_–K   \_\_\_\_+K \_\_–K

    FATHER SAY   HOT    MOTHER SAY   WARM   BABY SAY  COLD

"Father Bear said "(this is too) hot!" Mother Bear said "(mine is) warm." Baby Bear said "(mine is too) cold!"

Whereas no 3-, 4-, or 7-year-olds use this strategy (see figure 11.5), *all* of the 5-year-olds use SAY to introduce their quotes, in addition to the gaze shift and facial expression (as above). Since this lexical approach does not occur in the adult stories, and infrequently at ages other than 5, we inferred that it reflected a linguistic reorganization on the part of the child. The younger children (3–4 years old) are challenged by the complexity of the nonmanual signal, using facial expression often, but somewhat indiscriminately.

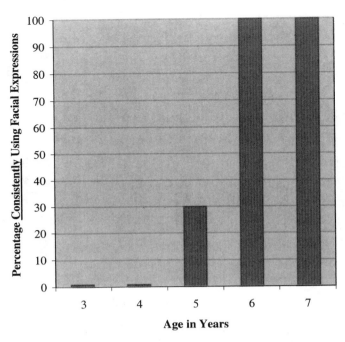

Figure 11-5. Consistency of facial behavior in children's direct quotes. Modified from Reilly (2000).

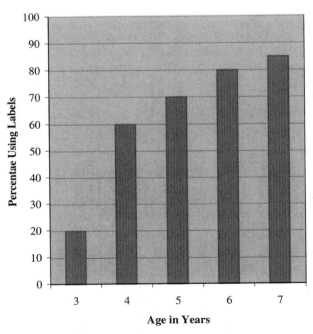

Figure 11-6. Labeling characters in direct quotes. Modified from Reilly (2000).

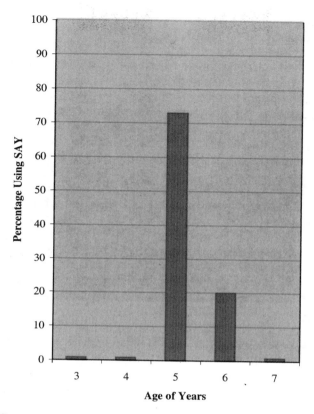

Figure 11-7. Use of the manual sign SAY in direct quotes. Modified from Reilly (2000).

SAY, a lexical alternative to nonmanually signaling direct quote, appears to function as a bridge in the reanalysis of emotional expression for new linguistic purposes. Again, as with negation, wh-questions, and conditional clauses, we see the manual channel functioning as a transition to the nonmanual behaviors.

## SUMMARY AND CONCLUSIONS

Looking over the children's data from the various studies presented, some persistent themes recur. Initially, at the one-sign stage, signs for emotions as well as other predicates and their nonmanual morphology are processed as holistic forms suggesting that hands and faces are initially acquired as a package. However, once syntax and multisign utterances emerge, earlier mastery of an isomorphic communicative form does not appear to play a role in acquiring the grammatical behaviors.

In fact, at this point, children appear to actively ignore what might be considered pertinent prelinguistic capabilities.

Children used the same acquisition strategy, hands before faces, whether the structure had a prelinguistically acquired communicative correlate or not. That is, after the one-sign stage, structures were approached with a linear manual sign before children tackled the co-occurring nonmanual morphology. This pattern holds true for negation, adverbials, wh-questions, and conditional sentences. Moreover, in direct quotes where facial expression conveys emotion, there, too, children make the transition from communication to language via a lexical manual sign.

To return to the original questions, the data suggest that the relations among affect, communication, and language change with development. Initially, these appear to all be served by one broad-based symbolic communicative system. Then, with the onset of syntax, sometime near the child's second birthday, there is a shift such that the developing linguistic system no longer has free access to communicative/affective behaviors, even when they are semantically and formally pertinent, as with negation. These behavioral changes imply a bifurcation such that the systems for language and affect are differentially mediated. Supporting evidence for this functional change comes from studies using Event Related Potential (ERP) of infants at two developmental time points (Mills, Coffey-Corina, & Neville, 1997). In the younger group (average age, 13 months), broad areas of both the left and right hemisphere of the brain are activated in the baby's electrophysiological response to words with which she is familiar. As children approach their second birthday (average age, 20 months), the response to known words is qualitatively different: Only the left hemisphere is activated, and the area is significantly more circumscribed. Another such discontinuity that occurs at this developmental point is the much discussed gesture/sign bifurcation noted by Volterra and her colleagues (Volterra & Iverson, 1995; Volterra, Iverson, & Castrataro, chapter 3 this volume). Together, the ERP and behavioral data raise the possibility that we are witnessing the evolution of brain specialization for language. As such, the acquisition of nonmanual morphology in deaf children has provided a unique opportunity to systematically track the reorganization of presumably innate behaviors emotional facial expressions for linguistic purposes.

The final issue concerns how deaf children address these unusual structures that are signaled across channels: hands and faces. These structures are unique to signed languages and present specific challenges to the learner. The data show that, once children are combining signs, rather than recruiting their prelinguistic affective or communicative abilities, they solve this problem by focusing on the hands for language. They invariably choose a linear lexical strategy to tackle these structures, similar to the approach children take to learning bound morphology in a spoken language. The pattern also suggests that the manual and nonmanual signals are being independently analyzed before children integrate the cross-channel productions. Thus, once the child has entered the grammar, even though the components are facial behaviors, used by the vast majority of the world's population to convey affect (Ekman, 1972), these, too, still fall under the constraints of basic language acquisition principles.

## APPENDIX

### Facial Action Coding System: Some Relevant Action Units (Ekman & Friesen, 1978)

AU1, Inner brow raise
AU2, Outer brow raise
AU4, Furrowed brows
AU5, Widened eyes
AU6, Cheek raise
AU7, Bottom lids tight
AU13, Cheek puff
AU15, Lip corner depress
AU18, Lip pucker
AU19, Tongue show
AU23, Lip tight
AU24, Lip press
AU25, Lips parted
AU26, Jaw drop
AU45, Blink
AU51, Head turn left
AU52, Head turn right
AU55, Head tilt left
AU56, Head tilt right
AU57, Head forward
AU58, Head back

## REFERENCES

Anderson, D. E., & Reilly, J. S. (1997). The puzzle of negation: How children move from communicative to grammatical negation in ASL. *Applied Psycholinguistics, 18,* 411–429.

Anderson, D. E., & Reilly, J. S. (1999). Pah! The acquisition of adverbials in ASL. *Sign Language and Linguistics, 1,* 117–142.

Anderson, D. E., & Reilly, J. S. (2002). The MacArthur Communicative Development Inventory for American Sign Language: The normative data. *Deaf Studies and Deaf Education, 7,* 83–106.

Bahan, B., & S. Supalla (1995). Line segmentation and narrative structure: A study of eye gaze behavior in ASL. In K. Emmorey & J. Reilly (Eds.), *Language, gesture and space* (pp. 171–191). Norwood, NJ: Lawrence Erlbaum.

Baker, C. (1977). Regulators and turn-taking in American Sign Language discourse. In L. Friedman (Ed.), *On the other hand: New perspectives on American Sign Language* (pp. 215–236). New York: Academic Press.

Baker, C., & Cokely, D. (1980). *American Sign Language: A teacher's resource text on grammar and culture*. Silver Spring, MD: T. J. Publishers.

Baker, C., & Padden, C. (1978). Focusing on the nonmanual components of American Sign Language. In P. Siple (Ed.), *Understanding language through sign language research* (pp. 27–57). New York: Academic Press.

Baker-Shenk, C. (1983). *A microanalysis of the non-manual components of questions in American Sign Language*. Unpublished doctoral dissertation, University of California, Berkeley.

Bellugi, U., & Klima, E. S. (1982). The acquisition of three morphological systems in American Sign Language. *Papers and Reports on Child Language Development, 21*, 1–35.

Bellugi, U., Lillo-Martin, D., O'Grady, L., & van Hoek, K. (1990). The development of spatialized syntactic mechanisms in American Sign Language. In W. Edmondson & F. Karlsson (Eds.), *Fourth International Symposium on Sign Language Research* (pp. 16–25). Hamburg: Signum-Verlag Press.

Borod, J. C. (2000). *The neuropsychology of emotion*. New York: Oxford University Press.

Brown, R. (1973). *A first language*. Cambridge, MA: Harvard University Press.

Campos, J., Barret, K. C., Lamb, M. E., Goldsmith, H. H., & Stenberg, C. (1983). Socioemotional development. In P. Mussen (Series Ed.) & M. Haith & J. Campos (Vol. Eds.), *Handbook of child psychology: Vol. 2. Infancy and development: psychobiology* (pp. 783–915). New York: Wiley Press.

Coulter, G. (1980). *American Sign Language typology*. Unpublished doctoral dissertation, University of California, San Diego.

de Haan, M. (2001). The neuropsychology of face processing during infancy and childhood. In C. A. Nelson & M. Luciana (Eds.), *Handbook of developmental cognitive neuroscience* (pp. 381–398). Cambridge, MA: MIT Press.

Ekman, P. (1972). Universal and cultural differences in facial expressions of emotion. In J. K. Cole (Ed.), *Nebraska symposium on motivation 1971* (pp. 207–283). Lincoln: University of Nebraska Press.

Ekman, P. (1979). About brows: Emotional and conversational signals. In M. von Cranach, K. Foppa, W. Lepenies, & D. Ploog (Eds.), *Human ethology* (pp. 169–248). London: Cambridge University Press.

Ekman, P., & Friesen, W. (1978). *Facial action coding system*. Palo Alto, CA: Consulting Psychologists Press.

Elman, J. L. (1996). *Rethinking innateness: A connectionist perspective on development*. Cambridge, MA: MIT Press.

Emmorey, K., & Reilly, J. (1998). The development of quotation and reported action: conveying perspective in ASL. In E. Clark (Ed.), *Proceedings of the Stanford Child Language Forum* (pp. 81–90). Stanford, CA: Center for the Study of Language and Information Publications.

Engberg-Pedersen, E. (1993). *Space in Danish Sign Language*. Hamburg: Signum-Verlag.

Engberg-Pedersen, E. (1995). Point of view expressed through shifters. In K. Emmorey & J. Reilly (Eds.), *Language, gesture, and space* (pp. 133–154). Hillsdale, NJ: Lawrence Erlbaum.

Erting, C., Prezioso, C., & O'Grady-Hines, M. (1990). The interactional context of deaf mother-infant communication. In V. Volterra & C. J. Erting (Eds.), *From gesture to language in hearing and deaf children* (pp. 97–106). New York: Springer-Verlag.

Goodglass, H. (1993). *Understanding aphasia*. San Diego: Academic Press.

Hiatt, S., Campos, J., & Emde, R. (1979). Facial patterning and infant emotional expression: happiness, surprise and fear. *Child Development, 50*, 1020–1035.

Liddell, S. (1978). Nonmanual signals and relative clauses in American Sign Language. In P. Siple (Ed.), *Understanding language through sign language research* (pp. 59–90). New York: Academic Press.

Lillo-Martin, D. (1999). Modality effects and modularity in language acquisition of American Sign Language. In W. C. Ritchie & T. K. Bhatia (Eds.), *Handbook of child language acquisition* (pp. 531–567). San Diego: Academic Press.

Lillo-Martin, D. (2000). Early and late in language acquisition: Aspects of the syntax and acquisition of wh-questions in American Sign Language. In K. Emmorey & H. Lane (Eds.), *The signs of language revisited: An anthology to honor Ursula Bellugi and Edward Klima* (pp. 401–414). Mahweh, NJ: Lawrence Erlbaum.

MacWhinney, B. (1975). Rules, rote, and analogy in morphological formations by Hungarian children. *Journal of Child Language, 2*(1), 65–77.

Mills, D. L., Coffey-Corina, S. A., & Neville, H. J. (1997). Language comprehension and cerebral specialization from 13–20 months. *Developmental Neuropsychology, 13*(3), 397–445.

Nelson, C. A. (1987). The recognition of facial expressions in the first two years of life: Mechanisms of development. *Child Development, 58*, 890–909.

Nelson, C. A., & de Haan, M. (1997). A neurobehavioral approach to the recognition of facial expressions in infancy. In J. A. Russell & J. M. Fernandez-Dols (Eds.), *The psychology of facial expression* (pp. 176–204). New York: Cambridge University Press.

Padden, C. (1986.) Verbs and role-shifting in ASL. In C. Padden (Ed.), *Proceedings of the Fourth National Symposium on Sign Language Research and Teaching* (pp. 44–57). Silver Spring, MD: National Association of the Deaf.

Pettito, L. A., & Martenette, P. F. (1991). Babbling in the manual mode: Evidence for the ontogeny of language. *Science, 251*, 1493–1496.

Pinker, S. (1999). *Words and rules*. London: Weidenfeld & Nicolson.

Poizner, H., Klima, E., & Bellugi, U. (1987). *What the hands reveal about the brain*. Cambridge, MA: MIT Press.

Poulin, C., & Miller, C. (1995). On narrative discourse and point of view in Quebec Sign Language. In K. Emmorey & J. Reilly (Eds.), *Language, gesture, and space* (pp.117–132). Hillsdale, NJ: Lawrence Erlbaum.

Reilly, J. (1982). The acquisition of conditional sentences in English. Unpublished doctoral dissertation, University of California, Los Angeles.

Reilly, J. (1983). What are conditionals for? *Papers and Reports on Child Language Development, 22*, 1–8.

Reilly, J. S. (1986). Acquisition of temporals and conditionals. In E. Traugott, A. ter Meulen, J. Reilly, & C. Ferguson (Eds.), *On conditionals* (pp. 309–332). Cambridge: Cambridge University Press.

Reilly, J. (2000). Bringing affective expression into the service of language: Acquiring perspective marking in narratives. In K. Emmorey & H. Lane (Eds.), *The signs of language revisited: An anthology in honor of Ursula Bellugi and Edward Klima* (pp. 415–432). Mahweh, NJ: Lawrence Erlbaum.

Reilly, J. S., & McIntire, M. L. (1991). WHERE SHOE: The acquisition of wh-questions in ASL. *Papers and Reports in Child Language Development, 30*, 104–111.

Reilly, J., McIntire, M. L., & Anderson, D. (1994, November). *Look who's talking! Point of view and character reference in mothers' and children's ASL narratives.* Paper presented at the Boston Child Language Conference, Boston, MA.

Reilly, J. S., McIntire, M. L., & Bellugi, U. (1986/1990). Faces: The relationship of language and affect. In V. Volterra & C. Erting. (Eds.), *From gesture to language in deaf and hearing children* (pp. 128–141). New York: Springer-Verlag; Washington, DC: Gallaudet.

Reilly, J., McIntire, M., & Bellugi, U. (1990). Conditionals in American Sign Language: Grammaticized facial expressions. *Applied Psycholinguistics, 11*(4), 369–392.

Reilly, J., McIntire, M., & Bellugi, U. (1991). BABYFACE: A new perspective on universals in language acquisition. In P. Siple (Ed.), *Theoretical issues in sign language research: Psycholinguistics* (pp. 9–24). Chicago: University of Chicago Press.

Rossini, P., Reilly, J., Febbretti, D., & Volterra, V. (2000). Aspetti non manuali nelle narrazioni LIS. In C. Bagnara, P. Chiappini, M. P. Conte, & M. Ott (Eds.), *Viaggio nella città invisibile. Atti del 2f Convegno nazionale sulla Lingua Italiana dei Segni* (pp. 112–119). Pisa: Edizioni del Cerro.

Scherer, K. (1986). Vocal affect expression; A review and model for future research. *Psychological Bulletin, 99*, 143–165.

Slobin, D. I., Hoiting, N., Anthony, M., Biederman, Y., Kuntze, M., Lindert, R., et al. (2001). Sign language transcription at the level of meaning components: The Berkeley Transcription System (BTS) (241K). *Sign Language and Linguistics, 4*, 63–96.

Smith, C., Lentz, E., & Mikos, K. (1988). *Signing naturally: Teacher's curriculum guide.* Berkeley, CA: Dawn Sign Press.

Traugott, E., ter Meulen, A., Reilly, J., & Ferguson, C. (Eds.) (1986). *On conditionals.* Cambridge: Cambridge University Press.

Volterra, V., & Iverson, J. (1995). When do modality factors affect the course of language acquisition? In K. Emmorey & J. Reilly (Eds.), *Language, gesture and space* (pp. 371–390). Norwood, NJ: Lawrence Erlbaum.

# 12

# Deaf Children's Acquisition
of Modal Terms

*Barbara Shaffer*

While it is important to continue to study cognitive development in children, we can never fully understand how children construe their worlds. Certain linguistic competencies, however, do provide a window into the child's developing mind and therefore contribute to our overall understanding of child development. Mastery in the use of modal terms (e.g., "have to," "should," "can") is a major linguistic feat, one that suggests much about a child's cognitive development and social awareness. This chapter explores the emergence of modal terms in deaf children. It focuses primarily on two types of modality: agent oriented and epistemic. Agent-oriented modals describe conditions placed on main clause agents (e.g., "John must go to the doctor"), while epistemic modals convey the speaker's beliefs regarding the truth of a proposition ("John could be at the doctor").

Modal utterances of both types are high in speaker subjectivity; that is, they actively place speakers within their own discourse. In addition, epistemic modals refer to the mental state of the speaker. Research is beginning to show that competent use of epistemic modals, in particular, requires specific cognitive skills, including theory of mind reasoning. Regardless of the language, in order to competently use words that express degrees of certainty, children must be aware that they have unique beliefs and desires that can be conveyed to others (see López-Ornat, Férnández, Gallo, & Mariscal, 1994; Moore & Frye, 1991; Pérez-Leroux, 1998).

While there are identifiable cross-linguistic tendencies in the acquisition of modal terms, deaf children are faced with the unique situation of modal notions coded manually (with a lexical sign) and nonmanually (with grammatical facial markers). In addition, information ordering, specifically topic-comment (or given-new, shared-new) ordering, has been shown to be critical to the interpretation of a modal in American Sign Language (ASL)[1] as either agent oriented (describing a condition, e.g., "have to") or epistemic (referring to speaker certainty, as in "maybe"; Shaffer, 2000, 2004).

Further, as Reilly, McIntire, and Belugi (1990, 1991) and others have suggested, the manual component of ASL grammar is acquired differently than the nonmanual component. Slobin (1973) has noted that, where both lexical (or periphrastic) and grammatical means of expressing a concept are available, children tend to initially opt for the lexical. Because ASL modals have both manual and nonmanual coding, this is of interest.

This chapter takes a holistic approach to the acquisition of modality by deaf children. The goal is not to describe a set of syntactic structures and chart a course of development. Instead, we explore the role of modality in language—how and why speakers use modals. Next, the cognitive, grammatical, and pragmatic prerequisites for modal use are discussed, for both hearing children acquiring spoken languages and deaf children acquiring a signed language. Signed-language–specific aspects of modal acquisition, such as the acquisition of topic-comment information ordering, and nonmanual marking, are also discussed, from both a pragmatic and a morphological perspective. Finally, possible next steps in child modal research are outlined. The result is a snapshot of the development of an extremely complex communicative function, in a unique linguistic situation.

## THE CONCEPTUAL DOMAIN OF MODALITY

The study of modality is as broad as it is complex, and a researcher must carefully choose how to delimit this broad domain for her investigation. Stephany (1986) provides a useful starting point for a definition of modality, stating that it is a semantic category that expresses concepts such as "possibility," "necessity," "obligation," "permission," and "intention." It is most often expressed in two main ways: with modal verbs (main verbs or auxiliaries, e.g., "may," "can," "must," "will") and with modal inflections (or moods, e.g., imperative, subjunctive, optative, conditional; Stephany, 1986, p. 375). Stephany (1986) notes that the function of modality is to enable speakers to either

---

[1] Although the issues addressed here are assumed to apply, generally, to all natural signed languages, research on modality acquisition does not appear to be available for languages other than ASL.

comment on the validity, truth, or factuality of what they say, or to indicate conditions such as permission, or ability (p. 375). Coates (1990) also comments on the cognitive underpinnings of modal expression:

> Modality has to do with notions such as possibility, necessity, ability, volition, obligation. It can be explained in terms of our ability to conceptualise parallel worlds; in so far as humans can imagine things being otherwise, they express awareness using forms whose essence is that they qualify the categorical. Many languages rely on the mood of the verb to express modal meaning, that is, on contrasts between indicative, subjunctive, imperative, etc. (p. 54)

The distinction between mood and modality is an important one. Bybee (1985) describes modality as a conceptual (semantic) domain, which may be expressed with words, such as auxiliaries (modals), or inflectional morphemes (mood). The distinction proves useful when studying the acquisition of modal notions by children, because, as mentioned above, inflectional processes and lexical processes are acquired in significantly different ways. A child may, for example, acquire the grammatical inflection that in adult discourse is used to signal epistemic modality, but in a child's language that inflection may have a different function or, in fact, no function at all. The significance of this is discussed further below in this chapter. It suffices here to say that the conceptual domain of modality is decidedly complex, with implications for the study of semantics, pragmatics, grammar, and discourse. It follows that the acquisition of modality would be equally complex.

Because modality is a broad category, any cogent analysis of it must be narrowed in scope. For this chapter, the discussion is limited to two subcategories of modality: agent-oriented modality and epistemic modality.

An agent-oriented modal describes a condition that is placed on the main clause agent regarding the act described by the verb. The condition can be either limiting or enabling and can be imposed by the speaker, the semantic agent of the clause, or someone else. In example 12.1, the English "must" is used to describe a limiting condition that has been by someone other than the agent (Tim):

(12.1) "Tim must pay his library fines by July 31st."

Example 12.1 profiles the limiting condition (obligation: "must") placed on the main clause agent (Tim) with respect to the completion of the predicate action (the paying of library fines). Example 12.1 contrasts with the examples of epistemic modality in examples 12.2 and 12.3, where no obligation or necessity is implied. Instead, the speaker of example 12.2 is using "must" to indicate his belief that "Tim is here." "Could" is used in example 12.3 to mark the speaker's limited certainty that "it is raining outside."

(12.2) "Tim must be here by now."

(12.3) "It could be raining outside."

De Haan (1999) defines epistemic modality as "concerning itself with the degree of commitment on the part of the speaker to his or her utterance" (p. 83). On the basis of that evaluation, a confidence measure is assigned. An epistemic modal is used to reflect this degree of confidence. The modal reflects the speaker's mental state. In example 12.2, the speaker is stating his fairly high degree of certainty that Tim is present. In example 12.3 the speaker expresses less certainty about the truth of what he is saying. Note that it is the speaker's conception of reality that is coded by the epistemic modal, not objective reality. That is, a speaker can view something as true or actual even when it is not, and he codes his utterance accordingly.

Of importance is the overall discourse effect of these two kinds of modality. While example 12.1 is a sentence about the semantic agent (Tim), examples 12.2 and 12.3 are subjective utterances about what the *speaker* thinks and believes. Lyons (1977) has described subjectivity as "devices whereby the speaker, in making an utterance, simultaneously comments upon that utterance and expresses his attitude to what he is saying" (p. 739). Examples 12.2 and 12.3 are higher in subjectivity than is example 12.1 because in these the speaker is making his perspective on the situation explicit. The analysis of the expression of the speaker's attitude or perspective is at the core of the discourse-based study of modality and is the foundation on which this chapter is based.

To summarize the discussion thus far: Modality is a conceptual area indicating possibility, ability, necessity, obligation, permission, and so forth. It expresses the speaker's belief state about the situation being discussed and is conveyed inflectionally (mood) or lexically (modals).

## WHY MODALITY?

From the discussion of modality above, it becomes clear that both agent-oriented and epistemic modals describe how the speaker construes a given situation. The choice of "must" versus "should" in the following sentences illustrates this point.

(12.4) "You must eat your vegetables."

(12.5) "You should eat your vegetables."

In example 12.4 the speaker uses "must" to try to impel the agent of the sentence to eat the vegetables. In example 12.5, however, the speaker merely suggests what ought to be done, and the utterance carries much less pragmatic force. Aside from the modal, all other aspects of the utterance, including the participants and grammatical and semantic relationships, remain the same. To further illustrate, consider the sentences in examples 12.6 and 12.7.

(12.6) "She must eat her vegetables."
(When uttered by one caregiver to another)

(12.7) "She must eat her vegetables."
(When uttered by one observer to another)

In example 12.6 the speaker (a caregiver) uses "must" to describe a limiting condition placed on (presumably) a child. In example 12.7, however, the speaker uses "must" to express confidence that the observation of (perhaps the health and vitality of) a third person is correct. Additionally, while example 12.6 is a sentence about a third person (the child), example 12.7 is about the *speaker's beliefs* about a third person.

What does the proficient use of modals by a child suggest about that child's development? By expressing modal notions, children are actively placing themselves within the discourse, whether consciously or unconsciously, and expressing a particular stand or personal perspective regarding what they are saying. They are using language to convey their mental state (perspective) to others. Agent-oriented modals select or profile specific relationships between the agent and the action, and their use suggests that the child is able to consider other alternative relationships. Epistemic modals express the speaker's stance regarding what she is saying. Simply put, they express the speaker's beliefs about reality, regardless of what is really true.

Modality, then, is the expression of a social and psychological construct. The distinction between agent-oriented and epistemic is an important one for studies of first language acquisition, because as discussed below, these two types of modality are acquired differently by children, even when expressed with the same forms. The analysis of modality in discourse raises the following questions about modal acquisition in deaf children:

(1) What are the underlying cognitive demands for modal use? What do children have to understand about themselves and their relationships to others in order to be able to use terms that describe conditions and evaluate the belief states of themselves and others?

(2) How does a child develop facility with grammatical constructions that are coded both manually and nonmanually?

(3) What can we predict about deaf children's acquisition from the available literature on the acquisition of markers of modality by hearing children?

(4) How would access to language in the home affect the course of modal development? Will deaf children who do not have access to language in the home show delays in the acquisition of modal terms?

## MODALITY IN ASL

In order to begin to answer these questions, it is helpful to review what is known about modality in ASL. Studies of modality in signed languages are rare (but see Ferreira Brito, 1990; Wilcox & Wilcox, 1995). Shaffer (2000) provides a framework for the analysis of adult modal use in ASL and suggests that modal notions are expressed in ASL discourse primarily by the words MUST/SHOULD, CAN/POSSIBLE, FUTURE, MAYBE, SEEM, FEEL, and OBVIOUS (see also Wilcox & Wilcox, 1995).[2] Negative modal notions are most often expressed with FORBID, CAN'T, IMPOSSIBLE, DOUBT, and NOT-SHOULD. Necessity markers in ASL (e.g., MUST/SHOULD) express the following discourse functions: authoritative obligation, more general types of necessity ranging from physical necessity to group necessity (i.e., pertaining to social mores), advisability, and finally root necessity (where the condition is inherent in the situation, rather than imposed) and epistemic necessity. The conceptual domain of possibility is most frequently expressed in ASL with CAN/POSSIBLE, and its discourse functions include notions of mental and physical ability, general ability, permission, root possibility, and epistemic possibility.[3] For both necessity and possibility, discourse function is viewed as being on a continuum, with agent-oriented modal use on one side and epistemic modal use on the other side.

In ASL, a modal's role in the discourse (agent-oriented or epistemic) correlates strongly with the information ordering of the construction (Shaffer, 2004). The more subjective the modal's function is (i.e., the more it expresses the speaker's belief state), the more likely the modal is to be in the comment of a topic-marked construction.

Modals that refer to the agent are most often found near the agent in the sentence, while modals that refer to the speaker's belief state are found later in the sentence, including those that mark speaker assertion. In the data reviewed in Shaffer (2004), epistemic modals were *only* found in the comment of a topic-comment construction. In a topic-comment construction, the shared or "given" information is presented in the topic, while the "new" information is in the comment. The comment is the information that is in focus, or what the utterance is about.

---

[2] Throughout, WORD refers to a signed word and parallels the terms spoken word and written word.

[3] Notions of possibility are also expressed with words such as SEEM, FEEL, and OBVIOUS.

In the case of epistemic modal use, the utterance is *about* the speaker's beliefs; thus, this information is in the comment. Examples 12.8 and 12.9 help illustrate this. In example 12.8 the speaker is using SHOULD to suggest what the library should do. The use is said to be agent-oriented because the speaker is describing a condition imposed on the library. The utterance is about the library. In example 12.9, however, the speaker is telling his addressee that he believes the library *does* have *Deaf Life* magazine. The modal serves an epistemic discourse function, and the utterance, while referring to the library, is really *about* the speaker (and his beliefs). It is in the comment of this topic-marked construction and is produced with a head nod and brow furrow. As noted in Shaffer (2004), the nonmanual marking serves to further convey the degree of the speaker's beliefs.

(12.8) LIBRARY SHOULD HAVE *DEAF LIFE* MAGAZINE
"The library should have *Deaf Life* magazine."

(12.9) [LIBRARY HAVE *DEAF LIFE* MAGAZINE]–top [SHOULD]–bf/hn[4]
"Surely the library has *Deaf Life* magazine."

As can be seen, the degree of the speaker's certainty is coded both manually (in this case with SHOULD) and with nonmanual markers, in particular, with a furrowing of the brow and a nodding (or shaking) of the head. Example 12.10 below helps to illustrate the importance of nonmanual coding in the expression of speaker certainty. If the manual sign SEEM were reduplicated, and the head nod and brow furrow more pronounced, the discourse effect would be increased certainty by the speaker to the likelihood that Tim and Jennifer will be divorcing soon.

12.10 [TIM, JENNIFER]–top [DIVORCE SEEM]–brow furrow/slow head nod
"It looks like Tim and Jennifer are going to get a divorce."
"I think Tim and Jennifer are going to get a divorce."

In summary, modal notions in ASL are expressed by a combination of manual signs and nonmanual marking. While the same words are used to express both agent-oriented and epistemic notions in discourse, modals that code the speaker's belief state tend to be found in clause final position, in the comment of a topic-comment construction. Nonmanual marking serves to further express the speaker's belief state. The following section addresses some of the cognitive skills that relate to the

---

[4] Instead of the traditional "overbars," discourse produced with concomitant nonmanual marking is bracketed. –bf/hn refers to brow furrow and head nod, respectively. –hs indicates a head shake. –wg indicates that the bracketed sign is produced with a wiggling of the fingers. –top refers to the part of the utterance marked with a brow raise indicating a discourse or utterance topic.

emergence of modal use in child language. Following that, the acquisition of modal terms in ASL is described, along with the acquisition of topic marking. Finally, some areas for future research are discussed.

## TRENDS IN MODAL DEVELOPMENT AMONG HEARING CHILDREN

### Cognitive Prerequisites for the Use of Modals

Regardless of the language being acquired, a child must have certain cognitive skills in order to appropriately use and comprehend modal terms. Among the important cognitive development milestones that affect modal acquisition is the ability to "refer to information that is spatially and temporally displaced from the location of the speaker and the listener" (Morford & Goldin-Meadow, 1997). This ability was termed "displacement" by Hockett (1960) and has been the focus of a number of studies of hearing children. Morford and Goldin-Meadow summarize three developmental stages related to the emergence of what they, and many others, refer to as "displaced reference": (1) reference to nonpresent objects, actions, attributes or locations; (2) reference to proximal events; and (3) reference to distal or nonactual events. Of particular importance here is reference to distal or nonactual events, as this requires that the child be able to distinguish between possibility and reality.

"Pretend play" is the label Piaget used to describe children's exploration of the notions of possibility and reality. In Piagetian terms, this distinction develops in the preoperational stage, which begins at approximately 2 or 3 years of age, and continues until approximately age 7 (Piaget, 1955). This exploration is expressed through the child's language.

Child development studies conducted on a number of languages have documented the use of the imperfect past, as well as some inflectional mood markers (e.g., the subjunctive, which is discussed below) by children engaged in pretend play (Stephany, 1986). These studies show that changes in the use of linguistic resources correspond to changes in the child's ability to manipulate different kinds of mental representations. The following findings are particularly striking in this regard.

(1) Children tend to use agent-oriented modals first, sometimes as early as their second birthday, usually to refer to themselves (Tomasello, 2003). While there is considerable variation, modals with second and third-person referents become increasingly common in the third and fourth year (Bliss, 1988).[5]

---

[5] French (1999) notes that children generally begin using language to refer to others more frequently during the third year.

(2) Children typically begin by discussing their own abilities, and intentions ("I can," "I need to," "I'm gonna"). In fact through age 5, ability and intention remain the most common uses (Bliss, 1988). Expressions requesting permission also appear early ("Can I?"), as do expressions of necessity ("I hafta," "you hafta"; see Stephany, 1986).

(3) Regardless of the language under investigation, it is consistently the case that epistemic expression emerges last (usually beginning with "I think," "I guess," "I know"). And, while children use epistemic modals with increasing frequency in the third and fourth year, they often do not fully comprehend the degrees of certainty entailed by the various epistemic modals until much later. Some studies suggest that children do not fully comprehend degrees of certainty until their fifth year (Noveck, Ho, & Sera, 1996).[6]

Another significant finding is that children often use modal forms that serve epistemic functions in adult language to express agent-oriented notions, which highlights the difference production versus comprehension. The tendency to master agent-oriented modality before epistemic modality is very clearly illustrated in an acquisition study on Antiguan Creole, which is spoken on Antigua, an island in the Caribbean. Modal notions are expressed primarily with modal auxiliaries in Antiguan Creole. These auxiliaries are English based; however, as is common in Creole situations, wide divergence in meaning, and therefore discourse function, has occurred (Shepherd, 1982). In English, modal auxiliaries are commonly used to express both agent-oriented and epistemic notions, while in Antiguan Creole certain forms are used exclusively to express agent-oriented modality and others serve epistemic functions. Only a few modals have both agent-oriented and epistemic meanings.

In the expression of necessity the following forms are used: *bounfu, hafu, mos, fi,* and *mosa. Bounfu, hafu,* and *mos* are derived from the English words "bound to," "have to," and "must," but as noted above, they do not share the same meanings as their standard English counterparts. *Bonfu* is the strongest of the forms indicating absolute obligation on the agent. *Hafu* expresses strong necessity. Next in declining strength is *mos. Mos* is used to convey a weaker sense of necessity than either *bonfu* or *hafu. Fi* ranks lowest on the scale and appears to have roughly the same uses as standard English "should" (Shepherd, 1982, p. 319).

---

[6] Other studies (summarized in Bliss, 1988) suggest that epistemic meanings may not be cognitively mastered until at least age 7.

(12.11) Ya *bonfu* do wha dem say fu do.
"You must do what they tell you to do."

(12.12) Ya wan me fu deal wi? *Ya hafu* ha money laka peas.
"If you want to deal with me you have to have lots of money."

(12.13) Me *mos* tap usin all dark color.
"I have to/ought to stop using/wearing all dark colors (because
they don't look good on me)."

Shepherd's data suggest that children acquiring Antiguan Creole do
not always use markers of modality to serve the same discourse functions as adults. For example, while *mosa* is only used to express epistemic beliefs in adult language, example 12.14 was uttered by a child 4
years 6 months of age (4;6). In example 12.14, *mosa* is agent-oriented,
expressing obligation.

(12.14) A-ya play wi de sudn, na. A-ya *mosa* gon play wi de sudn.
"You play with that thing, you hear? You have to go and
play with it." (Shepherd, 1982, p. 321)

Divergence in meaning among children and adults is not unique to
Antiguan Creole. Stephany (1986) and others (e.g., Choi, 1991, 1995),
for example, have suggested that children acquiring highly inflectional
languages may begin to use inflectional forms (that have modal meanings in adult language) at an earlier age than children acquiring iso-
lating languages. Yet, in child language these inflectional forms do not
serve modal functions. For example, López-Ornat et al. (1994) and
Pérez-Leroux (1998) show that children acquiring Spanish begin using
the form that in adult discourse is used to signal subjunctive mood at
approximately 2 years of age, but the child's use is nonsubjunctive in
nature. Subjunctive mood is the verbal inflection that portrays the state
of affairs described by the verb as "relative" or "contingent." It also
used in the coding of subjective evaluation including epistemic certainty. An example of the Spanish subjunctive is given in example
12.15. The copula (esté) is in the subjunctive. The speaker (presumably
an adult) is stating his beliefs regarding whether or not a third person is
asleep. Whether or not the person is actually asleep is not coded in the
grammar, only the speaker's belief about it.

(12.15) No pienso que esté dormida.
"I don't think she is asleep." (from Travis, 2003 p. 51)

Pérez-Leroux (1998) suggests that the appropriate use of subjunctive
mood requires that a child have what has previously been referred to as
a "theory of mind." She notes: "In order to talk about what is not
actual, and to master the morphological encoding of events as actual or
non actual, children must first understand that individuals, themselves

or others, can think of events as actual even if they aren't" (p. 600). Put another way, children must understand that each person has his own knowledge and beliefs before they can appropriately code belief states in their discourse.

## Theory of Mind

Theory of mind here refers to children's understanding of their own and others' mental states, including thoughts, beliefs, knowledge, and desires (Wimmer & Perner, 1983). Theory of mind reasoning typically emerges between the ages of 3 and 5 and becomes more sophisticated as children mature. Theory of mind research represents an interesting intersection of cognitive, social, and language development, because as theory of mind reasoning is maturing, the child's language is also developing in very important ways. Experiments are designed to get at exactly what a child at a specific age knows about the knowledge and beliefs of others, as well as the relationship between theory of mind reasoning and the comprehension and use of specific linguistic constructions (see Moore, Pure, & Furrow, 1990).

Many theory of mind experiments include a false belief task. Here, participants are asked to state how the character in a story will react or respond when something in the story is changed without the character's knowledge (e.g., when an object is moved). The story character, then, is said to have a false belief. A child with theory of mind reasoning will be able to distinguish between *his* knowledge and the false beliefs of story characters.

Theory of mind reasoning has only recently been examined in deaf and hard-of-hearing children. The findings have been mixed but suggest much about the relationship between theory of mind and language acquisition. In an early study, Gale, de Villiers, de Villiers, and Pyers (1996) examined theory of mind reasoning in young orally educated deaf children. The children in the study ranged in age from 3;9 to 8;9 and were of normal intelligence. Results of three experiments indicated that the orally educated deaf children were significantly delayed relative to hearing preschoolers (also tested) with respect to theory of mind reasoning. The delay noted was approximately 3 years. The authors suggest that the delays seen in theory of mind reasoning were due not only to the language needed to complete the task but also to a delay in a deeper conceptual understanding that underlies verbal and nonverbal tasks.

A similar study was conducted by Peterson and Siegal (1995, 1999) with deaf children in Australia who were being educated using a form of signed English. The children in this study ranged in age from 8 to 13 years and were also of normal intelligence. The authors reported that the deaf children tested were significantly delayed in mastery of the tasks presented. In fact, only 35% of the children (average age, 10;4) were able to complete the tasks successfully. These results were noted to be comparable to those previously found for autistic children of the same age and were much worse than the results obtained for mentally retarded (nonautistic) children.[7] Peterson and Siegal noted that deaf children with deaf parents did considerably better with the tasks presented, and hypothesized that in addition to having more access to language in general, deaf children with deaf parents may also have increased exposure to the language of the mind. That is, because deaf parents share a language with their children, they may engage in more conversations about what they are thinking, thus making their thoughts, including their beliefs and false beliefs, accessible to their children.

While the results of the Peterson and Siegal studies do add to our understanding of the emergence of theory of mind reasoning in deaf children, some experimental design issues were addressed in later studies. First, the children in the Peterson and Siegal studies were much older than those examined in most studies of hearing children. Comparisons, then, between deaf and hearing children must be made with caution. In addition, a signed language interpreter was used by the researchers to test the children. This suggests that children must not only be able to solve the tasks presented but must also have some degree of experience using interpreters.

More recent studies, such as those described in Schick, deVilliers, deVilliers, and Hoffmeister (2000), have suggested that deaf children whose parents are Deaf are not delayed in the emergence of theory of mind reasoning. The deaf children from Deaf families tested by Schick and her colleagues showed theory of mind reasoning between the ages of 4 and 5, well within the expected range. Schick et al. did not use signed language interpreters to conduct their study, instead relying on native signers communicating directly with the signing children.

Courtin (1998, 2000) examined theory of mind reasoning among deaf children in France. Courtin's study attempted to tease out potential effects caused by the use of interpreters in the experiment. As with the Schick et al. (2004) study, testing in Courtin's study was conducted by a fluent signer (in this case, a French Sign Language user). The results were similar in most regards to those reported by Schick et al., namely, that deaf children whose parents were Deaf performed similarly to their hearing peers. Deaf children who used a form of signed language but were not second-generation Deaf were not able to perform the tasks as well as second-generation deaf children. And,

---

[7] Steeds et al. (1997) obtained substantially better results when they attempted to replicate the findings presented by Peterson and Siegal.

finally, orally educated deaf children solved the tasks at a significantly later age than either the hearing children or the deaf children from deaf families.

An important component of theory of mind research looks at changes in language comprehension and production as theory of mind reasoning emerges and matures (see Moore et al., 1990; Noveck et al., 1996). In one such study, Moore et al. (1990) examined children's comprehension of modal terms and their ability to use terms such as "must" and "might" to solve hidden object tasks. The researchers presented children with epistemic sentences (e.g., "the ball could be in the basket") that served as hints toward solving "hidden location" theory of mind tasks. The children were then asked to choose a location for the hidden object. The results suggested that children (in this case acquiring English) were unable to use epistemic information to solve theory of mind tasks until age 4.

The implications here are clear. Children must be aware of the thoughts and beliefs of others before they are able to use language that assumes that thoughts and beliefs can be viewed as true, even when they are not. In addition, as the child's reasoning develops, his ability to manipulate the language used to describe mental states using modals or other mental state terms also develops. This also suggests that if there are delays in theory of mind reasoning, delays in language will also be seen, including the emergence of modal terms.

## MODALITY AND DEAF CHILDREN ACQUIRING ASL

To this point we have discussed the conceptual domain of modality, its expression in languages, and some of the important cognitive milestones that correlate with its emergence in child language. We turn now to a discussion of the unique characteristics of the acquisition of modality in ASL.

The expression of modal notions in ASL incorporates three key features: manual coding, nonmanual coding, and the ordering of information in the construction. The interplay of the three features determines the modal's role in discourse. How then does a child acquire these features?

There are no published studies describing the acquisition of modal notions by deaf children acquiring a signed language. However, Shaffer (2001) does report the initial findings of a study of the emergence of modality in a second-generation deaf child acquiring ASL from birth. The child was filmed from age 3;10 to 5;7, in a variety of settings with peers, adults, an ASL specialist, and her family. While no formal theory of mind testing was conducted with the child, her answers to questions that required theory of mind reasoning suggest that by 3;10 she had at least emerging theory of mind.

As has been reported for hearing children acquiring spoken languages, the child began by expressing agent-oriented notions first. She was seen first using a formal modal at the age of 3;11 (though cross-linguistic evidence suggests she was likely using modal terms prior to 3;11). While playing with a doll house she juxtaposed a doll and a toy dog and stated that the doll was permitted to sit on the doll house furniture, but the dog was not. She used CAN to indicate permission, and NO to indicate the denial of permission. Though Stephany (1986) reported that permission does tend to appear early in child language, the earliest modals are most often first-person agent oriented and used to assert ability or intention (e.g., "I can do it").

(12.16) CAN SIT FURNITURE
"(He) can sit on the furniture."

(12.17) NO CHAIR STAND
"(He's) not allowed on the chair he has to stand."

The data show this child using modals with first-person agents at 4;2, several months after her third-person use of these modals. In example 12.18 she asserts her own ability. In example 12.19 she uses FUTURE to assert her intention to join the family in an activity after the movie she is watching ends.

(12.18) I CAN SEE SMILE
"I can see a smiley (face)."

(12.19) FUTURE index center FINISH
"I will, when this is over."

From this point on, the child otherwise follows the general patterns seen for children acquiring spoken languages. She uses CAN to assert her abilities (example 12.18), as well as what is possible, and uses MUST to describe what others should or must do. And, by age 4;2, she uses CAN and CAN'T to express permission and denial of permission respectively. For example, at age 4;2 the child was filmed playing a game (that belonged to her) with her family. She uses CAN to grant permission to her sister.

(12.20) YOU CAN TEAR CARD
"You can tear that card."

At age 4;2 she engages the person filming her in a discussion of her two cats and notes that while one is allowed outside, the other is not. Here, CAN and CAN'T are used in the same utterance, both with permission readings.

(12.21) index (cat) CAN GO OUTSIDE WHITE CAT CAN'T
"This cat can go outside, but the white cat can't."

During the same game she expresses impossibility with CAN'T when she is accused of cheating.

(12.22) [CHEAT CAN'T]–top $_2$LOOKING$_1$[8]
"I can't cheat with you looking at me."

At age 4;2, then, the child uses many modals with a wide range of agent-oriented discourse functions. Stephany (1986) notes that examples of epistemic possibility and necessity have been found in child language from age 3;6 and that epistemic modals usually appear about 6 months after the emergence of agent-oriented forms. Here, the first documented epistemic use is seen approximately 3 months after the child's first documented agent-oriented uses, suggesting that, in fact, her use of modal terms began prior to the first filming at age 3;10. In example 12.23, a continuation of example 12.21 above, she makes two epistemic comments, one without a formal modal and one with a formal modal. First, she uses nonmanual coding (the head nod and brow furrow) to express her belief that the cat will suffer. Next she uses FUTURE to indicate her certainty that at a future time the cat will die. It is of interest that she uses FUTURE twice in this discourse segment: once in the topic of a topic-comment construction, to indicate a far off future time (a temporal reference), and once to indicate her beliefs about the cat. Each use of FUTURE has its own concomitant nonmanual coding adding distinct meaning to FUTURE.

(12.23) wave, index CAT [SUFFER]–hn/bf
[FUTURE]–top/wg OLD (aging) DIE [FUTURE]–hn
"This cat will suffer. He will get old. He will die."

While the child was using modal terms with some facility at age 4;2, by age 5;2 use of both agent-oriented and epistemic modals becomes more sophisticated, as does her language in general. Example 12.24 illustrates the growth in her language. She uses FEEL to mark the tortoise's suspicion that the hare was behind him. The child is expressing the *tortoise's* belief state instead of her own. Perhaps understanding the potential for confusion, she explicitly states "the tortoise" just prior to "feels."

(12.24) TORTOISE FEEL (the hare is gaining) (look behind, EEK) WALK
(fast) CROSS-LINE (finish line)
"The tortoise suspected it. He looked behind him. The hare
was gaining on him! He sped up and crossed the finish line."

In examples 12.25 and 12.26, the child is relating an experience she had to her parents. She describes how she saw a family friend's new car and asked if she could touch it. She uses eye gaze and body shifts to

---

[8] Here the subscripts 2 and 1 refer to second- and first-person, respectively, giving the meaning "you look at me."

indicate her perspective as she makes a request of the man and to indicate the visual perspective of the man as he responds to her request. She gazes toward her parents to comment to them on the discourse.

(12.25) NOT PERMIT TOUCH RUB (on car) CAR (mouth open in awe), [CAN'T]–head shake [WHY]–top [ROUGH*]–squint SCRATCH TOUCH (eye gaze down and left) LOOK-AT FIST (threatening) [CAN'T]– head shake NO
"I wasn't allowed to touch the car, because I might scratch it. He'd get mad if I did."

(12.26) I TELL (eyes center) (pause) (eye gaze up right) [I CAN I PUSH-KNOB]–y/n (eye gaze down and left) (nod) (eye gaze center) PUSH-KNOB (eyes widen) LOUD*
"I asked (the man) can I push (the radio knob). He said yes, so I did. It was loud!"

By 5;2 the majority of her utterances follow a shared-new, or topic-comment ordering, though not all pragmatically topical information is coded nonmanually. Examples 12.27–12.29 further illustrate her increased use of topic-comment ordering. While example 12.27 includes some topic marking, examples 12.28 and 12.29 do not; however, when considered in a discourse context, examples 12.28 and 12.29 follow a shared-new ordering. Both "goggles" and "sun" were mentioned earlier in the discourse and are now shared by the addressee.

(12.27) PLAY++ [SUN-SHINE (begins to shine)]–top [ ]–hs CAN'T [SUN-SHINE]–top CAN'T [WHY]–top RAIN++ FINE IF NONE FINE
"It's okay to play as long as it's raining. When the sun is shining, you can't."

(12.28) GOGGLES (on face) CAN FINE GOGGLES (on face)(look around) CAN
"If you have goggles it's fine. With goggles on you can see."

(12.29) SUN (shine on him) NOT-SHOULD
"(Goggles) aren't necessary when the sun is shining."

In summary, this deaf child's acquisition of modal terms appears to follow the general tendencies noted for children acquiring a spoken first language. She began using agent-oriented modals first, and as she gained facility with a wide variety of discourse functions (ability, intention, possibility, permission, necessity, etc.), she also began to use the modals to express her own certainty about what she was saying. By her fifth year she was also employing topic-comment ordering, with and without topic marking. Topic marking is complex linguistic feat that has specific grammatical, cognitive, and pragmatic components, which are reviewed below.

## Topic Marking

Recent studies of ASL (e.g., Janzen, 1998, 1999; Slobin, chapter 2 this volume) have suggested the utility of considering ASL discourse in terms of overall information ordering. ASL discourse, which involves the combining of multiple sentences, frequently employs a shared-new paradigm and thus parallels what is seen at the sentential level. Shaffer (2001) and Shaffer and Janzen (2002) suggest that in order to make full use of the shared-new paradigm, a signer, and in particular a child, must have a sophisticated understanding of what information is shared. In order to incorporate this in his discourse, a child must have well-developed theory of mind reasoning. That is, the child must understand that his beliefs are autonomous from the beliefs of others before he understands what is available for topic marking.

Early studies ASL of acquisition appear to support this notion. For example, Newport and Meier (1985) reviewed literature on language acquisition among signing children between the ages of 2 and 5 (reviewing Hoffmeister, 1978) and note that children show a strong tendency to use subject–verb (SV), verb–object (VO), SVO, VL (presumably location), and SVL early on. The data from Shaffer (2001) also provide insights into the information ordering strategies used by children.

The child from Shaffer (2001) was filmed beginning at the age of 3;10. Her first documented modal was at age 3;11. Her discourse at 4;2 contained numerous agent-oriented modals expressing notions such as ability (and inability), permission (and denial of permission), intention, possibility (and impossibility), and necessity. At 4;2 she was also using some topic-comment constructions, though all of her early topics make reference to people and things in close physical proximity to her. Finally, while no formal testing for theory of mind was conducted at 4;2, she does engage in conversations that suggest she is able to use theory of mind reasoning. For example, she tells her father during a game that she didn't cheat and, in fact, *cannot* cheat because he is watching her (example 12.20). This suggests that she understands that if her father were not watching, she *could* cheat, because he would not know. She was also able to accurately report the beliefs (and false beliefs) of story characters, belief states that differed from her own.

Previous studies (e.g., López-Ornat et al., 1994; Moore et al., 1990; Pérez-Leroux, 1998) and the data reported here all suggest that prior to developing theory of mind reasoning, a child is unlikely to appropriately use modals that express his belief state because to do so would require that he understand that others can hold differing beliefs. With respect to ASL acquisition, Shaffer and Janzen (2002) suggest that it is also unlikely that the child will competently use topic-marked constructions because the notion of "shared information" is central to the pragmatics of topic, and an understanding of what is shared relies on the awareness that others may have differing knowledge. Put another way, children must know what is shared before they can fully use topic-comment constructions.

How, then, do children get from utterances that merely juxtapose concepts to utterances that express speaker stance using a shared-new (topic-comment) ordering? Part of the answer is that they mature cognitively. In fact, Slobin (1973, p. 184) claimed that cognitive development is the pacesetter for linguistic growth. Clues to the answer also come from our understanding of how children acquire manual and nonmanual marking.

### The Acquisition of Facial Marking

To this point we have only discussed topic-marked constructions from a pragmatic perspective. But, as most who study a signed language know, topics are commonly coded nonmanually in ASL. Reilly, McIntire, and Bellugi (1990, 1991) and Reilly (chapter 11 this volume) have conducted perhaps the most thorough analysis of the acquisition of nonmanual marking by deaf children. Reilly et al. draw from research on the acquisition of affective facial expression, as well as work on facial affect in adults (see Ekman, 1972), but note that the while the acquisition of affective expression appears to be holistic in nature, *grammatical* facial marking develops componentially. And, while it has been suggested that grammatical facial markers share some characteristics with affective facial behaviors, those with grammatical properties are highly constrained and rule governed. Reilly and her colleagues provide solid empirical evidence to support the case for a disassociation between affective and grammatical facial marking.

The authors divide nonmanual markers into three categories: (1) nonmanual markers that are obligatory with single lexical items; (2) nonmanual adverbials, which appear to be productive in nature, combining with predicates; and (3) clause level nonmanual markers such as those marking topics and conditionals.

The data (Reilly et al., 1991) show the first nonmanual marking of topics at age 3;0. In contrast to the marking for topics, which the children acquired relatively early, nonmanual marking of conditionals appeared later. This is significant due to the obligatory nature of nonmanual marking of conditionals in adult ASL. In fact, the marking of conditionals is essentially identical to the marking of topics in ASL, consistent with Haiman's (1978) assertion that conditionals *are* topics. The children appeared to favor manual marking of conditionals using SUPPOSE, IF and the fingerspelled loan sign I-F, rather than nonmanual markers. Reilly et al. (1990) note that even during elicitation tasks young deaf children did not repeat the modeled conditional markers. When presented with conditional sentences without *lexical signs* marking the condition (i.e., those only marked with nonmanual signals), the children repeated them as two simple propositions. The authors suggest that this indicates that the children were not even cognizant that the nonmanual marking functioned to signal conditionals.

Children appear to be making a distinction between the essentially identical marking for topics and conditionals by opting for manual signals for conditionals, and nonmanual signals for topics. Slobin's (1973) uniformity principle helps us understand this complex development. Topics have no obligatory manual morphology, and thus, the nonmanual marking is the only option for topic. By contrast, a lexical signal is available for conditionals, along with the nonmanual coding. Children often exhibit a preference for free morphemes (words) to signal such things as past temporal events, prior to signaling them with the bound past-tense morpheme. Perhaps the same phenomenon is at work here.

While the studies conducted by Reilly and her colleagues suggest that children are able to mark topics nonmanually as early as 3;0, what has yet to be determined is the child's pragmatic *use* of topics. Put another way, can children who are 3;0 make full use of the shared-new paradigm, or do they simply mark as topical entities that are in the signing space, and are thus clearly "shared." If Shaffer and Janzen (2002) are correct in their assertion regarding children's use of topic-comment constructions, sophisticated use of topic-marking requires theory of mind reasoning, which typically develops between the ages of 3 and 5. This warrants further study.

## SUMMARY AND CONCLUSIONS

While there is still much to learn about how deaf children become proficient in the use of modal terms, some general conclusions emerge. Deaf children appear to acquire modals in much the same way hearing children do. Agent-oriented modals are acquired first, and over time, these terms come to serve varied discourse functions. Epistemic modality will be seen only after children are using agent-oriented modals with some degree of consistency. The evidence also suggests that children (deaf and hearing) do not begin to make true epistemic comments until they have theory of mind reasoning. A child must be aware that others have differing belief states before he will appropriately use language that expresses his own belief state.

While there are many cross-linguistic commonalities, there are also features of modal acquisition that are unique to children acquiring a signed language. ASL has been characterized as a topic prominent language (see Janzen, 1998, for a review). The shared-new (topic-comment) paradigm is pervasive in ASL discourse and serves a variety of pragmatic functions. One that is of importance here is the expression of speaker belief state. Specifically, the speaker's certainty regarding the truth of his proposition (expressed with an epistemic modal) is found in the comment of topic-marked constructions (Shaffer, 2004). Topic marking is a grammatical component of ASL. And, while Reilly and her colleagues note that topic marking is seen as early as age 3;0, Shaffer and Janzen (2002) suggest that in order to make full use of the shared-new paradigm, a child must have theory of mind reasoning. As with the relationship between theory of mind reasoning and epistemic modal use, appropriate use of topic is dependent on an understanding that people have different knowledge and beliefs, and an understanding knowledge and beliefs can be shared.

What we see then is a complex interaction of grammar, pragmatics, socialization, and cognitive development, all leading to the eventual linguistic expression of speaker perspective. This is what we know. What we don't know are the specifics of the development of each component, or how the components work together.

### What's Next?

It is clear that much has yet to be learned about deaf children and modal use. Some questions remain to be answered:

(1) At what age does the facial marking that accompanies epistemic modals become salient to children? At what age do they begin to use that marking themselves? When do children develop competence with the subtle degrees of commitment that are coded nonmanually?

(2) What more can we learn about the interaction of theory of mind and epistemic modal use? Do the semantic distinctions between notions such epistemic possibility (MAYBE) and epistemic necessity (MUST) develop as the child's theory of mind reasoning matures, as previous research would predict?

(3) At what age do semantic distinctions in the manual coding of modals become salient? For example, when do children come to understand that MUST expresses greater certainty than SHOULD? And, when do they develop competence in coding these distinctions in their own discourse?

(4) How does the notion of shared information mature? Do children develop this concept componentially? For example, does a child begin by realizing that entities in the shared physical space are also shared in cognitive space, and at a later age recognize that information can be shared even if it hasn't been physically shared with the addressee? Can the research on displaced reference (see Morford & Goldin-Meadow, 1997) help us understand the development of a child's understanding of the notion of "shared information"?

(5) Finally, how do delays in language acquisition in general manifest in deaf children's use and comprehension of modals?

The clear best approach for learning the answers to some of these questions is through well-designed experimental studies that consider modals within a discourse context. Moore et al. (1990) have begun this process for spoken English. For example experimental research shows that 4-year-olds are beginning to understand that beliefs may be held with differing degrees of certainty, but the concept of relative certainty appears to continue to develop even as children are reaching school age.

Empirical studies that tease apart lexical and grammatical expression, and manual and nonmanual expression are needed, as is further work on the relationship between the pragmatics of information ordering and cognitive construal. The study of the acquisition of modality in signed languages is a rich area for explorations of the interplay between conceptualization and linguistic expression.

## REFERENCES

Bliss, L. (1988). Modal usage by preschool children. *Journal of Applied Developmental Psychology, 9*(3), 253–261.

Bybee, J. (1985). *Morphology: A study of the relation between meaning and form.* Amsterdam: John Benjamins.

Choi, S. (1991). Early acquisition of epistemic meanings in Korean: A study of sentence-ending suffixes in the spontaneous speech of three children. *First Language, 11*, 93–119.

Choi, S. (1995). The development of epistemic sentence-ending modal forms and functions in Korean children. In J. Bybee & S. Fleishman (Eds.), *Modality in grammar and discourse* (pp. 165–204). Amsterdam: John Benjamins.

Coates, J. (1990). Modal meaning: The semantic-pragmatic interface. *Journal of Semantics, 7*, 53–63.

Courtin, C. (1998). Development of theories of mind in deaf children. In M. Marschark & M. D. Clark (Eds.), *Psychological perspectives on deafness* (Vol. 2, pp. 79–102). Mahwah, NJ: Lawrence Erlbaum.

Courtin, C. (2000). The impact of sign language on the cognitive development of deaf children: The case of theory of mind. *Journal of Deaf Studies and Deaf Education, 5*, 266–276.

de Haan, F. (1999). Evidentiality and epistemic modality: Setting boundaries. *Southwest Journal of Linguistics, 18*(1), 83–101.

Ekman, P. (1972). Universals and cultural differences in facial expressions of emotion. In J. Cole (Ed.), *Nebraska Symposium on Motivation 1971* (pp. 207–283). Lincoln, NE: University of Nebraska Press.

Ferreira Brito, L. (1990). Epistemic, alethic and deontic modalities in a Brazilian Sign Language. In S. D. Fischer & P. Siple (Eds.), *Theoretical issues in sign language research* (pp. 229–260). Chicago: University of Chicago Press.

French, M. (1999). *Starting with assessment: A developmental approach to deaf children's literacy.* Washington, DC: Gallaudet University Press.

Gale, E., de Villiers, P., de Villiers, J., & Pyers, J. (1996). Language and theory of mind in oral deaf children. In A. Stringfellow, D. Cahana-Amitay, E. Higher, & A. Zukowski (Eds.), *Proceedings of the 20th Boston University Conference on Language Development* (pp. 213–224). Boston: Cascadilla Press.

Haiman, J. (1978). Conditionals are topics. *Language, 59,* 781–819.

Hockett, C. (1960). The origin of speech. *Scientific American, 203,* 88–96.

Hoffmeister, R. (1978). *Word order in the acquisition of ASL.* Paper presented at the Boston University conference on language development, Boston, MA.

Janzen, T. (1998). *Topicality in ASL: Information ordering, constituent structure, and the function of topic marking.* Unpublished doctoral dissertation, University of New Mexico, Albuquerque.

Janzen, T. (1999). The grammaticization of topics in American Sign Language. *Studies in Language, 23*(2), 271–306.

López-Ornat, S., Férnández, P., Gallo, P., & Mariscal, S. (1994). *La Adquisicion de la lengua Española.* Madrid: Siglo XXI.

Lyons, J. (1977). *Semantics.* London: Cambridge University Press.

Moore, C., & Frye, D. (1991). The acquisition and utility of theories of mind. In D. Frye & C. Moore (Eds.), *Children's theories of mind: Mental states and social understanding* (pp. 1–13). Hillsdale, NJ: Lawrence Erlbaum.

Moore, C., Pure, K., & Furrow, D. (1990). Children's understanding of the modal expression of speaker certainty and uncertainty and its relation to the development of a representational theory of mind. *Child Development, 61,* 722–730.

Morford, J., & Goldin-Meadow, S. (1997). From here and now to there and then: The development of displaced reference in homesign and English. *Child Development, 68*(3), 420–435.

Newport, E., & Meier, R. (1985). Acquisition of American Sign Language. In D. Slobin (Ed.), *The cross-linguistic study of language acquisition* (Vol. 1, pp. 881–938). Hillsdale, NJ: Lawrence Erlbaum.

Noveck, I., Ho, S., & Sera, M. (1996). Children's understanding of epistemic modals. *Journal of Child Language, 23,* 621–643.

Pérez-Leroux, A. (1998). The acquisition of mood selection in Spanish relative clauses. *Journal of Child Language, 25,* 585–604.

Peterson, C., & Siegal, M. (1995). Deafness, conversation and theory of mind. *Journal of Child Psychology and Psychiatry, 36,* 459–474.

Peterson, C., & Siegal, M. (1999). Representing inner worlds: Theory of mind in autistic, deaf, and normal hearing children. *Psychological Science, 10*(2), 126–129.

Piaget, J. (1955). *The language and thought of the child.* New York: Meridian Books.

Reilly, J., McIntire, M., & Bellugi, U. (1990). The acquisition of conditionals in American Sign Language. *Applied Psycholinguistics, 11*(4), 369–392.

Reilly, J., McIntire, M., & Bellugi, U. (1991). Baby face: A new perspective on universals in language acquisition. In S. D. Fischer & P. Siple (Eds.), *Theoretical issues in sign language research: Vol. 2. Psychology* (pp. 9–23). Chicago: University of Chicago Press.

Schick, B., Hoffmeister, R., de Villiers, P., & de Villiers, J. (2000, July). *American Sign Language and Theory of Mind in Deaf children with Deaf or hearing parents.* Seventh International Conference on Theoretical Issues in Sign Language Research, Amsterdam, The Netherlands.

Shaffer, B. (2000). *A syntactic, pragmatic analysis of the expression of necessity and possibility in American Sign Language*. Ph. D. dissertation, University of New Mexico, Albuquerque.

Shaffer, B. (2001, September–October). *The acquisition of markers of modality by deaf children*. Paper presented at the 2001 National Symposium on Childhood Deafness, Sioux Falls, SD.

Shaffer, B. (2004). Information ordering and speaker subjectivity: Modality in ASL. *Journal of Cognitive Linguistics, 15*(2), 175–195.

Shaffer, B., & Janzen, T. (2002, July). *Topic marking: What signers know and interpreters don't*. Invited paper presented at the Association of Visual Language Interpreters of Canada national conference, Halifax, Nova Scotia.

Shepherd, S. (1982). From deontic to epistemic: An analysis of modals in the history of English, creoles, and language acquisition. In A. Ahlqvist (Ed.), *Papers from the 5th International Conference on Historical Linguistics* (pp. 316–323). Amsterdam: Benjamins.

Slobin, D. I. (1973). Cognitive prerequisities for the development of grammar. In C. A. Ferguson & D. I. Slobin (Eds.), *Studies in child language development* (pp. 175–208). Hillsdale, NJ: Lawrence Erlbaum.

Steeds, L., Rowe, K., & Darker, A. (1997). Deaf children's understanding of beliefs and dislikes. *Journal of Deaf Studies, 2*, 185–195.

Stephany, U. (1986). Modality. In P. Fletcher & M. Garman (Eds.), *Language acquisition* (2nd ed., pp. 375–400). Cambridge: Cambridge University Press.

Tomasello, M. (2003). *Constructing a language: A usage-based theory of language acquisition*. Cambridge, MA: Harvard University Press.

Travis, C. (2003). The semantics of the Spanish subjunctive: Its use in the natural semantic metalanguage. *Journal of Cognitive Linguistics, 14*, 47–69.

Wilcox, S., & Wilcox, P. (1995). The gestural expression of modality in ASL. In J. Bybee & S. Fleishman (Eds.), *Modality in grammar and discourse* (pp. 135–162). Amsterdam: John Benjamins.

Wimmer, H., & Perner, J. (1983). Beliefs about beliefs: Representation and constraining function of wrong beliefs in young children's understanding of deception. *Cognition, 13*, 103–128.

# 13

# The Development of Narrative Skills in British Sign Language

*Gary Morgan*

By the end of the preschool period, children have acquired a substantial portion of the generative language system commensurate with that of the adult. Despite this ability, there are still many challenges that remain in learning how to use language in different pragmatic contexts. This chapter focuses on the continued developments and refinements that occur in the production of deaf school-age children's narratives in British Sign Language (BSL). Although the data and psycholinguistic models discussed are based on narratives produced in BSL, it is intended that this work can be applied to other signed languages.

The chapter includes an exploration of the issues surrounding deaf children's mastery of the extended uses of signed language narrative (e.g., those needed for academic discourse). It is argued that these developments revolve around the bilingual relationship between literacy in signed and spoken language. School-based activities involving comparative narrative analysis are outlined at the end of the chapter.

## FROM FIRST WORDS TO FIRST STORIES

Children start to link sentences together in narrative only after a prolonged period of mastering the sentence-level linguistic devices of their

I thank Isabel Garcia, Ros Herman, and Nicola Grove for comments on earlier versions of this chapter. I am also very grateful for insightful comments provided by Brenda Schick and Marc Marschark.

314

language. Berman (1988) and Berman and Verhoeven (2002) have described this as one "paradox" of language development in that children progress from mature use of their language at one level to a complete lack of awareness of the new pragmatic demands made of the same linguistic forms at the level of discourse. Bamberg (1986), also writing about this transition, argued that

> Linguistic knowledge of lexical semantics and syntactic rules forms the building blocks out of which narrative is constructed; we expect the child first to acquire linguistic knowledge and then to apply this knowledge (in the form of semantics/syntactic building blocks) when acquiring the ability to tell narratives. (p. 1)

The production of narrative involves the coordination of at least three major cognitive domains. First, many linguistic devices are used within and across sentences and bigger discourse units (e.g., in episodes and settings). Some of these include the correct use of gender, number and tense agreement, the use of markers for direct discourse, and correct anaphoric and cataphoric reference (McCabe & Peterson, 1990). Second, pragmatic abilities are central in narrative production and comprehension, which require awareness of a conversation partner or addressee's information needs (Hudson & Shapiro, 1991). Third, domain-general cognitive abilities such as working memory and information processing are involved in narrative for the sequencing of large amounts of information (Eisenberg, 1985).

These domains are also involved in the construction of sign language narratives. Although less well documented than in spoken languages, work on sign language discourse has revealed how modality specific devices (e.g., eye-gaze shifts) are used to organize and structure extended signed texts (Bahan & Supalla, 1995; Gee & Kegl, 1983; Roy, 1989). The structure of narrative in signed language is probably more akin to similar texts produced in nonwritten languages with "oral" traditions (Bahan & Supalla, 1995). This difference between BSL and English will become more salient in the final section of this chapter.

The development of the cognitive abilities necessary for narrative begins with children's first attempts at moving from sentence level descriptions of the "here-and-now" to talking about past or fictional events in narrative. Narrative has its origins in the first proto-narratives that stem from children's experiences of picture book "reading" and play involving toys and other objects that occur in most homes in the years preceding entry to school. Good communication between parents and children during these activities would seem crucial. Successful development of proto-narrative skills is an issue if deaf children are not accessing all the important information in the spoken language addressed to them.

As abilities in sequencing events increase proto-narratives get larger (Applebee, 1978; Wigglesworth, 1997). Once children begin school, narrative gets entwined in other important developmental milestones such as theory of mind (Eaton, Collis, & Lewis, 1999).

## What Goes Into a Narrative?

The narratives produced by typically developing 3–5-year-olds are generally vague and not well constructed. They frequently centre on some event of personal and immediate significance. Often different character's actions in different episodes are not linked across the narrative; rather, the child describes each successive scene independently. By early school age (5–6 years), children are already able to consistently produce stories with certain key elements, such as where the narrative is set, and sometimes more optional and alternative information is provided (Applebee, 1978; Wigglesworth, 1997). By 5–6 years children can narrate with a basic story grammar and attempt to organize the flow of information in a hierarchical fashion. Other story elements such as the internal responses of characters including their motivations, intentions, goals, and plans for resolving conflicts emerge much later in development.

It is after 6 years that narratives that are more adultlike begin to develop; these contain plots, character development, and a logical sequence of episodes. As children mature, their narratives become longer, more detailed, and better organized and contain a greater number of episodes. The episodes are also more likely to be complete and to be embedded within larger discourse units (subplotting).

At around the age of 8 or 9 years, children can link stories between different sentences and obey the linguistic and pragmatic constraints imposed on them for telling a story to another person (Kemper, 1984). It is also around this age that the introduction of detail and variation through differential linguistic markers such as pronouns and the linking devices "and," "so," and "when" start to occur. More effort is also evident with increasing age to engage and keep the listener's attention. This is related to the child's development of discourse pragmatics.

The development of more complex narrative and pragmatic skills is interwoven into children's educational experience. As literacy abilities grow, so the links between "oral" narrative skills and the new extended, decontextualized uses of language encountered in written texts become more evident (Westby, 1998). Oral narrative skills encouraged in earlier classroom experiences are activities such as "show-and-tell" or fictional storytelling.

Narrative has long been considered important for later reading readiness and literacy in general (Debaryshe, 1995), so much so that in Britain, narrative development features in the government's "Early Learning Goals" (Botting, 2002). These guidelines suggest that prior to starting school, children should be able to use language to "imagine and recreate roles and experiences." It is important to point out that for many deaf children these language-based preschool activities may not be fully developed before children arrive at school because of issues to do with successful communication with their hearing parents.

Some studies also point out that the cultural biases in certain narrative skills are more preferable in mainstream education than others (Brice-Heath, 1983). Different cultures define and value varieties of narrative skills in different ways, meaning that "children from some backgrounds enter school with existing knowledge of the type of narrative structure that is valued in school; while children from other backgrounds do not" (Peterson, Jesso, & McCabe, 1999, p. 1).

## THE DEVELOPMENT OF DISCOURSE PRAGMATICS

Pragmatic competence involves the ability to use language appropriately in different social contexts. Most of what is discussed in this chapter concentrates on the pragmatic abilities involved in retelling events from storybooks. One part of pragmatics is knowing the principles that govern how information should be organized across a series of interrelated utterances in order to make the parts of a narrative cohesive or connected. In this chapter the narratives produced by deaf children are described by focusing on two aspects of pragmatics: (1) the marking with the appropriate reference form, the relative newness of information as a function of a specific referential function, and (2) the controlling of the sequence of episodes. In the following sections these two aspects of narrative are discussed in turn.

### Marking Reference Forms and Referential Functions

All languages use linguistic devices to pick out entities within discourse. English has a continuum of reference forms with different referential saliencies or dependencies. These include indefinite noun phrases (e.g., "a little boy"), definite noun phrases (e.g., "the dog"), pronouns (e.g., "the boy and the dog looked for the frog; *they* found some trees"), and zero or ellipsed forms (e.g., "he climbed up the tree and *zero* looked in the hole"). These forms carry out several referential functions during the telling of a story, including the introduction of a character as the discourse topic into the narrative for the first time, the reintroduction of a character into the narrative after leaving or after being replaced as the discourse topic by another character, and the maintenance of a character in the narrative as the discourse topic over stretches of several linked utterances.

Narrative involves the building up of layers of information about characters, places, and events. Givòn (1983) established the principle that the choice of form used in narrative is related to its function (e.g., introduction, reintroduction, or maintenance of reference). When retelling stories, narrators make choices about how a character will be focused on in the narrative (Slobin, 1996). The first time a character is introduced into the story, this is new information, and so reference is made through a salient or referentially unambiguous reference form (e.g., "a little boy"). There are two options available following an introduction: The character may stay as the discourse topic and hence be maintained or may leave the focus of attention temporarily, needing to be reintroduced at some later time. In these latter contexts, more subtle, less salient reference forms are used, for example, pronouns or zero forms. Previously given information for identifying the antecedent of the anaphoric form is assumed to be shared implicitly by both the narrator and the addressee. The use of reduced reference forms functions as a pragmatic signal or marker of this implicitness or relevance (Sperber & Wilson, 1995). The relationship between form and function for English can be shown as a hierarchy of explicitness shown in table 13.1.

*Person Reference in BSL*

While the reference forms in BSL[1] differ, it appears that they perform similar referential functions from those described for English (Morgan, 2000). There are several reference forms available to adult signers of BSL when narrating (see Sutton-Spence & Woll, 1999, pp. 271–274). The three relevant forms described here are noun phrases, entity or semantic classifiers, and role shift.

**Table 13-1: A Hierarchy of Explicitness in English**

| Form | Explicitness |
| --- | --- |
| Indefinite noun phrase | High |
| Definite noun phrase | |
| Pronoun | $\updownarrow$ |
| Zero form | Low |

[1] Signed sentences that appear in the text follow standard notation conventions. Signs are represented by SMALL CAP English glosses. Repetition of signs is marked by "+". Above the glosses, eyegaze markers such as blinks (ØØ), direction (left/right or neutral space) and gaze toward the addressee (><) are indicated by a vertical line across the affected segment. In later sections semicircles represent the fixed referential space with the flat edge nearest to the signer's perspective. The location of an entity classifier is shown by an "X" in the semicircle. A full circle represents the shifted referential space. Arrows indicate the direction of a sign's movement.

*Noun phrases*   As in many spoken languages (e.g., Russian), there is no lexical difference between indefinite and definite noun phrases in BSL. The distinction is marked through discourse pragmatics. Noun phrases can also be expressed through a finger spelt word, for example, T-O-M, or a name for one of the characters, for example, BIG-NOSE.

*Entity classifiers*   In narrative, entity or semantic classifiers (Supalla, 1990) mark the semantic category or the size and shape of the referent noun and are used for establishing referent identity, as well as describing topographical information (see Emmorey, 2003). For example, the classifier for vehicle is articulated in BSL with a B hand shape (a flat hand with the palm face down). In most narrative cases, classifiers are rarely used to introduce a new character, but instead, they are used to maintain reference to an entity previously mentioned through a noun phrase antecedent. The example shown in figure 13.1 relies on the signer previously signing CAR so that in the succeeding sentence the classifier for vehicle and its movement are clearly understood. On its own, the hand shape could also refer to other vehicles.

*Role shift*   In BSL narratives it is often the case that the words, actions, and thoughts of a character are described through direct discourse. This reference form is referred to in the literature by various terms such as "role shift" (Loew, 1984), "referential shift" (Emmorey & Reilly, 1998), and "constructed action" (a particular form of role shift; Metzger, 1994; Winston, 1995), among others. Metzger (1994) pointed out that when the signer switches to role shift to describe what someone said, did, or thought, the narrator's actions are not a direct copy of what the third person did but a constructed version of these actions. Role shift is used in narrative to maintain reference as its use relies on previous identification thorough a noun phrase antecedent. This referential

**Figure 13-1: "The car moves under the bridge."**

**Figure 13-2. "The dog jumps up at the beehive."**

device allows the signer to describe the actions of one of the characters in the narrative. The example in figure 13.2 shows the signer describing the actions of a dog jumping up at a beehive.

In the previous discourse, the narrator refers to the dog explicitly through a noun phrase and then shows how the dog jumped up at a swinging object. The signer represents the animal through both manual (the shape of her hands) and nonmanual means (the face). Importantly, this allows reference to the character to be maintained across a stretch of discourse (within an episode).

Reference forms in BSL, as in English, can be placed on a hierarchy of explicitness related to the amount of information they carry. This is shown in table 13.2, where the reference forms discussed are placed on a hierarchy related to how much previous information is required for their use.

This hierarchy means that if the signer signs BOY, the noun phrase requires very little previous information to identify the referent. Thus, it is the most salient or explicit of the reference forms available. Other reference forms require more previous information for their correct use in discourse, as they are less explicit. In BSL entity classifiers can be used to refer to both boys and dogs in discourse. Handshape distinguishes

**Table 13-2: A Hierarchy of Explicitness in BSL**

| Form | Explicitness |
| --- | --- |
| Noun phrase | High |
| Entity classifers | ↕ |
| Role Shift | Low |

between the two classes of animate entities: a "g-hand" (the index finger) for humans and a "bent v-hand" (a victory sign with fingers bent) for small animals. However, the entity classifier only refers to a class of semantically similar objects rather than a particular member of that group. The small-animal classifier does not distinguish between a dog and a cat, for example; this information must be given as an antecedent. Thus the classifier reference form requires more previous information for its correct identity than the noun phrase as it carries less explicit information. Lastly, the role shift reference form, because it uses the signer's whole body, cannot be used as easily to distinguish between human, vehicle, or flat object, and so forth. Because it is the least explicit in terms of the amount of identifying information it carries, this reference form requires the most amount of previous information from the narrator to ensure its correct identification by an conversation partner viewing the narrative (see Morgan & Woll, 2003).

*The Development of the Organization of Reference Forms in English*

Bamberg (1986) proposed stages in the development of reference form organization. Initially children choose explicit reference forms that unambiguously pick out characters even though they are maintaining reference rather than introducing or reintroducing. This can be seen in the second mention of the boy through a repeated noun phrase in the following example from a 5-year-old:

> (13.1) "The boy fell-out and the bees were flying after the dog, *the boy.*"

At the next stage of development, Bamberg described children as focusing on the organization of reference at the level of the sentence by using one character as the main or "thematic subject" perspective. In this way within small narrative units, the main character can be maintained as the discourse topic through reduced forms, for example, pronouns, but in a rigid, formulaic way, as in example 13.2:

> (13.2) "*The dog*'s sitting down, and *he* finds the beehive, and *he*'s looking at it, and the boy's looking through a hole, and then he goes to the branch, and the dog is sitting down" (6-year-old, from Wigglesworth, 1997, p. 298)

Bamberg's final stage is reached when children choose a form based not only on the nearness of an immediate mention but also by taking into consideration what is going on in the bigger discourse unit. In this way pronouns and zero forms can be used with full anaphoric functions stretching across intervening referents but relying on the wider pragmatic context (what is going on in the rest of the story beyond the immediate sentence) to provide coherence. This can be seen in example 13.3, where the child uses the pronoun (him) in the final sentence.

The pronoun is clearly understood as referring to the "boy" character despite there being intervening noun phrases:

> (13.3) " ... and *the boy* looked down a hole, and a beaver came out, and the dog was shaking the tree where the beehive was, and he made the beehive fall, and *the boy* was looking in a tree ... hole, and the owl, an owl came out and pushed *him* down" (10-year-old, from Wigglesworth, 1997, p. 294).

Adultlike use of this pragmatic knowledge continues to develop in the teenage years. The control of reference in order to carry out more complicated referential functions coincides with a major growth in the child's pragmatic abilities to assess the knowledge of the listener as well as monitor the narrative for ambiguity (Bamberg, 1986; Berman & Slobin, 1994). The development of literacy is important in making these connections clear through direct text analysis tasks. By seeing how reference functions across static written texts, children with good command of their first language can more easily build up knowledge of how complex narratives are made up from layers of information about characters, places, and events. Consequently, children are expected in school to construct their oral narratives and extended uses of language (debating, answering questions, or constructing explanations) based on the written narrative template. This way of speaking like you write, but also thinking like you write (Olson, 1994), becomes one of the more preferred and valued types of narrative skills in the school context (Peterson et al., 1999). As discussed in the final section of this chapter, this transference of narrative abilities from oral to written codes relies on nativelike knowledge of a first language, which is implicitly assumed in most hearing children but may not be the case in some deaf children.

### Reference Organization and Its Development in BSL

The narratives analyzed and presented here were collected from 12 deaf children and 2 deaf adults exposed to BSL from infancy from their deaf parents or in early childhood from their hearing parents. All the children attended a deaf-only day school, which had adopted a bilingual BSL/English policy. The hearing parents all signed with their children and were enrolled in adult sign language courses. In the school setting, all the children had good models of fluent adult BSL, including extensive examples of narratives and had been informally assessed as having age-appropriate levels of BSL.[2] The age of the

---

[2] At the time these data were collected, there was no standardized BSL assessment battery (see Herman et al., 2004). Deaf teachers carried out all language assessment through informal measures.

**Table 13-3: Child Narrators' Ages and Parental Hearing Status**

| Child | Age (year;month) | Parental Hearing Status |
|-------|------------------|-------------------------|
| 1     | 4;3              | Hearing                 |
| 2     | 4;9              | Deaf                    |
| 3     | 5;6              | Deaf                    |
| 4     | 5;7              | Hearing                 |
| 5     | 7;8              | Deaf                    |
| 6     | 9;6              | Hearing                 |
| 7     | 9;10             | Hearing                 |
| 8     | 10;4             | Hearing                 |
| 9     | 11;6             | Deaf                    |
| 10    | 11;10            | Hearing                 |
| 11    | 13;1             | Hearing                 |
| 12    | 13;4             | Deaf                    |

children ranged from 4 years 3 months (4;3) to 13;4, and none had any developmental impairments. Details of the children's ages and parental hearing status are given in table 13.3. For comparison, the children were grouped into three age groups as shown in table 13.4.

*Data Collection*

The narratives were elicited through a picture book retell task. The book, *Frog Where Are You?* (M. Mayer, 1969), consists of 24 wordless pictures of various scenes depicting the adventures of a young boy and his dog, as they search for an escaped frog. After familiarizing themselves with the book, children retold narratives from memory in BSL to their deaf class teacher. During the retell, the picture book was not present. This method for collecting the story was chosen because previous studies have shown that if the book is present, young children often use the surface of the picture book for reference, rather than linguistic devices (Baker, van den Bogaerde, Coerts, & Woll, 1999; Morgan, 2003). The narratives were recorded on a video camera positioned next to the addressee. Trained deaf and hearing signers transcribed the signed narratives.

**Table 13-4: Age Groups**

| Group | Age (years) | N |
|-------|-------------|---|
| 1     | 4–6         | 4 |
| 2     | 7–10        | 4 |
| 3     | 11–13       | 4 |

## General Narrative Organization

Looking at the development of narrative across the 12 children and 2 adults, the number of episodes produced in the narratives increased across the different age groups. The use of increasingly more episodes across the groups reflects the development of memory and planning processes. The percentage of the three reference forms (noun phrases, classifiers, and role shift) classified as ambiguous (not possible to identify the identity of the character the reference form referred to) conversely shows a uniform decrease across the groups. This information is summarized in table 13.5.

Next, the narratives were analyzed for the way the children and adults used particular referential forms.

*Coding Reference Forms for Particular Referential Functions*

In studies of BSL narrative development, for example, Morgan (1998, 2000) and Morgan and Woll (2003), reference forms appearing in narratives were coded for whether they introduced, reintroduced, or maintained reference to a character. This means that an introduction was the first mention of a character in the story. If a character went out of discourse focus because of an intervening referent, then when it was referred to again it was coded as a reintroduction. Maintenance constituted the continued reference to a character that remained in discourse focus. The ability to judge which reference forms are needed for which referential function is a pragmatic skill based on assessing the conversation partner's needs. Children developing BSL need to master this level of pragmatic knowledge in order to tell clear and interesting signed narratives.

## Results of the Age-Group Comparison for Reference Form and Function

A comparison of which referential function the noun phrases, for example, BOY, DOG, or FROG, in the narrative were performing revealed

### Table 13-5: General Narrative Development Across Age Groups

| Measure | Group 1 (4–6 years) | Group 2 (7–10 years) | Group 3 (11–13 years) | Adults |
|---|---|---|---|---|
| Episodes | 5.5 | 13.5 | 16.5 | 19 |
| References | 28 | 75 | 96 | 140 |
| Ambiguous reference | 16% | 8.8% | .2% | 0% |

Data are mean number of episodes in narratives, total number of reference forms used and mean ambiguous reference that in all age groups both children and adults used them mainly to introduce and reintroduce characters. There were differences across the groups however, the lowest percentage of use for maintenance was in the adults (6%) and the highest percentage use was in the youngest age group (22.5%). This is shown in figure 13.3. The inappropriate selection of a form that is very information explicit for light referential functions was most salient in the youngest children. The younger children also failed to use explicit noun phrases to introduce new characters, which adults did nearly 100% of the time.

The use of repeated salient reference, through noun phrases, in the 4–6-year-olds for maintenance maps onto the first stage in Bamberg's developmental model (Bamberg, 1986). At this age children are concerned with making sure characters are mentioned with explicit reference forms at the level of the sentence and are less able to balance demands for relevant reference across larger units of discourse. The more appropriate pattern of noun phrase use for referential function is clearer in the 7–10-year-olds. Interestingly even the oldest children in the groups (11–13 years) used noun-phrase forms for reintroduction and maintenance in a different way than the two adults, suggesting that narrative skills are still developing at this late age.

Turning to the other referential forms in the narratives produced by adults, nearly one third (31%) of the total number of tokens of reference maintenance was through entity classifiers, while only 4% of the total number of reference introductions was through this form (see figure 13.4). In cases where an adult used a classifier to introduce a referent,

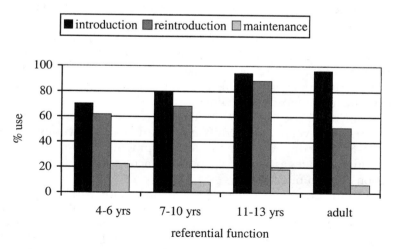

**Figure 13-3. A comparison of noun phrase use across referential function and age group as a total percentage of reference forms used.**

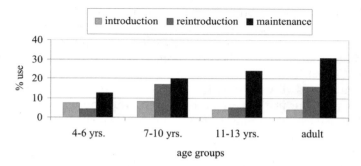

Figure 13-4. Adult and children's use of classifiers as a percentage of total number of reference forms across each referential function.

there was cataphoric reference; that is, they were immediately followed by a noun phrase identifying the referent explicitly. Entity classifiers, because of their low information explicitness, are important, therefore, for reference maintenance and to report old or already talked about information in narratives.

This pattern of form and function contrasts with the use of the same entity classifiers in the narratives produced by the children. The youngest children (4–6-year-olds) used entity classifiers markedly less for maintenance than the two adult signers (12.5% of total reference maintainers compared to 31% in the adults), and this use increased with age (20% for 7–10-year-olds, and 24% for the 11–13-year-olds). Conversely, the youngest children were twice as likely to choose an entity classifier to introduce a character, without the clarifying cataphoric or following noun phrase, as the adults were (8% of introductions in 4–6-year-olds compared to 4% in adult narratives).

These results suggest that while the youngest children are able to use entity classifiers at the single sentence level, they are still developing the necessary pragmatic knowledge for using these same forms with narrative functions. Adults and the oldest children (11–13 years) reserve their use mostly to maintain reference to characters in a narrative; thus, their use is anaphoric. This is pragmatically appropriate as classifiers carry very little identifying information. The youngest children (4–6 years) did not show this level of pragmatic awareness. Classifiers in the youngest children appeared across the three referential functions fairly uniformly.

The third reference form used for maintenance was role shift, as shown in figure 13.5. Role shift to refer to a character follows a similar functional distribution to that for classifiers. Across all age groups, it was used most predominantly for maintenance of discourse topic (59% of total reference maintainers in the adults). Role shift was used more

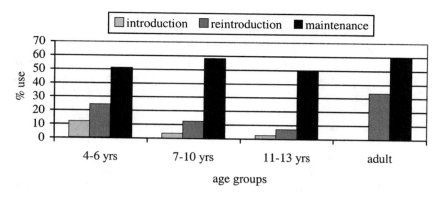

Figure 13-5. Adult and children's use of role shift as a percentage of total number of reference forms for each referential function.

than classifiers for maintenance of reference. The adult narrators repeated role shifts several times in parts of their narratives in order to maintain a focus on a particular referent. None of the adult narratives included role shift for introduction of referents, whereas in the 4–6-year old group, a significant percentage of reference introductions (11.25%) were made through this form. This was often the cause of referential ambiguity (see table 13.5), as the form does not carry enough referential information to successfully serve this function.

Concerning these results, it appears that even the youngest children understand that role shift is a referential form appropriate for referential maintenance. What marks the difference between an adult and child use of role shift is the subject of a separate chapter, but it appears that adult signers are able to keep track of where they are in a narrative and that this control triggers how overtly the role shift is made. Role shift can be signaled through overt or discreet changes in head, face, and body posture. The further into a narrative the adult narrator is, the more often role shift can be used to identify a referent but also the less overt these shifts to role shift can be (Morgan, 1999). This is not the case for child narrators who produced overt role shifts at all points in their narratives.

In general, control of the pragmatic role of entity classifiers and role shift in discourse develops gradually with initial mastery at the sentential level, where young children may use these constructions correctly but fail to use them appropriately in relation to their new referential functions in discourse (see also Loew, 1984, for American Sign Language).

Discussion now turns to the second aspect of narrative to be described in BSL—the control of sequences of events.

## Controlling the Sequencing of Episodes

This aspect of narrative involves the setting out of a series of episodes in a story clearly enough so that the conversation partner may follow what has happened as a logical sequence of related events across time (McCabe & Peterson, 1990). Some background on narrative is described first.

There are two overlapping times in a narrative: the external plot time and the passage of the internal episode sequences. While in the canonical story the plot time passes from the start of the story to some sort of completion, within the internal discourse units (parts of the story) episodes are not always sequentially organized. The ordering of single episodes through the course of the narrative may involve some overlapping, repetition, or adjustment of time forward or backward within the overall plot time.

### Controlling the Sequencing of Episodes in English

Within the overarching plot time, individual parts of the narrative being retold may contain overlapping pieces of information, for example, where two referents are involved in separate co-occurring activities. An example of this type of episode time overlap is depicted in the events in figure 13.6, A and B. These two pictures come from the storybook *Frog Where Are You?* (M. Mayer, 1969). In the complete story the plot revolves around two characters (a boy and a dog) and their eventful search and eventual discovery of an escaped frog. The plot time progresses through the picture book from an introduction of the main characters and initial realization of the frog's disappearance to the final rediscovery of the frog and the happy ending. Figure 13.6 shows one complicated subpart of the story: In A, the two main characters are seen searching for the frog in separate trees at the same time; in B, the two characters are involved in overlapping events where the boy discovers an owl in the hole he was looking into while the dog is chased by a swarm of bees. Across the "Frog story" there are several complicated episodes like the "owl and beehive scene" where events when retold in a narrative unfold in a nonlinear way. Describing this scene requires the narrator to express a sequence of events by overlapping, repeating, or moving parts of the episode backward in time while keeping the plot flowing forward.

In order to do this successfully a narrator chooses particular strategies to describe overlapping events that will make the description both internally consistent and understandable. An adult English speaker described the events in figure 13.6A in the following way: "To the dog's amazement, he knocked the beehive off the tree while the boy was searching the trunk" (example from Berman & Slobin, 1994).

6a

6b

Figure 13-6. The owl and beehive scene in *Frog Where Are You?* (M. Mayer, 1969). Pictures reproduced with permission from Dial Press, New York.

The speaker's description of the two parts of the episode is sequential, as speakers (naturally) can only talk about one part at a time, yet we interpret the two subparts of the event as taking place simultaneously or in overlapped episode time because of the connective "while." The ordering of the two events in the episode in this way allows the listener to move attention between the two character's actions sequentially but still take from the description an appreciation of the simultaneity.

*Controlling The Sequencing of Episodes in BSL*

The devices available to users of signed languages offer other possible strategies for talking about simultaneity: "One of the advantages of sign languages is that the visual-spatial modality enables the simultaneous presentation of not only more than one piece of information but also the information that these things are happening simultaneously" (Aarons & Morgan, 2003, p. 125).

In analyzing how a series of episodes are laid out in BSL narrative, Morgan (1999, 2002) describes how adult signers divide up the series of connected utterances between two types of linguistic sign space: (a) the fixed referential space (FRS) and (b) the shifted referential space (SRS; see also Aarons & Morgan, 2003; van Hoek, Norman, & O'Grady-Batch, 1987).

During a signed narrative these sign spaces are continually changing and being reused for reference to characters, to describe the physical layout of a scene and for expressing the passage of episode and plot time. The set of reference forms described in the preceding section get used within with these two sign spaces.

### The Fixed Referential Space

The FRS is an area of representational sign space. In narrative, signers may use specific locations in this sign space with noun phrases and subsequently link pronouns and verb inflections to these locations (Lillo-Martin, 2002). Signers also use the FRS to describe anaphoric and spatial relationships with entity classifiers (e.g., Emmorey & Falgier, 1999). The important feature of the FRS is its fixedness during a set part of a narrative episode. The locations of noun-phrase indexes or the classifier entities placed within the FRS may change through the duration of a narrative, but this reuse of the space is clearly indicated by the narrator by setting up new noun phrases and locations.

### The Shifted Referential Space

In the SRS the sign space is extended to include the signer's own body as a character in the narrative and not just as the articulator of the sign message (the narrator). Up to this point in this chapter, this use of space has been referred to through the term "role shift." The SRS becomes useful when the narrator uses direct discourse, for example, when the narrator wants to report what a character did by shifting to the character's point of view rather than through a description provided from the narrator's perspective. A common signal that the SRS is being used is a brief disengagement of eye gaze by the signer from his conversation partner; that is, the signer momentarily looks away from the conversation partner while articulating direct discourse in role shift (as shown in figure 13.2).

### Telling Stories Using the FRS and SRS

When describing a complicated sequence of events, such as in the owl and beehive scene, adult signers organize the narrative episodes by moving between the FRS and SRS. Some of the information is laid down in the FRS for character identity or particular locations and relations between objects and characters. More information about a character's actions from that character's or another character's perspective may be linked into this FRS space through direct discourse in the SRS. In this way the narrator describes how different episodes are to be understood as following a particular sequence and allows the signer to move between particular perspectives (both physical and temporal) on a scene. During the laying out of this information, it is common to see the narrator looking intently back and forward between areas of space relevant in the narrative as well as looking at the conversation partner. Looking at the conversation partner, when identifying particular characters and transitions between spaces, functions to stress that pieces of information in the narrative will be important for understanding the passage of events. In this way the narrator highlights as important particular parts of the narrative in a similar way that intonation does in spoken language narratives.

BSL has different ways of organizing episodes than that in English (for similar devices in other signed languages, see Engberg-Pedersen, 1995; Miller, 1994). In narrative, switching between or even overlapping referential forms in the FRS and SRS allows the signer to refer to two characters acting in the same episode. The use of duel perspectives on one scene has been described in the literature as SAME-TIME-WHILE (e.g., Valli, 1987).

To illustrate this, in figure 13.7, the signer describes two characters engaged in the same activity. First the boy is mentioned, followed by a direct discourse description of his actions LOOK-DOWN(1) through role shift in the SRS. Then the dog is mentioned explicitly and an entity classifier for small animal is placed in the FRS on the signer's

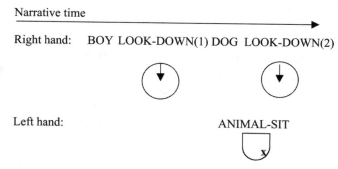

Narrative time

Right hand:    BOY LOOK-DOWN(1) DOG  LOOK-DOWN(2)

Left hand:                                    ANIMAL-SIT

'The boy looked down while the dog sat nearby'

Figure 13-7. Overlap of the FRS and SRS. Semicircles represent fixed referential space, with the flat edge nearest to the signer's perspective. The location of an entity classifier is shown by an X in the semicircle. Full circles represent the shifted referential space. Arrows indicate the direction of a sign's movement.

BOY   ENTITY-FALL(1) DOG  JUMP-UP BEES SWARM  BOY ENTITY-FALL(2)

'As the boy was falling, the dog made the bees angry and then the boy hit the ground'

**Figure 13-8. Using flashbacks to overlap subparts of an episode. Conventions are as in figure 13.7.**

nondominant left hand. The signer holds the left hand in sign space while returning to the action of the boy looking down LOOK-DOWN(2). The second utterance of LOOK-DOWN is understood as an anaphoric reference to the boy. The two parts of the episode overlap in the time frame but also in their articulation between the two sign spaces. The black arrow indicates the passage of narrative time over the gloss.

As well as combining the FRS and SRS simultaneously, adult signers often show the temporal flow of episodes sequentially through repeating different subparts. In this way the episode time moves backward. The completion of the first activity is not shown until the second referent is mentioned (Engberg-Pedersen, 2003; Morgan, 1999, 2002). This final discourse devise is akin to a "flashback" in cinematic terms. In figure 13.8, the first mention of the boy's fall through an entity classifier ENTITY-FALL(1) in the FRS was held in the air momentarily before the role shift to the dog in the SRS. The second fall, ENTITY-FALL(2), is articulated completely.

During these types of signing it is common to see adult signer's pay great attention to their conversation partner's uptake of the message (i.e., they look at their conversation partner more than in other parts of the narrative).

### The Development of Episode Sequencing in English

In hearing children's English narrative development, the overlapping of episode time through the use of "while" appears only after the associated concept of sequentiality and its markers, such as "then," "and," or "next" (Bamberg, 1986; Costermans & Bestgen, 1991):

(13.4) "The boy fell-out and the bees were flying after the dog."
(5-year-old, from Wigglesworth, 1997, p. 295)

This is thought to be because tracking more than one character in the same episode is more cognitively demanding in a narrative task (Aksu-Koç & von Stutterheim, 1994; Chen, 2002; Silva, 1991). Switching between characters influences the continuity of the narrative both at the episode level and the overall plot level. It is the ability to manage both these types of narrative time that identifies the mature user of a language. In older children, more detail is provided for each part of the episode but combining the two different subepisodes is still rare before 8 years:

> (13.5) "The dog's sitting down, and he finds the beehive, and he's looking at it, and the boy's looking through a hole, and then he goes to the branch, and the dog is sitting down." (6-year-old, from Wigglesworth, 1997, p. 298)

In the next stage of development children become more able to move back and forward between the two parts of the episode and attempt to embed the actions of the characters in one overlapped time. However, even 10-year-olds find it difficult to organize the sequence of events in a way that allows an overlapped interpretation of the different parts of the episode while at the same time not disturbing the overarching flow of the plot:

> (13.6) "... and the boy looked down a hole, and a beaver came out, and the dog was shaking the tree where the beehive was, and he made the beehive fall, and the boy was looking in a tree ... hole, and the owl, an owl came out and pushed him down." (10-year-old, from Wigglesworth, 1997, p. 294)

## The Development of Episode Sequencing in BSL

There are obvious differences between English and BSL in the form of the linguistic devices at narrators' disposal for organizing sequences of events in complicated narrative episodes. Despite these differences, mastery of this narrative skill poses a very similar problem for children developing BSL and, across children of different ages, presents clear developmental trends.

There have been few studies of children's development of this aspect of signed language narrative (Engberg-Pedersen, 2003; Morgan, 2002). In Morgan (2002), narratives produced by the same children and adults as described in the preceding section were analyzed for the use of the FRS and SRS. In the youngest children's narratives (4–6 years of age), the owl and the beehive scene was retold as a sequence of actions with no attempt to overlap or encode the simultaneity of the different parts of the episode. Typical examples from two children ages 5;6 and 5;7 are shown in English translations in examples 13.7 and 13.8, respectively. In both examples, only the dog's actions are referred to.

> (13.7) "The dog is walking along and he sees a tree fall, and the bees are coming out of the hive, the dog is biting and pushing at the bee hive, it falls down and they try to catch the dog."

(13.8) "The dog sees a tree with something hanging on the branch of the tree, the dog pushes at the tree which sways back and forward, the hive moves and falls off onto the ground and breaks, really gets squashed, the bees come flying out, the dog is scared and runs away."

The difficult task of overlapping the two parts of the episode means the youngest children focus on only one of the two parts of the beehive and owl event. This parallels findings on same age children's abilities in constructing spoken language narratives, for example, Aksu-Koç (1994). The difficulty in sequencing co-occurring events at this age appears therefore to be a general developmental issue, which includes children acquiring a signed language. When telling stories children at this age use many of the linguistic devices available in BSL for person reference, for example, entity classifiers, pronouns, verb inflections, and role shift, but all at the sentential level. They do not link these devices across their narratives.

In the narratives of the 7–10-year-old children, there continued to be a sequential description of the two parts of the scene, although by this age the children were able to include both characters involved in the episodes and switch between them. As the conversation partner finds out about what happened to the boy, the dog's actions (pushing at the hive) are not recounted. When we return to the dog, we see his actions not from where we left him, but from further into the narrative. This is seen in example 13.9 from a child age 7;8, again translated from BSL into English.

(13.9) "So over there the dog is walking and there is a hive and bees are coming out; the mouse, the man, I mean the boy, is looking into the hole on the tree; yes looking into the hole; an owl comes flying out which scares the boy; the dog runs past; the bees are following him."

The combination of the FRS and SRS and the "flashback" devices first appeared in the BSL narratives of the oldest children (11–13 years). An example from a child 11;10 of age of the "flashback" device is shown in example 13.10. The two repeated events are italicized in the translation.

(13.10) "Well, he climbs up and is looking into the hole; all of a sudden *he falls back* from the tree; in the hole there is an owl flapping away. The dog later on is over by the hive which has fallen from the branch on the tree and the bees are angrily coming out of the hive; the dog runs right through there, being chased by the swarm of bees who are colliding with him and stinging him. *The boy lands on the ground* and carries on walking, calling 'where is my dog?'"

DOG  RUN  PASS CL-G-DOG-RUN  #SEE BOY CL-FALL

# PAIN HURT-BOTTOM

'...suddenly the dog runs past seeing the boy falling onto the ground "ouch that was

painful on the bottom"...'

**Figure 13-9. Overlapping sign spaces to recount the activities of the boy and dog simultaneously. Conventions are as in figure 13.7.**

In another example from a child age 13;4, the simultaneous movement of the running dog and the falling boy are shown through several sequences of overlapped sign space, as shown in figure 13.9. The utterance begins with the noun-phrase reintroduction DOG and an entity classifier showing the direction of the animal as it runs, the 13-year-old signer then indicates that the dog sees the boy falling, at the same time the signer in role shift depicts the perspective of the dog running past the falling boy. The role shift to show the dog's perspective in the SRS is articulated simultaneously with an entity classifier in the FRS to show the trajectory of the boy falling. Finally, the 13-year-old switches to show the boy's constructed action during his fall through role shift in the SRS. An attempt to capture the complexity of this string of utterances is given in a sign gloss in figure 13.9. The part of the example where the 13-year-old describes the running dog through role shift, watching the falling boy, is shown by overlapping the semicircles (SRS) and ovals (FRS) in the gloss.

One of the reasons only the oldest children manage this aspect of sign narrative has to do with the cognitive demands of recounting a sequence of events involving the tracking of more than one character. In narrative, children have to remember and sequence the whole narrative plot as well as get the particular sequence of events in the right order. This information processing load explains the youngest children's preference for omitting one of the character's actions and the middle group of children (7–10 years) rigidly sticking to a sequential rather than simultaneous sequencing of this parts of the episode. These simplification strategies presumably reduce the cognitive demands.

The sequencing of episodes in signed narrative involves overlaying perspectives through the FRS and SRS articulated both simultaneously and sequentially. The signing strategies needed to recount narratives with complicated sequences of episodes, requires children to interactively create (through negotiation with their conversation partner) a rich textured set of perspectives on an event (Aarons & Morgan, 2003). Although not described in detail here, the younger children often fail while narrating to indicate how to interpret the switches they make between the FRS and SRS. They frequently tell the whole of this part of the narrative without looking once at their conversation partner. This in contrast was achieved by the adult narrators looking frequently to their conversation partner (Morgan, 2002).

## FURTHER DEVELOPMENT OF NARRATIVE-BASED LANGUAGE SKILLS

Summarizing the reviewed research on BSL narrative development and the pragmatic control of reference and episode sequencing, it seems that children can have mastery of linguistic devices at the level of individual sentences but continue to have great difficulty using these same forms in appropriate ( adultlike) ways when they are recruited for narrative. The main reasons for this stems from the development of the pragmatic awareness of the functions of reference, that is, telling a story for another, and also the child's still developing cognitive abilities in handling large stretches of information "online." The studies reviewed in this chapter point toward similar underlying patterns of development in English and BSL, which is interesting in itself when considering the major typological differences between signed and spoken languages. Despite these similarities, there are some major differences in narrative development and later uses of extended language between the two modalities that need to be discussed further.

It is often assumed in the literature on spoken language development that the development of extended uses of language is greatly influenced by the child's emerging literacy (e.g., Bamberg, 1986; Berman & Verhoeven, 2002; Gillam & Johnston, 1985). What is more it is also claimed that literacy has an effect on not only language use but on thinking itself (e.g., Olson, 1994). It is often argued (Bamberg, 1986; Berman & Verhoeven, 2002) that this influence is because becoming literate involves developing metalinguistic awareness.

Metalinguistic awareness allows the child to focus on and reflect on language as a "decontextualized object." Decontextualized language is characterized by the fact that the speaker and listener do not directly share the experience being communicated. Expanding literacy affects the child's skill in creating cohesive decontextualized language in both spoken and written modes. The uses of "oral" (as in not written but spoken or signed) language skills in school revolve around constructing complex texts with a heavy bias from written language organization (e.g., answering questions, debating, arguing, describing routines).

Taking these factors into account it would seem important to understand how extended uses of sign language could develop fully, if deaf children have less success in developing age-appropriate print literacy skills. In the typical scenario, literacy in a given language grows out of the child's abilities in spoken language skills in the same language. Because there is no agreed upon written version of BSL, many deaf children have less of an understandable mapping between the first language (e.g., BSL) and the written version of a different language (e.g., English).

These two factors are closely linked through feedback with each other. The full development of extended language use is influenced by literacy skills and literacy skills are themselves built on previous abilities in the same language in the "oral" mode. For the full-extended uses of signed language to develop (e.g., using BSL to describe the sequence of steps when carrying out an experiment in laboratory chemistry), further learning about discourse construction may have to come from literacy-based activities. Currently, it is not clear how literacy skills in signed or written language impact on the development of extended uses of signed language development. The transfer between BSL literacy skills (e.g., narrative) and English literacy skills may happen in both directions. BSL could facilitate the start of English literacy, but later English literacy would influence the further development of BSL narrative skills. In this concluding section, two issues are mapped out for further research: (a) transfer of first language skills into the start of literacy and (b) the continued development of extended signed language skills through the influence of literacy (in signed and spoken language)

## Transfer

There is much work describing deaf children's development of literacy as a difficult process (Allen, 1992) but not impossible (Mayberry, 1992; Mayberry & Chamberlain, 1994). What counts as literacy in these studies is not always clear; for example, is it the reading of single words and sentences or the writing of extended expositions? It emerges that deaf children with more first language abilities generally do better at developing English literacy. Presumably, this is because they are coming from a "position of strength" (Hoffmeister, 2000) although exactly how first language abilities in American Sign Language facilitate English literacy is not well understood (Mayberry, 1992; Singleton, Supalla, & Schley, 1998).

Although there are some perspectives that propose no useful transfer of sign abilities to written English development (e.g., C. Mayer & Wells, 1996), many more studies propose that underlying skills *will* transfer from extended signed language abilities to English literacy development. Lichtenstein (1998) argued that working memory and metalinguistic knowledge are important in learning to read for deaf children. Knowing how to construct a good, long and interesting narrative in BSL, in part, involves knowledge of the pragmatic dependencies that license the use of certain reference forms over others.

From the research reviewed above, it was concluded that the hierarchy of explicitness for forms and functions is organized similarly for BSL and English. This means that referential forms that pick out characters unambiguously are used mainly for introductions in narrative across both BSL and English. Similarly reference forms with low explicitness on the hierarchy (e.g., zero forms or role shift) are also chosen for the same functions (referential maintenance) across the two languages. It follows then that children with good narrative skills in sign therefore have the necessary underlying pragmatic and cognitive abilities to be able to understand and produce written narratives. This will follow if, and this is a big if, the written language code is clearly understood.

If there are shared processes underlying both BSL and English narrative production then transfer from first language to second is possible Strong & Prinz (2000). It would seem important therefore to ensure that a deaf child has exposure to examples of extended uses of BSL (e.g., debate, theater, explanation of scientific reasoning) in enough quantities and from fluent adult models. This will provide the child with the opportunity to develop potential cognitive flexibility and metalinguistic abilities in order to facilitate the development of English literacy skills.

*Continued Development of Extended Uses of Signed Language*

In order to promote the full development of extended signed language abilities and facilitate the transfer of potential common underlying abilities between the languages it is important to work on special narrative-based classroom practices within "bi-bi" (bilingual bicultural) programs (e.g., Hoffmeister, 2000; Kuntze, 1998, 2000; Mashie, 1995). Progress in this area can benefit from signed language research. There is a growing literature on the analysis of signed language texts (Bahan & Supalla, 1995; Gee & Kegl, 1983). More is being found out about the linguistic structures inherent in different genres of extended sign language use, for example, formal lectures, theater, jokes, frozen texts, anecdotes, and poetry (Valli, 1987). There are narrative assessment batteries for children under development (Herman et al., 2004). There is even some developmental work on the use of written signed language (Gangel-Vasquez, 1997). On the negative side, however, it has still not been demonstrated that signed language literacy skills (abilities in producing extended narrative texts) are useful for developing English written language skills.

If children are to see how their skills in signed narration transfer to written narratives in English, comparative narrative devices need to be taught explicitly to children by 6 or 7 years of age, once they have some sign language narrative skills and some knowledge about how the written English code works (e.g., Bailes, 1999, 2001). Explicit narrative analysis tasks involve children analyzing video recordings of BSL narratives and carrying out text analysis of written English narratives. This is followed by activities focusing on translation between languages.

Bialystock (1991) argued that there are three stages in children's development of literacy: (a) the "oral"/conversational stage, (b) a learning to read stage, and (c) a metalinguistic stage where children learn how to manipulate language. It is this third stage that is important to stimulate so that transfer skills between BSL and English can take place. Deaf children's metalinguistic knowledge of BSL has to be stimulated through focused BSL literacy classes. In this way, teachers can begin to point out the relationships between how narrative is BSL and English are differently organized. Contrastive narrative analysis classes would build on previous translation/decoding skills learned from initial reading classes. Contrastive text analysis is currently used in signed language interpreter training programs for hearing adults but is not in wide use in schools. Some research on comparative narrative analysis in schools has already suggested practical pedagogic strategies (e.g., Kuntze, 2000; Mather & Thibeault, 2000).

Currently, the educational system is asking deaf children to become bilingual users of extended texts but is not always providing the necessary metalinguistic skills with which to facilitate this movement to bilingualism. There is a lost opportunity here. Potentially, skills in written English such as constructing narratives, theater, and poetry could benefit greatly from properly informed deaf bilingual writers bringing another perspective into their English writing from BSL in a creative and truly bilingual way.

## REFERENCES

Aarons, D., & Morgan, R. (2003). Classifier predicates and the creation of multiple perspectives in South African Sign Language. *Sign Language Studies, 3,* 125–156.

Aksu-Koç, A. (1994). Development of linguistic forms: Turkish. In R. Berman & D. Slobin (Eds.), *Different ways of relating events in narrative: a crosslinguistic developmental study* (pp. 159–167). Hillsdale, NJ: Lawrence Erlbaum.

Aksu-Koç, A., & von Stutterheim, C. (1994). Temporal relations in narrative: Simultaneity. In R. Berman & D. Slobin (Eds.), *Different ways of relating events in narrative: a crosslinguistic developmental study* (pp. 393–455). Hillsdale, NJ: Lawrence Erlbaum.

Allen, T. (1992). Subgroup differences in educational placement for Deaf and hard of hearing students. *America Annals of the Deaf, 137,* 331–388.

Applebee, A. (1978). *The child's concept of story.* Chicago: University of Chicago Press.

Bahan, B., & Supalla. S. (1995). Line segmentation and narrative structure: A study of eyegaze behavior in American Sign Language. In K. Emmorey & J. Reilly (Eds.), *Language, gesture, and space* (pp. 171–191). Hillsdale, NJ: Lawrence Erlbaum.

Bailes, C. N. (1999). *Primary-grade teachers' strategic use of American Sign Language in teaching English literacy in a bilingual school setting.* Ph.D. dissertation, University of Maryland: College Park.

Bailes, C. N. (2001). Integrative ASL-English language arts: Bridging paths to literacy. *Sign Language Studies, 1*(2), 147–174.

Baker, A. E., van den Bogaerde, B., Coerts, J., & Woll, B. (1999, November). *Methods and procedures in sign language acquisition studies.* Paper presented at the Fourth Intersign Workshop, London.

Bamberg, M. (1986). A functional approach to the acquisition of anaphoric relationships. *Linguistics, 24,* 227–284.

Berman, R. (1988). On the ability to relate events in narrative discourse processes *11,* 468–497.

Berman, R., & Slobin, D. (1994). *Different ways of relating events in narrative: A cross-linguistic developmental study.* Hillsdale, NJ: Lawrence Erlbaum.

Berman, R., & Verhoeven, L. (Eds.). (2002). Cross-linguistic perspectives on the development of text-production abilities in speech and writing [Special issue]. *Written Language and Literacy, 5*(2).

Bialystock, E. (Ed.). (1991). *Language processing in bilingual children.* Cambridge: Cambridge University Press.

Botting, N. (2002). Narrative as a tool for the assessment of linguistic and pragmatic impairments. *Child Language Teaching and Therapy. 18,* 1–22.

Brice-Heath, S. (1983). *Ways with words: Language, life, and work in communities and classrooms.* New York: McGraw-Hill, Oxford University Press.

Chen, J. (2002). *Mandarin and English-speaking children's expression of temporality.* Doctoral dissertation, University of Manchester.

Costermans, J., & Bestgen, Y. (1991). The role of temporal markers in the segmentation of narrative discourse. *Cahiers de Psychologie Cognitive, 11*(3), 49–70.

Debaryshe, B. (1995). Maternal belief systems: Linchpin in the home reading process. *Journal of Applied Developmental Psychology, 16,* 1–20.

Eaton, J., Collis, G., & Lewis, V. (1999). Evaluative explanations in children's narratives of a video sequence without dialogue. *Journal of Child Language, 26,* 699–720.

Eisenberg, A. R. (1985). Learning to describe past experiences in conversation. *Discourse Processes, 8,* 177–204.

Emmorey, K. (2003). *Perspectives on classifier constructions in sign language.* Mahwah, NJ: Lawrence Erlbaum.

Emmorey, K., & Reilly, J. (1998). The development of quotation and reported action: Conveying perspective in ASL. In E. Clark (Ed.), *The Proceedings of the Twenty-ninth Annual Child Language Research Forum* (pp. 81–90). Stanford, CA: CSLI Publications.

Emmorey, K., & Falgier, B. (1999). Talking about space with space: Describing environments in ASL. In E. A. Winston (Ed.), *Story telling and conversations: Discourse in Deaf communities* (pp. 3–26). Washington, DC: Gallaudet University Press.

Engberg-Pedersen, E. (1995). Point of view expressed through shifters. In K. Emmorey & J. Reilly (Eds.), *Language, gesture and space* (pp. 133–154). Cambridge: Lawrence Erlbaum.

Engberg-Pedersen, E. (2003). How composite is a fall? Adults' and children's descriptions of different types of falls in Danish Sign Language. In K. Emmorey (Ed.), *Perspectives on classifier constructions in sign language* (pp. 311–332). Mahwah, NJ: Erlbaum.

Gangel-Vasquez, J. (1997). *Literacy in Nicaraguan Sign Language: Assessing word recognition skills at the Escuelita de Bluefields.* Unpublished master's thesis, California State University. Dominguez Hills.

Gee, J., & Kegl, J. (1983). Narrative/story structure, pausing and American Sign Language. *Discourse Processes, 6,* 243–258.

Gillam, R., & Johnston, J. R. (1985). Development of print awareness in language-disordered preschoolers. *Journal of Speech and Hearing Research, 2*(8), 521–526.

Givón, T. (1983). *Topic continuity in discourse: An introduction.* Philadelphia: Benjamins.

Herman, R. (2003). *The development of a British Sign Language assessment battery.* Unpublished doctoral dissertation, City University London.

Herman, R., Grove, N., Holmes, S., Morgan, G., Sutherland, H. & Woll, B. (2004). *Assessing BSL development: Production Test (Narrative Skills).* London: City University Press.

Hoffmeister, R. (2000). A piece of the puzzle: ASL and reading comprehension in deaf children. In C. Chamberlain, J. Morford, & R. Mayberry (Eds.), *Language acquisition by eye* (pp. 143–163). Mahwah, NJ: Erlbaum.

Hudson, J. A., & Shapiro, C. R. (1991). From knowing to telling: The development of children's scripts, stories and personal narratives. In A. McCabe & C. Peterson (Eds.), *Developing narrative structure* (pp. 89–136). Hillsdale, NJ: Lawrence Erlbaum.

Kemper, S. (1984). The development of narrative skills: Explanations and entertainments. In S. Kuczaj (Ed.), *Discourse development: Progress in cognitive development research* (pp. 99–122). New York: Springer-Verlag.

Kuntze, M. (1998). Literacy and Deaf children: The language question. *Topics in Language Disorders, 18*(4), 1–15.

Kuntze, M. (2000). Codeswitching in ASL and written-English language contact. In K. Emmorey & H. Lane (Eds.), *Signs of language revisited: An anthology to honor Ursula Bellugi and Edward Klima* (pp. 287–302). Mahwah, NJ: Lawrence Erlbaum.

Lichtenstein, E. (1998). Reading in deaf children. *Journal of Deaf Studies, 3,* 1–55.

Lillo-Martin, D. (2002). Where are all the modality effects? In R. P. Meier, K. Cormier, & D. Quinto-Pozos (Eds.), *Modality and structure in signed and spoken language* (pp. 241–262). Cambridge: Cambridge University Press.

Loew, R. (1984). *Roles and reference in American Sign Language: A developmental perspective.* Unpublished doctoral dissertation, University of Minnesota. Rochester.

Mashie, S. (1995). *Educating deaf children bilingually.* Washington, DC: Gallaudet University, Pre-College Programs.

Mather, S., & Thibeault, A. (2000). Creating an involvement-focused style in book reading with deaf and hard of hearing students: The visual way. In

C. Chamberlain, J. Morford, & R. Mayberry (Eds.), *Language acquisition by eye* (pp. 191–219). Mahwah, NJ: Erlbaum.

Mayberry, R. (1992). The cognitive development of deaf children: recent insights. In S. Segalowitz & I. Rapin (Eds.), *Handbook of Neuropsychology* (Vol. 7, pp. 51–68). Oxford: Elsevier.

Mayberry, R., & Chamberlain, C. (1994, November). *How ya gonna read the language ifya don't speak it? Reading comprehension in relation to sign language comprehension.* Paper presented at the 19th Annual Conference on Language Development, Boston, MA.

Mayer, C., & Wells, G. (1996). Can the linguistic interdependence hypothesis theory support a bilingual-bicultural model of literacy education for deaf students? *Journal of Deaf Studies and Deaf Education, 1*(2), 93–107.

Mayer, M. (1969). *Frog where are you?* New York: Dial Press.

McCabe, A., & Peterson, C. (1990). What makes a narrative memorable? *Applied Psycholinguistics, 8,* 73–82.

Metzger, M. (1994). Constructed dialogue and constructed action in American Sign Language. In C. Lucas. (Ed.), *Sociolinguistics in Deaf communities* (pp. 255–271). Washington, DC: Galaudet University Press.

Miller, C. (1994). Simultaneous constructions and complex signs in Quebec Sign Language. in I. Ahlgren, B. Berman & M. Brennan (Eds.), *Perspectives on sign language usage* (pp. 131–148). Durham, UK: ISLA Press.

Morgan, G. (1998). *The development of discourse cohesion in British Sign Language.* Unpublished doctoral dissertation, University of Bristol.

Morgan, G. (1999). Event packaging in BSL discourse. In E. Winston (Ed.), *Story telling and conversation: discourse in Deaf communities* (pp. 27–58). Washington, DC: Galluadet Press.

Morgan, G. (2000). Discourse cohesion in sign and speech. *International Journal of Bilingualism, 4,* 279–300.

Morgan, G. (2002). The encoding of simultaneity in children's BSL narratives. *Journal of Sign Language and Linguistics, 5*(2), 127–161.

Morgan, G., & Woll, B. (2003). The development of reference switching encoded through body classifiers in British Sign Language. In K. Emmorey (Ed.), *Perspectives on classifier constructions in sign languages* (pp. 297–310). Mahwah, NJ: Lawrence Erlbaum.

Olson, D. R. (1994). *The world on paper: The conceptual and cognitive implications of writing and reading.* Cambridge: Cambridge University Press.

Peterson, C., Jesso, B., & McCabe, A. (1999). Encouraging narratives in preschoolers: An intervention study. *Journal of Child Language, 26,* 49–67.

Roy, C. (1989). Features of discourse in an American Sign Language lecture. In C. Lucas (Ed.), *The sociolinguistics of the Deaf community* (pp. 231–252). San Diego: Academic Press.

Silva, M. (1991). Simultaneity in children's narratives: the case of when, while and as. *Journal of Child Language, 18,* 641–662.

Singleton, J., Supalla, S., & Schley, S. (1998). From sign to word: Considering modality constraints in ASL/English bilingual education. *Topics in Language Disorders 18,* 16–29.

Slobin, D. (1996). From "thought to language" to "thinking for speaking." In J. Gumperz & S. Levinson (Eds.), *Studies in the social and cultural foundations of Language: Vol. 17. Rethinking linguistic relativity* (pp. 70–86). Cambridge: Cambridge University Press.

Sperber, D., & Wilson, D. (1995). *Relevance: Communication and cognition*(2nd ed.). Oxford: Blackwell.

Strong, M., & Prinz, P. (2000). Is American Sign Language skill related to English literacy? In C. Chamberlain, J. P. Morford, & R. Mayberry (Eds.), *Language acquisition by eye* (pp. 131–142). Mahwah, NJ: Lawrence Erlbaum.

Supalla, T. (1990). Serial verbs of motion in ASL. In S. Fischer & P. Siple (Eds.), *Theoretical issues in sign language research: Vol. 1. Linguistics* (pp. 127–152). Chicago: University of Chicago Press.

Sutton-Spence, R., & Woll, B. (1999). *The Linguistics of BSL: an introduction.* Cambridge: Cambridge University Press.

Valli, C. (1987). The nature of a line in ASL poetry. In W. Edmondson & F. Karlsson (Eds.), *International studies on sign language and communication of the Deaf* (Vol. 10, pp. 171–182), Hamburg: Signum.

van Hoek, K., Norman, F., & O'Grady-Batch, L. (1987). *Development of spatial and non-spatial referential cohesion.* Working paper, Salk institute.

Westby, C. (1998). Assessing and Facilitating test comprehension problems. In H. Catts & A. Kahmi (Eds.), *Language and reading disabilities* (pp. 154–222). Boston: Allyn & Bacon.

Wigglesworth, G. (1997). Children's individual approaches to the organization of narrative. *Journal of Child Language, 24,* 279–309.

Winston, E. (1995). Spatial mapping in comparative discourse frames. In K. Emmorey & J. Reilly (Eds.), *Language, gesture and space* (pp. 87–114). Cambridge: Lawrence Erlbaum.

# 14

# Natural Signed Language Acquisition Within the Social Context of the Classroom

*Jenny L. Singleton & Dianne D. Morgan*

*Deaf parents with deaf children may provide important insights*
*for hearing parents and early interventionists regarding optimal strategies for*
*communicating with a deaf infant.*

—Koester, Papoušek, & Smith-Gray (2000)

For many deaf children born to hearing parents, the best opportunity for learning a natural signed language will take place in their classroom, and the primary linguistic model will be their teacher. Some parents will be eager to learn sign language and will take courses to develop proficiency. Others may learn some basic sign vocabulary to support only a functional level of communication. Whether or not a deaf child has signing parents, when she engages in daily interactions with a highly proficient signing teacher, that natural signed language may become her primary language, and that teacher will likely become an important role model in the child's language development.

The notion that a classroom is a context for language acquisition has considerable theoretical importance. Whereas learning a second language from one's teacher and peers in the classroom setting is not uncommon in the United States (e.g., a Spanish-speaking recent immigrant who attends an English-as-a-second-language program in the United States), most children do not learn their *primary language* in schools from their teachers. While a research base of linguistic studies focusing on deaf children acquiring a natural signed language, such as American Sign Language (ASL), from their deaf parents has accumulated, little research has been conducted on the acquisition of natural signed languages by deaf children of hearing parents in the social context of the classroom.

The goals of this chapter are to first highlight some of the social and linguistic practices that have been observed in deaf parent/deaf child and hearing parent/deaf child family contexts. Our review is influenced by a sociocultural theoretical framework in which engage-ment and guided participation support a child's development of lan-guage and identity. Second, we review what is known about classroom interactions in early childhood and elementary school contexts. Third, we discuss some practical considerations with respect to teachers em-ulating deaf caregiver–deaf child practices and consider some of the obstacles that may challenge this potential approach. Finally, taking together all of the research findings reviewed on caregiver–infant and teacher–student interaction, we end with a discussion in which we pro-pose a new conceptualization of an educator of the deaf whose primary focus would be to guide and promote, through everyday practice, the bilingual and bicultural identity development of deaf children using communication strategies modeled upon effective family engagement.

## LANGUAGE AND IDENTITY DEVELOPMENT IN THE FAMILY CONTEXT: A THEORETICAL FRAMEWORK BASED ON ENGAGEMENT AND GUIDED PARTICIPATION

Children are born into an engagement system that enables them to acquire the important meaning-making practices of their family and supports their identity development through increasing participation as a member of their community (Rogoff, 1990, 2003). *Practices* are mean-ingful actions, including language and cultural behaviors, that are re-peated and "packaged with values and are part of a group's identity" (Miller & Goodnow, 1995, p. 6). Two general processes in this meaning-making system, *intersubjectivity* and *appropriation*, enable a child to en-gage mutually with the caregiver and to experiment with the meanings of practices. According to Rogoff (1990), intersubjectivity involves the sharing of attention and intentions in the communicative practices be-tween caregiver and child. As communication is likely to be asymmet-rical between adults (experts) and children (novices), intersubjectivity is achieved when adaptations and shifts in understanding occur on the part of both adult and child. When there is intersubjectivity, a mutual understanding has been reached, and learning can take place. In this theoretical framework, learning is characterized as a child's growth in their participation in interaction.

Appropriation happens as a part of further activity between child and caregiver; it is characterized by the child imitating, experimenting, or trying the practices. Rogoff (1990) maintains that intersubjectivity and appropriation are essential for the development and growth of a child and are primarily realized through everyday social exchanges with care-givers within joint activities. Appropriation is different from simply internalizing something that is external. Rather, appropriation is tak-ing in or trying on *some* of the meanings that occur in actions; that is, a child's capacity to appropriate is supported (or limited) by her own sense-making and developmental level of involvement. Therefore, the appropriated practices do not exactly mirror the external practices, and the caregiver provides supportive scaffolding for those as yet-unappropriated elements. Through a process of increasing mutual structuring of participation, a child develops a sense of belonging (identity) and shares in the everyday practices (or *ways of being*) of one's community of practice (Rogoff, 1990; Wenger, 1998). A *community of practice* can be a family, a neighborhood, a business, or a larger community. The key idea is that a group of "expert" participants (e.g., adults) shares a set of everyday practices, and they support the increased participation of "novices" (e.g., children) into the joint enterprise.

Also important is the concept of *nonparticipation*. Wenger (1998) argues that an individual's nonparticipation can be defined in terms of *eventual* participation, with the expectation that they are still learning and growing. Nonparticipation, framed as *legitimate peripherality*, is part of a trajectory toward full participation in a community of practice (Lave & Wenger, 1991). By contrast, Wenger (1998) describes another identity in which nonparticipation is restrictive and is negatively construed: *marginality*.

These identity notions are relevant to our discussion of deaf children. For example, caregivers and educators are likely to encounter contexts in which a deaf child does not seem to achieve intersubjectivity or appropriate new behaviors, meanings, or forms of language. One can view nonparticipation as marginality or peripherality. In the case of marginality, a child is seen as not fitting into the community of practice. For example, hearing parents may see that their deaf child is not appropriating hearing ways of being and thus see them as not fitting in (i.e., deficit or pathological view of deafness). With respect to peripherality, a child is expected to appropriate the practice at some point in the future, but for now, the child legitimately participates more as an observer. A deaf child will at some point be able to appropriate *Deaf ways of being*, if guided by Deaf adults who view them as eventual full participants in their community of practice (i.e., cultural view of deafness).

Caregivers engage in this socialization system in intuitive ways with their children, reflecting the same ways in which they were engaged in their own childhood (Papoušek & Papoušek, 1987). The intuitive and propagating nature of the engagement system usually ensures that the communicative modes of the caregiver and child are well matched. For example, hearing caregivers, who have been engaged as children using primarily spoken language with some simultaneous visual communication (looking at an object or pointing), will engage hearing children using this intuitive combination and priority of modes. A deaf caregiver, engaged using primarily visual communication (language and eye gaze patterns) throughout his or her life, will engage a deaf child in matching ways. As an illustration of the unfolding of this engagement system, we review studies comparing "matching" caregiver–child interactions (deaf/deaf and hearing/hearing) and "mismatching" interactions (hearing caregiver/deaf child).[1]

## Matching Engagement in Caregiver–Infant Interactions

In early infancy, deaf mothers and hearing mothers both appear sensitive and responsive to their deaf and hearing infants, respectively, in specific ways that likely facilitate the processes of intersubjectivity and appropriation (Meadow-Orlans & Spencer, 1996; see Spencer & Harris, chapter 4 this volume). Hearing mothers, for example, use a variety of complex speech patterns to heighten the responsiveness of their hearing infant such as varying melodic contours, pitch ranges, rhythms, and repetitions (Koester, Papoušek, & Smith-Gray, 2000; Spencer, Bodner-Johnson, & Gutfreund, 1992).

In contrast, deaf mothers use visual communicative strategies in response to a deaf infant's interaction needs (Koester, Karkowski, & Traci, 1998; Loots & Devise, 2003; Waxman & Spencer, 1997). For example, some researchers have found that when an infant's eye gaze is directed toward a deaf mother in shared face-to-face interaction, the mother responds with visual behaviors such as facial exaggerations, nodding, finger play, and gestures (Koester, Brooks, & Traci, 2000; Koester et al., 1998).

At around 9 months of age, human infants seem to experience a kind of revolution in the way that they understand the world and engage with others and objects (Tomasello, 1999). Before this revolution, between 6 and 9 months of age, infants will interact with objects and people dyadically. That is, infants engage with an object but ignore the person who is present, or engage with a person (shared face-to-face attention) and ignore the object that is present. When the complexity of the engagement system is increased, between 9 and 12 months of age, an infant can now interact with objects and people triadically, also referred to as *joint attention*. Joint attention requires the infant to coordinate his behaviors between himself, the object, and the caregiver (Bruner, 1981; Tomasello, 1999).

There are some interesting differences in the nature of these joint attention episodes between deaf/deaf and hearing/hearing dyads. Across several studies, deaf/deaf dyads have been found to spend more time than hearing/hearing dyads engaged in coordinated joint attention

---

[1] It is important to acknowledge one other "mismatching" family: Deaf parents with hearing children ("codas"). Singleton and Tittle (2000) review some of the key issues facing language and identity socialization in this kind of family configuration. In short, codas have the potential to develop an auditory or visually based system of engagement. One or both systems can be developed depending on the nature of early experiences.

during play interactions (Koester, Brooks, & Traci, 2000; Meadow-Orlans & Spencer, 1996; Spencer et al., 1992). This longer duration is likely due to the sequential nature of caregiver–child–object interactions in the deaf/deaf dyads. As a deaf infant looks at an object, a deaf mother often waits for her child to look back at her before responding using sign language. By contrast, a hearing mother can talk while her hearing infant looks at an object. This simultaneous (visual and auditory) pattern can result in shorter engagement duration in hearing/hearing dyads, at least when engagement is scored using looking time measures. Spencer (2000) reported finding slightly higher mean times for coordinated joint attention between deaf/deaf dyads and hearing/hearing dyads; however, this difference was not statistically significant. The key point is that both hearing/hearing and deaf/deaf dyads appear to be functioning smoothly in their caregiver–infant interaction, utilizing patterns of attention and language that match the modalities they are using.

Deaf mothers may also shorten the length of their utterances in order to compensate for a child's developing use of triadic eye gaze coordination (Spencer et al., 1992). Mohay (2000) argued that using shorter utterances may be a response to increased memory demands on a child related to the shifting of visual attention between object and caregiver. Deaf caregivers also produce a visual version of child-directed speech, producing sign language and facial expressions that are unique to adult–child communication (Erting, Prezioso, & Hynes, 1990; Holzrichter & Meier, 2000; Masataka, 2000).

Deaf mothers seem to know intuitively how to get their deaf child's attention using a visual language and physical behaviors. Several studies have shown that deaf mothers use developmentally appropriate attention-getting strategies for engaging their deaf infants, strategies that are coordinated with both their attending behaviors and language use (Spencer, 1993; Swisher, 2000; Waxman & Spencer, 1997; Waxman, Spencer, & Poisson, 1996). These strategies include moving the object so that it is within the child's visual field, tapping the child or object, using a form of child-directed language (but visual), and waving or hitting the floor. As the child becomes more mobile, repeated tapping is used not only to signal attention but also to train the child to be available to the mother's communication (Waxman et al., 1996). Not surprisingly, hearing mothers with hearing children primarily rely upon vocalizations and child-directed speech to gain their infant's attention, even if they also gesture and manipulate objects.

With preschool-age children, deaf and hearing mothers appear similar in that they both extend and elaborate their child's communication as they engage (see Spencer & Harris, chapter 4 this volume). Deaf children of deaf families and hearing children of hearing families at this age typically exhibit the ability to engage fully in meaning-making through their use of questioning, symbolic references, and abstractly conversing about their own self and others, whether or not the people are present (Meadow, Greenberg, Erting, & Carmichael, 1981).

To summarize, mothers in matching caregiver–child dyads intuitively adjust their linguistic and cultural practices to the needs of young children, toward achieving intersubjectivity. In general, they experience successful attunement, coordinated joint attention to objects and people, and a dynamic system of engagement in which caregivers make available for the child opportunities to observe and participate in the practices of their community. Through mutual structuring (child influences caregiver, caregiver influences child), a child participates and increasingly becomes a more competent and central member of the community of practice. Through everyday interactions, a child will naturally appropriate a language and cultural identity.

### Mismatching Engagement in Caregiver–Infant Interactions: Hearing Mothers and Deaf Infants

For a deaf child born into a hearing family, there are considerable challenges in providing interactions that are equivalent in quality to those described for the matching dyads above. This mismatch in the engagement process may negatively affect the child's development and may impede the parents' ability to engage their deaf child using their intuitive resources (Meadow-Orlans, 1997). This suggestion is generally supported by a number of studies investigating early childhood interactions between hearing mothers and their deaf infants. Before summarizing these studies, three caveats must be offered. First, it must be acknowledged that some studies utilize group averages of hearing parents' practices that may mask within-group differences. Second, age of hearing loss diagnosis can make a difference, as more recent reports of dyads with a diagnosis in early infancy present more positive interactive patterns for hearing caregivers and their deaf infants (see Spencer & Harris, chapter 4 this volume). Finally, the studies reported here are not meant to represent all hearing parents' engagement practices. Instead, these comparisons serve mainly to support an argument that there are distinctive visually oriented engagement practices that may not "come naturally" to some hearing caregivers. Practices such as those observed between deaf/deaf dyads help us to understand what a deaf infant may need in his or her caregiving environment.

In past studies, hearing mother–deaf infant dyads have been found to exhibit less coordinated joint attention (compared to matching dyads), and the mothers often attempted to start new, unrelated, activities that interrupted their deaf infant's attention (Meadow-Orlans & Spencer, 1996; Spencer et al., 1992). While, as a group, hearing mothers of deaf infants used more visual communication strategies than hearing mothers of hearing children, many hearing mothers continued to use speech as the dominant mode in their attempts to engage their deaf infant (Lederberg & Everhart, 1998). For example, hearing mothers tend to rely on vocalizations when trying to regain their deaf child's attention, and are often unsuccessful. Even when hearing mothers tried to use signs in these studies, their deaf children did not always visually attend (Koester et al., 1998; Waxman et al., 1996). In addition, Spencer et al. (1992) found that hearing mothers used more directing kinds of interaction with their deaf infant and often began responding before their deaf infant had made eye contact, demonstrating their difficulties in coordinating visual attention and language with their child.

As compared to matching dyads, deaf children's interactions with their hearing mothers could be characterized as having a lower proportion of child-initiated linguistic constructions (Jamieson, 1994), a higher proportion of nonelaborated responses by the mother, and a higher proportion of time in which the child ignores the mother (Lederberg & Everhart, 1998; Meadow et al., 1981; Waxman et al., 1996). For deaf children, this mismatch within the engagement system in early childhood has been linked to a later underdeveloped sense of self (Traci & Koester, 2003), learned powerlessness from parental directiveness (Schlesinger, 1987), and self-reported decreased mental health functioning in adolescence (Wallis, Musselman, & MacKay, 2004). Specifically, the Wallis et al. (2004) study found that signing deaf adolescents raised by hearing caregivers who did not sign to them in early childhood or adolescence (mismatching) reported significantly higher rates of externalizing mental health problems, such as delinquency and aggressive behaviors, compared to signing deaf adolescents whose hearing mothers signed with them in early childhood (matching). These researchers speculated that one reason for the adolescents' externalizing behavior may have been a response to communication frustration beginning in their early years (p. 11).

At a core developmental level, based on the theoretical frameworks established by Vygotsky (1978), Bruner (1983), and Rogoff (1990, 2003), the system of caregiver–child engagement plays an essential role in the normal development of language and cognition, and as such, children in mismatched dyads may not have interactions that adequately support the processes of intersubjectivity and appropriation (Kuntze, 1998, p. 11). Hearing parents tend to use fewer practices that adapt to the child's visual communication needs, and it should not be surprising that hearing individuals would intuitively engage deaf children using "hearing" ways of being, the way they were engaged in their own childhoods and the way they see modeled in their everyday world. Yet, a deaf child may struggle to appropriate hearing ways of being and is simultaneously lacking in opportunity to engage in a shared visually based system of engagement with other deaf individuals. Many hearing parents either do not seek out opportunities for their deaf children to engage with deaf adults or do not have easy access to observation of the practices of deaf parents who have deaf children. Although some early-intervention programs may recommend interaction with deaf adults, in practicality, socialization into visually based engagement practices is not likely to happen in early childhood.

There is some evidence that training can help hearing parents understand the visual learning needs of their deaf child and learn to use some of these visual engagement techniques used by deaf/deaf dyads. For example, Mohay (2000) individually observed a group of hearing mothers once a week and provided them with prompts (regarding their communication strategies) as they interacted with their deaf infants. After 6 weeks, postintervention observations showed that the mothers did not incorporate the recommended strategies into their own repertoires. In the second intervention, Mohay observed just one family for a period of almost 1 year. Mohay provided the family with instructional materials: a set of 10 videotapes each dealing with specific methods to make language more visually accessible and meaningful to the deaf child. In addition to the instructional materials, a deaf assistant visited the hearing family's home for 1 hour a week, providing additional demonstrations beyond the training videotapes. Postintervention videotaping of spontaneous parent–child interaction revealed that the hearing mother was effectively incorporating many of the strategies modeled by the deaf assistant and instructional materials. Mohay reported that the mother had greater success communicating with her deaf child.

While Mohay's findings are of great interest, the notion of training hearing parents to engage in more Deaf ways of being needs further exploration from both theoretical and practical standpoints. Alternatively (and possibly in addition to parent training), early childhood and school programs may serve as a viable context in which the development of a visually based system of engagement could be supported. This alternative is examined in the remainder of this chapter.

## TRANSITION FROM HOME TO SCHOOL

The transition from home to school is a significant change for any child. Several researchers have highlighted some of the key differences in the discourse patterns of home versus school "talk" (Cazden, 1988; Heath, 1986; Tattershall & Creaghead, 1985). They have suggested that children whose parents used a more "schoollike" discourse style at home transitioned into school discourse more easily than children whose parents did not. This style includes asking the child questions, expecting family members to talk one person at a time, using more decontextualized speech, and engaging regularly in home literacy activities.

While many children experience discourse challenges during this transition, they still enter school having experienced a meaningful system of engagement with their caregivers in which they have *learned how to learn.* That is, based on their early years of mutual structuring of participation with their caregiver(s), children will have developed basic understandings, such as communication with a child being *valued*, a child's participation being *guided or structured* by a more expert other, and a community of practice in which the child is becoming a member. The community has certain ways of being that the child easily appropriates (owing to a matching system of engagement).

Given the establishment of a mutual and visually based system of engagement with their caregivers, deaf children born to deaf parents could be characterized as *knowing how to learn* and are poised to make a successful transition from home to school. However, all of this presupposes a schoolteacher in the classroom who *knows how to teach*. As we discuss in the next section, several studies investigating interactions in classrooms with deaf children indicate that effective teacher–student engagement is not often attained.

## INTERACTIONS IN CLASSROOMS WITH DEAF CHILDREN

Our review focuses on a selected set of classroom investigations that highlight (1) the dynamics of conversational control and level of deaf student participation, (2) discourse processes supporting effective teaching and learning, (3) visual and linguistic teaching strategies that are argued to be especially effective with deaf (signing) learners, and (4) the classroom as a context for the socialization of language and identity. In these selected studies, the classrooms include only deaf students (i.e., they are not in "mainstream" or inclusion settings) and are mostly qualitative in their methodology (which is not uncommon in classroom discourse research).

We then separately address communication issues faced by deaf students who are mainstreamed into "inclusive classrooms" with regular education teachers. Some of these students rely upon sign language interpreters for access to adult and peer interactions. Several investigations into the nature of interpreter communication and mainstreamed deaf students' classroom engagement experiences also are discussed.

Our review focuses on early childhood and elementary age students– the age range of primary language acquisition. Young adults are not experiencing the same linguistic challenges that a child faces, and adults may have different language learning strategies available to them in the classroom context (for examples of secondary- and college-level deaf classroom discourse research, see Kluwin, 1983; Stinson & Liu, 1999; Stinson, Liu, Saur, & Long, 1996). Furthermore, the scope of our classroom discourse review focuses on teacher–student interaction, leaving out deaf children's communication with their peers. Peers surely play an important role in language acquisition in the classroom context, yet at the same time, language competence is critical for being able to successfully engage peers and developing meaningful social relationships (for reviews, see Antia & Kreimeyer, 2003; Kluwin, Stinson, & Colarossi, 2002). Because of the importance of peer interaction in a child's development, further research on this topic is needed, especially as recommendations for student placement and program design are considered.

## Conversation Control and Participation in Deaf Education Classrooms

David and Heather Wood and their colleagues extensively observed deaf children in British oral and simultaneous communication (speech combined with signed English) classrooms during the 1980s and 1990s (Wood & Wood, 1991, 1997; Wood, Wood, Griffiths, & Howarth, 1986; Wood, Wood, & Kingsmill, 1991). We focus primarily on their study involving simultaneous communication classes, as this is the situation closest to the predominant educational setting in the United States. Wood and Wood (1991) and Wood et al. (1991) videotaped nine teachers intermittently over a period of 3 years as they engaged with their deaf students in naturally occurring classroom activities. The 33 children involved were between the ages of 4 years 7 months (4;7) and 11;8. The teacher evaluation measures in this research focused on power, conversation repairs, pace, and complexity of language used. The child evaluation measures included initiative, misunderstandings, and loquacity (mean length of turn).

These researchers found that the teachers, all of whom were hearing, did most of the initiating and exerted considerable control over the conversation with their deaf students. Specifically, the teachers often made requests for the children to repeat themselves and had high frequencies of question asking, consequently controlling the content of discourse and narrowing what would be considered appropriate contributions from deaf students. In addition, the length of the turn-taking sequences was short, with only rare occasions of extended discourse occurring between teacher and student. Moreover, the grammatical complexity of "teacher talk" did not increase with the age of the deaf students in the classroom, as it has been shown with hearing students (Wood et al. 1991, p. 321).

Teachers who used this type of communication style more often had deaf students who seldom contributed to the topic of conversation, rarely exercised "listener control" (i.e., asking for clarification if they could not understand the teacher), and rarely added to what their peers had said. One way to characterize the teacher–student engagement patterns in these classrooms might be to frame them as therapeutic interactions directed by teachers whose goals focused more on speech accuracy and auditory awareness than on meaningful and contingent conversation.

Erting has conducted several studies of teacher (or adult) interactions with deaf preschool children in the United States. In one study, Erting (1988) documented classroom interactions involving a hearing teacher, who primarily used simultaneous communication (but sometimes included ASL features in her discourse), and a deaf adult, both of whom interacted with three deaf preschool students using ASL and English (through varying representational forms). Erting found that the hearing teacher frequently asked children to repeat themselves and to use their voices while signing, and she often began signing before all the children were attending. In contrast, the deaf adult responded to the meaning of the children's utterances, rather than the form, and never commented on their use of voice. The deaf adult used visual and tactile signals to ensure that she had children's visual attention before she signed. In another study, Erting (1980) described how a deaf classroom aide averaged longer interactions (3 turns) with the preschool children than the hearing teacher (1.6 turns).

What is interesting about Erting's early research is her suggestion that the deaf adults in these studies used more effective and meaningful communication practices with deaf students compared to the hearing teachers she observed. Furthermore, these deaf/deaf classroom engagement patterns are strikingly different from the *therapeutic* teacher–student patterns reported by Wood and colleagues.

In the two decades that have followed these investigations, researchers have refined their questions regarding what constitutes teaching effectiveness and have begun to examine factors such as sign language proficiency and instructional discourse strategies (e.g., dialogic inquiry). With an increase in the number of deaf education programs adopting a bilingual/bicultural philosophy,[2] there has also been a growing interest in the roles and interactions of signed and spoken language in the classroom and in identifying and understanding the significance of visual and linguistic strategies that may be unique to classroom contexts with deaf, sign-language–using students.

---

[2] The bilingual/bicultural educational movement, begun in the early 1990s, offers a classroom environment in which deaf children are taught using a natural signed language, and spoken language is approached as a second language, recognizing the unique accessibility issues faced by deaf learners. Some European countries have taken this approach (e.g., Sweden), and in the United States, LaSasso and Lollis (2003) report that 24% of the residential schools they surveyed had adopted a bilingual philosophy, using ASL as the primary language of instruction. Most mainstream settings do not offer an ASL or a bilingual approach to deaf students in public schools. As examples, Schick et al. (2000) reported that less than 2% of the mainstream educational interpreters they evaluated, and Jones, Clark, and Stoltz (1997) found that 2.8% of the interpreters they surveyed used ASL in their practice.

These recent studies also reflect a shift in theoretical approach, following the trends taking place more generally in educational research of this period. That is, teaching and learning processes are now being examined from within a sociocultural (e.g., Vygotskian) framework, and effective teacher–student discourse practices are viewed as critical for the *joint* construction of knowledge (see Rogoff, 1990). More specifically, students are viewed as active participants in classroom discourse, and they should be given the opportunity to discuss meaningful and relevant problems. Teachers are considered to be guides who are contingently responsive to the needs of the learner and who scaffold their participation in the social process of learning (for overviews of this framework, see Cazden, 1988; Forman, Minick, & Stone, 1993; Moll, 1990).

## Teacher–Student Discourse and Dialogic Inquiry

Mayer, Akamatsu, and Stewart (2002) proposed a model for effective teaching practice with students who are deaf that focuses less on teacher sign proficiency or particular communication method employed and more on the processes of teacher—student discourse. Specifically, Mayer et al. proposed that effective teaching requires engaging in dialogic inquiry (in a Vygotskian sense). This approach frames teaching and learning as a collaborative enterprise, with teachers engaging students in active and joint construction of knowledge, solving problems, and answering questions that are meaningful. In their qualitative study, Mayer et al. videotaped 10 teachers of the deaf who were nominated by their supervisors as "exemplary." All were certified educators of the deaf, had a minimum of 5 years of teaching experience, and had advanced levels of sign proficiency in ASL or English-based sign communication. The teachers were videotaped over a 2-year period and were sampled across grade levels from kindergarten to high school, including both residential schools and public school self-contained classroom settings.

Mayer et al. (2002) identified exemplars of dialogic inquiry used by these teachers, regardless of the particular method of communication during their interaction. They reported examples of teacher–student exchanges in which participants were contingently responsive with each other. Their main point was that sign proficiency alone does not result in teaching effectiveness. A dialogic inquiry approach requires that teachers let the conversation influence the nature of the communication used, and rather than taking the role as "teller" who dictates knowledge to the students, teachers should guide students in their construction of knowledge. Nevertheless, communication proficiency does play an important role in dialogic inquiry as Mayer et al. (2002) suggest that "teachers who are comfortable in their manner of communicating will be better able to engage in dialogic inquiry because they will not be hindered by their own attempts to convey meaning in the language or code most suitable to their student and the pedagogical goals of the lesson" (p. 501). Some children will require a particularly skillful adult to scaffold interactions and to understand their communication intentions, which may not be grammatically well-structured or clear. Without such skill, teachers may be inclined to resign their efforts and turn to a "knowledge-telling" model of practice (p. 499).

## Unique Visual and Linguistic Strategies

There are researchers who contend that a teacher's proficiency in a natural signed language, such as ASL, and the use of particular linguistic and visual teaching strategies in the classroom, are *essential* to effective teaching practice with students who are deaf. The strategies described are reminiscent of some of the matching caregiver–infant interaction patterns discussed above.

Mather has conducted several investigations that describe teacher–student interactions in deaf classrooms (Mather, 1987, 1989, 1990). In this set of qualitative studies, Mather compared two teachers, one native signer of ASL (deaf) and one skilled nonnative signer (hearing), as they engaged a group of deaf preschool students, discussing a book that the teacher had already read to the class. Mather concluded that eye gaze patterns reflect visually oriented teaching strategies that support student's understanding of the dynamic discourse that occurs in classrooms. She argued that only the deaf native-signing teacher managed his eye gaze to direct children's attention to who was speaking. For example, the deaf teacher directed his eye gaze at an individual student when that student was expected to answer the question. When he was addressing a question to all of the students, and any student could respond, the teacher used an eye gaze pattern that was arclike and constantly moving. In contrast, Mather found that the nonnative-signing hearing teacher mixed her individual and group eye gaze patterns, resulting in some students not being sure whether they were supposed to respond.

Similar to the classroom discourse patterns reported by Erting (1988), Mather (1989) also found that the hearing teacher sometimes began signing before all the children were attending, whereas the deaf teacher was sensitive to the visual requirements of the deaf students and would regularly check on the status of the students' visual attention and sign READY? before proceeding to sign. Mather reported that the deaf teacher more typically asked the group a question first and then, after a student responded, asked follow-up questions with individuals. For students who answered incorrectly, the deaf teacher provided more clues and persisted with modified questions and discussion (i.e., scaffolding) until the struggling student could engage at his or her level of understanding. The deaf teacher more often asked questions that required students to participate and think actively in a discussion (e.g., "What happened?").

The hearing teacher asked questions that typically required a yes/no answer or asked for specific information (e.g., "What is the title?"). Mather found that in the one episode she analyzed (time length of this interaction was not reported), the deaf teacher asked 41 questions, all of which were eventually answered by the students. The hearing teacher asked nine questions, only two of which were answered by the students.

Mather (1989) also documented some linguistic strategies that seemed to take advantage of the rich narrative features inherent in ASL. For example, the deaf teacher engaged in role play, used many ASL classifier predicates, positioned himself at the toddler's eye gaze level for ease of perception, and produced "miniature signs" near or on the book to visibly connect the pictures to sign concepts, all of which were strategies rarely used by the hearing teacher.

Mather (1987, 1989) did not collect specific outcome measures of student learning in these qualitative studies; rather, her aim was to identify the visual and evocative teaching strategies used by deaf teachers who have high ASL proficiency and extensive personal experience as visual learners. And, it should be acknowledged that Mather selected this deaf teacher because he was considered to be a master teacher.

It is interesting to note that Mather focuses her research interpretations more on the issue of language proficiency (native vs. nonnative) rather than the hearing status of the teacher (deaf vs. hearing). She suggests that the hearing teacher she observed could learn these visually oriented and evocative teaching strategies provided that she attained a high level of ASL proficiency (Mather, 1987, 1989, p. 187). We also would add that it is important not to assume that any deaf teacher would necessarily use all of these linguistically rich and engaging discourse techniques in their practice. Similarly, not all hearing teachers fail to include visually oriented strategies.

Paired with an effective teacher, deaf children of deaf parents may provide us with insights into how successful visually based engagement could take place in a classroom with deaf students. In a qualitative study, Ramsey and Padden (1998) described a fourth-grade classroom led by a deaf teacher and analyzed how the teacher and students coordinated language and attention within a mixed classroom of what they term *natives* (deaf children born to deaf parents) and *newcomers* (deaf children born to hearing parents). They present one compelling observation of the complex visual coordination of a deaf child of deaf parents. Coming from a home where parent signed communication is embedded within the interests of everyday life, this child not only had been brought up to know where to look to get essential linguistic information, but also was expertly attuned to the timing patterns of the shifts of eye gaze between sources of information (e.g., objects, printed material, other people) and the person who was providing linguistic information about those sources. In short, this child was ready to engage with her teacher from her first day of school and knew how to construct new meanings (i.e., learn) based on her interactions and participation in the classroom context.

Ramsey and Padden (1998) also portrayed the contrasting example of a newcomer, a deaf child of hearing parents who had not had much success engaging in interaction in his previous school setting. He was a fairly recent arrival to the classroom, as well as new to interacting with deaf adults. The engagement patterns this child experienced could be characterized as disconnected and chaotic. He looked at the teacher's signing, then to his paper in front of him, but spent too much time with his eye gaze directed toward the paper. Once he looked up again, the teacher was already in mid-sentence and he had missed critical information. In a footnote, Ramsey and Padden remarked that in their follow-up visit to this school 3 years later, this particular student had made significant progress and showed great improvement in his visual/ attentional coordination and engagement.

### Classroom Socialization of Language and Identity: The Importance of Deaf Role Models

Earlier in this chapter, we presented a sociocultural framework theorizing how children engage with their caregivers, attain intersubjectivity, and appropriate certain ways of being as they are socialized (through language, action, and participation) into their communities of practice (Rogoff, 1990, 2003; Wenger, 1998). It would therefore be interesting to consider how the context of the deaf education classroom may create opportunities for a child to develop ways of being that are consistent with being a visual communicator and consistent with a trajectory toward full participation in a Deaf bilingual community of practice.

Historically, when the majority of deaf children in the United States were educated in residential schools, they were socialized into the Deaf community primarily through naturally occurring interactions in the dormitories with deaf children from deaf families and deaf adults working on the campus (Padden & Humphries, 1988). Since the 1970s, however, fewer deaf children stay as boarding students at residential schools due to the increased mainstreaming of deaf students into regular education classrooms in their local school districts. As a consequence, this historical mode of cultural and linguistic transmission is now diminishing (Padden, 1996a). Furthermore, the changing structure of deaf education has resulted in fewer deaf teachers being employed and thus fewer opportunities for a deaf child to have contact with deaf adults (Lou, 1988; Marschark, 1997). Yet, in spite of these diminishing opportunities, there are several key studies that address the importance of deaf role models in the schooling experiences of young deaf children and examine how deaf teachers may engage deaf students in visually oriented and meaningful ways.

Erting (1980) emphasized the special multiple roles of the deaf aide in the preschool classroom she studied. For example, the aide supported the students by correcting their "babysigns" (misarticulated signs produced by the children) and modeled standard signs when a child produced "homesign" or a gesture to express their ideas. The deaf aide supported the hearing teacher with whom she worked by helping her to understand some of the children's signing by "interpreting" and also was a resource ("a sign language authority") for the teacher when she was unsure of a sign for a particular concept. Moreover, not being officially responsible for English instruction in the classroom, the deaf aide was liberated to simply engage the preschoolers in natural and contingently responsive ways. However, Erting did report that this deaf aide did model some English to the preschoolers, using strategies that we describe later in this chapter with respect to bilingualism.

Another critical role for culturally Deaf teachers is that of providing a learning environment that enhances deaf students' opportunities to understand what it means *to be Deaf,* leading to the students' potential appropriation of such practices. Findings from our own research (Morgan, 2004; Singleton & Morgan, 2004), in which we observed and videotaped three deaf teachers engaged in their everyday classroom activities in an ASL-using bilingual/bicultural preschool, suggest that deaf teachers explicitly express through their everyday narratives what it means to be Deaf, and they demonstrate how to interact effectively with hearing people as a bilingual/bicultural individual.

In one example, a deaf teacher and a five-year-old deaf child are looking at a book together in a comfortable corner of the classroom. The child spontaneously decides to pick up a toy telephone on the table next to her. The child holds the handset to her ear as she no doubt has seen her hearing parents engage in this activity. After the teacher asks her several questions in ASL (e.g., Who is on the phone? What are they saying?), the child then hands the phone to the teacher. The teacher shakes her head "No" and responds in ASL, "I can't hear, I use this (and she grabs a TTY on the table)."[3] The teacher then begins a pretend play interaction where she *calls* the child's hearing parent on the TTY, signing *out loud* what she is typing (description and translation of videotaped example from Singleton & Morgan, 2004).

Through her discourse and actions, this teacher modeled her solution to the using-the-telephone obstacle and demonstrated that she can

---

[3] A TTY is a device that connects to a telephone and allows a typed conversation.

successfully exchange information with the child's hearing parents using the TTY. Later in this episode, the child brought the TTY to her own lap and continued the pretend play, trying to make her own TTY call to her parents. Applying Rogoff's (1990, 2003) notions to this interaction, the teacher was structuring the situation, supporting the child's participation and understanding of what it means to be Deaf through a natural, responsive style of engagement.

The deaf teachers in our study also made comments to the preschoolers about everyday activities in their lives—comments that did not necessarily highlight deafness. What may seem mundane conversation to some was exactly the kind of "everyday talk" that many deaf children of hearing parents lack in their home settings. For example, during one observation, a teacher was playing an interactive game with two children during a free choice activity time in the classroom. One 5-year-old child, who has hearing parents, pointed to a bracelet on the teacher's wrist with her eyebrows raised in a surprised expression. The teacher then signed (in ASL):

> "Oh! My new bracelet! Isn't it pretty? A few days ago I was shopping, [begin role play shopping] just looking around, when I spotted this beautiful bracelet. I said "COOL!", so I bought it [end role play], and now I'm wearing it! See the swirl design and beads? Isn't it pretty?" (description and translation of videotaped example from Singleton & Morgan, 2004).

The teacher responded to the child's curiosity with a narrative that detailed not only how she acquired the bracelet but, through role play, also revealed an emotional component of what it is like to discover something wonderful. Thus, the adult, influenced by the child's initiation, is using a culturally meaningful practice, narration, to reference her actions and reactions. This type of everyday narrative supports meaning-making for the child (Miller & Goodnow, 1995; Rogoff, 1990, 2003).

### Teacher–Student Interactions in Inclusive Classroom Settings

A majority of students with hearing loss in the United States are now being educated in public schools with hearing children (including regular education classrooms, resource rooms, and self-contained classrooms; Karchmer & Mitchell, 2003). A growing number of these students rely upon educational interpreters and other support staff. In Schick, Williams, and Bolster's (2000) study, 93% of the 59 educational sign language interpreters they surveyed reported that they predominantly used a manual code for English (73%) or some form of pidgin Sign English (20%) in their practice.

In theory, an educational interpreter conveys everything a regular education teacher says to her students, and everything the students in the classroom say. However, in practice, an interpreter makes decisions about what speech in the classroom environment will be interpreted (Cawthon, 2001). According to Ramsey (1997), selections, deletions, and breakdowns occur in the translation process because "the spoken discourse and the bidding for and distribution of turns outpaces the interpreted version" (p. 61). Furthermore, an educational interpreter tends to have an expanded role compared to interpreters in other settings. Educational interpreters tend to be more "instructional" in their translations. For example, they may repeat or rephrase the hearing teacher's statements if they feel the deaf student has not understood or needs content accommodation. They also might comment on the deaf child's classroom behavior. Cawthon (2001) found that the two educational interpreters in her qualitative study of a kindergarten/first grade classroom (seven deaf and nine hearing students) and a second/third-grade classroom (2 deaf students and 12 hearing students) also played a supporting role to the hearing students in the classroom, guiding their behavior and responding to their requests for assistance when the regular teacher was attending to another student.

Based on her comparison of a group of second grade deaf students who divided their school day attending both self-contained and mainstreamed classrooms, Ramsey (1997) suggested that "an interpreted education is very unlike interacting directly with a teacher, and the deaf children were naturally less engaged in the mainstreaming classroom than they were in the self-contained classroom" (p. 61). Cawthon (2001) reported that the two hearing teachers in her study directed fewer interactions toward the deaf students in the class, as compared to the hearing students. Similarly, the hearing teacher in Ramsey's study expressed discomfort that the deaf students' eyes were not trained on her; instead, they were looking at the interpreter. She found it hard to engage the deaf students without experiencing direct eye contact. The teacher also felt that on many occasions she had to alter the pace and organization of her talk to accommodate the interpreting situation. Ramsey also stated that it was understandably difficult for the second-grade deaf children she observed to keep their attention fully toward the educational interpreter for extended periods, simply due to developmental limitations on their attention span. Consequently, an educational interpreter often has to deal with fatigued children and must find ways to accommodate what they missed when they averted their eye gaze.

Finally, of great concern is the fact that many educational interpreters have inadequate sign language and interpreting skills and lack professional training specific to children. For example, Schick et al. (2000) conducted comprehensive evaluations of 59 educational interpreters and found that 56% of those assessed did not possess the minimal skills sufficient to serve as an interpreter in the classroom. In this study, minimal skill was defined as "intermediate" and conformed to the skill level established by several states for interpreting in a classroom setting. Moreover, Schick et al. believed that their findings most likely underestimated the percentage of inadequate educational interpreters because the assessment was voluntary; presumably some individuals with extremely low interpreting skills might not volunteer to be assessed for a research study perhaps out of fears about criticism and job security.

Taken together, what appear to often be lacking between a regular education hearing teacher, an educational interpreter, and a deaf child are the processes of shared participation, contingent exchanges, and negotiated meaning-making using a natural language. This situation will differ, of course, depending upon the language skills and preferred language mode(s) of an individual child, the skill and personal understanding of "role" of an individual interpreter, and other aspects of specific classroom contexts. Because information to date is based on limited numbers of observations, it should not be generalized; however, this is an area in special need of additional research.

## PRACTICAL CONSIDERATIONS REGARDING NATURAL SIGNED LANGUAGE ACQUISITION IN THE CLASSROOM

We propose an alternative conceptualization of an educator of the deaf whose primary function is to guide deaf children's development toward the aims of native or near-native natural signed language proficiency and full participation in an ASL/English bilingual community. Given the constraints of the educational interpreter situation summarized above, we are currently unable to see how these aims could be fully achieved by a deaf child with limited language proficiency who is integrated into a mainstream classroom. It may be that this new kind of educator could support deaf children within different kinds of educational placements; however, the context that seems most compatible with this model is one where deaf children would be educated together, in a "natural language immersion" kind of setting for a considerable portion of each day, and where they would have significant exposure to deaf adults in their educational experience.

We begin exploring this new conceptualization by considering how a teacher could engage his/her deaf students, emulating deaf caregiver language socialization practices, including visual attunement, rich exposure to a natural signed language, and meaningful bridging to multiple (and visually accessible) representations of a spoken language (for a discussion of Deaf-informed indigenous classroom practices, see Humphries, 2004). Moreover, the fact that a classroom has more participants than the caregiver–infant context makes the interactions more complex and may therefore necessitate different engagement strategies for the learner than the home setting requires. We also consider cultural identity issues as these are deeply connected to language development and the context of Deaf and hearing "worlds."

## Visual Attunement Considerations

Just as with caregiver–infant dyads, one-to-one interactions between teacher and deaf student require establishing a visual connection. For example, a teacher may kneel down to get within a small child's visual field to increase the child's chance of attuning to the teacher's signing. And, when a child's eye gaze shifting is not yet fully coordinated, and he or she consequently misses the teacher's signed comment, the teacher may have to repeat the utterance, or hold their signing until the child is looking. One could view the child's lack of eye gaze coordination in a negative light, by characterizing the child as easily distractible and not paying attention (i.e., a deficit model), or one could view this as a developmental issue and characterize the child as a *peripheral* (yet moving toward fully participating) member of the community of practice who is still appropriating the skills of knowing where to look for linguistic input (Singleton & Morgan, 2004; Wenger, 1998). Like caregivers, teachers could also produce their signing very close to the object being discussed in order to facilitate the child's development of eye gaze coordination.

Attention should also be given to the physical layout and visual organization of the classroom. Each deaf student needs a direct line of sight to the teacher. When multiple classmates are participating in a discussion, it is helpful if the teacher points or uses a "LOOK-over there" sign to mark which individual has the conversational turn (i.e., to "direct the visual and linguistic traffic"). Visual displays (e.g., a calendar or a writing board) need to be situated close to the teacher so that when children look to the display, they can still see the teacher's signing within their field of view or with a minor shift in eye gaze direction. If taking in the visual display requires extended looking time, then the teacher needs to pause her signing so as not to present conflicting visual source demands to the child. Exciting new educational technologies such as SMART boards and LCD or overhead projectors can also support proximal visual displays (for a full set of recommendations generated from the Star Schools Project, see Nover, Andrews, Baker, Everhart, & Bradford, 2002).

As evident from the studies conducted by Mather (1987, 1989) and Ramsey (1997), the development of an effective system of visual engagement becomes even more complicated as multiple sources of information require a child's attention, often without clear onset signals. For example, several students could be signing all at once. Thus, a teacher will likely play an important role in scaffolding the visual detection skills necessary to see who is talking and to know when the "floor" is available for the taking. Structuring and guiding children's participation will also be a more complex task for the teacher as he or she handles multiple children each at different points along a trajectory toward developing an effective system of engagement and participation.

## Exposure to Natural Signed Language

When using a natural signed language, such as ASL, in an early childhood or elementary school classroom, a teacher may emulate caregiver language practices such as a "motherese" register and expansions and elaborations of a child's utterances (for discussions of such practices with deaf caregiver–deaf infant dyads, see Erting et al., 1990; Holzrichter & Meier, 2000; Masataka, 2000). Mather (1987, 1989, 1990) and Singleton and Morgan (2004) both described how an ASL-proficient deaf teacher often capitalized on ASL's rich grammatical and narrative structures such as role play, classifiers, and facial expression to engage their preschool students. The key is that a teacher's talk, unlike the classroom language practices observed by Wood and his colleagues (Wood & Wood, 1991, 1997; Wood et al. 1986, 1991), should be *contingently responsive* and become more linguistically complex as the child develops.

Another important classroom objective is to expose deaf students to complex meanings through "everyday talk," as was shown in Singleton and Morgan's (2004) example of a teacher discussing with her student how she acquired her new bracelet and the feelings connected with her discovery. Through narratives, teachers can share real-world experiences and hypothetical situations and analyze complex situations with their students. It is important to emphasize that this kind of rich exposure is not accomplished by having an ASL storyteller visit a classroom on a weekly basis; this kind of meaning-making should be jointly constructed in virtually every conversation held between teacher and student.

## Toward a Bilingual Self

In addition to primary linguistic competence, it is important to begin building concepts of bilingualism/biculturalism early on because most deaf children are members of hearing families and all deaf children are living within a predominantly hearing society whose members are not proficient in signed language. The notions of bilingualism and biculturalism are complex when considering a deaf individual's development of signed and spoken language proficiency and their identity relationship with Deaf and hearing worlds or cultures. Padden (1996a) describes the term "bicultural" in the deaf and hearing context as "not to be competent in two cultures, as bilingualism is to be competent in two languages..., but to negotiate tensions between competing and profoundly contradictory beliefs, lives, and activities, those that are embedded in the lives of hearing people on one hand and those of Deaf people on the other" (p. 87). Thus, it makes sense to gather expertise from Deaf adults, who are experienced visual communicators, to understand *how to be Deaf in a hearing world* and how to negotiate tensions to become a proficient user of the dominant language within that hearing society.

One group of "experts," bilingual deaf adults, has been studied by Padden (1996b) and Erting, Thumann-Prezioso, and Sonnenstrahl Benedict (2000). These researchers have discussed the different ways that culturally Deaf parents model English to their Deaf children through the use of various forms of English embedded in naturally occurring ASL-based discourse. Indeed, some studies have suggested that deaf children born to deaf parents generally attain higher levels of English proficiency than do deaf children born to hearing parents (for a review, see Israelite, Ewoldt, & Hoffmeister, 1992), although some researchers contend that this assertion may not be grounded by the strongest of empirical studies (Marschark, Lang, & Albertini, 2002). Some examples of bilingual discourse strategies observed in ASL-using deaf families include code switching, fingerspelling, and chaining/sandwiching in which multiple representations (signing, fingerspelling, pointing to object) of the same meaning are produced sequentially in the same utterance (Blumenthal-Kelly, 1995; Erting et al., 2000). In their case study, Erting et al. (2000) documented that the deaf parents they observed began fingerspelling to their deaf infants even as young as 5 weeks of age. In this family, child production of fingerspelling, in "scribble spelling" attempts, was documented as young as age 1;6.

Classroom studies have documented deaf teachers using some of these bilingual discourse strategies as well. For example, Erting's (1980) study described how the deaf aide used contrastive ("chaining"-like) examples to highlight to her students how ASL and English were different. Padden (1996a) observed that one deaf teacher in a bilingual/bicultural program used fingerspelling (plus a facial expression of puzzlement) as a discourse device to distance a particular word, "funnel," to set it up as an unknown term, something for the class to consider and discuss. Another strategy used by this teacher was "linking." The teacher showed the students a box of baking soda, fingerspelled it, and then linked this box to the fact that perhaps they may have this same box at home in their refrigerator to absorb odors (p. 91). The deaf teacher skillfully switched between ASL signing, fingerspelling, and pointing to printed text, all to demonstrate equivalences across these multiple representations. "The teacher plays the role of modeling a bicultural life, showing how to link the parts together and how to understand them relative to one another . . . she teaches students how to understand English, science, and other practices of the larger society" (Padden, 1996b, p. 94).

Padden and Ramsey (1998, 2000) found that the three deaf teachers they observed used twice as much fingerspelling as did four hearing teachers (although hearing teachers working in residential school settings fingerspelled more than those working in public school settings). The deaf teachers predominantly used fingerspelling within a string or a chain of equivalent structures including print and signed forms. This chaining technique "seems to be a process for emphasizing, highlighting, objectifying, and generally calling attention to equivalences across texts and languages" (Padden & Ramsey, 1998, p. 40).

In our study (Singleton & Morgan, 2004), the three preschool deaf teachers we observed also appeared to be promoting a *bilingual self* and modeled to their students strategies for communicating with hearing individuals through ASL and through multiple modes of English (primarily through fingerspelling and print English). For example, one teacher reported to us that when she took her preschool students on a field trip and interacted with hearing individuals (e.g., a tour guide at a museum), she explicitly told her students how she planned to communicate (e.g., use paper to write back and forth or communicate through an interpreter), and she also "interpreted back into ASL" any statements that were rendered in English that might not have been fully accessible to these preschool-age children.

These kinds of explicit comments regarding representational forms of English, the production of contrastive examples of ASL and English, and the chaining of equivalent forms in classroom discourse serve to raise children's levels of metalinguistic awareness (i.e., knowing and thinking about the two languages in their lives). Nevertheless, Nover, Christensen, and Cheng (1998) argued that further research is needed regarding how ASL/English bilingual teachers engage in code-switching and whether certain discourse strategies might be particularly effective for students of different age levels.

## CHALLENGES FOR NATURAL SIGNED LANGUAGE ACQUISITION IN THE CLASSROOM

We must recognize that there are certain aspects of a classroom setting that clearly distinguish it from a family setting and that these features may require that we consider natural language and identity socialization in classrooms with deaf children as a special process of its own. First, there are far fewer opportunities for one-to-one interactions in classrooms, as compared to what occurs in a caregiver–child context. Second, perhaps we place too much emphasis on the teacher as the primary linguistic and socialization partner. Other deaf peers surely play an important role in this process. Would a critical mass of deaf students be important for successful language and identity development? For example, would it be advisable to recommend a minimum of five deaf students per program? How important is it that deaf children of hearing parents interact with deaf children of deaf parents to optimally develop a *bilingual and culturally competent* identity?

We also face the reality that in deaf education settings, we must still be prepared to engage older children who enter an immersion or bilingual program after having experienced several years of failure to thrive in their previous educational placements. Is there a limited window of opportunity, or a critical period, in which we can successfully engage a deaf child visually and linguistically? Can teachers make up for the experiential and linguistic deprivation that some deaf children have endured? And, what about identity? Is it an educator's primary objective to support the development of a *Deaf self* when that deaf child is being raised in a hearing family? What about supporting the child's appropriation of some elements of their hearing family's ways of being?

These questions are not simple to answer. Each deaf child and his or her family is unique in that they have some existing system of engagement (even if inadequate) and certain choices to make in terms of what linguistic, educational, and social opportunities the parents will deem appropriate for their deaf child. Adding to this uniqueness, we must not neglect the other communities of practice in which a deaf child participates (e.g., racial and ethnic identity, social and economic class, and geographical context [urban, suburban, rural]).

## IMPLICATIONS FOR TEACHER EDUCATION

In this new conceptualization, an educator of the deaf creates an instructional context that aims to build visual attunement, emotional understanding and competence, proficiency in a natural signed language supported primarily through engagement in "everyday talk" and some explicit instruction, and competence in multiple modes of English that are accessible to a visually oriented learner. This immersion approach includes teacher modeling and structuring of the child's development of linguistic and sociocultural competence in their worlds (both hearing and Deaf). An important message to convey is that educational placement should not be perceived as tracking a child into either "a Deaf world" or a "hearing world." If teachers in all educational settings aimed toward developing a deaf child's bilingual/bicultural competence, then that child would be equipped to negotiate his way successfully in both worlds, or at least possess the linguistic and cognitive competence to make his own decision about identity group participation.

This bilingual/culturally competent model raises an important, and perhaps somewhat controversial, issue. Are Deaf adults the individuals most qualified to support the linguistic and cultural development of a deaf child? Borrowing from Rogoff's (1990) framework of guided participation, we would contend that Deaf individuals would certainly have a primary role in the education and socialization of young deaf children. Recall that Rogoff argued that through everyday practice, adults (experts) guide children (novices) into increased participation in their community of practice. Deaf adults' expertise is based upon a lifetime of experience validating and affirming their visual culture and navigating their way in a "hearing world" (Johnson & Erting, 1989; Padden, 1996a).

However, with changes in the professional preparation of educators of the deaf, could a hearing teacher increase his or her knowledge and skills to more effectively engage a deaf preschooler both visually and linguistically? Recall that Mather (1989) suggested this might be accomplished provided a hearing teacher began with a high level of ASL proficiency. Mohay's (2000) research with hearing mothers suggested that working with a deaf mentor who models such engagement strategies may be important as we consider different approaches to professional development.

Deaf education professional preparation programs could include activities in which hearing preservice teachers: (1) engage in reflective analysis of their own hearing ways of being and how that affects their teaching practice, (2) observe and reflect on the practices of deaf teachers, and (3) design a rationale and implementation plan for collaboration with deaf teachers and/or paraprofessionals. Hearing teachers with high proficiency in ASL may be able to learn to appreciate and respond to the visual and linguistic needs of a deaf child. For example, according to the admissions web page for University of California San Diego's master's degree program in "Deaf Education with a Bilingual Emphasis," the program "recognizes that deaf and hard of hearing children need teachers who are themselves bilingual and knowledgeable about the role of culture in human development." The program also requires ASL fluency to gain admission. Such professional knowledge and competencies would surely enhance a deaf or hearing teacher's effectiveness in their teaching practice (Humphries, 2004a).

But most important, a hearing teacher cannot, and should not, speak to what it is like *to be Deaf*. One might therefore suggest a team-teaching approach, pairing up every hearing teacher with a Deaf teacher who could serve as a role model to the students. Unfortunately, this is probably an impractical solution, as Allen and Karchmer (1990) have estimated that approximately 20% of educators working in residential schools and only 1% of teachers working in nonresidential settings are deaf. There are not enough deaf teachers in the work force to set up team teaching at all age levels across residential and public school settings. However, two suggestions to address this issue would be, first, to place more deaf teachers in early childhood settings, and second, to increase efforts to recruit deaf teachers to the field.

Another possibility is to include more deaf paraprofessionals in the deaf education classroom. There are surely many wonderful deaf adult role models who have not had the opportunity to complete degree requirements for teacher certification who could serve in a teacher's aide or paraprofessional capacity. One of the primary points of this chapter is that young deaf children are missing out on "everyday talk" in their home environments and that it is precisely this kind of discourse that enables children to achieve intersubjectivity and appropriate linguistic and cultural understandings. This is the kind of discourse that a paraprofessional could easily provide, and further professional development of deaf paraprofessionals could support their understanding of concepts such as visual engagement, bilingual/biculturalism, the structuring of a child's participation in classroom discourse, and effective collaboration with teachers (especially those who are hearing) in the classroom.

If a school adopts a deaf paraprofessional approach in order to enhance the quantity and quality of deaf role model interactions for deaf students, an important issue must be raised. With a deaf paraprofessional, there is often an imbalance of power in the classroom environment, as the hearing teacher tends to make all the language choice decisions and establishes discourse rules in a bilingual classroom. Deaf aides (like hearing teacher aides) often have not completed postsecondary education and are sometimes not empowered enough to challenge the authority of a hearing classroom teacher. Therefore, we recommend that professional staff hold open discussions together about the (sometimes changing) roles of the adults in the deaf education classroom and to be mindful of inadvertent oppression that might occur. For deaf students, observing the daily negotiations between hearing and deaf adults would no doubt be beneficial in promoting metalinguistic awareness and development of their own bilingual/ bicultural competence.

## SUMMARY AND CONCLUSIONS

With early identification of childhood deafness, we have the opportunity to begin engaging deaf infants as visual communicators. In a classroom-based model of natural language socialization and acquisition, deaf children born to hearing parents begin as legitimate peripheral members of a bilingual/bicultural community. In such a setting, a young deaf child will observe deaf and hearing adults as they interact using a natural signed language. When appropriate and feasible, teachers may emulate the visual, linguistic, and bilingual practices observed in deaf-parented families and engage their deaf students in contingent and responsive ways. As deaf children appropriate the adults' everyday indigenous practices (and those of peers as well), they will thereby increase their own participation in what Padden (1996a) and Humphries (1996, 2004b) have described as a modern bicultural deaf community, and will be expected to successfully negotiate the boundaries between Deaf and hearing ways of being.

We look forward to future qualitative and quantitative studies that ask (1) how a visually based system of engagement can best be modeled in the social context of the classroom, (2) how effective is a bilingual/ cultural competence model with respect to deaf children's linguistic, academic, and social progress, (3) which visually based strategies are most effective across different age levels of deaf children, and (4) how different educational settings and configurations of professional staff would best incorporate the concepts promoted by this model.

## REFERENCES

Allen, T. E., & Karchmer, M. A. (1990). Communication in classrooms for deaf students: Student, teacher, and program characteristics. In H. Bornstein (Ed.), *Manual communication: Implications for education* (pp. 45–66). Washington, DC: Gallaudet University Press.

Antia, S., & Kreimeyer, K. H. (2003). Peer interaction of deaf and hard-of-hearing children. In M. Marschark & P. E. Spencer (Eds.), *Oxford handbook of deaf studies, language, and education* (pp. 164–189). New York: Oxford University Press.

Blumenthal-Kelly, A. (1995). Fingerspelling interaction: A set of deaf parents and their deaf daughter. In C. Lucas (Ed.), *Sociolinguistics in deaf communities* (pp. 62–73). Washington, DC: Gallaudet University Press.

Bruner, J. S. (1981). The pragmatics of acquisition. In W. Deutsch (Ed.), *The child's construction of language* (pp. 39–55). New York: Academic Press.

Bruner, J. S. (1983). *Child's talk: Learning to use language.* New York: Norton.

Cawthon, S. (2001). Teaching strategies in inclusive classrooms with deaf students. *Journal of Deaf Studies and Deaf Education, 6*(3), 212–225.

Cazden, C. (1988). *Classroom discourse: The language of teaching and learning.* Portsmouth, NH: Heinemann.

Erting, C. J. (1980). Sign language and communication between adults and children. In C. Baker & R. Battison (Eds.), *Sign language and the Deaf community: Essays in honor of William Stokoe* (pp. 97–106). Silver Springs, MD: National Association of the Deaf.

Erting, C. J. (1988). Acquiring linguistic and social identity: Interactions of deaf children with a hearing teacher and a deaf adult. In M. Strong (Ed.), *Language learning and deafness* (pp. 192–219). New York: Cambridge University Press.

Erting, C. J., Prezioso, C., & Hynes, M. (1990). The interactional content of deaf mother-infant communication. In V. Volterra & C. Erting (Eds.), *From gesture to language in hearing and deaf children* (pp. 97–106). New York: Springer-Verlag.

Erting, C. J., Thumann-Prezioso, C., & Sonnenstrahl Benedict, B. (2000). Bilingualism in deaf families: Fingerspelling in early childhood. In P. E. Spencer, C. Erting, & M. Marschark (Eds.), *The deaf child in the family and at school* (pp. 41–54). Mahwah, NJ: Lawrence Erlbaum.

Forman, E. A., Minick, N., & Stone, C. A. (1993). *Contexts for learning: Sociocultural dynamics in children's development.* New York: Oxford University Press.

Heath, S. B. (1986). What no bedtime story means: Narrative skills at home and school. In B. B. Schieffelin & E. Ochs (Eds.), *Language socialization across cultures* (pp. 97–124). New York: Cambridge University Press

Holzrichter, A. S., & Meier, R. P. (2000). Child-directed signing in American Sign Language. In C. Chamberlain, J. P. Morford, & R. I. Mayberry (Eds.), *Language acquisition by eye* (pp. 25–40). Mahwah, NJ: Lawrence Erlbaum.

Humphries, T. (1996). Of deaf-mutes, the strange, and the modern deaf self. In N.S. Glickman & M.A. Harvey (Eds.), *Culturally affirmative psychotherapy with deaf persons* (pp. 99–114). Mahwah, NJ: Lawrence Erlbaum.

Humphries, T. (2004a, April). *An alternative approach to classroom practice: A California experimental program.* Paper presented at the annual meeting of the American Educational Research Association, San Diego, CA. Accessed January 29, 2005 from http://www-tep.ucsd.edu/admission/madeaf.shtm.

Humphries, T. (2004b). The modern Deaf self: Indigenous practices and educational imperatives. In B.J. Brueggemann (Ed.), *Literacy and Deaf people: Cultural and contextual perspectives* (pp. 29–46). Washington, DC: Gallaudet University Press.

Israelite, N., Ewoldt, C., & Hoffmeister, R. (1992). *Bilingual/bicultural education for deaf and hard-of-hearing students: A review of the literature on the effective use of native sign language on the acquisition of a majority language by hearing impaired students.* Toronto: MGS Publications Services.

Jamieson, J. R. (1994). Instructional discourse strategies: Differences between hearing and deaf mothers of deaf children. *First Language, 14,* 153–171.

Johnson, R. E., & Erting, C. J. (1989). Ethnicity and socialization in a classroom for deaf children. In C. Lucas (Ed.), *The sociolinguistics of the deaf community* (pp. 41–83). San Diego, CA: Academic Press.

Jones, B. E., Clark, G. M., & Stoltz, D. F. (1997). Characteristics and practices of sign language interpreters in inclusive education programs. *Exceptional Children, 63,* 257–268.

Karchmer, M. A., & Mitchell, R. E. (2003). Demographic and achievement characteristics of deaf and hard-of-hearing students. In M. Marschark & P. E. Spencer (Eds.), *Oxford handbook of deaf studies, language, and education* (pp. 21–37). New York: Oxford University Press.

Kluwin, T. (1983). Discourse in deaf classrooms: The structure of teaching episodes. *Discourse Processes, 6,* 275–293.

Kluwin, T., Stinson, M. S., & Colarossi, G. M. (2002). Social processes and outcomes of in-school contact between deaf and hearing peers. *Journal of Deaf Studies and Deaf Education, 7*(3), 200–213.

Koester, L. S., Brooks, L., & Traci, M. A. (2000). Tactile contact by deaf and hearing mothers during face-to-face interactions with their infants. *Journal of Deaf Studies and Deaf Education, 5*(2), 2127–2139.

Koester, L. S., Karkowski, A. M., & Traci, M. A. (1998). How do Deaf and hearing mothers regain eye contact when their deaf infants look away? *American Annals of the Deaf, 143,* 5–13.

Koester, L. S., Papoušek, H., & Smith-Gray, S. (2000). Intuitive parenting, communication, and interaction with deaf infants. In P. Spencer, C. Erting, & M. Marschark (Eds.), *The deaf child in the family and at school* (pp. 55–71). Mahwah, NJ: Lawrence Erlbaum.

Kuntze, M. (1998). Literacy and deaf children: The language question. *Topics in Language Disorders, 18*(4), 1–15.

LaSasso, C., & Lollis, J. (2003). Survey of residential and day schools for deaf students in the United States that identify themselves as bilingual-bicultural programs. *Journal of Deaf Studies and Deaf Education, 8*(1), 79–91.

Lave, J., & Wenger, E. (1991). *Situated learning: Legitimate peripheral participation.* New York: Cambridge University Press.

Lederberg, A. R., & Everhart, V. (1998). Communication between deaf children and their hearing mothers: The role of language, gesture, and vocalization. *Journal of Speech, Language, and Hearing Research, 41,* 887–899.

Loots, G., & Devise, I. (2003). The use of visual-tactile communication strategies by deaf and hearing fathers and mothers of deaf infants. *Journal of Deaf Studies and Deaf Education, 8*(1), 31–42.

Lou, M. W. (1988). The history of language use in the education of the deaf in the United States. In M. Strong (Ed.), *Language learning and deafness* (pp. 75–98). New York: Cambridge University Press.

Marschark, M. (1997). *Raising and educating a deaf child.* New York: Oxford University Press.

Marschark, M., Lang, H. G., & Albertini, J. A. (2002). *Educating deaf students: From research to practice.* New York: Oxford University Press.

Masataka, N. (2000). The role of modality and input in the earliest stage of language acquisition: Studies of Japanese Sign Language. In C. Chamberlain, J. P. Morford, & R. I. Mayberry (Eds.), *Language acquisition by eye* (pp. 3–24). Mahwah, NJ: Lawrence Erlbaum.

Mather, S. M. (1987). Eye gaze and communication in a deaf classroom. *Sign Language Studies, 54,* 11–31.

Mather, S. M. (1989). Visually oriented teaching strategies with deaf preschool children. In C. Lucas (Ed.), *The sociolinguistics of the deaf community* (pp. 165–187). San Diego, CA: Academic Press.

Mather, S. M. (1990). Home and classroom communication. In D. F. Moores & K. P. Meadow-Orlans (Eds.), *Educational and developmental aspects of deafness* (pp. 232–254). Washington, DC: Gallaudet University Press.

Mayer, C., Akamatsu, T., & Stewart, D. (2002). A model for effective practice: Dialogic inquiry with students who are deaf. *Exceptional Children, 68*(4), 485–502.

Meadow, K., Greenberg, M., Erting, C., & Carmichael, H. (1981). Interactions of deaf mothers and deaf preschool children: Comparisons with three other groups of deaf and hearing dyads. *American Annals of the Deaf, 126,* 454–468.

Meadow-Orlans, K. P. (1997). Effects of mother and infant hearing status on interactions at twelve and eighteen months. *Journal of Deaf Studies and Deaf Education, 2*(1), 27–36.

Meadow-Orlans, K. P., & Spencer, P. E. (1996). Maternal sensitivity and the visual attentiveness of children who are deaf. *Early Development and Parenting, 5*(4), 1213–1223.

Miller, P. J., & Goodnow, J. J. (1995). Cultural practices: Toward an integration of culture and development. In J. J. Goodnow, P. J. Miller, & F. Kessel (Eds.), *Cultural practices as contexts for development* (pp. 5–16). San Francisco, CA: Jossey-Bass Publishers.

Mohay, H. (2000). Language in sight: Mothers' strategies for making language visually accessible to deaf children. In P. E. Spencer, C. J. Erting, &

M. Marschark (Eds.), *The deaf child in the family and at school* (pp. 151–166). Mahwah, NJ: Lawrence Erlbaum.

Moll, L. C. (1990). *Vygotsky and education: Instructional implications and applications of sociohistorical psychology.* New York: Cambridge University Press.

Morgan, D. D. (2004). *Deaf teachers' practices: Supporting and enabling preschool deaf children's development of a participative identity.* Unpublished doctoral dissertation, University of Illinois at Urbana-Champaign.

Nover, S., Andrews, J., Baker, S., Everhart, V., & Bradford, M. (2002). *Star Schools final project report (1997–2002).* Albuquerque, NM: New Mexico School for the Deaf. Accessed January 29, 2005 from http//www. star-online. org/de/resources/project.jsp.

Nover, S., Christensen, K. M., & Cheng, L. L. (1998). Development of ASL and English competence for learners who are deaf. *Topics in Language Disorders, 18*(4), 61–71.

Padden, C. (1996a). From the cultural to the bicultural: The modern deaf community. In I. Parasnis (Ed.), *Culture and language diversity and the deaf experience* (pp. 79–98). New York: Cambridge University Press.

Padden, C. (1996b). Early bilingual lives of deaf children. In I. Parasnis (Ed.), *Culture and language diversity and the deaf experience* (pp. 99–116). New York: Cambridge University Press.

Padden, C., & Humphries, T. (1988). *Deaf in America: Voices from a culture.* New York: Cambridge University Press.

Padden, C., & Ramsey, C. (1998). Reading ability in signing deaf children. *Topics in Language Disorders, 18*(4), 30–46.

Padden, C., & Ramsey, C. (2000). American Sign Language and reading ability in deaf children. In C. Chamberlain, J. P. Morford, & R. I. Mayberry (Eds.), *Language acquisition by eye* (pp. 165–189). Mahwah, NJ: Lawrence Erlbaum.

Papoušek, H., & Papoušek, M. (1987). Intuitive parenting: A dialectic counterpart to the infant's integrative competence. In J. D. Osofsky (Ed.), *Handbook of infant development* (2nd ed., pp. 669–720). New York: John Wiley & Sons.

Ramsey, C. (1997). *Deaf children in public schools: Placement, context, and consequences.* Washington, DC: Gallaudet University Press.

Ramsey, C., & Padden, C. (1998). Natives and newcomers: Gaining access to literacy in a classroom for deaf children. *Anthropology and Education Quarterly, 29*(1), 5–24.

Rogoff, B. (1990). *Apprenticeship in thinking: Cognitive development in social context.* New York: Oxford University Press.

Rogoff, B. (2003). *The cultural nature of human development.* New York: Oxford University Press.

Schick, B., Williams, K., & Bolster, L. (2000). Skill levels of educational interpreters working in public schools. *Journal of Deaf Studies and Deaf Education, 4*, 144–155.

Schlesinger, H. S. (1987). Deafness, mental health, and language. In F. Powell, T. Finitzo-Hieber, S. Friel-Patti, & D. Henderson (Eds.), *Education of the hearing-impaired child* (pp. 103–116). San Diego, CA: College Hill.

Singleton, J. L., & Morgan, D. D. (2004, April). *Becoming Deaf: Deaf teachers' engagement practices supporting deaf children's identity development.* Paper presented at the annual meeting of the American Educational Research Association, San Diego, CA.

Singleton, J. L., & Tittle, M. D. (2000). Deaf parents and their hearing children. *Journal of Deaf Studies and Deaf Education, 5*(3), 221–236.

Spencer, P. E. (1993). Communication behaviors of infants with hearing loss and their hearing mothers. *Journal of Speech and Hearing Research, 36,* 311–321.

Spencer, P. E. (2000). Looking without listening: Is audition a prerequisite for normal development of visual attention during latency? *Journal of Deaf Studies and Deaf Education, 5*(4), 291–302.

Spencer, P. E., Bodner-Johnson, B. A., & Gutfreund, M. K. (1992). Interacting with infants with a hearing loss: What can we learn from mothers who are deaf? *Journal of Early Intervention, 16*(1), 64–78.

Stinson, M., & Liu, Y. (1999). Participation of deaf and hard-of-hearing students in classes with hearing students. *Journal of Deaf Studies and Deaf Education, 4*(3), 191–214.

Stinson, M., Liu, Y., Saur, R., & Long, G. (1996). Deaf college students' perceptions of communication in mainstream classes. *Journal of Deaf Studies and Deaf Education, 1*(1), 40–51.

Swisher, M. V. (2000). Learning to converse: How deaf mothers support the development of attention and conversational skills in their young deaf children. In P. E. Spencer, C. J. Erting, & M. Marschark (Eds.), *The deaf child in the family and at school* (pp. 21–39). Mahwah, NJ: Lawrence Erlbaum.

Tattershall, S., & Creaghead, N. (1985). A comparison of communication at home and school. In D. Ripich & F. Spinelli (Eds.), *School discourse problems* (pp. 29–51). San Diego, CA: College Hill Press.

Tomasello, M. (1999). *The cultural origins of human cognition.* Cambridge, MA: Harvard University Press.

Traci, M. A., & Koester, L. S. (2003). Parent-Infant interactions: A transactional approach to understanding the development of deaf children. In M. Marschark & P. E. Spencer (Eds.), *Oxford handbook of deaf studies, language, and education* (pp. 190–202). New York: Oxford University Press.

Vygotsky, L. S. (1978). *Mind in society: The development of higher psychological processes* (M. Cole, V. John-Steiner, S. Scribner, & E. Soubernam, Eds.). Cambridge, MA: Harvard University Press.

Wallis, D., Musselman, C., & MacKay, S. (2004). Hearing mothers and their deaf children: The relationship between early, ongoing mode match and subsequent mental health functioning in adolescence. *Journal of Deaf Studies and Deaf Education, 9*(1), 2–14.

Waxman, R. P., & Spencer, P. E. (1997). What mothers do to support infant visual attention: Sensitivities to age and hearing status. *Journal of Deaf Studies and Deaf Education, 2*(2), 104–114.

Waxman, R. P., Spencer, P. E., & Poisson, S. S. (1996). Reciprocity, responsiveness, and timing in interactions between mothers and deaf and hearing children. *Journal of Early Intervention, 20,* 341–355.

Wenger, E. (1998). *Communities of practice: Learning, meaning, and identity.* New York: Cambridge University Press.

Wood, D., & Wood, H. (1991). Signed English in the classroom, I. Teaching style and child participation. *First Language, 11,* 189–217.

Wood, D., & Wood, H. (1997). Communicating with children who are deaf: Pitfalls and possibilities. *Language, Speech, and Hearing Services in Schools, 28,* 348–354.

Wood, D., Wood, H., Griffiths, A., & Howarth, I. (1986). *Teaching and talking with deaf children*. New York: John Wiley & Sons.

Wood, D., Wood, H., & Kingsmill, M. (1991). Signed English in the classroom, II. Structural and pragmatic aspects of teachers' speech and sign. *First Language, 11*, 301–325.

# Author Index

# Subject Index

ability, expressing, 307
Abkhaz, 175
abstract thought, conveying in sign
    language, 7
academic performance, educational
    method and, 9
acknowledgment, 73
activity, relation between speech
    and, 73, 75, 85
addition errors, 216–217
adolescence, mental health
    functioning in, 350
adverbs
    facial, 264, 271, 273–275
    fingerspelled, 190
affect, modifying, 78
affective expressions, 266
agent arguments, overt, 249
agent-oriented modality, 293, 295,
    298, 303–304, 306, 309
agglutinative morphology, 24
Agricola, Rudolphus, 5
amalgams, 270
*American Annals of the Deaf and
    Dumb*, 7
American School for the Deaf, 6
American Sign Language, 137, 223

acquisition of, 155
definition of, 12, 13
features in manually coded
    English, 121–122
frequency of fingerspelling, 190
glossing, 31
grammatical features, 22, 39
lexical development of, 138–142
modality in, 292, 296–298
morphemic layering, 83
morphology, 104–121, 245–246
negation in, 271–273
nonmanual morphology, 264–266
origins of, 6
proficiency of teachers, 368
referential shifts in, 116–119
slips in, 212
topic marking, 307
using narrative features of, 357
verb marking in, 35
verb specificity, 26
anaphoric reference, 118, 126, 318
animal names, in first words and
    signs, 141
Antiguan Creole, modality in,
    299–300
aphasia, 213